James Madison

JAMES MADISON

Philosopher, Founder, and Statesman

Edited by John R. Vile, William D. Pederson, and Frank J. Williams

OHIO UNIVERSITY PRESS ATHENS

Ohio University Press, Athens, Ohio 45701
www.ohioswallow.com

Printed in the United States of America
Ohio University Press books are printed on acid-free paper ♾ ™

15 14 13 12 11 10 09 08 5 4 3 2 1

Library of Congress Cataloging-in-Publication Data

James Madison : philosopher, founder, and statesman / edited by John R. Vile, William D. Pederson, and Frank J. Williams.

p. cm.

Selected papers from a conference held Oct. 19–21, 2006 at Louisiana State University, Shreveport.

Includes bibliographical references and index.

ISBN 978-0-8214-1831-4 (cloth : alk. paper) — ISBN 978-0-8214-1832-1 (pbk. : alk. paper)

1. Madison, James, 1751–1836—Congresses. 2. Madison, James, 1751–1836—Influence—Congresses. 3. Presidents—United States—Biography—Congresses. 4. Statesmen—United States—Biography—Congresses. 5. United States—Politics and government—1783–1809—Congresses. 6. United States—Politics and government—1809–1817—Congresses. I. Vile, John R. II. Pederson, William D., 1946– III. Williams, Frank J.

E342.J357 2008

973.5'1092—dc22

[B]

2008027391

Contents

Introduction: More Than Just a President vii
John R. Vile, William D. Pederson, and Frank J. Williams

ONE: BECOMING JAMES MADISON

Madison and Philosophy: His Coursework and His Statesmanship 3
David Nordquest

More Than an Intellectual Scribe: The Political Drives and Traits of James Madison 21
Craig Grau

TWO: MADISON, THE CONSTITUTIONAL CONVENTION, AND CONSTITUTIONAL DESIGN

James Madison and Constitutional Paternity 37
John R. Vile

Inventing the Extended Republic: The Debate over the Role of Madison's Theory in the Creation of the Constitution 63
Alan Gibson

A Portrait of James Madison's Views on Citizenship and Leadership in Popular Government 88
Gordon P. Henderson

THREE: MADISON AND THE BILL OF RIGHTS

James Madison and Religious Freedom 105
Rodney A. Grunes

James Madison's *Report of 1800:* The First Amendment, Freedom of the Press, and the Common Law 133
John R. Vile

Mirroring Madison: The Historic and Continuing Influence of James Madison on the U.S. Supreme Court 157
Steven P. Brown

FOUR: MADISON AS A PARTY LEADER

Madison and Hamilton: The End of a Friendship 175
Mary Stockwell

James Madison and Impeachment: Theory and Practice 193
Stefano Luconi

James Madison, David Hume, and Modern Political Parties 209
John Allphin Moore, Jr.

FIVE: MADISON AS PRESIDENT

James Madison: Brilliant Theorist, Failed Tactician 229
Byron W. Daynes and Mark P. Hopkins

The Legislative Messages of the Madison Administration 250
Samuel B. Hoff

President James Madison's Appointments to the U.S. Supreme Court 261
Henry J. Abraham

SIX: MADISON AS ELDER STATESMAN

Madison's Response to Nullification 269
James H. Read

Selected Bibliography 285
Contributors 293
Index 295

Introduction

More Than Just a President

The face of James Madison, Jr., is not carved in stone on Mount Rushmore, nor is Madison commemorated with a pavilion in Washington, DC. Yet he remains a pivotal figure for understanding the American experiment in constitutional government. Born in 1751 in Port Conway, Virginia, reared on a plantation in Orange, Virginia, tutored by Donald Robertson, and educated at the College of New Jersey (now Princeton), Madison was among the most cerebral of the founders. His contemporaries quickly realized that his pen was a weapon of liberty, and they appointed him to a committee headed by George Mason to write the Virginia Declaration of Rights. He also served on the Governor's Council and then in the Continental Congress and the Virginia state legislature, respectively.

While in the two latter institutions, Madison recognized that the weaknesses of the Articles of Confederation were threatening the hard-won freedoms secured by the American Revolution and joined with other nationalists who pressed first to strengthen the Articles and then to replace them. Madison was among the delegates to the Annapolis Convention who pushed to call the Constitutional Convention, and, when the Convention was called, he worked both within Congress to secure its success and outside it to persuade George Washington to attend.

Madison was the first out-of-state delegate to arrive in Philadelphia for the Convention in 1787, and he worked as hard as any delegate there to craft its work. Believed to be the central author of the Virginia Plan, Madison positioned himself near the front of the assembly so that he could become its unofficial secretary. Although the delegates rejected some of Madison's pet ideas, including proposals for a Council of Revision and a congressional veto, as well as some ideas, such as proportional representation in both houses of Congress, that he shared more widely with others from states similarly situated to Virginia, Madison departed from the Convention resolved to fight for constitutional ratification. He then authored some of the most famous essays in the *Federalist Papers* and participated in the critical debates in Richmond, where he helped beat back Patrick Henry's attacks on the new Constitution. Then, heeding a promise that he had made to his own constituents, Madison worked as a member of the first House of Representatives for the adoption of the Bill of Rights, a project that he once had pronounced to be unnecessary.

Madison later served as secretary of state for both terms of Thomas Jefferson's administration before his own election as a two-term president. Even in retirement, Madison remained abreast of current affairs, and his home beckoned travelers to the Virginia Piedmont. Despite frail health, the sickly "Jemmy" survived all the other delegates to the Constitutional Convention, and his wife, who had dominated the social scene and eased interpersonal relationships during Jefferson's and Madison's presidencies, remained popular after his death in 1836.

A Madison Conference

In 2006 the International Lincoln Center for American Studies, with the help of the Louisiana Endowment for the Humanities, the Lincoln Forum, and Phi Kappa Alpha (the National Political Science Honor Society), hosted a conference on James Madison, Jr., at the Louisiana State University Shreveport campus on October 19 through 21. As in the case of previous triennial conferences, professors assembled from a variety of disciplines and perspectives for scholarly exchange in a collegial environment that was enhanced by the presence of students and members of the community. Most sessions were plenary, encouraging scholars to interact with one another and with the attentive lay audience. Appropriate to a Louisiana conference, there was lagniappe: a costume portrayal of Madison, a speech by a recent biographer of Dolley Madison, and the presentation of at least one rap song on Madison's presidency!

It is not perhaps uncommon to collect papers at such conferences, but its sponsor greatly aided the likelihood of a book first by having chosen panels for the conference that complemented one another and then by making it clear that only the choicest essays would be published in book form. These submissions were then culled and edited, and this volume is the result. Like the distinctive flavors of spicy Cajun cuisine and the varied styles of music that participants in the Madison conference sampled in Shreveport, this volume accentuates the diversity of Madison's contributions to American political life and the diversity of interpretations that surround his work.

Becoming James Madison

This book is divided into six sections arranged in rough chronological order. The first focuses on the development of Madison the man and features essays by David Nordquest and Craig Grau.

After completing his studies with Donald Robertson at a nearby plantation, Madison and his family had to decide where he would attend college. Although the College of William and Mary in Williamsburg, Virginia, was near home, Madison may have been troubled by its association with the established Anglican Church of Virginia. Or he may simply have been attracted by the opportunity to study under John Witherspoon, the Scottish divine who was heading the College of New Jersey. Madison flourished in this environment, compressing the normal four-year course of study into about two years and then staying on for graduate study with Witherspoon.

In the lead essay of this book, Nordquest examines how "the child is father to the man," through examining the handwritten notes of Madison and his contemporaries from two college philosophy classes. Madison's contemporaries recognized his ability to do justice to multiple sides of an issue, and these class notes provide clues as to the method he adopted for understanding and incorporating rival points of view in the *Federalist* and subsequent writing. They clarify his role as a philosophical statesman.

Today's scholars often portray Madison as a short, bookish man with little personality, but his contemporaries more frequently recognized him as a "philosophical politician," who blended study with practical politics. Grau confirms that Madison had both a lifelong passion for religious liberty and a patriot's heart. Madison found reinforcement for his identity through a career in politics that spanned nearly his entire adult life. Grau further demonstrates how Madison's even temper, his ability to collaborate with others, his sense of humor, and his willingness to let others take credit for mutual achievements contributed to his political success and helped him achieve the political position that he needed to put his theories into action.

Madison, the Constitutional Convention, and Constitutional Design

Madison is perhaps best known as the "father" of the Constitution, and the second section of this book describes his role at the Constitutional Convention. John Vile canvasses the views of leading authorities on the Constitutional Convention to assess Madison's role there. Although such authorities agree that he was one of the most, if not *the* most, important contributor, Madison himself never claimed primary authorship. Not only did he fail to get a number of his key proposals adopted, but he also recognized that the document would be more embraced, and thus more likely to succeed, if the people accepted it as a collective work. Although his credentials clearly show him to have been "first among equals," he did not seek the title of father of the Constitution, and it should be bestowed on him only with appropriate reservations.

If Madison is not the father of the Constitution, should he be designated as its central "architect"? Alan Gibson utilizes his considerable historical skills to tease out the manner in which Madison might be responsible for the overarching constitutional design. Probably no writing by any founding father better captured the imagination of American political scientists than Madison's famed *Federalist* No. 10, with its elegant theory of factions and the manner in which an extended republic might serve to check such factions. Drawing from the best of contemporary scholarship, Gibson demonstrates that while this theory, which historian Charles Beard has probably done the most to popularize, was important to Madison, it does not appear to have been particularly influential at the Convention or in subsequent ratifying debates. Madison was much more concerned with injustices at the state level than many other delegates, and attempts to follow Madison too closely on this point might actually sidetrack scholars from matters that other delegates considered to be more prominent. Indeed, consistent with emerging scholarship in the area, Gibson suggests that contemporary scholars might understand the Convention better if they viewed it less as an attempt to reconcile majority rule and individual rights and more as what he describes as "a means of creating a stronger and more structurally sound national government, enhancing national security, and preventing the states from going to war with each other."

Gordon P. Henderson further attempts to understand Madison's constitutional vision by examining his views on citizenship and leadership. Although scholars generally associate Madison with the observations that "the seeds of faction are . . . sown in the nature of man" and the corollary that "enlightened statesmen will not always be at the helm," Henderson shows that Madison's views were much more complex. Approaching the topic of citizenship variously as a political scientist, a cultural anthropologist, and a political engineer, Madison believed that popular government could protect liberty and enhance American virtues while keeping baser behavior in check. Madison held that democratic leaders had a responsibility to design the political system efficiently, while citizens had the responsibility to retain sufficient oversight to restrain their leaders.

Madison and the Bill of Rights

As Nordquest's lead essay in this book demonstrates, Madison was passionately committed to civil liberties. Accordingly, the next section of this book treats Madison and the Bill of Rights. Initially unconvinced that such parchment barriers would succeed, Madison soon viewed the addition of such a bill as essential to head off the movement for another constitutional convention that might negate the work of the first. Correspondence with Thomas Jefferson further persuaded him of the efficacy of such a bill. Madison gathered and organized proposals for a Bill of Rights and successfully led the fight in the first Congress for its adoption.

Because of the primacy of the First Amendment within the Bill of Rights, it is fitting that two essays in this section focus on Madison's views of this amendment. Rodney Grunes's essay explores Madison's stances toward religious freedom. He divides Madison's thoughts on religious freedom into prepresidential, presidential, and postpresidential phases. In the first phase, which dates to his late youth and is perhaps best reflected in Madison's "Memorial and Remonstrance against Religious Assessments," Madison articulated the idea that religious liberty is a God-given inalienable natural right that predates the formation of civil society. Madison proved somewhat more willing to accommodate religious exercise when he served as president, especially when facing the exigencies of the War of 1812. After leaving the presidency, however, Madison questioned some of the accommodations that he had made in the office. While he appears to have maintained fairly stable convictions, he sometimes adapted them to accommodate perceived political realities.

Vile follows up on Grunes's essay by examining Madison's views of freedom of speech and freedom of the press as expressed in the Report of 1800 that Madison wrote for the Virginia Assembly defending the Virginia and Kentucky Resolutions. Significantly, his writing marked the first occasion on which an American founding father offered an extensive interpretation of the First Amendment. In this report, Madison made three arguments against the constitutionality of the Sedition Act of 1798. He argued that it represented the exercise of a power that the Constitution did not delegate to Congress, specifically violated the First Amendment, and affected the right of publicly examining public men and public measures. Madison argued that the First Amendment offered much wider protection for the rights of speech and the press than English common law. In arguing that the First Amendment should be so interpreted, Madison also seemed to suggest that state guarantees should be interpreted likewise. On this score, he expressed a view more libertarian than those held by his contemporaries and perhaps even more libertarian than that which the Supreme Court articulated in *New York Times Co. v. Sullivan* (1964), its most important twentieth-century opinion on libel.

No interpretation of the Bill of Rights could be complete without a discussion of the U.S. Supreme Court, and Steven P. Brown provides this discussion with his essay on Madison's continuing influence on the Court. Although the Court is generally interpreted as having censured Madison and Jefferson in *Marbury v. Madison* (1803), the case that asserted judicial review over national legislation, Madison's contributions to the Court are among his most enduring. The institution of judicial review mirrors Madison's belief in the need for a powerful check that would prevent legislative tyranny and monitor the relationship between the national government and the states. In enforcing the Bill of Rights, the Court applies the principles that Madison identified to specific cases. The Court has also come to accept Madison's view that such rights should limit the actions of both state and national governments, while recognizing that few, if any, rights are absolute. Like Madison, the modern Court has recognized the primacy of the rights within the First Amendment. Although Madison would undoubtedly decry some aspects of modern jurisprudence, Brown demonstrates that he would likely find much comfort, and some degree of familiarity, with the Supreme Court.

Madison as a Party Leader

Few transformations seemed less likely than Madison's evolution from a philosophical statesman into a party leader, but Madison was at the forefront of the development of the American political party system. He and Thomas Jefferson cofounded the Democratic-Republican Party. Mary Stockwell leads off this section of the book by reminding readers of how closely Madison had worked with Alexander Hamilton (soon the leader of the Federalist Party) in Congress prior to the time when, partly at Madison's own suggestion, Washington elevated Hamilton to the position of secretary of the treasury. She further traces the breach that this position opened between Madison and Hamilton. Although some of their differences may have arisen from simple jealousy and differences in interests between the geographic sections they represented, Hamilton largely attributed their falling-out to Jefferson's increasing influence on Madison. Stockwell reminds readers to consider the manner in which personalities interacted with ideas to influence early American politics.

In the succeeding essay, Stefano Luconi further explores the connection between Madison's theory and practice by examining his views of impeachment. Luconi demonstrates that Madison's concept of impeachment at the Constitutional Convention, where he opposed this punishment for mere "maladministration," was generally consistent with his actions during his subsequent role as a party leader. Despite some of his disagreements with Hamilton, Madison opposed impeaching him for perceived improprieties as secretary of the treasury, disfavored the Senate plan to impeach William Blount after expelling him, and opposed the use of impeachment as a partisan weapon against Federalist judges. Madison's opinion that impeachment should be limited to cases of serious malfeasance in office has largely prevailed and has undoubtedly been salutary.

The dominant view is that the American framers, for the most part, disfavored political parties. John Allphin Moore, Jr., argues a contrary finding that Madison's arguments in various essays, including *Federalist* Nos. 10 and 51, not only show that he heavily borrowed from David Hume on the subject but also testify to Madison's knowledge that parties and factions were inevitable. They further reveal Madison's belief that a republican system could be established to tame the passions of extreme factions and channel them into effective government. Moore thus demonstrates that Madison's own practical service on behalf of the

Democratic-Republican Party was consistent with his earlier theoretical writings on the subject.

Madison as President

Before Thomas Jefferson died, he directed that only three achievements be noted on his tombstone: his writing of the Declaration of Independence and the Virginia Statute for Religious Liberty, and his founding of the University of Virginia. He did not include his presidency. Similarly, Madison's other achievements appear to overshadow his accomplishments as president. The section on Madison as president shows that scholars continue to be divided in their assessment of Madison's achievements in this position.

Byron W. Daynes and Mark Hopkins probably reflect the prevailing consensus in portraying Madison as a "brilliant theorist" but a "failed tactician." Examining Madison's presidential roles as opinion/party leader, legislative leader, chief executive, chief diplomat, and commander in chief, the authors conclude that Madison's performance was fairly lackluster. Although his presidency was notable for preserving civil liberties and for flexibility in applying republican principles, the authors believe that Madison's lack of interpersonal skills, his views of the presidency, and his introverted personality were not ideally suited to the crises he faced, especially with respect to relations with Great Britain.

Samuel B. Hoff provides a much more positive assessment of the Madison presidency by focusing on Madison's legislative messages. Hoff points especially to Madison's persistent use of presidential proclamations and to his exercise of both the regular and the pocket veto as a way of preserving the institutional presidency.

Henry J. Abraham rounds out the picture of Madison's presidency and casts further light on Brown's earlier observations regarding Madison's contributions to the judiciary by examining Madison's appointments to the high court. Although he was able to fill only two vacancies, scholars recognize Madison's successful nomination of Joseph Story as one of the greatest judicial appointments in American history. Madison's choice of Gabriel Duvall was less heralded and was followed by a twelve-year period in which there were no more vacancies on the Court.

Madison as Elder Statesman

In his day, contemporaries sought to appropriate Madison for their own purposes. A constant procession of visitors came to visit the famous former president and to share his and his wife's hospitality. Madison's mind remained agile, and he tried to organize his papers. As Grunes's earlier chapter demonstrated, Madison spent some of his retirement reflecting on, and sometimes second-guessing, decisions that he had made as president.

Madison was the only founding father alive to contest the uses to which advocates of nullification and secession, most notably South Carolina's fire-breathing John C. Calhoun, were putting the Virginia and Kentucky Resolutions. Madison sought through private correspondence and public writings to rebut allegations that he and Jefferson had ever defended the right of a single state to nullify state laws or to secede from the Union. He further argued that Calhoun's theories would elevate minority rights over majority rule. In the book's final essay, James H. Read argues that even though Madison showed that Calhoun's theories differed significantly from his own, Madison's arguments neither succeeded in getting Calhoun to back down from his own argument nor persuaded most of Calhoun's supporters. Read convincingly asserts that Madison almost surely intended for his parting warning to his country about disunion to include Calhoun.

In the end, Madison's warnings against disunion and secession proved inadequate, and the Civil War began less than twenty-five years after his death. In part because of the leadership of another great president, the forces of the constitutional Union ultimately prevailed and Madison's dream survived.

After he died, widow Dolley's debts forced her to sell the family estate. As a consequence, for many years, Madison's home, Montpelier, was a private residence, open to the public only on special days. Over the last generation, the Duponts bequeathed this house and its many additions to the nation, and Montpelier was restored recently to its eighteenth-century simplicity, with its greatest ornament perhaps being Madison's second-story study where he retreated to read and write. The editors of, and contributors to, this volume hope that this book, like the restored Montpelier, will stimulate further interests in Madison and continue to provide insight into this remarkable, humble man who spent most of his life in politics and dedicated his life to the pursuit of freedom.

John R. Vile
William D. Pederson
Frank J. Williams

ONE

Becoming James Madison

DAVID NORDQUEST

Madison and Philosophy

His Coursework and His Statesmanship

In coursework and study at the College of New Jersey from 1769 until 1772, James Madison acquired much of the grasp of philosophy that distinguishes his statesmanship. He took with him from Princeton, as well, the ideal of the philosopher-statesman that his good friend and fellow alumnus William Bradford would soon find realized in the work of the Continental Congress. In August 1774, anxious for news of the sessions of Congress then being held in Bradford's Philadelphia, Madison appealed to his friend for reports. Bradford's enthusiastic reply professed confidence that Congress's measures would be "wisely plan'd," because they "debate on them like philosophers." He reported that Congress had chosen a place to meet with ready access to a fine library, and he had learned from a talk with the librarian that the delegates were making constant use of the collection and were taking "Vattel, Barlemaqui[,] Locke & Montesquieu" as "the standar[d]s to which they refer either when settling the rights of the Colonies or when a dispute arises on the Justice or propriety of a measure."[1] Very soon, Madison would himself be recognized as, perhaps, the foremost practitioner of this statesmanship based on philosophical analysis and scholarship. For good reason, Adrienne Koch has called him the "prime master of political logic."[2]

Madison completed two philosophy courses at the College of New Jersey—logic, probably taught to sophomores by James Thompson, and moral philosophy, taught to seniors, and just possibly also to juniors, by college president John Witherspoon.[3] (Because Madison doubled up on his work to finish early, he could hardly have taken the course more than once.) Madison's seriousness in regard to his studies suggests that his coursework may have been quite influential. He wrote a former teacher soon after arriving in Princeton that he was "perfectly pleased" to be facing "three years confinement" because of "the advantages" he hoped to gain from it. He almost destroyed his health by sleeping but "four or five hours a night" for "weeks at a time" as he devoted himself single-mindedly to his work.[4] It was all worth it, of course. Indeed, Madison was so convinced of the value of this intense study that he made it the model for his statesmanship. He learned, as J. C. A. Stagg put it, "to prepare for public business by researching policy questions as thoroughly as possible."[5] In their accounts of ideas, language, reason, and method, the logic notes taken by Madison help clarify why he thought such study necessary. They also cast light on his political prudence and institutional craftsmanship.

Logic

Madison's logic course was much wider in scope than the traditional survey of syllogistic reasoning. Adrienne Koch calls it a study in logic and epistemology.[6] She might have more accurately termed it a course in "the art of thinking." Its structure mirrors that of the influential seventeenth-century classic by Arnaud and Nicole, *Logic or the Art of Thinking.* According to those authors, logic has four divisions corresponding to the principal operations of the mind: conceiving, judging, reasoning, and disposing or ordering, that is, method.[7] The more immediate source for Madison's course was Isaac Watts's *Logick,* which relied on Arnaud and Nicole and listed the same four operations as, first, perception, conception, or apprehension; second, judgment; third, argumentation or reasoning; and, fourth, disposition.[8] Madison's course notes identify divisions of logic named for these same operations: "the art of Logick consists of four parts: The first of ideas and their origins: the Second of Judgment & proposition: The third of Discourse & Syllogism; and the last of Method or Order."[9]

Evident in the notes is the wide influence of both Watts's popular work, which provided frequent examples, and Locke's *Essay Concerning Human Understanding.* The notes range widely into such questions as the origins of ideas in sensation and reflection, their differences in complexity and adequacy, their representation by signs, the propositions that affirm their agreements and disagreements, the reasonings by which individuals move from some propositions to others, and the methods by which humans organize their thinking. The notes also give attention to aspects of metaphysics. Of particular interest are the explanations of how disagreements originate in differences in ideas. Discovering how to surmount these disagreements in good republican fashion was a key challenge for Madison's statesmanship.

Scholars are fortunate to have 122 pages of manuscript notes in Madison's own hand of what was covered in his logic course. The editors of his *Papers* convincingly argue that the manuscript dates from Madison's college years, although biographer Irving Brant supports a precollege origin.[10] This earliest full example of Madison's great note-taking lets readers follow his thinking as he mastered a central area of philosophy.[11] The detail and care of the notes testify to their importance to Madison. There is also substantial evidence that the ideas the notes record became a fundamental part of Madison's mind, helping shape how he thought about a host of political problems.

The editors of Madison's *Papers* published only brief excerpts from the notes because they did not consider the work to be Madison's own creation but rather that of his teacher, possibly supplemented by Madison's own references to other philosophical works.[12] Adrienne Koch, however, argues that the notes are more original than his editors supposed. As an example, she points out that the notes criticize even "the great Mr. Locke," and she maintains they "reveal Madison's very early capacity . . . for philosophic analysis and the intellectual trait that remained with him throughout his life of independent scrutiny of supposedly 'received' and 'authoritative' opinion."[13] The clarity of the notes surely does suggest Madison's "capacity . . . for philosophic analysis." However, absent the discovery of the instructor's notes for the course, it is difficult to see how one might determine whether the "independent scrutiny" was Madison's or his teacher's—unless one can take Madison's brackets around a criticism of Locke as a sign it was his own.[14]

The most important benefit of the course for Madison was probably a general one—the chance it gave him to make his reason fully his own. Thomas Jefferson saw the significance of this self-mastery in his estimate of Madison on the eve of the Constitutional Convention. Jefferson reported that Madison had "acquired a habit of self-possession, which placed at ready command the rich resources of his luminous and discriminating mind, and of his extensive information." This self-possession "rendered him the first of every assembly, afterwards, of which he became a member."[15]

Self-possession can mean self-discipline, but here it means more. It involves an awareness of the proper use of the mind, of reason, and explains why, as Jefferson put it, Madison never wandered "from his subject into vain declamation" but pursued each issue "closely, in language pure, classical, and copious."[16] His speech and writing thus came to exemplify what a commentator on Plato sees as philosophy itself, "the reasonable use of words in thinking."[17] Part of the importance of the notes lies in the glimpses they provide of the process by which Madison achieved this "self-possession," or, as the philosopher Bernard Lonergan would put it, self-appropriation.[18] Lonergan sees "self-appropriation" accomplished by reflectively running over and over the operations involved in knowing. A logic course, like Madison's, organized around the operations of the mind, would facilitate this self-appropriation, giving Madison a standard and a template for future knowing, speech, and writing.

A crucial distinction in the notes—that between natural and artificial logic—taught Madison the necessity of such a reflective and critical grasp of human reason. He records in the notes that "Natural Logic is that faculty of thinking, reasoning and arguing which a Man has by Nature without any other help but his own Sagacity and Experience." It is uncritical, unreflective, unsystematic thinking. "Artificial Logick," on the other hand, "is a collection of the observations and Experience of many Ingenious Men concerning the discovery or Illustration of truth & Error, digested into order for ready use." According to the notes, the two differ in fruitfulness "as a piece of Ground dispos'd and cultivated by a careful & Skilful Planter differs from the same sort of Ground left uncultivated in the State of Nature."[19] The comparison between cultivated and uncultivated land comes from Locke's *Second Treatise,* which attributes 9/10 or 99/100 of the value of land to cultivation.[20] Watts's *Logick,* the likely immediate source, makes the contrast between a cultivated and an uncultivated mind even more extreme. Watts contends that, although God gave reason to all men, "acquired improvements," the artificial logic of Madison's notes, can improve people's reason enough to place them above so-called savages almost as much as those unfortunates are placed above "the birds, the beasts, and the fishes."[21] A similar comparison may be found in the moral philosophy lectures. John Witherspoon mentions, but does not assert, the view that men brought up "without instruction" have been "scarcely superior to Brutes."[22]

Because reason is both natural and strongly dependent on cultivation and method, it is necessary to read Madison's comments on the subject with care. If reason's strength here or there is said to be weak, that implies little as to its overall possible strength. With cultivation and support, its power relative to the passions may be substantially increased. In time, Madison came to see that institutional devices, too, may serve to make effective the largely potential rationality humans are born with and can thereby help transform both individual minds and polities. Madison's recognition of the partly contingent character of reason was a necessary prerequisite for his search for the institutional conditions necessary for its flourishing.

The logic notes begin with ideas, considered as the objects of all human thinking. Ideas are said to be excited in the mind by impressions, by substantial forms, by vibrations of the nerves, or by some process producing tiny canals in the brain. Although their precise cause is a matter of "unfathomable speculation," ideas somehow result from what are called both the faculties and also the operations of sensation and reflection.[23] Imagination, apprehension or understanding, judgment, remembrance, and the other operations involved in thinking are all defined by reference to ideas, which are considered to be pictures or images. Philosophers no longer consider the focus on ideas, the assumed faculty psychology, and the picture-thinking present in this account to be adequate. Despite its flaws, however, the account casts some very useful light on matters of political importance, such as the nature of human disagreements. Indeed, Madison may well have had the analysis in the notes, as well as Hume's *Essays,* in mind when he probed the sources of factions in *Federalist* No. 10.

The notes argue that "if all men Had the same Ideas and expess'd them by the same words, there wou'd be neither difference in sentiment, nor controversy in discourse. But so it is that the same object in different persons and at different times in the same Persons excite [*sic*] different Ideas."[24] The argument is similar to the contention in *Federalist* No. 10 that "as long as the reason of man continues fallible, and he is at liberty to exercise it, different opinions will be formed."[25] The logic notes indicate that because no two persons have the same simple ideas, "this diversity occasions an irreconcilable difference of Sentiments, which cannot be justly charg'd to the imperfection of words."[26] The result is differences in judgment. The notes see no prospect of resolving such disagreements, because, if one party lacks some simple ideas, there is, to that extent, nothing in common to which another may appeal. *Federalist* No. 10 sees no prospect of eliminating factions for similar reasons—because to do so would require eliminating the freedom that permits the diverse experience, which inevitably gives rise to different ideas, opinions, sentiments, and judgments. The understanding of the origins of ideas in the notes seems a likely source for the argument in *Federalist* No. 10 that the causes of faction are sown in the nature of man.

The notes classify complex ideas as "either partial or adequate." Disagreements over complex ideas occur frequently because their very complexity increases the likelihood of partiality: "there are very few things of which we have adequate Ideas," where "adequate" is a division of complex ideas. Fortunately, such disagreements may be mitigated by applying proper method: if you "see one side of a House," "you can form but a partial and imperfect Idea of the house: whereas if you attentively visit it on every side and examine every Chamber, your Idea is adequate and Compleet."[27] Madison recommended this technique in the *Federalist,* when he stated the need, in considering the Constitution, of "examining it on all its sides; comparing it in all its parts, and calculating its probable effects."[28] The need for viewing matters comprehensively was also a key motive for Madison's own extensive scholarship. Thus, he asked Jefferson to send him a collection of books from Paris so he could view confederations on all sides as he prepared for the Constitutional Convention. He also supported features of the new constitutional system because of the comprehensive viewing they provide. To ensure that policy proposals receive the thorough examination needed to avoid partial and inadequate ideas and judgments, Madison favored granting multiple institutions with varying perspectives shaped by their different institutional arrangements and memberships the power to review such measures. Such devices make it probable that enough varied attention will be given to measures to minimize the chance anything material is overlooked.

Federalist No. 37 offers a lengthy analysis of another factor leading to disagreements—the weakness of language as an instrument for expressing complex ideas. To put such an elaborate analysis in a work of political persuasion shows how relevant Madison thought a wider logic might be to practical politics. The relevant passage from the *Federalist* reads as follows:

> The use of words is to express ideas. Perspicuity therefore requires not only that the ideas should be distinctly formed, but that they should be expressed by words distinctly and exclusively appropriate to them. But no language is so copious as to supply words and phrases for every complex idea, or so correct as not to include many equivocally denoting different ideas. Hence, it must happen, that however accurately objects may be discriminated in themselves, and however accurately the discrimination may be considered, the definition of them may be rendered inaccurate by the inaccuracy of the terms in which it is delivered. And this unavoidable inaccuracy must be greater or less, according to the complexity and novelty of the objects defined. When the Almighty himself condescends to address mankind in their own language, his meaning, luminous as it must be, is rendered dim and doubtful by the cloudy medium through which it is communicated.[29]

In writing this passage, it is likely that Madison recalled the following sentences in his logic notes: "As no human Invention is compleat but partakes more or less of the imperfection of the Inventor, so it fares with Speech. Which by the infirmity more than by the perversity of human nature, is very far from being a certain and incontestible Indication of the sentiments of the mind. For what Law either human or Divine is so correctly worded, as not to leave room for a controverted explication, not only among those who are litigious and Intoxicated, but even among the calm and candid?"[30] The notes thus refer to the same uncertainty in revelation that Madison mentions in the *Federalist*.

A remedy for conflicting, inadequate, or partial ideas lies in the "Explication of a Word to limit and determine its precise meaning," this by definition and division. The notes mention three methods of accomplishing this: by resort to Etemology [*sic*], to *genus* and *differentia*, and to division into "the several simple Ideas of which it is composed."[31] A splendid example of Madison's application of the latter technique may be found in his all-important encounter with Patrick Henry at the Virginia ratifying convention. The triumph of Madison's reason and logic over Henry's bombast may have prevented the convention from rejecting the Constitution. Madison summed up both Henry's method and his own in the following words: "He told us that this Constitution ought to be rejected because it endangered the public liberty, in his opinion, in many instances. Give me leave to make one answer to that observation: Let the dangers this system is supposed to be replete with be clearly pointed out: if any dangerous and unnecessary powers be given to the general legislature, let them be plainly demonstrated, and let us not be satisfied with general assertions of danger, without examination."[32] Madison thus undermined Henry's strategy or habit of avoiding particulars by deconstructing his woefully incomplete ideas. The *Federalist* itself is, of course, largely an explication of words to counter partial and inadequate ideas about the Constitution.

The recognition within the notes of the inevitable differences among humans due to different sets of simple ideas and to complex ideas that are inadequate in different ways seems to have had an important influence on Madison's views of the freedoms of speech and religion. Thus, when simple ideas differ, the notes find that there is no hope of conversion or unity of sentiment and therefore opt for freedom: "The only remedy is toleration."[33] Madison articulated this same perspective in a letter he wrote to Jefferson following Madison's extraordinary success in defeating a plan for religious assessments in Virginia. Madison claimed to have stopped forever "the ambitious hope of making laws for the human mind."[34] Because of his understanding of how human minds came to have ideas, he thought it impractical and oppressive to try to impose ideas and convictions on others. In his *Memorial and Remonstrance,* he based the right to freedom of religion and of thought generally on this empiricism: "This right is in its nature an unalienable right. It is unalienable, because the opinions of men, depending only on the evidence contemplated by their own minds cannot follow the dictates of other men."[35]

The account of knowing in the logic notes probably helped shape Madison's perspective on proper institutional arrangements, as well. The epistemology of the notes begins with sensation, from which perception proceeds, followed by judgment. In the long epistemological passage of *Federalist* No. 37 referred to above, Madison listed the faculties of the mind in the same order: "sense, perception, judgment, desire, volition, memory, imagination."[36] The first three constitute an individual's cognitive process. For Madison, the policy process of the national government is, to a significant extent, that cognitive process writ large. The people's experience leads to the refined perceptions of the House, followed by the exercise of critical judgment by the Senate and then by the president. More detailed influences on Madison's epistemological accounts of mixed government may be found in notes taken by students during Witherspoon's moral philosophy lectures, an account of which follows.

Moral Philosophy

Madison's second philosophy course was an impressive, wide-ranging survey of moral and political philosophy, taught by the college president, John Witherspoon.

The course covered the following: human nature; the nature, foundation, and obligation of virtue; human relations and duties to God, others, themselves, and the material order; and the principles of domestic and civil society. The law of nature and nations and jurisprudence also received extended treatment. Jack Scott points out that Witherspoon's organization owes much to Francis Hutcheson's *System of Moral Philosophy.*[37] After lecturing on these topics, Witherspoon elaborated on them during recitations, so a student as attentive as Madison likely had Witherspoon's analysis stamped firmly on his mind.[38] Nor was Madison the only theorist or statesman strongly influenced by Witherspoon. Jeffrey Morrison has written recently that the influence of the lectures "on early American political thought (and practice) is difficult to overestimate."[39]

The number of specific parallels between the lectures and Madison's writings makes it probable that parts of the lectures entered into the habitual texture of his thinking. Parallels are evident between the lectures and the *Federalist* concerning human nature, the passions, bias, reason, the affections, institutional virtues, and balanced government. Witherspoon's lectures may also have served as a conduit into the *Federalist* for a sprawling system of thought called faculty psychology.

Witherspoon identified "two great branches" of moral philosophy, ethics and politics, the latter of which includes jurisprudence. Because he believed the principles of moral obligation "must be drawn from the nature of Man," he began with a philosophical anthropology, one full of realism, good sense, and balance.[40] It provides an admirable foundation for the account of political philosophy found later in the work. The most striking feature Witherspoon found in human nature was its character as "a compound of body and spirit." In words Madison likely remembered in writing *Federalist* No. 10, Witherspoon contended that "the Body and the Spirit have a great reciprocal Influence one upon another."[41] In *Federalist* No. 10, Madison observed that human "opinions and passions will have a reciprocal influence on each other."[42] The similarity of phrase seems too close to be coincidental. Witherspoon's direct reference to the reciprocity between opinion and passion in a later version of the lectures may reflect the kind of elaboration he provided during recitations in Madison's day: "as the influence [between truthfulness and goodness] is reciprocal, malignity of disposition, even with the greatest natural powers, blinds the understanding, and prevents the perception of truth itself."[43]

Witherspoon argued that the sources of the passions, in the acts of the will, "may be reduced to the two great Heads Desire & Aversion."[44] "The Passions," as a result, "are very numerous and may be greatly diversified; because every thing, however modified, that is the Object of Desire or Aversion, may grow by Accident, or Indulgence to such a Size as is called, or may be called deservedly a Passion." The causes of passions are thus "implanted in our Nature."[45] In *Federalist* No. 10, Madison argued that the causes of factions, passions writ large, are "sown in the nature of man" and went on to consider the astonishing variety of factions that develop around the most varied objects of desire, even around purely fanciful distinctions. Witherspoon's account of how anything can become the object of a passion may well have been a source for Madison's similar analysis, although Madison used repeated examples rather than a universal definition to show the pervasiveness of passions, thus making his account more memorable:

> A zeal for different opinions concerning religion, concerning government, and many other points, as well of speculation as of practice; an attachment to different leaders ambitiously contending for pre-eminence and power; or to persons of other descriptions whose fortunes have been interesting to the human passions, have, in turn, divided mankind into parties, inflamed them with mutual animosity, and rendered them much more disposed to vex and oppress each other than to cooperate for their common good. So strong is this propensity of mankind to fall into mutual animosities, that where no substantial occasion presents itself, the most frivolous and fanciful distinctions have been sufficient to kindle their unfriendly passions and excite their most violent conflicts. But the most common and durable source of factions has been the various and unequal distribution of property. . . . A landed interest, a manufacturing interest, a mercantile interest, a moneyed interest, with many lesser interests, grow up of necessity in civilized nations, and divide them into different classes, actuated by different sentiments and views.[46]

The lectures say that because the passions are propensities, they tend to carry human judgments along with them: "as far as they differ from a Calm deliberate Decision of the Judgment, or Determination of the Will, they may be called strong Propensities, implanted in our nature, which not a little bias the Judgment, or incline the Will."[47] In the *Federalist,* Madison found this bias unavoidable in the presence of passions of interest: "No man is allowed to be a judge in his own cause because his interest would certainly bias his judgment, and, not improbably, corrupt his integrity."[48] Other passions have similar results. Because the relation between body and spirit is reciprocal, however, reason can correct the affections, even those that become passions. A well-known passage from *Federalist* No. 49 illustrates the two-way, if here slightly indirect, commerce: "The *passions* therefore not *the reason,* of the public, would sit in judgment. But it is the reason of the public alone that ought to controul and regulate the government. The passions ought to be controuled and regulated by the government."[49]

Although Witherspoon found "most English writers of the last age" relying on reason as the standard of virtue, he took note of several thinkers of his own age who looked to the moral sense as the standard. It seemed to him to be identical to conscience or "the law which our Maker has written upon our hearts" that "both intimates and enforces duty, previous to all reasoning." Witherspoon thought the existence of the moral sense as a "principle of our nature" was as obvious as that of the gross external senses or of the reflex senses, such as the sense of beauty. However, he did not follow Hutchinson in opposing those who would "make Reason the Principle of virtuous Conduct."[50] Both the moral sense and reason play a role; Witherspoon summarized with apparent approval the argument of advocates of reason that "Reason does often controul, & alter Sentiment; whereas Sentiment cannot alter the clear decisions of Reason." He provided a striking illustration: "Suppose my heart dictates to me any Duty, as for example, to have Compassion upon a Person detected of a Crime; yet if upon cool Reflection, I perceive that suffering him to go unpunished will be hurtful to the Community, I counteract the Sentiment from the Dictates of Reason."[51]

A March 1820 letter from Madison to James Monroe provides a charming example of a similar and very self-conscious correction of a sentiment by reason. Madison asked Monroe to give special consideration to his nephew for a government position but called attention to "the personal relation which may be supposed to bias me." To counteract and correct this bias, Madison consulted justice and the public good and concluded: "however agreeable it must of course be to me to see his interests promoted, I can neither expect nor wish it farther than his pretensions may bear the test applied to those of others and those that public considerations will authorize."[52] Another example is found in remarks that an aged Madison made in the Virginia Convention of 1829. He observed that some, "consulting the purity and generosity of their own minds," would find security against tyranny in the social feelings. Unfortunately, conscience can be "misled . . . into acts which an enlightened conscience would forbid."[53]

Daniel Walker Howe argues that Madison learned Thomas Reid's faculty psychology from Witherspoon and applied it extensively in the *Federalist*. In a first account, Madison portrays a hierarchy in the psyche of, from the top down, conscience or the moral sense, then prudence, and, finally, the baser and stronger animal powers of the emotions and passions.[54] In a second account, he puts reason at the top instead of the moral sense.[55] In both versions, he sees the power of the faculties as inversely proportional to their rank order, so the passions easily out-muscle the moral sense and reason. Because the conscience is so weak, there is no hope of a nation of philosophers or even of rule by philosopher-kings. The *Federalist* therefore relies on and appeals to the more numerous group of those swayed by enlightened self-interest, by an interested, prudential reason.[56]

Although Madison frequently referred to the faculties in his writings, he probably viewed them more flexibly than Howe's account might suggest. Indeed, Witherspoon taught his students to doubt the very idea of a hierarchy of separate faculties: "the Faculties of the mind are commonly divided into these three kinds, the Understanding, Will & Affections. Tho perhaps it is proper to observe that these are not three qualities wholly distinct; as if they were three different things; but different ways of exerting the same simple [Principle.]" For Witherspoon, "it is the Soul or Mind that understands, wills, or is affected with Pleasure, and Pain."[57] Apparently, Madison had no need to consider the matter directly, but a passing reference to how the faculties of the mind shade into each other in *Federalist* No. 37 does suggest he saw an overlap or partial unity.[58] In any case, if the "faculties" are, indeed, "different ways of exerting" the single soul, as Witherspoon contended, then they are not really faculties but operations. From such a perspective, the "faculty" language would be used with a certain tentativeness. A passage in Madison's logic notes suggests the same lesson. It teaches that the names of mental operations are all similes and metaphors, as is most apparent in an ancient language such as Hebrew, and it finds that the imprecision of these figures is a cause of disputes.[59]

A Witherspoon discussion of discriminating complex objects makes a related point important for Madisonian prudence. In an aside, while weighing what is distinctive about human nature, Witherspoon observed the continuity in nature, which involves gradations such as the "glimmerings of reason" in the brutes, as well as their possession of a limited kind of speech. Because of this continuity, Witherspoon opposed reducing the distinction between men and other animals to "one peculiar incommunicable Characteristic," where "incommunicable" would deny continuity and gradation.[60] In a passage that does not appear in the notes of Madison's fellow students but only in the later published version of the lectures, Witherspoon explained that here and elsewhere nature presents "a beautiful and insensible gradation from one thing to another, so that the highest of the inferior is, as it were, connected and blended with the lowest of the superior class." Thus, "birds and beasts are connected by some species, so that you will find it hard to say whether they belong to the one or the other—So indeed it is in the whole vegetable as well as animal kingdom."[61] This may have been one of the points Witherspoon elaborated on in recitations Madison attended, before incorporating it into his lectures. In any case, Madison found such a gradation a significant consideration for the statesman.

He made use of the idea in *Federalist* No. 37 while discussing the difficulty of precisely discriminating among legislative, executive, and judicial powers. The parallel with Witherspoon suggests how thoroughly he remembered his lectures. According to Madison, the problem of separating the powers of government is merely one particular example of the general difficulty of discriminating "objects extensive and complicated in their nature." He found such difficulties an inevitable result of limited human faculties and of the complexity of objects such as the faculties of the mind and the divisions of nature. He then applied what was likely Witherspoon's analysis: "The boundaries between the great kingdoms of nature, and, still more, between the various provinces, and lesser portions, into which they are subdivided, afford another illustration of the same important truth. The most sagacious and laborious naturalists have never yet succeeded, in tracing with certainty, the line which separates the district of vegetable life from the neighboring region of unorganized matter, or which marks the termination of the former and the commencement of the animal empire. A still greater obscurity lies in the distinctive characters, by which the objects in each of these great departments of nature, have been arranged and assorted."[62]

The implication is that statesmen should not worry excessively about the inevitable imprecision in such matters but should consult prudence instead.[63] An interesting application of this lesson is found in a letter of January 6, 1831, to Reynolds Chapman on interpreting the Constitution: "It is not to be wondered that doubts & difficulties should occur in expounding the Constitution of the U. States. Hitherto the aim, in well-organized Governments, has been to discriminate & distribute the Legislative, Executive, and Judiciary powers; and these sometimes touch so closely or rather run the one so much into the other, as to make the task difficult, and leave the lines of division obscure. A settled practice, enlightened by occurring cases, and obviously conformable to the public good, can alone remove the obscurity. The case is parallel in new statutes on complex subjects."[64]

The parallels between Witherspoon's lectures and Madison's writings are especially obvious in Witherspoon's treatment of political institutions. If Madison did not need to learn Locke from Witherspoon, at least he received an excellent refresher course on the state of nature, natural rights, the social contract, the establishment of government, and the right of revolution. Witherspoon's particular influence seems to have been greater in his account of mixed government. He assessed forms of government according to their ability to provide wisdom; fidelity to the public good; secrecy, expedition, and dispatch; and institutional unity and concord. According to Witherspoon, monarchy best supplies unity, secrecy, and dispatch; aristocracy, wisdom; and democracy, fidelity to the public good. In an argument that must have intrigued Madison, Witherspoon argued that because simple forms meet only one or another of the requirements of good government, governments must be complex in form to be fully good.[65] Complex governments permit institutions to be structured and joined so that particular bodies can meet different standards and the government as a whole thereby meet them all.

This is the same view Madison took of the new constitutional system. In *Federalist* No. 62 he discussed the need for blending forms. He argued that "a good government implies two things: first, fidelity to the object of government, which is the happiness of the people; secondly, a knowledge of the means by which that object can be best attained." Madison found some governments "deficient in both these qualities," most deficient in fidelity to the public happiness, and existing American governments deficient in the wisdom needed to reach ends. He argued that the federal Constitution "avoids this error" and provides for wisdom in a way that also supports republican fidelity.[66]

Federalist No. 37 also explained the difficulty of blending institutional virtues properly:

> Energy in Government is essential to that security against external and internal danger, and to that prompt and salutary execution of the laws, which enter into the very definition of good government. Stability in Government, is essential to national character, and to the advantages annexed to it, as well as to that repose and confidence in the minds of the people, which are among the chief blessings of civil society. An irregular and mutable legislation, is not more an evil in itself, than it is odious to the people. . . . On comparing, however, these valuable ingredients with the vital principles of liberty, we must perceive at once, the difficulty of mingling them together in their due proportions.[67]

Madison appears to have drawn on Witherspoon's account of the peculiar virtues of monarchy, aristocracy, and democracy in his discussion of the strengths of the presidency, Senate, and House. Thus, he argued in *Federalist* No. 37 that "energy in Government requires not only a certain duration of power, but the execution of it by a single hand." In *Federalist* No. 62 he argued for the value of the Senate's special wisdom: "What indeed are all the repealing, explaining, and amending laws, which fill and disgrace our voluminous codes, but so many monuments of deficient wisdom; so many impeachments exhibited by each succeeding, against each preceding session; so many admonitions to the people of the value of those aids which may be expected from a well-constituted senate?" Finally, he made an extended argument for republican fidelity and its benefits in *Federalist* No. 39.[68] Lance Banning has, of course, provided conclusive evidence of Madison's constant devotion to republicanism in *The Sacred Fire of Liberty*.[69]

Witherspoon recommended a balance of institutions for another reason, as well—so that when self-interest manifests itself, the harm may be limited: "Every good form of Government must be complex, so that the one Principle may check the Other. It is of Consequence to have as much Virtue among the particular Members of a Community as possible; but it is folly to expect that a State should be upheld by Integrity in every one that has a Share in managing it. They must so be balanced, that when every one Draws to his own Interest or Inclinations, there may be an even Poise upon the Whole."[70] Witherspoon maintained that some *nexus imperii* making them necessary to each other was required to provide this balance.

This argument is strikingly similar to Madison's all-important argument in *Federalist* No. 51:

> But the great security against a gradual concentration of the several powers in the same department, consists in giving to those who administer each department, the necessary constitutional means and personal motives, to resist encroachments of the others. The provision for defense must in this, as in all other cases, be made commensurate to the danger of attack. Ambition must be made to counteract ambition. The interest of the man must be connected with the constitutional rights of the place. It may be a reflection on human nature, that such devices should be necessary to control the abuses of government. But what is government itself, but the greatest of all reflections on human nature? If men were angels, no government would be necessary. If angels were to govern men, neither external nor internal controls on government would be necessary.[71]

The key elements of this argument—a standard of integrity, a human nature unable to meet it, a complex form of government, checks among the parts to remove opportunities for abuse, and a co-opting of the sources of the problem to play a part in the solution—are all present in the Witherspoon passage just quoted.

The Legacy of Madison's Study of Philosophy

Madison's study of philosophy at the College of New Jersey provided him several important benefits. It helped him gain a highly self-conscious appreciation of his own reason. This self-possession or self-appropriation made Madison a "master of political logic" by giving him a standard against which to test his own arguments and those of others. It also suggested analogies between the cognitive process and government decision making, implying that similar methods, like reviewing, might apply to both.

The fundamental distinction between natural logic, which is inherent and weak, and artificial logic, which is acquired and potentially strong, taught Madison the partial contingency of rationality and may have suggested, along with Witherspoon's account of mixed government, the importance of congenial institutional settings. The lesson Madison learned was not to abandon reason in favor of reliance on the passions but to seek settings that would favor reason in its competition with the passions.

Madison's study of the origins of ideas suggested the futility of trying to make laws for the human mind. What he learned of simple and complex ideas and of their expression taught him the difficulties involved in symbolizing human experiences and intentions and the inevitability of disagreements based on differing simple ideas and on inadequate complex ideas. He was taught some methodological palliatives for these afflictions, but he learned that something well short of precision is all that can be expected of language. Such considerations help explain the prudential character of his political thought.

His study of human nature, especially in the moral philosophy course, impressed on his mind the reciprocal influence of opinions and affections, or passions. The implications of this reciprocity are that reason requires a suitable context in order to be properly effective and that reason itself can help make its context suitable. It can do so for the individual through the proper arrangement of ideas, that is, through method, and it can do so for society through the proper institutional arrangements. Madison's own reason was, of course, a significant factor in arranging the American political system so that it would be more conducive to the exercise of reason.

Madison learned, partly from Witherspoon, the theory of balanced interests that he soon applied with spectacular success in arguments for the large republic in *Federalist* No. 10 and for the policy of mutually checking interests in *Federalist* No. 51. The lessons he learned about the importance of reason's context and about the particular virtues of different institutional forms were necessary background for his institutional craftsmanship at the Constitutional Convention and for his defense of the Constitution afterward. Because he recognized that natural logic can be strengthened many times over by proper method and that institutions can be structured to facilitate some particular aspect of method, such as deliberation, Madison was able to develop what might be called an epistemological theory of mixed and balanced government.

Notes

1. James Madison, *The Papers of James Madison,* ed. William T. Hutchinson et al. (Chicago: University of Chicago Press; Charlottesville: University Press of Virginia, 1962–91), 1:126 (hereafter cited as *Papers*).

2. Adrienne Koch, *Madison's "Advice to My Country"* (Princeton, NJ: Princeton University Press, 1966), 113.

3. Ralph Ketcham, *James Madison: A Biography* (New York: Macmillan, 1974), 32; Francis L. Broderick, "Pulpit, Physics, and Politics: The Curriculum of the College of New Jersey, 1746–1794," *William and Mary Quarterly,* 3rd ser., 6 (January 1949): 43. Broderick says moral philosophy was taught to juniors and repeated by seniors. However, Witherspoon's account of the curriculum in his "Address to the Inhabitants of Jamaica," written while Madison was in residence at Princeton, says only that the course was taught to seniors. See Witherspoon, "Address," in *The Works of the Rev. John Witherspoon,* 2nd ed. (Philadelphia: Woodward, 1802), 4:193.

4. Quoted in Ketcham, *Madison,* 28; other information ibid., 45.

5. J. C. A. Stagg, "An Introduction to the Life and Papers of James Madison," Madison Papers, American Memory, Library of Congress, http://memory.loc.gov/ammem/collections/madison_papers/essayStagg.pdf.

6. Koch, *"Advice,"* 166–67n5.

7. Antoine Arnaud and Pierre Nicole, *Logic or the Art of Thinking,* trans. Jill Vance Buroker (Cambridge: Cambridge University Press, 1996).

8. Isaac Watts, *Logick or the Right Use of Reason in the Inquiry after Truth* (Philadelphia: Thomas Dobson, 1787).

9. James Madison, "A Brief System of Logick," MS. Madison Papers, Library of Congress, http://memory.loc.gov/ammem/collections/madison_papers/mjmser6.html (hereafter cited as *Brief System*).

10. *Papers,* 1:33; Irving Brant, *James Madison: The Virginia Revolutionist* (Indianapolis, IN: Bobbs-Merrill, 1941), 77.

11. Madison could have copied the notes from a master copy, as other students may have copied Witherspoon's moral philosophy lectures. See Jeffrey H. Morrison, *John Witherspoon and the Founding of the American Republic* (South Bend, IN: University of Notre Dame Press, 2005), 49. However, no similar copies of the logic notes have been discovered, and Madison's notes show evidence of later editing.

12. *Papers,* 1:35.

13. Koch, *"Advice,"* 12, 166–67n5.

14. *Brief System,* 12–14.

15. Quoted in Ketcham, *Madison,* 189.

16. Ibid.

17. "Plato," *Concise Encyclopedia of Philosophy,* ed. J. O. Urmson (New York: Hawthorn Books, 1960).

18. Bernard J. F. Lonergan, *Understanding and Being,* ed. E. A. Morelli and M. D. Morelli, in *Collected Works of Bernard Lonergan* (Toronto: University of Toronto Press, 1990), 5:3–21.

19. *Brief System,* 1–2. Madison may have become familiar, either in this course or later on, with the distinction that Sir Edward Coke, the chief justice of the English Court of Common Pleas, had drawn between "natural reason" and the "artificial reason and judgment of law" in questioning the judgment of James I. John V. Orth has observed that "Coke emphasized that 'long study and experience' of the law were required 'before that a man can attain to the cognizance of it.'" See Orth's *How Many Judges Does It Take to Make a Supreme Court?* (Lawrence: University Press of Kansas, 2006), 17.

20. John Locke, *Two Treatises of Civil Government,* ed. Peter Laslett, rev. ed. (New York: New American Library, 1960), 338, 340.

21. Watts, *Logick,* 13.

22. John Witherspoon, *Lectures on Moral Philosophy,* 1771–72: notebook, containing manuscript notes by Andrew S. Hunter, C0199–#538, Department of Rare Books and Special Collections, Princeton University Library, 5. I will quote and cite Hunter's notes because they are closest in time to the lectures Madison heard. The best published editions of the lectures are *Lectures in Moral Philosophy,* ed. V. L. Collins (Princeton, NJ: Princeton University Press, 1912), and *An Annotated Edition of Lectures on Moral Philosophy by John Witherspoon,* ed. Jack Scott (Newark: University of Delaware Press, 1982). Scott uses Collins's text but corrects occasional errors, as he explains at 61n175. I will therefore also cite Scott's edition, as well as the most accessible version, which is found in the 1802 edition of Witherspoon's works cited in note 3 above, which is now readily available without charge in digitized form from Google Books. Subsequent citations will thus refer to *Lectures* MS; Scott, *Lectures;* and *Works,* respectively.

23. *Brief System,* 5.

24. Ibid., 24.

25. Alexander Hamilton, James Madison, and John Jay, *The Federalist,* ed. Jacob E. Cooke (Cleveland: World, 1961), 58 (hereafter cited as *Federalist*).

26. *Brief System,* 24.

27. Ibid., 8.

28. *Federalist,* 231.

29. Ibid., 236–37; see also Gary Rosen, *American Compact: James Madison and the Problem of Founding* (Lawrence: University Press of Kansas, 1999), 23–24.

30. *Brief System,* 23.

31. Ibid., 27.

32. James Madison, *James Madison: A Biography in His Own Words,* ed. Merrill D. Peterson (New York: Newsweek, 1974), 157.

33. *Brief System,* 33.

34. *Papers,* 8:474.

35. Ibid., 8:299.

36. *Federalist,* 235.

37. Scott, *Lectures,* 27.

38. See the publisher's note introducing the *Lectures* in *Works,* 3:366.

39. Morrison, *Witherspoon,* 48.

40. *Lectures* MS, 7; Scott, *Lectures,* 66; *Works,* 3:369.

41. *Lectures* MS, 15; Scott, *Lectures,* 70; *Works,* 3:372.

42. *Federalist,* 58.

43. Scott, *Lectures,* 71; *Works,* 3:374.

44. *Lectures* MS, 19; Scott, *Lectures,* 72; *Works,* 3:375.

45. *Lectures* MS, 20, 19; Scott, *Lectures,* 72; *Works,* 3:374.

46. *Federalist,* 58–59.

47. *Lectures* MS, 19; Scott, *Lectures,* 72; *Works,* 3:374.

48. *Federalist,* 59.

49. Ibid., 343.

50. *Lectures* MS, 44, 31; Scott, *Lectures,* 84, 78; *Works,* 3:384, 379.

51. *Lectures* MS, 44; Scott, *Lectures,* 84; *Works,* 3:384.

52. Madison Papers, Library of Congress, Series 1, Image 494, http://memory.loc.gov/ammem/collections/madison_papers/mjmser.html.

53. Quoted in Ketcham, *Madison,* 297.

54. Daniel Walker Howe, "European Sources of Political Ideas in Jeffersonian America," *Reviews in American History* 10, no. 4 (December 1982): 37–38.

55. Daniel Walker Howe, "The Political Psychology of *The Federalist,*" *William and Mary Quarterly,* 3rd ser., 44 (June 1987): 491.

56. Howe, "European Sources," 37.

57. *Lectures* MS, 17; Scott, *Lectures,* 71; *Works,* 3:373. I have inserted the singular "Principle" because the other versions of the lectures all disagree with Hunter here and because the plural Hunter writes defeats the point Witherspoon is making.

58. *Federalist,* 235.

59. *Brief System,* 25–26.

60. *Lectures* MS, 9–10; Scott, *Lectures,* 66; *Works,* 3:370.

61. Scott, *Lectures,* 66; *Works,* 3:370.

62. *Federalist,* 234–35.

63. An elaborate and interesting account of Madisonian prudence from a somewhat different angle may be found in Rosen, *American Compact,* especially at 105 on the present passage.

64. Madison Papers, Library of Congress, MS, Series 1, Image 524, http://hdl.loc.gov/loc.mss/mjm.23_0523_0524.

65. *Lectures* MS, 192–97; Scott, *Lectures,* 144; *Works,* 3:435.

66. *Federalist,* 419. See also Howe, "Political Psychology," 499.

67. *Federalist,* 233–34.

68. *Federalist,* 234, 419.

69. Lance Banning, *The Sacred Fire of Liberty* (Ithaca, NY: Cornell University Press, 1995).

70. *Lectures* MS, 198; Scott, *Lectures,* 144; *Works,* 3:435.

71. *Federalist,* 349.

CRAIG GRAU

More Than an Intellectual Scribe

The Political Drives and Traits of James Madison

Although recent scholars and popularists have devoted a great deal of attention to the founding period of the United States, they have directed less attention to James Madison than to many of his major contemporaries. The last three decades of the eighteenth century encompass major events in America's history, including the Revolutionary War, the writing and ratification of the Constitution, the adoption of the Bill of Rights, the launching of the government based on the Constitution, and the advent of the two-party system. Among the "founders" six are of special focus: John Adams, Benjamin Franklin, Alexander Hamilton, Thomas Jefferson, James Madison, and George Washington. In recent decades Madison has been more likely to lead the others in the number of times that indexes of political science textbooks list him, but he trails the others among best-selling biographies.[1]

There are reasons for Madison's popularity among political scientists. He is often regarded in introductory political science texts as the father of the Constitution, author of the Bill of Rights, and the most important "explainer" of the Constitution, especially through *Federalist* Nos. 10 and 51. Advanced political science courses may also refer to Madison in American interest group, political party, and political theory classes.

Interestingly, few political scientists or biographers provide reasons beyond Madison's intellect for his historical titles or political successes. Indeed, common descriptions of Madison's personal traits might lead one seriously to wonder why he became active politically and succeeded, either at the time of the founding or today. He seemed to lack both driving political passions and personal attributes for political success.

A Man without a Personality?

James Madison is often portrayed in less than flattering personal terms. In a nation that often elevates men who are tall, healthy, and action-oriented, Madison was short, sickly, and sedentary. Scholars often describe him as bookish, cold, and provincial. Joseph Ellis, for instance, in his deservedly popular book *Founding Brothers,* writes that "'little Jemmy Madison' had the frail and discernibly fragile appearance of a career librarian or schoolmaster, forever lingering on the edge of some fatal ailment." Indeed, Madison "seemed to lack a personal agenda because he seemed to lack a personality," making attacks by opponents difficult and resulting in Madison victories.[2]

In his book *James Madison,* Garry Wills describes Madison as not only provincial but also "a prodigious worker at his desk, an omnivorous reader" who did not date until he was thirty-one years old and, when rebuffed, did not try again for a dozen years.[3] Gary Rosen refers to Madison as "the nerdy founder, the note-taker and committeeman . . . a rather dull, proper Virginia squire whose ideas sparkled far more than his domestic life or public persona."[4] Compared to the other more action-oriented founders, Madison lacked physical stature, military victories, or dueling experience. The closest popular connection between the name Madison and passion today may be sports fans in a namesake state capital or a fictitious sexual relationship in a namesake county known for its covered bridges.[5]

Adding to the Problem

It is certainly possible that being well informed on issues and underestimated by one's political opponents can be tactical advantages, but something seems missing in the current image of James Madison. He was active in the political arena for nearly four decades. It was not an easy time. One has to wonder what drove a man continually referred to as small, shy, and sickly into the rough political arena and what personality traits accounted for his successes.

Madison himself does not provide many clues. His papers that have survived are not as helpful as they could be. James Madison apparently felt that only documents and correspondence related to public matters should be saved for posterity. His wife edited letters in like manner.[6] Indeed, exceptions seem to prove the rule. Some letters escaped destruction thanks to their being in another's possession, such as those he wrote to William Bradford when he was a young man, which were kept by Bradford's relatives and show evidence of the author's emotions.[7] In order to explore a more personal Madison, scholars must supplement his papers with writings of his contemporaries.

Another factor that has inhibited such inquiry has been the academy's fixation on the *Federalist,* especially on Madison's *Federalist* No. 10. As Alan Gibson shows in a later chapter in this book, insights from these most famous of Madison's writings have captivated intellectuals since the 1910s.[8] In No. 10 Madison warns that one must guard against the mischief of minority and, especially, majority factions, which in modern terms roughly correspond to interest groups and political parties. Separation from such political organizations may suggest purity in the advocate, but lack of involvement in parties and interest groups leads one to wonder about the basis of Madison's political power. Similarly, the image of Madison as sickly and introverted conforms to the stereotype of a well-read introvert, hardly that of a major political force.

Scholar and Politician

There is little doubt that James Madison was short, shy in large crowds, and afflicted with a variety of physical maladies. He was also as well read in the studies of government as most of his contemporaries.[9] All of this is true, yet incomplete.

Contemporaries of Madison did not refer to him as a "scholarly philosopher" but as one who blended study with practical politics. In 1787 Madison's fellow delegate to the Constitutional Convention, William Pierce of Georgia, noted that Madison "blends together the profound politician with the Scholar."[10] Three years earlier the Reverend James Madison, the second cousin of the founder, advised young John Breckinridge that the reverend's relative was "the truly philosophic Politician—but you will discover it rather from private than public Conversation."[11] More than two centuries later, in the preface to his 2004 book on George Washington, Joseph Ellis chooses interesting words when describing the other founders. Ellis indicated his belief that Washington was the major founder but was not as "wise" as Franklin, as "brilliant" as Hamilton, as "well read" as Adams, as "intellectually sophisticated" as Jefferson, or as "politically astute" as Madison.[12] With exceptions like the above, modern scholars have too often underemphasized the "profound politician" known by his contemporaries more in private than in public. Important moments in the development of his political personality provide a good starting point for understanding Madison as a political actor.

An Identity Crisis

At age twenty-one James Madison had finished his college training at the College of New Jersey, today's Princeton University. He returned to Virginia to live at his family's estate, Montpelier, in Orange County, Virginia. As often occurs at this time in life, Madison was searching for his role in what he referred to as "our first entrance on the Theatre of Life."[13]

Madison was teaching his brothers and sisters, which could not have been that exciting, and he referred to the study of law as "course and dry."[14] When his collegiate friend William Bradford asked him about careers, Madison suggested the importance of "Advocates in the cause of Christ."[15] Madison, though, seemed initially more concerned that "sensations for many months have intimated to me not to expect a long and healthy life."[16] By the time he had turned twenty-two, his health had improved as he studied less and engaged in more activity in his "Obscure Corner."[17]

Madison seems to have been going through what twentieth-century psychologist Erik Erikson called an "identity crisis," which corresponds to "a variably intense period of psychosocial distress, normative in adolescence but often prolonged into adulthood, when a person is struggling more or less consciously for a clear sense of unified self and role in society." One of Erikson's best-known studies focused on the "identity crisis" of Martin Luther in the 1500s who found his identity as a monk who opposed the Roman Catholic religious establishment.[18] Taking on the religious establishment (of Virginia) would be Madison's first political cause as well.

Issue Drive: Church and State

The hardest early evidence we have of a politically passionate Madison is a letter he wrote to William Bradford shortly before the Revolutionary War. Madison wrote the letter at the age of twenty-two when the colonists were opposing the British tea tax. Madison, though, was more upset about religious persecution. He passionately wrote in this January 4, 1774, letter:

> Poverty and Luxury prevail among all sorts: Pride ignorance and Knavery among the Priesthood and Vice and Wickedness among the Laity. That is bad enough But It is not the worst I have to tell you. That diabolical Hell conceived principle of persecution rages among some and to their eternal Infamy the Clergy can furnish their Quota of Imps for such business. This vexes me the most of any thing whatever. . . I have neither patience to hear talk or think of any thing relative to this matter for I have squabbled and scolded abused and ridiculed so long about it, [to so lit]le purpose that I am without common patience.[19]

Although Madison wrote this letter in 1774, the jailing of Baptists had begun in June 1768 in the region of Virginia where the Madisons made their home.[20] Having spent his college years (1769–72) in the Mid-Atlantic region where more religious liberty existed, Madison declared his hope in the letter of visiting his Pennsylvania friend so that he could once again "breathe your free Air."[21]

Among those who Madison debated without effect on the subject may have been his relatives, including a master Virginia politician, Edmund Pendleton. Pendleton was related to Madison through his paternal grandmother, and Pendleton's ward, John Taylor of Caroline County, had attended a college preparatory school with Madison.[22] In 1771, when Baptist John Young was sentenced to jail for preaching the gospel at a person's house without having been licensed by the established church, Edmund Pendleton was one of "his majesty's justices."[23] An early twentieth-century Madison scholar has noted that Madison had a personal experience with the Baptist persecution: "An incident in his youth which made a deep impression on him was his standing outside the jail in the village of Orange and listening to several Baptists preach from the window of the cell in which they were confined because of their religious opinions."[24]

Elected at the age of twenty-five from Orange County to the 1776 Virginia Convention, which would deal with the subject of political independence from Britain, Madison's first political success would leave his mark on the issue of freedom of conscience. He sought to amend the Declaration of Rights, which George Mason had proposed. The original proposal on the subject of religion called for toleration of a person's religious beliefs. Whereas the term "toleration" suggests a power of the state to forbear from persecution, Madison saw freedom of conscience as a right. Patrick Henry carried his idea, but when confronted with the possibility that Madison's original wording would have called into question the established church, Henry retreated. Changing the wording to stress the entitlement "to the free exercise of religion," Edmund Pendleton, the presiding officer, supported Madison's amendment, and the convention adopted it.[25]

The convention became the Virginia legislature, and in the next session Madison continued his interest in the issue of state preference of one religious sect over others. With allies from Presbyterian and Baptist churches and with petitions arriving from dissident churches, Madison and his new ally Thomas Jefferson confronted the established church's supporters, including Edmund Pendleton and Robert C. Nicholas. The resulting compromise settled not on disestablishment but on suspension of pay by the government to the church for a year.[26]

Eight years later, in 1784, after the Revolution had ended, Patrick Henry led a group of Virginians who became concerned about a breakdown of morality. Henry suggested taxing Virginians for money to give to Christian teachers. Having returned to the Virginia legislature from national legislative service, Madison opposed Henry's idea. Initially, delay seemed the best strategy. Then, as his allies encouraged him to write a petition through which citizens could express their displeasure, James Madison wrote his now famous *Memorial and Remonstrance*. When the Virginia legislature returned in 1785, it was swamped with petitions against Henry's proposal, and Henry had been "promoted" to Virginia's weak governorship. The Christian teacher tax died without a vote, but Madison, sensing an opportunity, reintroduced Jefferson's Religious Liberty proposal, which had languished for six years but finally passed.[27] Madison then notified Jefferson, who was serving as ambassador to France, and he was thrilled. Jefferson notified others of the victory, and when he designed his own gravestone decades later, he placed the accomplishment second only to his authorship of the Declaration of Independence.[28]

Throughout Madison's political life, religious liberty remained an important touchstone. In his last State of the Union message as president (1816), Madison expressed his gratitude for the devotion to true liberty by the American people and "a Government which watches over the purity of elections, the freedom of speech and of the press, the trial by jury, and the equal interdict against encroachments and compacts between religion and the state."[29]

In his late sixties, after having left the presidency, Madison summarized the effects of the separation of government from religion in Virginia. Madison noted that while some had argued that the state and religion could not function without mutual help, this had not proven to be the case. As he observed in a letter to a resident of Pennsylvania, "The Civil Govt. tho' bereft of everything like an associated hierarchy possesses the requisite stability and performs its functions with complete success; Whilst the number, the industry, and the morality of the Priesthood, & the devotion of the people have been manifestly increased by the total separation of the Church from the State."[30] Madison biographer Ralph Ketcham has written, "religious liberty stands out as the one subject upon which Madison took an extreme, absolute, undeviating position throughout his life."[31]

Issue Drive: Nationalism

Madison was clearly moved to end religious persecution, but it was not his only political drive. He opposed British dominance of the colonies and thought the colonies should stick together and expand west of the Appalachians. Once again evidence of this nationalism can be found as he entered adulthood. Writing to his father from college in 1770, James Madison reported that although New York merchants had resumed importing merchandise from Britain, those graduating from his college wore "American Cloth."[32]

Madison's first political post was as a member of his home (Orange) county's Committee of Public Safety, and in 1775 this committee supported Patrick Henry's efforts against the British governor Lord Dunmore. In addition, the committee stated that a British military blow to Massachusetts was "a hostile attack on this [Virginia] and every other colony, and a sufficient warrant to use violence and reprisal, in all cases where it may be expedient for our security and welfare."[33] In 1780 Madison, in his late twenties, left the safety of his home state of Virginia, where he was sitting as a member of the Governor's Council, to serve as delegate to the national congress at a perilous time for the revolutionary effort. This is hardly a natural action for a person known to be a bookish introvert, unless he were moved by a strong passion.

In the mid-1780s a fear of a national breakup led Madison to champion a new constitution to strengthen the national government. He would not, however, keep the original states together by selling out the West. Making sure that the West had access to foreign markets led him to obtain access to New Orleans when he was secretary of state. His first presidential term would begin with Madison clothed in American cloth at his inauguration.[34] His second term would include a difficult war with Britain. His belief in nationalism was clear in a note to his country written in 1834 to be read after his death, which occurred two years later: "The advice nearest to my heart and deepest in my conviction is that the Union of the States be cherished and perpetuated."[35]

Choosing an Occupation and Positive Reinforcement

Madison's political passions of separating church and state as the United States declared independence from Great Britain occurred at the same time that he was searching for a career. His father was in charge of the family estate, and although Madison studied the law, he was not drawn to it as a profession. The ministry may have been a possibility. His family, though, was active in the established church, the Church of England, with which he was upset, and while he supported other religious sects politically, he expressed no desire to join them. Despite Madison's love of books, he never sought a career as an author or writer as did his college friend Philip Freneau.

He chose service in the government as a career. For a person who was shy, a political career would not appear to be a prime choice. Given the way scholars often describe Madison, it is equally surprising how successful he was at his career. From his first election in 1776 until he left the presidency in 1817, he was in governmental service for all but short periods. Madison found a career in government, championing the cause of religious dissenters and developing his own political identity. He took his stance against the privileged position of the established church in which relatives were active members.

Madison's parents were active in the established church. According to a cleric, who became a bishop in it, James Madison's mother was a stalwart of her local parish and one of the "few faithful witnesses" even when the church "was downtrodden and depressed." His father was a vestryman of the church, and even after the Baptist persecutions had ended, he wrote a letter to a Baptist minister in 1781 rejecting his request to use the neighborhood church though there was no resident minister of the established church at the time.[36] Edmund Pendleton, a relative, was one of the most ardent supporters of the established church in the Virginia legislature. Taking a stand for religious dissenters allowed Madison to be "his own man." Politics would allow him to act to "right a wrong."

A political career also helped Madison keep contacts with some of his collegiate friends. At college Madison not only read books and listened to lectures but also was active in a student organization and enjoyed himself. He belonged to a group called the American Whig Society, whose members skirmished with a rival group called the Cliosophic Society, attacking each other through poems. These Whigs included Philip Freneau and Henry "Light Horse Harry" Lee, who achieved historical fame.[37] Two other collegiate acquaintances, Caleb Wallace and Samuel Stanhope Smith, became Presbyterian ministers and settled in Virginia. By the time Madison became a member of the state legislature, Wallace had returned to minister among the Presbyterians in southern and western Virginia. Smith, a native Pennsylvanian, relocated to southern Virginia and in 1775 founded a school in Prince Edward County that become known as Hampden-Sidney College. Smith would be rector and Wallace a member of the board of directors. In 1776 additional members were added to that board, including Patrick Henry and James Madison.[38] That same year, when Madison was attempting to aid the Presbyterians and Baptists, an eloquent petition arrived, which was a memorial requesting the free exercise of religion according to one's conscience. It came from Prince Edward County and the Hanover Presbytery, of which Caleb Wallace was a clerk. Wallace came to Williamsburg for six to eight weeks during the session that began in October while Madison was a representative serving on the Committee on Religion.[39]

Although quiet and shy, Madison made more acquaintances in Williamsburg at the legislature. Edmund Randolph, a member of the legislature and two years younger than Madison, noted that the quiet Madison became somewhat of a magnet: "In convention debate his lips were never unsealed, except to some member who happened to sit near him; and he who had once partaken of the rich banquet of his remarks did not fail to wish daily to sit within the reach of his conversation."[40] Madison wanted to stay in this new position, but when he ran for reelection, he lost. Scholars have attributed his election defeat in 1777 to his failure to supply liquor to the voters. It is harder to explain how the House of Delegates then selected this shy introvert to sit on the Governor's Executive Council a few months later, and why he accepted that post.[41] The obvious answers are that in the short time he was in Williamsburg, Madison made a good impression, and he also enjoyed serving in government.

In two years (1776–77) James Madison had accomplished a great deal for a young man in his mid-twenties. His choice of career had been positively reinforced. He had successfully amended a statement of rights in Virginia's new constitution, and he had fought the politically powerful Edmund Pendleton to a draw on financing the established church. Those with whom he differed on the church issue may have agreed with him about splitting from Britain. Although his constituents did not reelect him to the legislature, the legislature had elected him to the Governor's Executive Council.

Madison would receive more positive reinforcement for nearly four more decades serving in many governmental capacities, never losing another election, and succeeding in increasing religious liberty and a stronger nation-state. Yet political passion and positive reinforcement are not all that account for political success. Other personal factors can include political knowledge, political skills, and positive personal attributes.

Political Learning

Madison's political knowledge was of two types, that which came from reading and that which came from experience. Scholars often emphasize the former. Indeed, he spent time acquiring knowledge of ancient and modern governments as well as political theories. In writing personal sketches of fellow members of the Constitutional Convention in 1787, William Pierce of Georgia noted in describing Madison that "from a spirit of industry and application which he possesses in a most eminent degree, he always comes forward the best informed Man at any point in debate."[42] He also possessed a thirst for knowledge and a strong work ethic. Madison was fortunate to have had excellent academic teachers, including Donald Robertson and John Witherspoon, the influence of whom David Nordquest has ably documented in the previous chapter.[43]

Witherspoon also provided Madison with a participatory model as an active delegate to the Continental Congress. He was not Madison's sole practical political model. Two others were Edmund Pendleton and James Duane. As Madison biographer Ralph Ketcham points out, Madison and Pendleton admired each other and were on the same side of most major issues, other than those involving church and state.[44] Pendleton was in his mid-fifties when Madison arrived in the Virginia legislature at half Pendleton's age, but Madison was not the only young man there. Edmund Randolph, for instance, was two years younger than Madison. When Madison was elected at twenty-six to the council to the governor, he again was not the youngest.[45] Virginians appear to have made an effort to "bring along" younger members in the legislative process.

Elected to the Continental Congress in 1780, Madison found lodging in Philadelphia in a boarding house at the corner of Fifth and Market streets, where he stayed when in that city for more than a decade. Among his fellow delegates who also stayed there was James Duane from New York. Biographer Ketcham writes that Madison seems to have become influential "in Congress first as a supporter and then as a lieutenant of Duane." By the time Madison left the Congress in 1783, the Revolution was over, and he had become an important legislator and leader in his own right.[46]

Political Skills and Attributes

Success in politics in a republic often requires the skill of working with others in order to accomplish goals. Most famously, Madison has been associated with Thomas Jefferson, yet in the years when the Constitution and the Bill of Rights were passed, Madison also worked closely with George Washington and Alexander Hamilton.[47] These, however, were only the most famous of his associates. Madison worked with many others, including George Nicholas, Edmund Randolph, and even James Monroe, who opposed him electorally yet was chosen by Madison as his secretary of state.[48] Madison had certain personality traits that made him not only a good collaborator but also a good legislator and legislative leader. He worked well with others politically because he did not require public credit for political achievements. He was not arrogant and he conveyed truthfulness. In small settings he was friendly and funny, and to most he was fair.

Seeking credit for political successes is relatively common in politics.[49] Conflict can occur when politicians struggle for such credit. James Madison did not exhibit this need; in fact, Jefferson referred to him as extremely modest.[50] Madison appeared less concerned with getting credit and more with achieving political objectives. A good example is his role in the passage of the Bill for Establishing Religious Freedom in Virginia. Certainly, he considered the bill to be important, and he played a critical role in its passage, but Jefferson claimed authorship on his tombstone, and the bill's passage undoubtedly aided the Jefferson-Madison friendship and collaboration.

Madison did not draw attention to himself. He anonymously authored *Memorial and Remonstrance* in 1785 and anonymously coauthored the *Federalist.* Largely because of his discretion, historians remain unsure about how much of the Virginia Plan, which led off proceedings at the Constitutional Convention, he authored.

Madison also had an extremely fair debating style. A Baptist minister, John Leland, who had supported Madison in some of his Orange County elections, indicated to an acquaintance, G. N. Briggs, that in debate Madison, "after stating, in the clearest manner, the positions and arguments of his opponent, if that opponent had omitted any thing that would strengthen his side of the case, he would add it, and then proceed to meet and answer the whole." Leland used words such as "candor" and "integrity" in describing Madison.[51] Jefferson referred to his "pure and spotless virtue."[52] Seeing all sides of an argument may lead some to think of Madison as "wishy-washy." Ketcham, however, quotes Albert Gallatin: "Mr. Madison is, as I always knew him, slow in taking his ground, but firm when the storm rises."[53]

In small groups Madison exhibited a sense of humor. According to biographer Ralph Ketcham, Madison's acquaintance, Mrs. Francis Few, stated that the founder's conversation was "lively and interesting."[54] Similarly, Drew McCoy quotes congressman and University of Virginia professor George Tucker, who noted that Madison's "unwonted gentleness and suavity of manner" along with his "large fund of anecdote" made him "one of the most companionable men in existence."[55]

A More Complex James Madison

Today scholars view James Madison as a reader of books, a scribe, and a writer of essays, but those who knew him well would have seen those attributes as only part of a more complex man. In addition to being well read, he was passionate about key political issues, and he was a learned, trusted, and delightful companion. His knowledge and his style aided him in becoming an important political force and a successful politician.

Madison clearly succeeded as a Virginia legislator and a member of the Continental Congress. He sparked the calling of the Constitutional Convention, the writing of the Constitution, and its ratification. He saw to it that the Bill of Rights was proposed and that the government under the Constitution was organized, and he helped form a political party. He helped accomplish all of this during the founding period, which ended when the Democratic-Republicans, the party that first coalesced under Madison's leadership in the 1790s, took control of the executive and legislative branches of the national government in 1800–1801 as the opposing party, the Federalists, started down the road to oblivion. Yet as historian Gordon Wood has written, "It is lamentable that Americans do not remember Madison as well as they should especially when we reflect on who he was and what he achieved."[56] Similarly, author Richard Labunski has unequivocally written in reference to Madison, "It is fair to say that no other person in the nation's history did so much for which he is appreciated so little."[57]

Labunski and a few others have succeeded in putting forth a view of a more political James Madison. Noble Cunningham, Jr., pointed out that in the mid-1790s, contemporaries designated the political party that opposed Hamilton and Adam's Federalists as "Madison's party."[58] James Yoho added new insights into Madison's stance on factions in *Federalist* No. 10 by pointing out that Madison was active in what today would be called interest group activity.[59] Labunski highlighted Madison's leadership in obtaining ratification of the U.S. Constitution at the Virginia convention against forces led by Patrick Henry.[60]

Madison neither restricted himself to writing political essays nor did he fit the stereotype of the "overly intellectual theorist." Some other pop psychology stereotypes do not fit him, either. A short man, he did not conform to his contemporary's "Napoleonic complex." A great political collaborator, he did not prostrate himself to those with more stature or terrorize those below himself in status. Indeed, his slave Paul Jennings said that he "never knew him [Madison] to strike a slave. . . . [He would] admonish them privately, and never mortify them by doing it before others."[61]

Madison was not known for losing his temper, challenging others to duels, or having promiscuous sex. This does not mean he lacked passions or valuable character traits. Senator Thomas Hart Benton described Madison's characteristics as "purity, modesty, decorum,—a moderation, temperance and virtue in every thing."[62] These are not bad characteristics for those who seek a personal or political model.

Understanding Madison's writings is not enough. The better citizens and scholars understand Madison the person, the more insights they may discover into not only his theories but also the founding period and the resulting political system, which is so often called a Madisonian democracy. This task is not an easy one, but we need to spend less time simplifying and summarizing what we know about James Madison and more time exploring the wide variety of characteristics of this complex founder.

Notes

1. See, for example, Kenneth Jada, Jeffrey M. Berry, and Jerry Goldman, *The Challenge of Democracy* (New York: Houghton Mifflin, 2005), A77–A100; Gary Rosen, "The Federalist," review of *James Madison and the Struggle for the Bill of Rights,* by Richard Labunski, *New York Times,* July 16, 2006.

2. Joseph J. Ellis, *Founding Brothers* (New York: Alfred A. Knopf, 2001), 53.

3. Garry Wills, *James Madison* (New York: Times Books, 2002), 5–6.

4. Rosen, "Federalist."

5. Robert James Waller, *The Bridges of Madison County* (New York: Warner Books, 1992).

6. Introduction to *The Papers of James Madison,* ed. William T. Hutchinson et al. (Chicago: University of Chicago Press; Charlottesville: University Press of Virginia, 1962–91), 1:xv–xvii (hereafter cited as *Papers*).

7. Editorial introduction to letter of William Bradford to James Madison, October 13, 1772, ibid., 1:71–72.

8. Charles A. Beard, *An Economic Interpretation of the Constitution of the United States* (New York: Macmillan, 1913); Lance Banning, *The Sacred Fire of Liberty* (Ithaca, NY: Cornell University Press, 1995), 205; Jack Rakove, *James Madison and the Creation of the American Republic* (New York: Longman, 2002), 238.

9. When asked, Madison appears to have supplied a list of books for the Continental Congress in 1782. See "Report on Books for Congress," in *Papers,* 6:62–117.

10. Pierce quoted in *The Records of the Federal Convention of 1787,* ed. Max Farrand (New Haven, CT: Yale University Press, 1937), 3:94.

11. (Reverend) James Madison to John Breckinridge, May 24, 1784, Breckinridge Family Papers, Library of Congress.

12. Joseph J. Ellis, *His Excellency: George Washington* (New York: Alfred A. Knopf, 2004), xiv.

13. James Madison to William Bradford, November 9, 1772, *Papers,* 1:74.

14. Ibid., 1:76; James Madison to William Bradford, January 24, 1774, *Papers,* 1:105.

15. James Madison to William Bradford, September 24, 1773, *Papers,* 1:96.

16. James Madison to William Bradford, November 9, 1772, *Papers,* 1:75.

17. James Madison to William Bradford, April 28, 1772, *Papers,* 1:84.

18. Erik H. Erikson, *Young Man Luther* (New York: W. W. Norton, 1962); *Random House College Dictionary,* s.v. "Identity crisis," 659.

19. James Madison to William Bradford, January 24, 1774, *Papers,* 1:106.

20. Lewis Peyton Little, *Imprisoned Preachers and Religious Liberty in Virginia* (Lynchburg, VA: J. P. Bell, 1938), 93–98.

21. James Madison to William Bradford, January 24, 1774, *Papers,* 1:106.

22. Ralph Ketcham, *James Madison: A Biography* (Charlottesville: University Press of Virginia, 1990), 4, 19.

23. Little, *Imprisoned Preachers*, 236.

24. Gaillard Hunt, "James Madison and Religious Liberty," *Annual Report of the American Historical Association* 1 (1901): 167.

25. Ketcham, *Madison,* 72–73.

26. Ibid., 75–76.

27. Ibid., 162–65.

28. Dumas Malone, *Jefferson the Virginian* (Boston: Little, Brown, 1948), 278–80; Thomas Jefferson, "Epitaph [1826]," in Merrill D. Peterson, ed., *Thomas Jefferson: Writings* (New York: Library of America, 1984), 706–7.

29. Fred L. Israel, ed., *The State of the Union Messages of the U.S. Presidents, 1790–1966* (New York: Chelsea House, 1966), 1:146.

30. James Madison to Robert Walsh, March 2, 1819, in *The Writings of James Madison,* ed. Gaillard Hunt (New York: G. P. Putnam's Sons, 1900–1910), 8:432.

31. Ketcham, *Madison,* 165.

32. James Madison to James Madison, Sr., July 23, 1770, *Papers,* 1:50.

33. "Address to Captain Patrick Henry and the Gentlemen Independents of Hanover," *Papers,* 1:147; Ketcham, *Madison,* 63–65.

34. Ibid., 176–81, 475.

35. James Madison, "Advice to My Country," in *James Madison: Writings,* ed. Jack N. Rakove (New York: Library of America, 1999), 866; Ketcham, *Madison,* 671.

36. Bishop Meade, *Old Churches, Ministers and Families of Virginia* (Baltimore, MD: Genealogical Publishing, 1966), 2:94, 87.

37. Jacob N. Beam, *The American Whig Society of Princeton University* (Princeton, NJ: American Whig Society, 1933), 21, 23, 25, 43, 47.

38. Ketcham, *Madison,* 34; William H. Whitsitt, *The Life and Times of Judge Caleb Wallace* (Louisville, KY: John P. Morton, 1888), 64.

39. Whitsitt, *Wallace,* 49, 50.

40. Edmund Randolph, *History of Virginia,* ed. Arthur M. Shaffer (Charlottesville: University Press of Virginia, 1970), 235. The original manuscript was compiled ca. 1809–10.

41. Ketcham, *Madison,* 77, 78.

42. Pierce quoted in Farrand, *Records,* 94.

43. See also Ketcham, *Madison,* 19–21, 41–44.

44. Ibid., 103, 69.

45. "Session of Virginia Council of State," *Papers,* 1:217.

46. Ketcham, *Madison,* 88, 104, 143.

47. Adrienne Koch, *Jefferson and Madison: The Great Collaboration* (New York: Alfred A. Knopf, 1950); Stuart Leibiger, *Founding Friendship* (Charlottesville: University Press

of Virginia, 1999), 1; Ron Chernow, *Alexander Hamilton* (New York: Penguin, 2004), 173–76, 247–57.

48. George Nicholas to James Madison, July 7, 1784, *Papers,* 8:316–17; Edmund Randolph to James Madison, June 12, 1786, ibid., 9:75–76; and Wills, *Madison,* 2, 3, 39.

49. Richard F. Fenno, Jr., *Home Style: House Members in Their Districts* (New York: HarperCollins, 1978), 139.

50. Thomas Jefferson, "Autobiography," *Jefferson: Writings,* 37.

51. B. T. Welch, "John Leland," in *Annals of the American Pulpit,* ed. William B. Sprague (New York: Robert Carter and Brothers, 1877), 6:180.

52. Jefferson, "Autobiography," 37.

53. Gallatin quoted in Ketcham, *Madison,* 473.

54. Few quoted ibid., 620, 476.

55. Tucker quoted in Drew R. McCoy, *The Last of the Fathers: James Madison and the Republican Legacy* (New York: Cambridge University Press, 1989), 29.

56. Gordon S. Wood, *Revolutionary Characters: What Made the Founders Different* (New York: Penguin, 2006), 143.

57. Richard Labunski, *James Madison and the Struggle for the Bill of Rights* (Oxford: Oxford University Press, 2006), 263.

58. Noble E. Cunningham, Jr., "The Jeffersonian Republican Party," in *History of U.S. Political Parties,* ed. Arthur M. Schlesinger, Jr. (New York: Chelsea House, 1972), 1:246.

59. James Yoho, "Madison on the Beneficial Effects of Interest Groups: What Was Left Unsaid in *Federalist* 10," *Polity* 27, no. 4 (Summer 1995): 587–605.

60. Labunski, *Bill of Rights.*

61. Paul Jennings, *A Colored Man's Reminiscences of James Madison* (Brooklyn, NY: G. C. Beadle, 1865), 15.

62. Benton quoted in McCoy, *Last of the Fathers,* 34.

TWO

Madison, the Constitutional Convention, and Constitutional Design

JOHN R. VILE

James Madison and Constitutional Paternity

James Madison's multifaceted work in connection with the U.S. Constitutional Convention may have been the most important of his life. Because of this work, scholars have often designated him, either singly or in conjunction with others, as a founding father. Although Madison was as worthy of this designation as anyone else, he did not apply the term "founding father" to himself. The term has layers of meaning that nonetheless illumine the role that Madison and his contemporaries played.

James Madison's Constitutional Credentials: A Brief Survey

Most accounts of the Constitutional Convention and of the early republic justifiably devote considerable attention to Madison.[1] His credentials, many of which this volume delineates in other chapters, included the following: serving actively in the Continental Congress; fighting for religious liberty, and against religious assessments, in his home state of Virginia; attending the Annapolis Convention, which issued the call for the Constitutional Convention; helping persuade Virginia to appoint delegates to the Constitutional Convention and convincing George Washington to attend; serving as the chief inspiration for, and probably chief author of, the Virginia Plan, which contained the first and most influential set of proposals introduced at the Convention; ably participating in the debates and taking the best records of the proceedings;[2] coauthoring the *Federalist* (including the remarkable essays Nos. 10 and 51), which explained and defended the new document against Anti-Federalist assaults; arguing for the Constitution at the Virginia ratifying convention, where Patrick Henry was among its most prominent foes; serving as a speechwriter for President Washington; shepherding the Bill of Rights through the First Congress;[3] founding and leading (both with the help of Thomas Jefferson) the Democratic-Republican Party; defending freedom of speech and freedom of the press in opposition to the Alien and Sedition Acts; serving as Thomas Jefferson's secretary of state during the period that included the Louisiana Purchase; spending two terms as U.S. president; helping oversee the University of Virginia; attending the Virginia state constitutional convention; and reaching out, almost as if from the grave, with an exhortation to his countrymen to cherish the Union.[4]

As Craig Grau's chapter has demonstrated, James Madison was a physically small man who was often troubled by fears over his health.[5] Thirty-six years of age at the time of the Constitutional Convention, and not yet married, he lived to be eighty-five. When he died in 1836, he was the last of the individuals who attended the Constitutional Convention. Like George Washington, Madison is not known to have fathered any children, but toward the end of Madison's life, his age highlighted the role that he had played as one of the "fathers" of the Constitution. Drew McCoy has observed that in a letter to Jared Sparks, dated June 1, 1831, Madison quipped, "Having outlived so many of my contemporaries, I ought not to forget that I may be thought to have outlived myself."[6]

Designations of Madison as a Founding Father

Repeating an encomium that his contemporaries had bestowed on him, Irving Brant called Madison "father of the Constitution" in a 1950 volume.[7] Robert A. Rutland, author of a popular Madison biography, has designated him as "*the* founding father."[8] And Marvin Meyers labeled a book of Madison's writings as reflecting "the mind of the Founder." Although Meyers did not, like Rutland, italicize the word "the" before the Founder, he indicated that if one could revisit only one of the founding fathers, it might well be Madison. Meyers identified Madison as "Washington's contriving hand at Philadelphia, Hamilton's reflective alter ego of the *Federalist,* [and] Jefferson's long-headed partner in Republican experiment." Meyers further observed that "Madison taught prudence to democrats, democracy to nullifiers, law to legalists, a reflective and generous patriotism to all breeds of the partisan, the provincial, the doctrinaire."[9] Meyers clearly intended to point to Madison's preeminence, at least with regard to writing and interpreting the U.S. Constitution.

Many other writers have followed these examples.[10] Journalist Bruce G. Kauffmann has designated Madison as the "Godfather" of the Constitution.[11] Ray Suarez conducted an interview for *The NewsHour with Jim Lehrer* with prominent scholars on the 250th anniversary of James Madison's birthday for an episode titled "Founding Father." In his opening remarks, Suarez observed that Chief Justice William Rehnquist called Madison "the Father of U.S. Constitutional Government."[12]

The Predecessors of the Founding Fathers

Jewish, Christian, and Muslim scriptures all assign a hallowed place to patriarchs in establishing peoples and nations. They variously designate Adam, Noah, Abraham, Jacob, Esau, and Moses as among the "fathers" of humanity, the Jews, the Arabs, or other nations and peoples.[13]

Just as all patriarchs other than Adam can trace their ancestry to earlier ones, those who Americans now laud as fathers or forefathers had their own forefathers, most notably the early settlers of America. Keith Stavely and Kathleen Fitzgerald have described how in 1769 Plymouth held its first annual "Forefathers' Day," something like a modern Fourth of July, to honor "the first landing of our worthy ancestors in this place."[14] Daniel Webster delivered one of his most famous orations in 1807 at the bicentennial of the landing of the Pilgrims at Plymouth.[15]

More recently, Francis Bremer authored a biography of John Winthrop subtitled "America's Forgotten Founding Father," while Edwin Bronner referred to William Penn as a "17th Century Founding Father," and Carole Marsh authored a book on Virginia's John Rolfe subtitled "Famous Founding Father." Mary Beth Norton has written a book on *Founding Mothers and Fath*ers that focuses on English settlement in America from about 1620 to 1670.[16] Abraham Lincoln's evocation of "our fathers" in the Gettysburg Address further indicates the historical continuity of the term.

The Origins and Uses of the Term "Founding Fathers"

Scholars had long used the words "fathers" and "founders" separately to designate individuals who had contributed to the formation of the nation and/or the Constitution. As improbable as it may seem, the otherwise lackluster president Warren G. Harding and his speechwriter (the first to be paid for the service), Judson Welliver, were the first to juxtapose the terms "fathers" with "founders," to create the expression "founding fathers."[17] Kenneth B. Umbreit subsequently used the term in 1941 for a book title describing the roles of Thomas Jefferson, John Adams, John Hancock, Samuel Adams, Patrick Henry, and George Washington.[18]

Scholars now routinely use the term, along with an architectural term, "framers,"[19] to designate early American patriots, and especially the fifty-six men who signed the Declaration of Independence and the thirty-nine who signed the U.S. Constitution.[20] Max Farrand titled one of his accounts of the Constitution *The Fathers of the Constitution,* Nathan Schachner called his history of the first decade of the new republic *The Founding Fathers,* and Selma R. Williams titled a book on the U.S. Constitutional Convention *Fifty-five Founders.*[21] Many subsequent books about individual American statesmen and groups of statesmen have used this title.[22]

Somewhat unusual variations of the above include Maurice Ross's inclusion of France's Louis XVI (the king of America's chief ally) as a "founding father" and

Joseph Ellis's reference to "founding brothers."[23] Cokie Roberts has recently reminded readers of a major defect of the term "founding fathers" (and brothers) by authoring a book on "founding mothers."[24] However, she acknowledges that the public roles of women were limited in the founding era.

George Washington as "Father" of the Nation

Scholars and citizens generally agree that the Constitution is important. Those who designate Madison or others as the father or fathers of the Constitution generally intend to honor them. However important the task of fathering the Constitution and its machinery of state was, those who created it did not, like the God of Genesis, do so *ex nihilo.*

Emphasizing the fathers' fathers, Michael Lind, who fairly consistently uses the more gender-neutral term "founders" instead of "founding fathers," thus distinguishes between "state-founders, or the drafters of the Constitution, and culture-founders, who bequeath the ideologies and norms that shape a nation for generations afterwards."[25] Further comparing culture-founders to "Lawgivers," Lind suggests that Constitution drafters and elected legislators are of secondary importance: "Framers improve the government of a people; Founders created the people in the first place."[26] Lind suggests that John Winthrop, Sir William Berkeley, Sir William Penn, Richard Allen ("the father of the Negro"), and Brigham Young are among America's prominent culture-founders.

In fashioning a "trans-American Pantheon," Lind suggests focusing on Alexander Hamilton, Franklin D. Roosevelt, and Frederick Douglass. Seeking further to diversify American icons, Lind also proposes adding Henry Highland Garnet, William Lloyd Garrison, Sojourner Truth, Wendell Phillips, Samuel Ringgold Ward, Thaddeus Stevens, Charles Sumner, Elizabeth Cady Stanton, Susan B. Anthony, A. Philip Randolph, Martin Luther King, Jr., Bayard Rustin, Franz Boas, Horace Mann, and Jane Addams.[27]

It is probably more traditional to focus on the founding of the nation rather than the culture, and most commentators would probably view the drafting of the specific structure of government as less important than the founding of the nation, which came first. Abraham Lincoln accordingly dated the conception of the nation—his "four score and seven years"—from the Declaration of Independence, which he identified with the principle of equality (the "apple of gold") rather than with the Constitution (the "frame of silver").[28] Associating the capital with the nation's founding rather than with the writing of the Constitution, George Will has observed that Americans designate it as Washington, DC, rather than Madison, DC.[29]

Although Thomas Jefferson was the primary author of the Declaration of Independence,[30] Americans almost universally bestow the title of father of the nation on George Washington, whom Henry Lee designated as "first in war, first in peace, and first in the hearts of his countrymen."[31] Washington, who had earlier served in the French and Indian War, won this designation for leading the patriot forces in the Revolutionary War, putting down his arms and returning to private life after the war ended, presiding over the Constitutional Convention, and serving two terms as the first U.S. president.[32]

Although such designations are common in the Western Hemisphere, where most nations were born from revolutions against mother countries, not every nation has a solitary founder or lawgiver or even a meeting or convention to which they can trace their political ancestry.[33] Thus, although it celebrates a variety of monarchs and military leaders, Great Britain, which traces its origins to the mists of time and celebrates the mores and customs of an unwritten constitution, has no equivalent to George Washington or a convention.[34] By contrast, a scan of WorldCat, an Internet database of books and other library records, shows several books on founding fathers of Australia, a nation, like the United States, with a written constitution formulated in a constitutional convention.[35] A number of biographies also feature U.S. state or county founding fathers.

Madison's Response to Authorship

In 1834 Madison received a letter from an individual whom Rutland designates as an "admiring citizen." The correspondent referred to Madison as "the writer of the Constitution of the U.S." Madison responded modestly: "You give me a credit to which I have made no claim." In denying sole authorship, he linked such authorship to paternity by observing that the Constitution "was not, like the fabled Goddess of Wisdom, the offspring of a single brain. It ought to be regarded as the work of many heads & many hands."[36]

Madison's response was consistent with his own support of republicanism and with his argument in *Federalist* No. 38 where he had contrasted the writing of many ancient constitutions by a single lawgiver with the American precedent of choosing "a select body of citizens, from whose common deliberations more wisdom, as well as more safety, might have been expected."[37] Although he professes to be somewhat uncomfortable with the word he coins, William Lee Miller thus observes in a book on Madison's role at the Convention that "one might say that the Americans resisted monofounderism . . . as they did monarchy, on republican principles—the republican principle that was the moral content of their Revolution and of the founding of the nation."[38]

Altogether, twelve states chose seventy-four delegates to represent them at the Convention that met in Philadelphia; fifty-five of these delegates attended. In responding to his admirer, Madison shared authorship, or paternity, by pointing to the collective nature of the enterprise of writing (and ratifying) the Constitution. Benjamin Franklin, who is also widely associated with republicanism, had sounded a similar theme in one of the most winsome speeches on the last day of the Convention, where, however, he failed to achieve the unanimity he sought. Arguing that "when you assemble a number of men to have the advantage of their joint wisdom, you inevitably assemble with those men, all their prejudices, their passions, their errors of opinion, their local interests, and their selfish views," Franklin professed pleasure in finding "this system approaching so near to perfection as it does."[39]

Although he would hardly have wanted to revisit such controversies, Madison could further have pointed to a number of key defeats that he suffered at the Convention. Forrest McDonald has found that Madison was on "the losing side" on forty of seventy-one specific proposals that he advocated there.[40] These included the delegates' repudiation of his proposal for a Council of Revision and for a congressional veto of all state legislation, both of which were key provisions of his original Virginia Plan.[41]

Relationship between "Father" and "We the People"

One might conceptualize the Declaration of Independence and the Constitution as the birth certificates of the nation. In such connection, one might further look for the name of the documents' father, or fathers, in the documents themselves.[42]

Although Thomas Jefferson was the chief author of the Declaration of Independence, the opening paragraph of that document identifies itself as "The unanimous Declaration of the thirteen united States of America" and purports to speak for an entire "people" who seek the "separate and equal station to which the Laws of Nature and of Nature's God entitle them." Jefferson later defended the Declaration not as his own idiosyncratic view but as "an expression of the American mind."[43] Delegates to the Second Continental Congress from all of the states signed the Declaration of Independence; the flamboyant signature of John Hancock (who was then president of the Second Continental Congress) is far more recognizable than that of Jefferson.

There are two obvious places to look for the paternity of the U.S. Constitution, namely, the Preamble and the list of signers attached to the end of the document. The latter lists delegates not as individuals per se but as representatives of the states. The first signature on the Constitution was that of the Convention secretary, William Jackson, presumably attesting to the authenticity of the document. It was followed by that of George Washington, who signed as "Presidt [*sic*] and deputy from Virginia." Thirty-eight additional signatures—one, that of John Dickinson, given by proxy—follow under the names of states, which delegates listed (if one begins from the right where the signatures started and continue from top to bottom down the column and then from top to bottom down the one to its left) from north to south. By referring to "the Unanimous Consent of the States present," delegates attempted to minimize the fact that Rhode Island had not sent delegates and that delegates Elbridge Gerry of Massachusetts and Edmund Randolph and George Mason of Virginia, who remained at the Convention on the last day, refused to sign the document.[44]

The majestic opening words of the preamble of the Constitution refer to the role of "We the People of the United States" in "ordain[ing]" and "establish[ing]" the Constitution.[45] The delegates to the Convention chose these words quite deliberately.[46] Those who composed the Constitution viewed the people as a whole as even less capable of *writing* the fundamental law (hence the need for their representatives to assemble in Philadelphia) than they would be of *writing* legislation—a task that the document clearly entrusts to a bicameral legislature, elected directly or indirectly by the people, and subject to a qualified executive veto. Still, the role of the people in constitutional *ratification* was important enough that, in one of his most important pronouncements on original intent, Madison argued that the "sense of that body [the Constitutional Convention] could never be regarded as the oracular guide in expounding the Constitution." He explained that "as the instrument came from them it was nothing more than the draft of a plan, nothing but a dead letter, until life and validity were breathed into it by the voice of the people speaking through the several State Conventions." He further observed that "If we were to look, therefore, for the meaning of the instrument beyond the face of the instrument, we must look for it, not in the General Convention, which proposed, but in the State Conventions, which accepted and ratified the Constitution."[47]

Delegates to the Second Continental Congress had written, debated, and modified the Articles of Confederation, which they had forwarded to state legislatures for ratification. Many of these legislatures had, in turn, both written and approved their own state constitutions. The Articles did not officially go into effect until the last state (Maryland, which had held out until larger states gave up their extensive western land claims) ratified in 1781.

In actions that some scholars still from time to time characterize as illegal,[48] the framers deliberately bypassed the amending mechanism under the Articles of Confederation. Although it required the unanimous consent of the state legislatures,[49] those who drafted the Constitution provided in Article VII that it would go into effect, but only among the states agreeing to it, when conventions in nine or more states ratified it. The delegates chose this convention mechanism both because they thought state legislatures were more likely to guard their existing powers, some of which they would be forfeiting, and because they thought that conventions specially called for the purpose had a better claim to representing popular wishes than did legislatures, whose members had been selected chiefly to make laws.[50]

New York's John Lansing, who favored the New Jersey Plan, argued that the Convention lacked authority to propose alterations as significant as those that the

Virginia Plan outlined.[51] Pennsylvania's James Wilson responded, "With regard to the *power of the Convention,* he conceived himself authorized to *conclude nothing,* but to be at liberty to *propose any thing.*"[52] On July 23 James Madison further observed "the difference between a system founded on the Legislatures only, and one founded on the people, to be the true difference between a league or treaty and a *Constitution.*" Later in the Convention he argued that "the people were in fact, the fountain of all power, and by resorting to them, all difficulties were got over. They could alter constitutions as they pleased. It was a principle in the Bills of rights, that first principles might be resorted to."[53]

The procedures for proposing and ratifying constitutional amendments in Article V of the Constitution further clarify the document's paternity. Consistent with its own origins, the document contains an unused mechanism through which Congress must call a convention at the request of two-thirds of the states to propose amendments; otherwise, two-thirds majorities of both houses of Congress have power to propose them. In either case, a select body of representatives takes the initiative of introducing the amendments. To become law of the land, three-fourths of the states must in turn ratify such amendments, acting, at congressional specification, either through their legislatures or, as in the cases of the adoption of the Constitution itself and the Twenty-first Amendment repealing national alcoholic prohibition, through special ratifying conventions.[54]

The ability to make the law is often associated with sovereignty. Lester Orfield has accordingly suggested that "in the last analysis, one is brought to the conclusion that sovereignty in the United States, if it can be said to exist at all, is located in the amending body."[55] The amending provisions, like those for ratification, point to supermajorities representing the people in Congress and in either state conventions or state legislatures as the ultimate "fathers" and (since ratification of the Nineteenth Amendment in 1920) "mothers" of the Constitution. While the reputation for patriotism and wisdom of those who formulated constitutional provisions might commend what they wrote and enhance the authority of the document, both in its original incarnation and in its amended form, its ultimate legitimacy rests not, as in ancient Greek republics, on the reputation of the lawgiver, but on the sanction of the people.

Assessments of Convention Delegates

Although the Constitution resulted from compromises among a number of delegates, analysts might still designate one or more such delegates who contributed substantially more than others as the "father" or "fathers" of the document. Many individuals who have written accounts of the Constitutional Convention have assessed the relative contributions of the delegates. Although few scholars arrive at identical lists of leaders, most agree that Madison was among them. One problem with assessing the proceedings is that they were originally held in secret; the most complete notes of the Convention, those of James Madison, were not published until 1841, and these were not combined with notes and letters from other delegates until the twentieth century, when Max Farrand published his *Records of the Federal Convention of 1787*.[56]

In 1861, in what may have been the first scholarly analysis of the Convention proceedings, George Ticknor Curtis identified nine individuals who he thought were most important and six others who made substantial contributions to the Convention. Curtis listed Madison as third on his top list, behind George Washington and Alexander Hamilton.[57] However, Curtis's inclusion of Hamilton (who missed much of the Convention) on his first list and Robert Morris (who hardly spoke at the proceedings) on his second suggests that Curtis may have based his assessments, which came before Farrand's careful compilation of Convention records, on the overall reputations of the delegates rather than their actual contributions to the Convention.

Max Farrand listed Madison as the preeminent person at the Convention and ranked James Wilson and George Washington just behind him.[58] Charles Warren identified Virginia as one of the five states that provided the "ablest delegations" and listed Madison among ten delegates who provided the final "form" to the Constitution.[59] Sol Bloom, who directed sesquicentennial celebrations and helped compile a book on the Constitution, characterized Washington as "the most important man in the convention," Madison as "the principal architect of the Constitution," and Franklin as "the seer of the convention."[60] Writing about the same time, historian Frank Garver listed Madison, with Wilson and Gouverneur Morris, in the top of three tiers.[61]

Merrill Jensen gave special credit to twelve delegates according to their ideologies. He listed Madison, Wilson, and Gouverneur Morris as "the outstanding national leaders."[62] Clinton Rossiter has written the most thorough classification of delegates. He designated Madison, Wilson, Washington, and Gouverneur Morris as among what he calls "the Principals," the highest among eight categories.[63] Choosing to sort delegates by their perceived talents, Broadus Mitchell and Louise Pearson Mitchell included Hamilton, Franklin, Madison, Mason, Robert Morris, Gouverneur Morris, Washington, and Wilson as being in "the first order of ability."[64]

Margaret Horsnell highlighted eleven delegates in an article she wrote for the constitutional bicentennial. They were Washington, Randolph, Sherman, Rutledge, Wilson, Gouverneur Morris, Mason, Martin, Paterson, Johnson, and Madison.[65] Seeming to list delegates in the order of their importance (although Hamilton's ranking would certainly be quite questionable), Carol Berkin identifies the twelve individuals she believes were "critical participants" at the Convention as Madison, Hamilton, Franklin, Sherman, Gouverneur Morris, Wilson, Gerry, Paterson, Dickinson, Charles Pinckney, Randolph, and Mason.[66]

Analysis of the Rankings

One of the striking features of these analyses is that all twelve studies include Madison within the top rank of delegates. The only other two delegates with a similar record are Gouverneur Morris and James Wilson, both representing Pennsylvania at the Convention. Ten of twelve studies rank Connecticut's Roger Sherman in the highest category, nine put Virginia's George Washington there, and eight include Virginia's George Mason and Pennsylvania's Benjamin Franklin.

One way to assess influence is to determine how frequently delegates spoke. Not surprisingly, there is considerable overlap between the number of times that records indicated that delegates spoke and their historical assessments. An elusive nineteenth-century survey of Convention speeches indicates that the most loquacious speakers were Gouverneur Morris, who was recorded as speaking 173 times; James Wilson, who spoke 168 times; James Madison, who spoke 161 times; Roger Sherman, who spoke 138 times; George Mason, who spoke 136 times; and Elbridge Gerry, who spoke 119 times.[67]

Other Contenders

One way of assessing Madison's contributions to the Constitution is to compare them to the contributions that others made there. A number of delegates are believed or are known to have exerted special influence at the Constitutional Convention.

Washington and Franklin

Commentators on the Constitutional Convention generally agree that the two delegates who had worldwide reputations were George Washington and Benjamin Franklin. Federalists subsequently cited their participation as a way of securing support for ratification. One of the difficulties of ranking George Washington at the Convention was his relative silence. He gave a short acceptance speech after the delegates selected him as president of the Convention and then went without giving a recorded speech until the last day of deliberations. Although better known for his qualities of character than for his intellect, Washington's vision for America corresponded in significant ways with the document that the Convention produced.[68] The cover of *Liberty* magazine for February 29, 1936, designed by Carl Pfeufer, depicts Washington holding a scroll titled, "Rights Guaranteed to Every American Under the Constitution."[69] Most portraits of the Convention give a prominent place to Washington, corresponding to his role as its presiding officer; many focus specifically on the signing of the document.[70]

Like the role of Washington, the role of Benjamin Franklin is difficult to assess, in part because of his age (at eighty-one, he was the oldest member of the Convention) and poor health (he had gout and stones). A year after the Convention, Franklin observed that had he died at seventy, he "would have cut off twelve of the most active years of my life." At several critical points at the Convention, Franklin emerged as a key conciliator, and the most detailed account of Franklin's role at the Convention concludes that he deserves to be seen as quite important.[71]

Gouverneur Morris

In addition to his having spoken the most frequently, Gouverneur Morris's influence on the Committee of Style that put the finishing touches on the document might give him an edge in being designated the "father" of the Constitution. Morris wrote a letter to Timothy Pickering on December 22, 1814, in which he claimed that the Constitution had been "written by the fingers, which write this letter."[72] James Madison confirmed Morris's role when he observed in a letter to Jared Sparks dated April 8, 1831, that "The *finish* given to the style and arrangement of the Constitution fairly belongs to the pen of Mr Morris; the task having, probably, been handed over to him by the chairman of the Committee, himself a highly respectable member, and with the ready concurrence of the others. A better choice could not have been made, as the performance of the task proved."[73] Although he spoke frequently and influenced the final style of the Constitution, Morris did not, like Madison, advance a major plan at the Convention, and he clearly did not play the subsequent role in American politics that Madison and some other delegates did.

Alexander Hamilton

Although Mary Stockwell demonstrates in a subsequent chapter of this volume that the friendship between James Madison and Alexander Hamilton was short-lived, a recent book by Charles Cerami has highlighted the influence that both men had on the Constitution.[74] Although Cerami does an excellent job of showing how these men pushed for both the convening of the Constitutional Convention and the ratification of the resulting Constitution, Hamilton clearly played a subordinate role to Madison in terms of the actual constitutional provisions he introduced at the Convention. As part of a divided state delegation that neutralized his influence, he absented himself through much of the Convention proceedings. Clinton Rossiter, who has published both an account of the Convention and a biography of Hamilton, classified Hamilton, with Robert Morris, as two of the Convention's "inexplicable disappointments."[75]

Roger Sherman

David Brian Robertson has recently advanced an exciting reinterpretation of the Constitutional Convention that focuses on the important role that Madison's opponents, especially Connecticut's Roger Sherman, had in modifying the central elements of the Virginia Plan. Robertson convincingly argues that the result was a distinctively more federal arrangement with less explicit guarantees of powers to Congress and a more ambiguous relationship between it and the states than that which the Virginia Plan, which Madison had supported, had originally proposed.

Distinguishing Madison's "principal role in bringing the Constitution into existence" and his "singular influence on Constitutional development" from his limited success in "designing its provisions," Robertson emphasized that "the original Constitution's design is not the product of a systematic philosophical plan, but the by-product of a path-dependent sequence of political compromise largely forced on Madison and his allies by their Convention opponents."[76] The fact that Robertson continues to take the Virginia Plan as the Convention's point of departure suggests, however, that Robertson underlines Madison's role, albeit as part of a larger whole, as much as he undermines it.

Other Important Contributors

From time to time, authors have advanced other individuals for consideration as the most important constitutional fathers. Hannis Taylor thus once wrote a pamphlet, now generally discredited, claiming that James Madison had largely been influenced by a pamphlet that Pelatiah Webster, a Philadelphia merchant, had written in 1783, titled *A Dissertation on the Political Union and Constitution of the United States of America.*[77] Collier and Collier have revived the accusation that Madison's notes underemphasized the role of South Carolina's Charles Pinckney, the egotistical young defender of slavery who is believed to have had a plan ready for the opening day of Convention business but whose later claims of constitutional influence appear to have been wildly exaggerated.[78]

James Wilson certainly deserves recognition, especially for the contributions that he made to the American presidency, but again, his overall role was subordinate to that of Madison. Observing Wilson's important contributions, one scholar notes that, especially in his attachment to the nation rather than to a state (Wilson was a Scottish immigrant), he "was in many ways quite atypical of the framers, almost sui generis."[79]

The importance of delegates like George Mason, Martin Luther, Edmund Randolph, and Elbridge Gerry, while at times considerable, is undercut by the fact that they either left before the proceedings were over or decided not to sign. To some extent, Madison and his colleagues gained even partial credit for Anti-Federalist ideas by ultimately choosing to support, rather than obstruct, proposals for a bill of rights.

Later Founders

In 1933 the Constitutional Educational Association of Chicago, an organization that also published and distributed the Atwood Books on the Constitution, produced a large illustrated print of the U.S. Constitution.[80] As is common in such prints, the outside border of the document portrays various framers who contributed to the Constitution. One of the unique aspects of this print is that the publisher did not limit himself to portraying individuals who attended the Convention.

While surprisingly omitting Madison altogether, the print pictures George Washington as responsible for the "Creation" of the Constitution; Benjamin Franklin (perhaps for his role in the Albany Plan of Union and for his work as a diplomat) for the "Preparation" of the Constitution; and Alexander Hamilton for the "Ratification" of the Constitution. Continuing (with the possible exception of Franklin) in this Federalist vein, it then proceeded beyond delegates to the Convention to cite John Marshall as the "Interpreter" of the Constitution, Daniel Webster as the "Expositor" of the Constitution, and Abraham Lincoln as the "Preserver" of the Constitution.[81] In yet another variation of this theme, a print published in 1866 inscribed the faces of Union generals Grant, Sherman, Meade, Thomas, and Sheridan through calligraphy into the constitutional text, visually equating their deeds with preservation of the document.[82]

These prints emphasize that an individual does not have to have been a member of the founding generation, or even a member of the Constitutional Convention, in order to have influenced the Constitution. Some understandings of today's Constitution are as much the work of Abraham Lincoln and Franklin Roosevelt[83] as of George Mason and Edmund Randolph. Mount Rushmore, a distinct American icon, notably links two founding presidents (Washington and Jefferson) with two later ones (Lincoln and Theodore Roosevelt); similarly, a memorial to Franklin D. Roosevelt in the nation's capital now joins those to Washington, Jefferson, and Lincoln. As "We the People" have expanded to include Native Americans, African Americans, women, and others, those who have contributed to understandings of the Constitution have also expanded.

The Authority of the Founding Fathers as a Constitutional Support

Although no one appears to have coined the term "founding fathers" in Madison's day, he would almost surely have appreciated its appeal to antiquity, which many people in turn tie to sagacity.[84] In *Federalist* No. 49 Madison critically examined a proposal that Thomas Jefferson had offered for calling a constitutional convention whenever two-thirds of the members of two branches of government thought such a convention was appropriate. Madison raised a number of arguments against this arrangement, but the most interesting and relevant for the purposes of this chapter was his argument that frequent appeals to the people would undermine constitutional authority. Madison observed that "as every appeal to the people would carry an implication of some defect in the government, frequent appeals would, in great measure, deprive the government of that veneration which time bestows on everything, and without which perhaps the wisest and freest governments would not possess the requisite stability." Madison hoped and believed that the age of the Constitution (and perhaps of its founders) would reinforce constitutional norms: "When the examples which fortify opinion are *ancient* as well as *numerous,* they are known to have a double effect." Madison recognized that in "a nation of philosophers . . . reverence for the laws would be sufficiently inculcated by the voice of an enlightened reason," but he hastened to add that "a nation of philosophers is as little to be expected as the philosophical race of kings wished for by Plato. And in every other nation, the most rational government will not find it a superfluous advantage to have the prejudices of the community on its side."[85]

In his more famous *Federalist* No. 10, in addition to emphasizing the pluralistic nature of the expansive government with a multitude of factions that the Constitution was creating, Madison further separated the generation that secured the Revolution and wrote the Constitution from those that might follow. Emphasizing the need for formalized mechanisms to secure the rights of minority factions, Madison observed that "it is in vain to say that enlightened statesmen will be able to adjust these clashing interests and render them all subservient to the public good. Enlightened statesmen will not always be at the helm."[86] The framers clearly designed the provisions in Article V for supermajority proposal and ratification of amendments to guard the Constitution against temporary passions on the part of the people.

Fame and the Founding Fathers

For more than a hundred years, most interpretations of those who had attended the Constitutional Convention were highly laudatory.[87] Scholars portrayed the drafters as wise and far-sighted statesmen, and, perhaps, even as divinely inspired.[88] In the early twentieth century, Charles Beard shook both popular and scholarly understandings of the proceedings by claiming that the founding fathers had largely sought to protect their financial interests.[89] Beard's thesis was more than a historical exercise; it pulled a psychological punch. Fathers who sire children merely to work their farms or mines or to take care of them in their old age are not as noble, or as worthy of praise, as those who sacrifice on behalf of their posterity.

Subsequent scholars have successfully challenged any simple equation between the motives of the founders and individual economic self-interests,[90] but they remain divided as to whether to attribute the delegates' actions to philosophic principles or to more wily political maneuverings.[91] Gouverneur Morris was among the delegates at the Convention who argued that "the love of fame is the great spring to noble & illustrious actions,"[92] and Alexander Hamilton referred to fame in *Federalist* No. 72 as "the ruling passion of the noblest minds."[93] Among modern scholars, Douglass Adair has arguably done the most to direct attention to the way in which the founding fathers' (and it seems significant that he chose to use this term to describe them) desire for fame transformed "egotism and self-aggrandizing impulses into public service." Distinguishing fame, which is the regard of wise men and posterity, from mere popularity, Adair hypothesized, in language that especially resonates with the paternalistic reference to founding fathers, that "the love of fame encourages a man to make history, to leave the mark of his deeds and his ideals on the world; it incites a man to refuse to be the victim of events and to become an 'event-making' personality—a being never to be forgotten by those later generations that will be born into a world his actions helped to shape."[94]

When scholars refer positively to founding fathers, they are helping the framers achieve the immortality that many of them sought. Although the dead cannot presumably enjoy such honors except perhaps as ethereal observers, the living may aspire to them. An emphasis on plural fathers, and the increasing attention given to founding mothers, further points present-day seekers of glory to more collective, and more democratic, pathways than would an emphasis on a single father.

Madison as a Scholar's Scholar: The Geek Factor

Like members of other occupations, modern political scientists and historians share common assumptions and values that stem from their professions. One of the author's colleagues has suggested that scholars highly value Madison precisely because he so epitomizes their own academic strengths. One could certainly argue whether Alexander Hamilton, Thomas Jefferson, John Adams,[95] or James Madison was the smartest, but Madison probably came closest to epitomizing the scholar. As Craig Grau documents in the previous chapter of this book, Madison was not a dashing Revolutionary War hero like Washington or Hamilton, a world traveler or polished speaker like John Adams, or a debonair diplomat like Jefferson. The most physically diminutive of the four, he prepared for the Constitutional Convention chiefly by reading books that he had asked Jefferson to send from France and by writing essays. Madison was shy and awkward around women, yet he married the quintessential entertainer and went on to occupy the highest office in the land. Kauffmann, who has high praise for Madison, has appropriately lauded him as "A Bookworm's Bookworm."[96]

Although scholars more frequently apply the term "father" of American political science to John Burgess, a Columbia professor of a century later, Madison's authorship of *Federalist* No. 10 would certainly qualify him for that role. The American Political Science Association has named both a lecture and scholarships after him. Not only did Madison embody republicanism,[97] but he also seems to confirm that political analysis and political writings matter. As long as individuals continue to recognize Madison as *the* founding father, or at least as prominent among those who are so designated, contemporary scholars can keep alive the hope that fame might also smile upon them and that the work they have done in the cloister could influence future public policy in positive directions.

The Implications of Vindicating Joint Paternity

Biological paternity by one father precludes biological paternity by another. One can have multiple sires (and grandsires) only if they represent different generations. Political paternity, especially in a republic, which broadens participation in politics, is not so exclusive. The nation has had more founding fathers than it has had presidents. It does not detract from James Madison's reputation to recognize Roger Sherman's part in modifying his ideas at the Convention, George Washington's contribution in presiding over and lending his prestige to the proceedings, James Wilson's role in shaping the presidency, Gouverneur Morris's role in polishing the Constitution's prose, the Anti-Federalists' importance in insisting on a bill of rights, John Marshall's role in interpreting the document in the early court, Abraham Lincoln's part in preserving the Union, or Earl Warren's or Martin Luther King, Jr.'s, roles in contemporary understandings of the document.

This chapter thus vindicates Warren G. Harding's use of the plural designation in founding fathers (if widened to include women and minorities) and Madison's own willingness to share credit with others. When it comes to a government as complex as that of the United States, the term "founding fathers" remains both historically more accurate and more in accord with republican theory than attempts to seek out a single founder. In terms of constitutional paternity, James Madison certainly is at or near the top of any list of founding fathers or brothers, but he is at best first among equals, or *primus inter pares.*[98]

Notes

1. And, needless to say, some such accounts make Madison the central focus. See, for example, William Lee Miller, *The Business of May Next: James Madison and the Founding* (Charlottesville: University Press of Virginia, 1992).

2. Madison not only took the best notes of the Convention but also wrote one of the earliest accounts of its formation. See "Preface to Debates in the Convention of 1787," in *The Records of the Federal Convention of 1787,* ed. Max Farrand (New Haven, CT: Yale University Press, 1966), 3:539–51. For a more recent edition of Madison's notes, see Edward J. Larson, *The Constitutional Convention: A Narrative History from the Notes of James Madison* (New York: Random House, 2005).

3. Madison is arguably more correctly designated as the father of the Bill of Rights than of the Constitution itself. For his role, see Robert Goldwin, *From Parchment to Power: How James Madison Used the Bill of Rights to Save the Constitution* (Washington, DC: AEI Press, 1997).

4. In 1834 Madison wrote his "Advice to My Country," which the *National Intelligencer* appropriately published in 1850, a year in which controversies over slavery dominated. In this posthumously published address, Madison said that "the advice nearest to my heart and deepest in my conviction is that the Union of the States be cherished and perpetuated. Let the open enemy to it be regarded as a Pandora with her box opened; and the disguised one, as the Serpent creeping with his deadly wiles into Paradise." Marvin Meyers, ed., *The Mind of the Founder: Sources of the Political Thought of James Madison* (Indianapolis, IN: Bobbs-Merrill, 1973), 576.

5. Madison appears to have come close to suffering an emotional breakdown during his student days. Not long after, he wrote a friend in November 1772 indicating that his "sensations for many months past have intimated to me not to expect a long or healthy life." Quoted in Jack N. Rakove, *James Madison and the Creation of the American Republic,* 3rd ed. (New York: Pearson Longman, 2007), 4–5.

6. Quoted in Drew R. McCoy, *The Last of the Fathers: James Madison and The Republican Legacy* (New York: Cambridge University Press, 1989).

7. Irving Brant, *James Madison: Father of the Constitution, 1787–1800* (Indianapolis, IN: Bobbs-Merrill, 1950). Michael Lind, who almost treats Madison with contempt in *The Next American Nation: The New Nationalism and the Fourth American Revolution* (New York: Free Press, 1995), traces the emphasis on Madison to the 1940s and 1950s (376). This would roughly correspond to the time when book titles appear to list Madison as the father of the Constitution. In contrast to Lind, who sees the designation of Madison as father as largely ideological, this author would trace such attribution to more widespread scholarly knowledge of the Constitutional Convention, much of which followed Max Farrand's compilation of Convention records and subsequent narratives of the proceedings.

8. Robert A. Rutland, *James Madison:* The *Founding Father* (New York: Macmillan, 1987). Emphasis in the original.

9. Meyers, *Mind of the Founder,* xviii, xix.

10. See, for example, Frank R. Donovan, *Mr. Madison's Constitution: The Story behind the Constitutional Convention* (New York: Dodd, Mead, 1965); Katharine E. Wilkie and Elizabeth R. Moseley, *Father of the Constitution: James Madison* (New York: Messner, 1963); Barbara Mitchell and Alex Tavoularis, *Father of the Constitution: A Story about James Madison* (Minneapolis, MN: Carolrhoda Books, 2004); and Brent P. Kelly and Arthur M. Schlesinger, Jr., *James Madison: Father of the Constitution* (Philadelphia: Chelsea House, 2001).

11. Bruce G. Kauffmann, "James Madison: Godfather of the Constitution," *Early American Review* (Summer 1997), http://earlyamerica.com/review/summer97/madison.html.

12. "Founding Father," *The NewsHour with Jim Lehrer,* PBS, March 22, 2001, transcript online at http://www.pbs.org/newshour/bb/white_house/jan-june01/madison_03-22.html.

13. For an effective, but unusual, use of the term "father" that seeks to combine paternal and maternal roles, see Aaron Wildavsky, *The Nursing Father: Moses as a Political Leader* (Tuscaloosa, AL: University of Alabama Press, 1984).

14. Keith Stavely and Kathleen Fitzgerald, *America's Founding Food: The Story of New England Cooking* (Chapel Hill: University of North Carolina Press, 2004).

15. Robert V. Remini, *Daniel Webster: The Man and His Time* (New York: W. W. Norton, 1997), 178–87.

16. Francis Bremer, *John Winthrop: America's Forgotten Founding Father* (New York: Oxford University Press, 2003); Edwin B. Bronner, *William Penn, 17th Century Founding Father: Selections from His Political Writings* (Wallingford, PA: Pendle Hill Publications, 1975); Carole Marsh, *John Rolfe: Famous Founding Father* (Peachtree City, GA: Gallopade International, 2002); Mary Beth Norton, *Founding Mothers and Fathers* (New York: Alfred A. Knopf, 1996). Norton's title is especially appropriate because she specifically focuses on family relations during this period.

17. Hendrik Hertzberg, interview by Terry Gross, broadcast on *Fresh Air*, July 14, 2004. Also see William Safire, *Safire's New Political Dictionary: The Definitive Guide to the New Language of Politics* (New York: Random House, 1993), 263.

18. Kenneth B. Umbreit, *Founding Fathers: Men Who Shaped Our Tradition* (New York: Harper and Brothers, 1941). The *Oxford English Dictionary* attributes the origin of the term "founding fathers" to Umbreit, but it does so by incorrectly citing the publication date of the Umbreit volume as 1914 rather than 1941. Relying on the *OED*, Safire repeats this mistake at page 263 of his *New Political Dictionary*.

19. For reflections on this term, see John R. Vile, "Framers," in *The Constitutional Convention of 1787: A Comprehensive Encyclopedia of America's Founding* (Santa Barbara, CA: ABC-CLIO, 2005), 2:288–89, and Akhil Reed Amar, "Architecture +," *Indiana Law Journal* 77 (Fall 2002), 671–700. The term "framers" fits nicely with the idea of a Constitution that "constitutes." See William F. Harris II, *The Interpretable Constitution* (Baltimore, MD: Johns Hopkins University Press, 1993). In a wise book, Derek Davis designates individuals who drafted the Constitution and the Bill of Rights as "framers" and the wider group of members of early congresses as "founding fathers" or "founders." See *Religion and the Continental Congress, 1774–1789* (New York: Oxford University Press, 2000), xiv.

Consistent with this analogy, the city of Philadelphia hosted a "Federal Procession" to honor the new Constitution on July 4, 1788. The procession featured a long parade of craftsmen, and Francis Hopkinson wrote a song for the event titled "The Raising: A Song for Federal Mechanics." See Laura Rigal, "'Raising the Roof: Authors, Spectators and Artisans in the Grand Federal Procession of 1788," *Theatre Journal* 78, no. 3 (1997): 253–77.

20. A total of fifty-five men attended the Convention. As will be apparent in this essay, scholars sometimes include individuals who attended but did not sign among those whom they designate as "founding fathers." The titles cited in the text are intended to be representative rather than exhaustive. Many other titles include the phrase "founding fathers."

21. Max Farrand, *The Fathers of the Constitution: A Chronicle of the Establishment of the Union* (New Haven, CT: Yale University Press, 1921); Nathan Schachner, *The Founding Fathers* (New York: Capricorn Books, 1954); Selma R. Williams, *Fifty-five Fathers: The Story of the Constitutional Convention* (New York: Dodd, Mead, 1970).

22. Richard Morris, has subtitled his book *Seven Who Shaped Our Destiny* (New York: Harper and Row, 1973) "The Founding Fathers as Revolutionaries"; M. E. Bradford titled his biographies of the individuals who attended the Constitutional

Convention of 1787 as *Founding Fathers: Brief Lives of the Framers of the United States Constitution* (2nd rev. ed.; Lawrence: University Press of Kansas, 1994); and Bruce Ackerman's book on the election of 1800 refers to *The Failures of the Founding Fathers* (Cambridge, MA: Belknap, 2005). Ray B. Browne and Glenn J. Browne have edited a book titled *Laws of Our Fathers: Popular Culture and the U.S. Constitution* (Bowling Green, OH: Bowling Green State University Press, 1986); Bill Adler has edited *America's Founding Fathers: Their Uncommon Wit and Wisdom* (Lanham, MD: Taylor Trade Publishing, 2003); David L. Holmes has edited *The Faiths of the Founding Fathers* (New York: Oxford University Press, 2006), which includes three individuals who attended the Constitutional Convention and three that did not; Steven Waldman focuses on the faith of Franklin and the first four presidents in his *Founding Faith: Providence, Politics, and the Birth of Religious Freedom in America* (New York: Random House, 2008); Bernard I. Cohen has authored *Science and the Founding Fathers: Science in the Political Thought of Jefferson, Franklin, Adams, and Madison* (New York: W. W. Norton, 1995); Stuart E. Leibiger has written *Founding Friendship: George Washington, James Madison, and the Creation of the American Republic* (Charlottesville: University Press of Virginia, 1999); and, in a theme that has become increasingly popular among students of the revolutionary generation, Charles C. Tansill has more daringly written a book titled *The Secret Loves of the Founding Fathers* (New York: Devin-Adair, 1964). Several other books, such as Frank W. Fox's *The American Founding,* 2nd ed. (Boston: Pearson, 2003), refer more generally to the "founding."

Many individual biographies of the revolutionary generation also used the "founding father" moniker. A review of the online listings of WorldCat reveals the following examples: Richard Brookhiser, in *Founding Father: Rediscovering George Washington* (New York: Free Press, 1996), calls George Washington a "founding father"; Paul Johnson, in *George Washington: The Founding Father* (New York: HarperCollins, 2005), distinguishes him as "the founding father"; and Janice Connell, in *Faith of Our Founding Father: The Spiritual Journey of George Washington* (New York: Hatherliegh, 2004), calls Washington "our founding father." Titles and subtitles of books often indicate an author's designation of the subject as a founding father. See, for example, Marvin R. Zahniser, *Charles Cotesworth Pickney: Founding Father* (Chapel Hill: University of North Carolina Press, 1967); James Strodes, *Franklin: The Essential Founding Father* (Washington, DC: Regnery, 2002); Leila Foster, *Benjamin Franklin: Founding Father and Inventor* (Springfield, NJ: Enslow, 1997); Page Smith, *James Wilson, Founding Father, 1742–1798* (Chapel Hill: University of North Carolina Press for the Institute of Early American History and Culture, 1956); George Billias, *Elbridge Gerry: Founding Father and Republican Statesman* (New York: McGraw-Hill, 1976), despite Gerry's opposition to adoption of the Constitution; Betsy M. Ross, *From Loyalist to Founding Father: The Political Odyssey of William Samuel Johnson* (New York: Columbia University Press, 1980); Walter Stahr, *John Jay: Founding Father* (New York: Hambledon and London, 2005); Sarah R. Riedman, *Benjamin Rush: Physician, Patriot, Founding Father* (New York: Abelard-Schuman, 1964); Lisa DeCarolis, *Alexander Hamilton: Federalist and Founding Father* (New York: PowerPlus Books, 2003); Brenda Haugen, *Alexander Hamilton: Founding Father and Statesman* (Minneapolis, MN: Compass Point Books, 2005); E. Merton Coulter, *Abraham Baldwin: Patriot, Educator, and Founding Father* (Arlington,

VA: Vandamere, 1987); Mildred C. Sargent, *William Few, a Founding Father: A Biographical Perspective of Early American History* (New York: Vantage, 2004).

For the bicentennial of the American Revolution, *Newsweek* produced *The Founding Fathers,* a series of two-volume biographies of selected founders taken mostly from their own writings. They included Adams, Franklin, Hamilton, Jefferson, Madison, and Washington and were published by Harper and Row of New York from 1972 to 1974. Similarly, Arlington House of New Rochelle, New York, issued a set of volumes in 1970 called *Giants of America, The Founding Fathers.* The set included biographies of Adams, Franklin, Jefferson, Hamilton, Henry, Madison, Monroe, Gouverneur Morris, and Washington.

23. Maurice Ross, *Louis XVI, America's Forgotten Founding Father, With a Survey of the Franco-American Alliance of the Revolutionary Period* (New York: Vantage, 1976); Joseph J. Ellis, *Founding Brothers: The Revolutionary Generation* (New York: Alfred A. Knopf, 2000).

24. Cokie Roberts, *Founding Mothers: The Women Who Raised Our Nation* (New York: William Morrow, 2004).

25. Lind, *Next American Nation,* 364. David Hacket Fischer, in *Albion's Seed: Four British Folkways in America* (New York: Oxford University Press, 1989), engages in a similar cultural focus.

26. Lind, *Next American Nation,* 364.

27. Ibid., 368–69. Attributing the rise to ideological strategies in the 1940s and 1950s, Lind suggests that "the earlier image of Madison as a relatively inconsequential figure was accurate" (377).

28. Taken from Lincoln's response to Alexander Stephens, vice president of the Confederate States, who had cited the words of Proverbs 25:11, "A word fitly spoken is like apples of gold in pictures of silver." Referring to the statement of principle in the Declaration of Independence that "all men are created equal," Lincoln had said: "The expression of that principle in our Declaration of Independence was the word 'fitly spoken' which has proved an 'apple of gold' to us. The Union and the Constitution are the picture of silver subsequently framed around it. The picture was made not to conceal or destroy the apple; but to adorn and preserve it. The picture was made for the apple, not the apple for the picture." Quoted in Forrest Church, "The American Creed," *Nation,* September 16, 2002, http://www.thenation.com/doc.mhtml?i=20020916&c=3&s=church.

29. George F. Will, "The Madison Legacy," *Newsweek,* December 7, 1981, 124. This argument is not altogether convincing since Washington actually played an important role in *both* founding events.

30. Carl L. Becker, *The Declaration of Independence: A Study in the History of Political Ideas* (New York: Vintage Books, 1970); Garry Wills, *Inventing America: Jefferson's Declaration of Independence* (New York: Doubleday, 1978).

31. Quoted in Brookhiser, *Founding Father,* 199.

32. David Ames of New York produced a print for the centennial of the Declaration of Independence in 1876 that features a portrait of George Washington (rather than Jefferson) in the middle of a transcript of the Declaration of Independence and Abraham Lincoln in the middle of a transcript of the Emancipation Proclamation. In the print, Washington's deeds as commander of the forces responsible for securing

independence thus take precedence over Jefferson's words justifying independence. Another print of the Declaration of Independence, labeled at the bottom as "The Great Centennial Memorial," depicts a standing Washington in the middle of the print and a smaller bust of Jefferson at the bottom. The penman, Gilman B. Russell, had entered the piece in 1866 in the clerk's office of the District Court of the Eastern District of Pennsylvania. The Knights of Mecca have subsequently reprinted and redistributed the print (no date listed). David McCullough's *1776* (New York: Simon and Schuster, 2005) puts far greater focus on Washington's deeds as commanding officer than on Jefferson's words.

33. Wikipedia thus associates José de San Martín and Manuel Belgrano with the founding of Argentina, Simón Bolívar with Bolivia and Colombia, Tiradentes with Brazil, Bernardo O'Higgins and José Miguel Carrera with Chile, and so on. Another Wikipedia entry lists the United States as one of forty-six nations, from Albania through Venezuela, that have designated an individual as a national father. See "Father of the Nation," http://en.wikipedia.org/wiki/Father_of_the_Nation. Another entry, labeled "Pater Patriae," designates twenty-four Roman leaders whose subjects referred to them as *Parens Patriae,* or "Father of the Fatherland." See http://en.wikipedia.org/wiki/Pater_Patriae. The fact that this list includes the emperor Nero suggests that for a time Romans used the title to designate living rulers, and not necessarily especially good ones, instead of praising an individual responsible for birthing the empire. Yet another entry titled "List of people known as the father or mother of something," lists literally hundreds of such individuals. It thus designates Albert Einstein as the father of relativity, Herodotus as the father of history, Hippocrates as the father of medicine, J. Robert Oppenheimer as the father of the atomic bomb, and so on. See http://en.wikipedia.org/wiki/List_of_people_known_as_the_father_or_mother_of_something. On conventions, see John R. Vile, "Three Kinds of Constitutional Founding and Change: The Convention Method and Its Alternatives," *Political Research Quarterly* 46 (December 1992): 881–95.

34. Responding in part to claims that the English monarchy was based on the "divine right of kings," Thomas Paine made a brilliant attempt to turn the tables by recalling William the Conqueror's invasion of England and observing that "no man in his senses can say that their claim under William the Conqueror is a very honorable one." He continued: "A French bastard landing with an armed banditti, and establishing himself king of England against the consent of the natives, is in plain terms a very paltry rascally original." See Thomas Paine, *Common Sense* (1776; New York: Penguin Books, 1976), 78.

35. See Lyn Spillman, "'Neither the Same nor Different nations': Constitutional Conventions in the United States and Australia," *Comparative Studies in Society and History* 38 (January 1996): 149–81.

36. Robert A. Rutland, "The Virginia Plan of 1787: James Madison's Outline of a Model Constitution," *This Constitution* 4 (Fall 1984): 23.

37. Alexander Hamilton, James Madison, and John Jay, *The Federalist Papers,* ed. Clinton Rossiter (New York: New American Library, 1961), 232–33. Ratification further broadened the base of the Constitution. In a statement that contemporary scholars could apply to either the Constitutional Convention or those that ratified it, Aristotle

observed that "there is this to be said for the Many. Each of them by himself may not be of a good quality; but when they all come together it is possible that they may surpass—collectively and as a body, although not individually—the quality of the few best. Feasts to which many contribute may excel those provided at one man's expense. In the same way, when there are many, each can bring his share of goodness and moral prudence." See *The Politics of Aristotle*, ed. and trans. by Ernest Barker (New York: Oxford University Press, 1958), 123.

38. Miller, *Business of May Next*, 146.

39. Farrand, *Records*, 2:642.

40. Forrest McDonald, *Novus Ordo Seculorum: The Intellectual Origins of the Constitution* (Lawrence: University Press of Kansas, 1985), 208–9. McDonald accordingly refers to "the myth" that Madison was "the father of the Constitution" (205). David Brian Robertson further elaborates on these defeats in "Madison's Opponents and Constitutional Design," *American Political Science Review* 99 (May 2005): 232.

41. See Charles F. Hobson, "The Negative on State Laws: James Madison, the Constitution, and the Crisis of Republican Government," *William and Mary Quarterly*, 3rd ser., 36 (April 1979): 214–35.

42. Some ideas from this section, albeit no direct quotations, come from Michael Warner, *The Letters of the Republic: Publication and the Public Sphere in Eighteenth-Century America* (Cambridge, MA: Harvard University Press, 1990), especially 97–117.

43. Quoted from a letter of 1825 to Richard Henry Lee in Becker, *Declaration of Independence*, 25.

44. Farrand, *Records*, 2:643. Similarly, because Alexander Hamilton was the only one of three New York delegates present, New York was not recorded as ratifying the Constitution, and Hamilton thus could attest only to his own approval and not that of his state.

45. The Constitution is ratified by, but not written by, the people. Significantly, the U.S. Constitution has no mechanism equivalent to the initiative for introducing either legislation or constitutional amendments. Both processes take place through representatives.

46. By contrast, the preamble to the Articles of Confederation listed states individually. See Winton Solberg, ed., *The Federal Convention and the Formation of the Union* (Indianapolis, IN: Bobbs-Merrill, 1958), 42.

47. Jack N. Rakove, *Original Meanings: Politics and Ideas in the Making of the Constitution* (New York: Alfred A. Knopf, 1996), 17–18.

48. See, for example, Bruce Ackerman and Neal Katyal, "Our Unconventional Founding," *University of Chicago Law Review* 72 (Spring 1995): 475–573; Richard S. Kay, "The Illegality of the Constitution," *Constitutional Commentary* 4 (Winter 1987): 57–80. For an effective rejoinder, see Jack N. Rakove, "The Super-legality of the Constitution, or a Federalist Critique of Bruce Ackerman's Neo-federalism," *Yale Law Journal* 108 (June 1999): 1931–58.

49. Article XIII of the Articles of Confederation thus specified: "nor shall any alteration at any time hereafter be made in any of them [the Articles]; unless such alteration be agreed to in a Congress of the United States, and be afterwards confirmed by the legislatures of every State."

50. In his *Notes on the State of Virginia* (New York: Harper and Row, 1964; originally published in 1787), 115–19, Thomas Jefferson had criticized his state's constitution in part for having been both written and approved by the state legislature. In 1780 Massachusetts became the first state to use to convention mechanism to ratify its constitution.

51. Lansing had observed that "he was decidedly of opinion that the power of the Convention was restrained to amendments of a federal nature, and having for their basis the confederacy [the Articles] in being." Quoted in Farrand, *Records,* 1:249.

52. Ibid., 1:253. Emphasis in original. In similar fashion, Alexander Hamilton argued that "we can only propose and recommend—the power of ratifying or rejecting is still in the states." Ibid., 1:295.

53. Ibid., 2:93, 476.

54. Although the Conventions that ratified the Constitution could make recommendations—for example, the addition of a bill of rights—they simply took up or down votes, albeit in some cases after weeks of debate. By contrast, the conventions that ratified the Twenty-first Amendment performed a largely plebiscitary role, often meeting to do little more than vote. See Everett S. Brown, "The Ratification of the Twenty-first Amendment," *American Political Science Review* 29 (December 1935): 1005–17.

55. Lester B. Orfield, *The Amending of the Federal Constitution* (Ann Arbor: University of Michigan Press, 1942), 154. Also see Max Radin, "The Intermittent Sovereign," *Yale Law Journal* 30 (1930): 514–31.

56. This section largely follows analysis in the entry on "Delegates, Individual Rankings," in Vile, *Constitutional Convention of 1787,* 1:219–22. For history of the *Records,* see ibid., 2:665–67.

57. George Ticknor Curtis, *History of the Origin, Formation, and Adoption of the Constitution of the United States with Notices of Its Principal Framers* (New York: Harper and Brothers, 1862), 1:380–486.

58. Max Farrand, *The Framing of the Constitution of the United States* (New Haven, CT: Yale University Press, 1913), 197–98.

59. Charles Warren, *The Making of the Constitution* (Boston: Little, Brown, 1928), 56–57.

60. Sol Bloom, *The Story of the Constitution* (Washington, DC: United States Sesquicentennial Commission, 1937), 19. A colorful presidential proclamation printed by the Sesquicentennial Commission proclaiming the celebration was illustrated with pictures of the signers, with those of George Washington and James Madison enlarged at the top and those of Benjamin Franklin and Alexander Hamilton enlarged at the bottom. Another print of the text of the Preamble of the Constitution by J. R. Rosen and illustrated by A. E. Hilton, done sometime after 1937, pictures Franklin and Washington at the top and Madison, Robert Morris, and Hamilton at the bottom. A print by the same two artists of the Bill of Rights, distributed at an unknown date by West Publishing Company, pictures Madison, Henry, and Jefferson.

61. Frank H. Garver, "Leadership in the Constitutional Convention of 1787," *Sociology and Social Research* 21 (1936–1937): 553.

62. Merrill Jensen, *The Making of the American Constitution* (Malabar, FL: Robert E. Krieger Publishing Company, 1958, 1969).

63. Clinton Rossiter, *1787: The Grand Convention* (New York: W. W. Norton, 1966), 247–52.

64. Broadus Mitchell and Louise Pearson Mitchell, *A Biography of the Constitution of the United States: Its Origin, Formation, Adoption, Interpretation* (New York: Oxford University Press, 1964), 46–47.

65. Margaret Horsnell, "Who Was Who in the Constitutional Convention? A Pictorial History of Its Leading Figures," *This Constitution* 15 (Summer 1987): 38–41.

66. Carol Berkin, *A Brilliant Solution: Inventing the American Constitution* (New York: Harcourt, 2002), 51.

67. "Constitutional Convention, 1787," *Historical Magazine,* 1st ser., 5 (January 1987): 18. Another way of evaluating the delegates is according to their attendance. The most thorough review is that of Rossiter, *1787,* 164–66. Almost all delegates regarded as the most important attended most or all of the days on which the Convention was in session.

68. For Washington's constitutional vision, see Glenn A. Phelps, *George Washington and American Constitutionalism* (Lawrence: University Press of Kansas, 1993).

69. The specific rights transcend those in the original document. Notably, the first refers to "Equality Before the Law." Others that are listed are "Religious Freedom," "Free Speech and Press," and "Trial by Jury."

70. Junius Brutus Stearns did a portrait in 1856 that pictured Washington addressing the Convention (something he rarely did); Thomas P. Rossiter did a painting in the 1860s entitled *Signing of the Constitution of the United States;* Louis Glanzman did another painting of the signing of the Constitution that is now displayed in the waiting room of Independence Hall. He paints Madison just to the right of George Washington, who is in the center of the picture. See Vile, *Constitutional Convention of 1787,* 2:37.

71. Quoted in William G. Carr, *The Oldest Delegate: Franklin in the Constitutional Convention* (Newark: University of Delaware Press, 1990), 5 (unnumbered in text).

72. Farrand, *Records,* 3:420.

73. Ibid., 3:499.

74. Charles Cerami, *Young Patriots: The Remarkable Story of Two Men, Their Impossible Plan and the Revolution That Created the Constitution* (Naperville, IL: Sourcebooks, 2005). Darren Staloff, in *Hamilton, Adams, Jefferson: The Politics of Enlightenment and the American Founding* (New York: Hill and Wang, 2005), has further described Hamilton as "the most important figure in the founding of the American republic" (125).

75. Rossiter, *1787,* 252.

76. Robertson, "Madison's Opponents and Constitutional Design," 240. Robertson has elaborated on this thesis in *The Constitution and America's Destiny* (New York: Cambridge University Press, 2005).

77. Hannis Taylor, *The Real Authorship of the Constitution of the United States Explained: James Madison and Pelatiah Webster Defended by Hannis Taylor against Attack* (Washington, DC: Government Printing Office, 1912).

78. Christopher Collier and James Lincoln Collier, *Decision in Philadelphia: The Constitutional Convention of 1787* (New York: Random House, 1986), 64–74. For further explanation of this plan, see Vile, *Constitutional Convention of 1787,* 2:580–81.

79. Richard J. Ellis, ed., *Founding the American Presidency* (Lanham, MD: Rowman and Littlefield, 1999), 15.

80. "The Constitution of the United States," M. B. Atwood, 1933. The poster may well have been published with the sesquicentennial of the Constitution (1937) in mind.

81. Although Lincoln undoubtedly helped preserve the Union, accuracy would probably require that Lincoln be designated not simply as the "preserver" but as the "transformer" of the Constitution. Unlike some changes in constitutional understandings (those of the New Deal, for example), Lincoln's were directly incorporated into Amendments Thirteen through Fifteen, eliminating chattel slavery, guaranteeing rights of citizenship to all persons born or naturalized in the United States, and prohibiting denials of the right to vote on the basis of race, respectively.

82. Duval Swader & Co., "Constitution of the United States" (Philadelphia, 1866). The outer rim of the document is illustrated with various scenes of Civil War battles. It is possible that this document served as something of a campaign document, since Grant ran for the presidency in 1868.

83. Significantly, however, Roosevelt's agenda was not, like much of Lincoln's, embodied in the constitutional text. Bruce Ackerman has sought to account for this through his idea of "constitutional moments," not all of which are embodied in constitutional amendments. See his *We the People: Transformations* (Cambridge, MA: Belknap Press of Harvard University Press, 1998). For worthy reservations about this idea, see David E. Kyvig, *Explicit and Authentic Acts: Amending the U.S. Constitution, 1776–1995* (Lawrence: University Press of Kansas, 1996), xvii.

84. The term "father" further personalizes the Constitution, making it less abstract but also something, perhaps like an heirloom, not to be casually tampered with.

85. Hamilton et al., *Federalist Papers*, 314–15.

86. Ibid., 80. Madison never appears to have persuaded Jefferson of the unwisdom of constant constitutional revision. In a letter to Samuel Kerchival in 1816 advocating the rewriting of the Virginia state constitution, Jefferson thus observed that "some men look at constitutions with sanctimonious reverence, and deem them like the arc [*sic*] of the covenant, too sacred to be touched. They ascribe to the men of the preceding age a wisdom more than human, and suppose what they did to be beyond amendment. I knew that age well; I belonged to it, and labored with it. It deserved well of its country. It was very like the present, but without the experience of the present; and forty years of experience in government is worth a century of book-reading; and this they would say for themselves were they to rise from the dead." See Thomas Jefferson, *The Works of Thomas Jefferson*, ed. Paul Leicester Ford (New York: G. P. Putnam's Sons and Knickerbocker Press, 1905), 12:11. Curiously, in a letter to John Adams, Jefferson had once described the members of the Convention as "an assembly of demigods." Quoted in Farrand, *Framing of the Constitution*, 39.

87. In his own sketch of the Convention, Madison had proclaimed: "I feel it a duty to express my profound and solemn conviction, derived from my intimate opportunity of observing and appreciating the views of the Convention, collectively and individually, that there never was an assembly of men, charged with a great and arduous trust, who were more pure in their motives, or more exclusively or anxiously devoted to the object committed to them, than were the members of the Federal Convention

of 1787, to the object of devising and proposing a constitutional system which should best supply the defects of that which it was to replace, and best secure the permanent liberty and happiness of their country." See Farrand, *Records,* 3:551.

88. The most comprehensive survey of such attitudes remains Michael Kammen's *A Machine That Would Go of Itself: The Constitution in American Culture* (New York: Alfred A. Knopf, 1987).

89. Charles Beard, *An Economic Interpretation of the Constitution of the United States* (1913; New York: Macmillan, 1949). For a recent effort to resuscitate Beard's thesis, see Robert A. McGuire, *To Form a More Perfect Union: A New Economic Interpretation of the United States Constitution* (New York: Oxford, 2003).

90. See especially Robert E. Brown, *Charles Beard and the Constitution: A Critical Analysis of "An Economic Interpretation of the Constitution"* (Princeton, NJ: Princeton University Press, 1956).

91. John P. Roche, "The Founding Fathers: A Reform Caucus in Action," *American Political Science Review* 55 (December 1961): 799–816.

92. Farrand, *Records,* 2:53.

93. Hamilton et al., *Federalist Papers,* 437.

94. Douglass Adair, "Fame and the Founding Fathers," in *Fame and the Founding Fathers: Essays,* ed. Trevor Colbourn (New York: W. W. Norton, 1974), 8, 11. To put such statements in perspective, it should be noted that American framers feared that the desire for fame could be insatiable and that they "tended to treat politics as an instrument for the protection of inherent human rights and not as an end in itself." See Peter McNamara, *The Noblest Minds: Fame, Honor, and the American Founding* (Lanham, MD: Rowman and Littlefield, 1999), 16. McNamara further points to the founders' frequent references to the "burdens" of public service (26–29).

95. Because he did not attend the Constitutional Convention, this paper has not emphasized the role of John Adams, but he was the chief author of the Massachusetts constitution of 1780, which served as a model for the U.S. Constitution. For this and other contributions, George W. Carey and James McClellan, in their "Editor's Introduction" to *The Federalist* (Indianapolis, IN: Liberty Fund, 2001), xxixn19, have accordingly argued that Adams was "in many respects the father of American constitutionalism."

96. Kauffmann, "James Madison."

97. George F. Will refers to *Federalist* No. 10 as establishing a "sociology of freedom." See "James Madison Remembered," *Newsweek,* March 19, 2001.

98. Consistent with the fatherhood analogy, it might be appropriate to identify Madison's role as "seminal."

ALAN GIBSON

Inventing the Extended Republic

The Debate over the Role of Madison's Theory in the Creation of the Constitution

On Thursday, November 22, 1787, James Madison's argument for an extended republic was first published when the tenth *Federalist* paper appeared in the New York City newspaper the *Daily Advertiser.*[1] Only the most sophisticated of his readers would not have been struck by the novelty of Madison's remarkable case for a "well constructed Union."[2] The "prevailing prejudice" at the time that Madison wrote, known in the United States through the writings of the French philosopher Baron de Montesquieu, was that republican governments must be confined within a small geographical area.[3]

A month earlier, the Anti-Federalist Brutus had tutored New Yorkers with a particularly astute and elaborate variation of this argument.[4] The greatest political thinkers had concluded and the experience of history confirmed, Brutus warned, that free governments could not succeed in a geographical area as vast as the United States. An extensive republic, Brutus further suggested, would be impossible to implement. If the legislature were sufficiently large to allow representatives to know the minds of their constituents and thus speak for their views, it would become so numerous and unwieldy that it would not be able to transact the public business. Furthermore, the legislature in an extended republic would not be able to attend to the array of concerns and desires of the different parts of the United States or promptly execute laws that were passed.

A republic, Brutus continued, echoing Montesquieu, must have a similarity of manners, sentiments, and interests unless there is to be a "constant clashing of opinions." But the United States already contained a large variety of climates, productions, manners, habits, and laws and customs. A legislature formed of representatives from these distant and diverse parts would be "composed of such heterogeneous and discordant principles, as would constantly be contending with each other."[5] Finally, in an extended republic, Brutus warned, the people would not develop an attachment to their government or rulers and would be unable either to monitor their representatives or to act in concert to throw them out of office if necessary. Instead, public officials—especially executive officers—would escape public control and use their offices to pursue their interests and ambitions.

Although we will never be certain, it is plausible that Madison adapted his argument of *Federalist* No. 10—already thoroughly developed in the writings that he had prepared for the Constitutional Convention and his famous October 24, 1787, letter to Thomas Jefferson—to respond directly to Brutus.[6] Certainly, Madison's now classic defense of an American union through the creation of a compound republic over a large geographical area covered much of the same ground but came to strikingly different conclusions. The homogeneity of interests and views that Brutus and Montesquieu sought, Madison maintained, was impossible in any government that granted liberty. As the experience of ancient democracies and the state governments formed in America after independence illustrated, the primary threat to liberty in republican governments was not ambitious or interested rulers but majority factions that could use the constitutional system to violate private rights and pass legislation that was opposed to the common interest. "Curing the mischiefs" of these factions while still preserving "the spirit and form of popular government," Madison argued, constituted the "great desideratum" that republican government had perennially faced and recommended the extended republic that Brutus loathed.[7]

Most important, this problem could be addressed only in an extended republic. In an extended republic, Madison argued, the number of representatives in proportion to constituents could be fewer than in a small republic. A large republic therefore opened the possibility of elections from large electoral districts. Such a scheme, Madison hypothesized, would increase the chances for the selection of a "chosen body of citizens, whose wisdom may best discern the true interest of their country, and whose patriotism and love of justice, will be least likely to sacrifice it to temporary or partial considerations." These representatives would be qualified to "refine and enlarge the public views."[8]

The most effective device for blocking the "plans of oppression" posed by "an interested and over-bearing majority" while preserving popular government, however, was the series of obstacles—including greater distance, a greater number of citizens, and a greater diversity of interests—posed by the extended republic.[9] The obstacles that Brutus had feared would make it impossible for citizens to monitor their representatives effectively and coordinate opposition to the government would, according to Madison, make it more difficult for majority factions to form, help prevent them from acting in concert, and have a salutary effect on the administration of the government.

Today, Madison's theory is widely viewed as "American sacred scripture," accepted as a foundational statement of American political thought, praised as perhaps the most important contribution by an American to the history of political thought, and seen as a guide to the "basic rationale for the American political system."[10] With the exception of the Declaration of Independence and the Constitution itself, none of the documents of the founding era has generated such intense interest, nor been the object of such close textual exegesis or the subject of such profound and persistent scholarly disputation. This scrutiny and discussion has led to almost universal praise for the eloquence of Madison's exposition and the originality and brilliance of his theory.[11] In particular, Madison's contention that factions or interests were ineradicable and could be constructively used to prevent majority tyranny is often viewed as a watershed in the transition from a classical conception of republicanism rooted in virtue to a "new science of politics" rooted in the reality of interest group politics. Scholars are equally effusive in their praise for the prescience of Madison's insights. As Akhil Reed Amar has written, "bristling with insights, No. 10 indeed has something for everyone today—an explicit reference to property rights and class conflict, a celebration of demographic and religious diversity, a sophisticated account of interest groups and electoral dynamics, and a prophetic sketch of the federal government's role in protecting minority rights."[12]

Existing scholarship, however, also contains a strong and increasingly popular countercurrent against another contention often made in support of the enormous attention given to Madison's theory: the claim that it was influential in the formation and ratification of the Constitution. Until relatively recently, most Madison scholars have assumed that Madison's contemporaries accepted his argument and that it had an immediate impact on the events of 1787–88. Developed in a brilliant burst of creative political thinking, Madison's theory, according to this account, is said to contain the underlying logic behind the constitutional reform package that the "father of the Constitution" took to the Philadelphia Convention. At Philadelphia, many scholars further suggest, Madison's theory "was very much at the center of the debate," especially during the first seven weeks of the Constitutional Convention. Here, it helped Madison convince his colleagues of the need to address the problems that he believed were most pressing (namely, the protection of individual rights against the threat of majority factions), shaped the form of the Constitution, and thus embodied the theory immanent in the U.S. Constitution.[13] Once the Convention sent the Constitution to the states for adoption, Madison's theory, according to many scholars, provided the leading Federalist response to the Anti-Federalists' adaptation of the small republic thesis.

A contrary line of scholarship on Madison's theory has, however, suggested that these claims are at best dubious and that they have rested upon inverted logic. Beginning in the 1970s, several scholars—including Michael Zuckert and Christopher Wolfe—expressed doubts that Madison's theory was influential or even widely understood at the Constitutional Convention. More recently, Akhil Reed Amar has stated flatly that Madison's theory of an extended republic "had remarkably little impact on Madison's contemporaries."[14] Larry Kramer has similarly stated that "the theory of the extended republic, particularly those aspects that are important to theorists today, played essentially *no* role in shaping the Constitution or its ratification."[15] The premise of these statements is that original ideas rarely have immediate impact on historical events. Thus, however brilliant or prophetic, Madison's theory was too novel to have been generally accepted by his colleagues, to provide the rationale for constitutional reform, to explain the underlying logic of the original Constitution, or to have significantly impacted its ratification. Indeed, according to Kramer, few people either understood or closely considered Madison's argument in his own day.

This essay examines the debate over whether Madison's vaunted theory was influential at the Constitutional Convention, was widely adopted during the ratification struggle, and can be said to contain the theory underlying the framers' Constitution of 1787.[16] These claims about the immediate historical impact of Madison's theory are distinct from the contentions that Madison's theory was a conceptual innovation that marks a watershed in the history of political thought, the most philosophically sound response to Montesquieu's small republic theory set forth during the struggle over the ratification of the Constitution, and a remarkable prophecy about the future character of American democracy. This essay outlines the traditional case for the immediate historical importance of Madison's theory and the argument of the challengers to this standard interpretation. It further makes some preliminary observations about how this debate might be clarified, what claims about Madison's theory have been eviscerated and which ones have survived, and the implications of recent challenges to the historical significance of Madison's theory for current debates over the original meaning of the Constitution and for scholarship on the American founding.

The Case for the Significance of Madison's Theory

The traditional case for the immediate historical influence of Madison's theory contains three distinct—though certainly not mutually exclusive—claims: (1) the argument that Madison's case for an extended republic was central in his political thought, especially the constitutional reform program that he developed in preparation for the Constitutional Convention; (2) the claim that the theory was important at the Constitutional Convention in focusing debate and shaping the content of the Constitution and thus can be said to contain the theory underlying or immanent within it; and (3) the claim that Madison's theory afforded the most important argument during the ratification struggle for countering the Anti-Federalists' case for a small republic.

The case for the centrality of Madison's theory within his own political thought rests on the presumption that in his argument for an extended republic, Madison identified the central reasons why he sought constitutional reform in the 1780s and explained the character of that reform. Madison, according to this account, diagnosed two distinct sets of problems with government under the Articles of Confederation: (1) the impotence of the national government brought about by its structural defects and absence of coercive power and exemplified in its inability to collect taxes, keep the states from violating treaties, or prevent the states from encroaching upon federal authority, *and* (2) the multiplicity, mutability, and injustices of laws passed *within* the states.[17] In both his private correspondence and at the Convention, Madison argued that the injustices of the laws within the states "contributed more to that uneasiness which produced the Convention, and prepared the public mind for a general reform, than those which accrued to our national character and interest from the inadequacy of the Confederation to its immediate object."[18]

Madison's central contribution to the debates in 1787, and the most sweeping contribution of his theory of an extended republic, according to this account, was to bring these two sets or problems together within a single reform package. Transferring essential powers from the states to the national government, Madison maintained, would transform a confederacy of independent states into an extended republic. Since majorities would be gathered from the large and diverse population of the extended republic, Madison's theory maintained, the national legislature would not be subject to the vicissitudes that had led to the hasty drafting of contradictory and unjust laws within the state governments.[19]

As suggested earlier, another important claim made about the historical impact of Madison's theory has focused on the role that the theory is believed to have had in shaping the form of the Constitution during debates at the Constitutional Convention. Martin Diamond forcefully set forth this argument.[20] The first stage of the debates in the Constitutional Convention, Diamond argued, was driven by the confrontation of "true federalists" and nationalists. "True federalists" accepted Montesquieu's proposition that republican government could be sustained only in a small geographical area and thus believed that the United States must remain essentially a confederation with only limited powers ceded to the national government. Led by James Madison, nationalists hoped to create an extended republic and believed that the national government should serve many purposes, including protecting individual rights within the states.

Madison "extorted acquiescence" from the "true federalists," according to Diamond, because he was able to show that the goals that they also had for the union—especially the protection of property rights and stability—could be achieved only by an essentially national government. Madison, Diamond maintained, convinced his fellow delegates that small republics incubated class conflicts, were unstable, and led to the violations of individual rights. He also, according to Diamond, not only established that republicanism was compatible with an extended republic, but he convincingly argued that largeness was necessary to preserve republicanism. In this way, Madison showed his fellow delegates how they could "have their cake and eat it too."[21] He showed them, in other words, how they could have the more extensive powers in the national government that their experience had suggested were necessary to the survival of the American experiment and yet retain a republican government—the only form that was consistent with the genius of the American people and the ethos of the Revolution.

Diamond thus credited Madison's famous June 6 Convention speech in favor of an extended republic—Madison's first public presentation of this theory—with liberating delegates from the assumptions of the small republic thesis and paving the way for the creation of a truly national government. This "fundamental theoretical issue" over size and the character of government and not, primarily at least, squabbles between delegates advancing the interest of large or small states over whether one or both branches of the legislature would have proportional representation was at the core of the dynamics of the debate in the first half of the Convention.[22] Most important, Diamond's account of these dynamics suggested that the delegates not only shared Madison's concern for the effects of majority factions within the state governments and believed that violations of individual rights by such factions were the principal reason that the Convention had been called but also accepted Madison's remedy for this problem—an extended republic that dispersed majority factions across an extended republic.

More recently, Jack Rakove has argued that Madison's theory of an extended republic was important at the Convention, not because it was at the center of the deepest theoretical dispute at the meeting but because it was integral to Madison's defense of proportional representation. Madison's defense of the extended republic was important to his vindication of proportional representation in at least two ways, according to Rakove. First, the extended republic argument suggested that *every* interest—including those within the small states—would be protected by the greater size and diversity of the nation and the wiser and more able representatives who would be elected in the proposed Constitution. The small states' claim that they needed equal representation in at least one branch of the legislature to protect their interests was thus unfounded.

Second, Madison's theory, according to Rakove, struck at the very idea of the states as interests that deserved representation. An array of economic interests and religious beliefs, Madison's theory suggested, divided each state and were the real or objective interests that merited representation in the national councils. Interests, in Madison's view, were the attributes of individuals. States, by contrast, were artificial corporate entities that allowed for convenient administration and did not demand equal representation in the national government.[23]

Most important, the arguments that leading nationalists—including Hamilton, Rufus King, Edmund Randolph, and James Wilson—used to defend their agenda of proportional representation and direct election from large electoral districts were, according to Rakove, "fundamentally consistent if not identical with the comprehensive theory that Madison had forged before the convention, and they were arrayed in essentially the same interlocking configuration." Nationalists countered objections to the direct election of representatives by arguing that these elections would be safe if conducted in large districts; they fought against election of senators by the state legislatures, saying that this would do nothing to bring men of weight and property into the legislature. Throughout the debate on proportional representation, Hamilton, Wilson, and Madison argued that small states had nothing to fear from a combination of large states, which had no common interests merely as a result of their size. This argument essentially restated Madison's theory that real factions or interests were individual, not corporate, in character.[24]

A third common claim about the historical impact of Madison's theory is that it was also central in the "great national discussion" that took place during ratification.[25] Madison's argument for an extended republic, according to this claim, was the leading response to the most profound objection to ratification of the proposed Constitution. With the possible exception of the argument that the Constitution had no bill of rights, the contention that a republican form of government could not be adapted to the sprawling American continent was the most frequently voiced objection to ratification of the Constitution. Madison's response thus played an important role in countering the Anti-Federalists' case against the Constitution.

In short, then, the traditional view of the significance of Madison's theory suggests first that the extended republic argument was central to Madison's own constitutional reform program in 1787. Commentators have further suggested that Madison expressed ideas or concerns that were commonly held, particularly about the dangers of majority factions within the states. Madison's persistence and, even more, his brilliance, much existing commentary suggests, led other delegates to accept his theory and embody it within the Constitution. Having won over the Convention to his ideas, Madison then took his ideas out into the ratification struggle where they were important in countering Anti-Federalist claims for the small republic.

Challenges from a Cluster of Contexts

While many of the claims within the traditional defense of the influence of Madison's theory are still widely taught and steadfastly defended, important challenges have been made against each of them. In direct contrast to the claims made by traditional defenders of the historical impact of Madison's theory, a number of other scholars have suggested that the very novelty of Madison's argument was an indication of its lack of resonance, let alone effect, among Madison's contemporaries. Christopher Wolfe, Michael Zuckert, and Kramer have all pursued this argument in various ways and degrees. Wolfe and Zuckert have countered Martin Diamond's suggestion that Madison's theory was important at the Convention.[26] Kramer has provided the most sweeping and challenging argument that Madison's theory was unimportant both at the Convention and during the ratification process that followed.

In particular, in 1977, Christopher Wolfe published a pioneering essay that challenged Diamond's assertion that Madison's theory had provided the framework for debate at the Constitutional Convention. According to Wolfe, Diamond's account of the early stages of the debate at the Convention as a contest between nationalists who accepted Madison's theory of an extended republic and "true federalists" who held to the small republic thesis was untenable. The small republic thesis, Wolfe argued, was not presented directly at the Convention. Furthermore, Madison's argument for an extended republic brought no opposition from other delegates. "Is it likely, then," Wolfe asked, "that this one speech [Madison's June 6 speech laying out his theory], which was not explicitly attacked or defended, would have changed the theoretical opinions of men of such standing as [Oliver] Ellsworth, one of the Convention's finest debaters and thinkers?"[27] It is true, Wolfe observed, that Madison proposed arguments late in the Convention that presupposed his theory of an extended republic. In particular, Madison argued that the national government should guarantee good internal legislation and internal tranquility to the states by preventing the violation of individual rights. Nevertheless, the Convention rejected the provision that Madison hoped to use to achieve these goals—his universal negative of state laws.

Contrary to Diamond's suggestion that a deep theoretical dispute controlled debates in the opening stages of the convention, then, in Wolfe's words, the "truly critical division during the first part of the Convention was the division between large and small states." Madison's theory was not important in persuading delegates to add powers to the national government or to have it act directly on the people in the first place, Wolfe argued, because delegates generally agreed on the scope of federal power and that the newly created national government would exercise its powers directly on the people. As traditional accounts suggested, the small states fought for equal representation in the Senate to preserve their power within the national government and to prevent the large states from dominating them. The objections of those who proposed the New Jersey Plan, Wolfe contends, were thus "not small-republican objections for the most part, but small state objections to the failure of nationalists to provide for the small states' security."[28]

In a series of articles on Madison's political thought, Michael Zuckert has further eroded Diamond's claims about the role of Madison's theory at the Convention and suggested that Diamond's interpretation of Madison's theory has fostered misunderstandings about the character and purposes of the American political system.[29] Zuckert's challenge to Diamond follows from his pioneering scholarship on the relationship between the theory of the extended republic and Madison's pet proposal for a sweeping universal veto of state laws.

Briefly put, Zuckert and Charles Hobson (then an editor of *The Papers of James Madison*) were the first scholars to notice that the universal negative was the constitutional means by which Madison hoped to achieve a republican solution to the republican problem of majority faction.[30] Madison's experiences with the states during the 1780s led him to conclude that majority factions were most dangerous in small republics and indeed would threaten individual rights in inverse proportion to the size of the republic. Madison also concluded that the only effective way to counter the multiplicity, mutability, and injustices of the laws of the states was to arm Congress with a sweeping universal veto of all state laws. Such a power, Madison argued, would not only prevent state encroachments on the prerogatives of the national government but also have the "happy effect" of protecting individual rights within the states.[31] Although this was the same power that the king of England had exercised (and abused) against the colonies and that Parliament had reaffirmed in the Declaratory Act of 1766, Madison believed that it was "the least possible abridgement of the State Sovereignties" that was consistent with the constitutional reforms that were necessary.[32]

Nevertheless, Madison had to explain why the national government could safely exercise a universal veto even though it, like the state governments, would operate on the basis of the principle of majority rule. Madison answered that question with his theory of an extended republic. According to Zuckert, Madison believed that the extended republic afforded two advantages over a small republic in the creation of nonfactious majorities. First, in an extended republic, a greater number and variety of interests would be represented in the republican legislature. An interest that had a majority at the state level would be outnumbered in the national legislature by representatives who were uninterested in the divisions within that state and thus qualified to serve as disinterested umpires of disputes there.

Second, the obstacles established in the extended republic—including distance, a greater number of individuals, and a greater variety of interest—would force the construction of artificial majorities. Whereas majority factions would easily communicate and concert their plans of oppression in a small republic, popular majorities created in the extended republic could now be constructed only from coalitions of minority interests. In order to cooperate and coalesce, these interests would have to seek common ground in their shared interests. The process of transformation that would take place as artificial majorities were formed would help ensure the formation of good majorities. Most important, both of these factors would increase the probability that factious majorities would not control the national legislature and, in turn, make Congress qualified to exercise the universal negative to protect individual rights from the threat of majority factions within the states.[33]

All of this, Zuckert points out, was part of a more general problem in governance that Madison was addressing with the aid of Montesquieu: how could the government be made sufficiently neutral between the interests of the society to arbitrate neutrally among them and yet be sufficiently dependent on society to ensure that it would not sacrifice the interests and rights of the people? A monarch, Madison observed, was sufficiently neutral between the interests of society but might sacrifice them to the monarch's own personal ambition and avarice. A small republic, in contrast, would be sufficiently dependent on the society to prevent it from violating the rights and interests of all but not sufficiently neutral among them. Since the citizens of that society do not have the same interest, and the majority has the power to enact laws in a republic, the majority interest would control the legislature and often violate the rights of minorities or promote its interests as common interests.

Montesquieu's solution to this problem was a limited monarch involving a king whose power was controlled by a popular assembly. The king would supply neutrality but be restrained by the legislature from acting irresponsibly. Madison, however, had to propose an entirely republican solution to the problem of majority faction. He found this solution not, as many commentators think, by simply adopting an extended republic. Instead, according to Zuckert, Madison combined the extended republic and the small republic in such a way as to achieve both neutrality and popular control. In much the same way that in Montesquieu's scheme a popular assembly could temper the power of a limited monarchy and achieve both neutrality and safety, the extended republic would ameliorate the problems of the small republic.

In the American federal system, the extended republic would promote the quality of disinterestedness in Congress. Congress would play the role of the neutral arbiter assumed by the hereditary king in the British system. It would have limited positive powers to legislate based upon objects that the Constitution enumerated. Over and above these limited powers, it would also exercise the universal veto within the states. But the lion's share of legislative power would remain within the states. The state legislatures would thus supply the popular ingredient within the regime. "The constitutional scheme Madison projects," Zuckert argues, "mimics the Montesquieuean model by combining the Congress of the government of the Union, playing the part of the monarch, but being itself a republican body, with the small republics of the states, playing the part of Parliament."[34]

What does this have to do with the reception of Madison's theory at the Convention and Diamond's interpretation? First, Madison went to the Convention with all of this systematically worked out, but he was never able to convince his fellow delegates of the value of the universal negative or more generally of his conception of federalism. Madison first failed, Zuckert observes, to get the Virginia delegation to include the universal veto in the Virginia Plan. Whereas Madison's version of the negative would have empowered the national government to veto state laws in "all cases whatsoever," the version of the negative included in the Virginia Plan provided only that the national government should be able to veto laws passed by the states that were "contravening in the opinion of the National Legislature the articles of Union."[35]

Madison's pioneering June 6 speech in which he first set forth his case for an extended republic was really a trial run to get the Convention to accept his universal veto, not the limited veto provided in the Virginia Plan. Far from "transforming the Convention and winning the others over" as Diamond suggested, however, Madison's speech met with "resounding silence."[36] Madison's speech fell flat at the Convention, according to Zuckert, because the power on which it was premised—the universal veto—was repudiated by his fellow delegates (and later by his friend Thomas Jefferson) as impractical and excessive. It also involved too much interference by the national government within the states and too much interaction between levels of government to be acceptable to his colleagues.

Furthermore, contrary to Diamond's suggestion and the interpretation presented in most analyses, Madison did not, according to Zuckert, advocate consolidating the republic or expanding the prerogatives of the national government. He never suggested that all of the numerous and various concerns of the states could be brought within the purview of a national government. He also did not say, as Diamond suggests, that republicanism "not only permits but requires taking away from the states responsibility for the security of private rights, and the steady dispensation of justice, else rights and justice will perish under the state governments."[37] The universal negative that Madison hoped to lodge in Congress was a power akin to an executive veto, not a positive power in which the national government would legislate within the states. Madison saw Congress as a neutral umpire of decisions made elsewhere, not a decision-making body for the states.

Larry Kramer's important and still unanswered essay, "Madison's Audience," represents a culmination of the challenges begun by Wolfe and Zuckert to the traditional account of the importance of the extended republic at the Constitutional Convention. Kramer then extends this challenge to the ratification struggle. Madison's theory, Kramer points out, might have been relevant in three decisions at the Constitutional Convention: the decision to abandon the Articles of Confederation and replace it with a truly national government; the debate over the universal veto of state laws; and the decision over how to structure the national legislature.

Madison's theory, Kramer argues, was not the rationale for adding powers to the national government. Indeed, Madison was not even able to get the Virginia Delegation to adopt his theory. Randolph's speech introducing the Virginia Plan focused on widely perceived national problems, not using federal reform to address problems within the states. Throughout the debate, none of the delegates recounted Madison's theory—either to challenge or support it—and none of them agreed with Madison that the problems in the states had to be addressed by federal reform. Instead, they continued to believe that state reforms should take place at the state level. Indeed, the records of the Convention suggest that only Alexander Hamilton even understood Madison's arguments.

In terms of the universal negative, few of the delegates grasped its relationship to Madison's theory and most rejected the negative, not simply because they were concerned about problems that would arise in implementing it, but also because they abhorred the very idea of a universal veto. In particular, Madison had given two justifications for the negative: its defensive role in protecting federal prerogatives from encroachments by the states and its supervisory role in protecting individual rights within the states. The delegates "failed to credit the negative's supervisory purpose at all and believed that the defensive purpose supported an unlimited negative weakly at best."[38]

The one area where Madison's theory might have had a limited impact on a few delegates, Kramer acknowledges, is in debates over the composition of Congress, especially the apportionment of representatives among the states. Even here, however, Kramer suggests, commentators have had to strain to find a role for Madison's theory. Jack Rakove's argument that delegates from the large states used Madison's theory to suggest that equal representation of the small states was unnecessary (because the extended republic offered to protect all the interests of the nation) and undeserved (because states were not real interests meriting representation), Kramer suggests, is more of a shrewd innovation by Rakove, an ex post facto effort to establish how Madison's theory might have buttressed the case of the large-state delegates, than a description of a line of argumentation that Madison, Hamilton, and James Wilson actually pursued at the Convention. The best that Rakove can say, Kramer argues, is that these arguments are "consistent with Madison's general theory," not that they were directly derived from or influenced by it.[39] Most of the delegates from large states, according to Kramer, opposed equal representation in the Senate on principle, not because they followed the logic of Madison's understanding of faction or understood its implications.

Finally, Kramer argues that Madison's theory was equally unimportant in the ratification process.[40] The Anti-Federalist bromide that a republic could survive only in a small geographical area, Kramer points out, provided Federalists with the perfect opportunity to evoke Madison's defense of an extended republic containing a multiplicity of interests. Far from being commonplace, however, Madison's observations about the structure of American society and the ameliorating effects of the extent of territory as a means of dispersing majority factions are present only in the *Federalist* papers and in essays by "Americanus" and "Harrington." Otherwise, Kramer argues, Madison's theory was reflected in scattered comments in the ratification process and made "appearances" in a couple of ratifying conventions such as those in New York and Virginia, where they were voiced by allies of Hamilton and Madison. Still, "by far the favorite Federalist retort to Antifederalist charges that a large republic was unthinkable was to throw Montesquieu back in their faces" and to argue that even he agreed that a confederate republic like that proposed in the Constitution could be extended over a large territory.[41]

In short, then, Madison's theory was "an insignificant detail, an unappreciated ingredient in the larger sweep of events."[42] Madison's theory *became* important to contemporary scholars after Charles Beard focused attention upon it because it addresses issues that contemporaries find important, not because it expressed issues that were important to the founding generation. Madison's theory was too far out in front of his contemporaries to have won them over. Scholars who have claimed otherwise have mistaken the prescience of Madison's argument for its significance.

The studies of Zuckert, Wolfe, and Kramer suggest that if the extended republic cannot be said to have been central at the Convention or in the ratification struggle, then it can hardly be said to explain the theory underlying the Constitution. But wasn't this theory at least central to Madison's political thought, especially in the preparations that he made for the Constitutional Convention and how he defended the Constitution in 1787? Kramer ultimately acknowledges that Madison's theory was important to Madison, though he also argues that Madison did not come to believe that the national government should address the problems within the states or connect this goal to extension of the sphere of the republic until "mere weeks before the Convention opened, and they reflected a rather sharp change in his thinking." Kramer also suggests that Madison's theory was important to Madison only in a brief moment and that he abandoned it after ratification, "mentioning it no more than once or twice during the entire rest of his life."[43]

Did Madison's Theory Have an Impact? Observations and the Implications

What, then, are we to make of this debate? Can any of the traditional claims for the importance of Madison's theory survive the challenges by scholars to its place in the formation and ratification of the Constitution? First, the most decisive challenge to the traditional view of Madison's theory has been lodged against the claim that it was important at the Constitutional Convention. As both Michael Zuckert and Christopher Wolfe first suggested, the small republic theory had no champions at the Constitutional Convention and was not even mentioned. It thus posed no conceptual barrier that delegates had to hurdle. With the exception of Madison, few of these delegates conceived of national constitutional reform as a vehicle for addressing the problems posed by majority factions within the states. Conversely, most of the delegates accepted the idea that a few essential powers—especially commercial regulation and the power of taxation—had to be added to the national government if it was going to address the goals that they wanted it to achieve. Convention delegates also understood that these powers would be exercised directly on individuals rather than on the states in their corporate capacity. Madison's theory was not necessary for delegates to reach these conclusions.

More broadly, since Madison's theory played at best a minor role at the Convention, it cannot be shown to contain the theory immanent in the Constitution. As Michael Zuckert has observed, it is a useful heuristic in this regard to ask, if Madison's theory of an extended republic underlies the Constitution, then in what clauses is it embodied? The only candidates are Article I, Section 10, which contains a series of prohibitions against the states, including prohibitions against coining money and against passing bills of attainder, ex post facto laws, or laws impairing the obligation of contracts; and Article I, Section 2, which provides for the direct election of the House of Representatives and their apportionment among the states based on population.

The prohibitions in Article I, Section 10, are a residual of the universal negative and represent an effort to address Madison's concern for the problems of majority factions within the states. The passage of these prohibitions suggests that many of Madison's colleagues shared his concerns with majority factions even as they rejected his remedy of the universal negative. Still, the differences between these prohibitions and the universal negative are stronger than their similarities. Madison's version of the universal negative was a plenary power given to Congress to review the laws of the states. In contrast, the provisions in Article I, Section 10, were specific, constitutionally enumerated limitations and were judicially enforced.[44]

With regard to proportional representation, it is clear that Madison's theory could have been used along the lines that Jack Rakove has suggested to buttress the case of large-state delegates for representatives to be apportioned among the states based upon population. Delegates may have used Madison's theory to arrive at the conclusion that the interests within the small states were protected by the extended republic (and thus that the small states did not need equal representation as a defensive power) and that states were not units that merited direct representation within the government.

Still, not even Madison made direct recourse to his theory in his opposition to claims of delegates to the small states. His argument that there was little danger of a coalition of the large states against the small because the large states shared no common interests as a result of their size and had never previously acted in concert against the small states was perhaps, as Rakove has suggested, rooted in the deeper structure of his theory. But his broader case against equal representation—the case echoed by other large-state delegates—was that this scheme of apportionment violated fundamental principles of justice and equity. Equal representation, Madison argued, would allow the small states to obstruct the wishes and interests of a majority of the American people, extort measures from Congress that a majority of the people opposed, and even impose measures in the Senate opposed by the majority of Americans (because the Senate had unique powers not subject to control by the House, and small-state senators would have a majority).[45]

Madison's theory might be said to have ensured the direct election of the House because, it could be argued, delegates to the Convention knew that such elections would take place from large districts and across an extended republic. In other words, it could be argued that the extended republic theory assured delegates that direct election of members of the House from large districts would help prevent the formation of a national legislative body with the same sets of problems that had plagued the state legislatures during the mid-1780s. This argument can be strengthened by pointing out that Madison first set forth his theory of an extended republic on June 6 at the Convention during debate on the direct election of representatives.

Still, it seems more likely that direct election of at least one branch of the legislature was a fundamental tenet of republicanism for most of the delegates than a principle they were led to accept on the basis of Madison's theory. Furthermore, many delegates were doubtlessly counting primarily on separation of powers to control abuses by majority factions, not on an extended republic. At any rate, even if it is granted that the prohibitions against the states in Article I, Section 10, apportionment based upon population, and direct election of representatives were justified on the basis of Madison's theory, it is difficult to see how these together constitute the theory underlying the Constitution.[46] In short, then, the cases made by Wolfe, Zuckert, and Kramer about the role of Madison's theory at the Convention are—for now, at least—decisive. Unless some scholar can convincingly show how the theory framed debate at the Convention in some way not previously considered and provide a convincing account tying provisions in the Constitution to the theory, then it is implausible to suggest that it was at the center of the debate in Philadelphia or was "incorporated in the underpinnings" of the Constitution.[47]

If we turn to the ratification struggle, it seems clear that current disagreements about whether Madison's theory was historically significant in the "great national discussion" that accompanied the adoption of the Constitution depend, in large part, on which of Madison's claims we consider to be the core of his theory.[48] At roughly the same time that Amar and Kramer concluded that Madison's theory had no resonance in the ratification struggle, Bernard Bailyn and Woody Holton suggested just the opposite, namely, that Madison's theory was really only the most eloquent version of quite common contentions. Holton speaks for Bailyn also when he argues that scholarship on the debate in the early republic over the size of the political sphere tends to portray Madison as a "pioneering soloist" when he was actually only "one voice in a choir." In particular, Holton has established that Madison's claims about the benefits of elections from large districts were part of a much broader debate in the early republic (reinvigorated by the ratification contest) about the effects of the size of electoral districts on the kind of representatives elected and policies proposed and adopted.[49]

Similarly, in an epilogue that he added in 1992 to his famous work *The Ideological Origins of the American Revolution,* Bernard Bailyn has argued that Madison gave the extended republic thesis "its ultimate range, depth, and intellectual elegance" and that no other commentator in the ratification debate had Madison's "cogency, penetration, knowledge, and range." Still, Bailyn observes, there were numerous other defenses of the extended republic during the ratification struggle by, among others, James Wilson, Edmund Randolph, Francis Corbin, Alexander Hamilton, James Bowdoin, Charles Pinckney, and especially John Stevens in his "Americanus" essays. "Nothing he [Madison] had to say about factionalism or its material basis," according to Bailyn, "was new or controversial."[50] Furthermore, like Madison, Stevens and the other Federalists recognized the inevitability of factions, believed that the government had to adjust these jarring factions if the republic was to survive, and concluded that republican government in the United States would be made stronger and safer through extension, not contraction, of the sphere of the republic. In short, then, in Holton's and Bailyn's estimation, the Federalists in general—not simply Madison—turned Montesquieu on his head.

Obviously, Amar's and Kramer's suggestions that Madison's theory of an extended republic had little resonance in the ratification debate on the one hand, and Holton's and Bailyn's claim that it was widespread on the other, can be squared only if these scholars are pointing to different aspects of Madison's theory. And indeed they are. Holton and Bailyn are suggesting that Madison's claims about the virtues of expanded electoral districts and the material basis of politics were the core points of Madison's theory and were commonplace arguments in the ratification struggle. Amar and Kramer are focusing on Madison's unorthodox contentions about the problems created by majority factions within the states, the novelty of his understanding of the social structure of the young republic, and the uniqueness of his belief that the multiplicity of interests within the extended republic would increase stability and protect liberty. Once this is realized, one can understand that the accounts by both sets of scholars are not only possible but plausible. It is, of course, feasible that the claims made by Madison in

Federalist No. 10 about the material basis of politics and his hypotheses about the benefits of elections from large districts were widely understood but that his signature arguments about the character of society and the salutary effects of a multiplicity of economic interests were stunningly original and expressed almost exclusively by Madison himself.[51]

If recent scholarship has given us a tempered and accurate assessment of the role of the theory of the extended republic at the Convention and in the ratification struggle, revisionists are nevertheless mistaken in downplaying the role this constellation of ideas played within Madison's own political thought. It is true, as Kramer suggests, that Madison did not come to believe that the national government should address the problems within the states or connect this goal to extension of the sphere of the republic until "mere weeks before the Convention opened, and they reflected a rather sharp change in his thinking." It is false, however, to say that Madison's theory was important to him only in a brief moment and that he abandoned it after ratification, "mentioning it no more than once or twice during the entire rest of his life."[52]

Actually, Madison returned to his theory of an extended republic in the essays that he wrote for the *National Gazette* in the 1790s. Here, rather than simply defending an extended republic, he engaged in a broader analysis of the effect of the size of a nation on the character, form, and conduct of the government. This analysis also involved an explicit investigation into the role of public opinion in the operations of government, especially the American republic.[53] In addition, during the early 1790s Madison continued to defend the principle of impartial representation or administration—the core conception of representation defended in *Federalist* No. 10.[54] Concretely, this meant that representatives would act impartially by equally protecting the rights of all citizens, equally distributing public benefits and burdens between interests, and impartially advancing the public good when choices between interests had to be made. In the First Congress, Madison embodied the idea of an impartial representative and encouraged his colleagues to follow his example. In debates on impost duties, for example, he attempted to construct a scheme of taxation that impartially distributed burdens among the products of the nation in such a way as to burden equally each interest and section of the nation. Madison's position on discrimination between the primary and secondary holders of the debt was similarly an effort to "hold the balance between" the opposing interests giving to each party what it justly deserved. Finally, Madison's essays for the Jeffersonian newspaper the *National Gazette*—especially his essay titled "Property"—resonate with this theme of justice as impartiality.[55] In short, far from abandoning his theory, Madison applied it to the operations of the new government and thought through the relationship of size and republicanism and the requirements of impartial representation from the new context of his role as a national party leader.[56]

Why does any of this matter? Why is it important whether Madison's theory had an immediate impact on the events of 1787 or 1788 and whether it was central to his political thought or little more than a passing interest to him? First, as Kramer notes, the rejection of the centrality of the argument of *Federalist* No. 10 to the American founding suggests that nothing less than a new interpretation of the formation of the Constitution is necessary. The Madisonian interpretation of the formation of the Constitution, which has been set forth most famously in Gordon Wood's *The Creation of the American Republic,* has been in place for almost forty years now. Wood's massively influential work accepts Madison's contention that the problems created by majority factions within the states were the central issue that led to the calling of the Constitutional Convention. It also suggests that Madison's theory of the extended republic was incorporated in the structure of the original Constitution as the proper solution to that problem and then used during the ratification struggle as the primary defense against the leading objection to the Constitution.[57]

But challenges to the immediate impact of Madison's theory—along with other trends in recent historiography—suggest that scholars are now breaking decisively with Wood's interpretation of the founding and thus also with Madison's characterization of the reasons for constitutional reform and the character of the framers' Constitution. In particular, the displacement of the theory of an extended republic from scholarship on the American founding suggests that, unlike Madison, most of the founders were either not particularly concerned with the problems of majority tyranny within the states or at least content to address them at the state level. More generally, it suggests that the problem of reconciling majority rule with the protection of individual rights is much more important to us than it was to the founding generation. In contrast, the founders may well have simply seen constitutional reform—and eventually the new Constitution—as a means of creating a stronger and more structurally sound national government, enhancing national security, and preventing the states from going to war with each other.[58]

Arguments against the historical significance of Madison's theory of an extended republic thus also challenge or at least diminish our familiar and comfortable characterization of Madison as the father of the Constitution and suggest that we need to revise our understanding of its creation. To be sure, Madison will always have a central role in the story. He was, after all, the principal author of the Virginia Plan, a participant in debate on most major questions at the Convention, the "semi-official reporter" of the Convention debates, the author of twenty-nine *Federalist* papers, the leading defender of the Constitution at the Virginia ratifying convention, and the architect of the Bill of Rights.[59] It is hard to argue that anyone was more productive than Madison during the crucial years of 1787–88 or to imagine anyone who had a better understanding of the constitutional structure created.

Nevertheless, much of Madison's reputation as the father of the Constitution also rests on the premise that his theory of the extended republic explained the rationale for constitutional reform and the theoretical structure of the Constitution. If this is untrue, if other founders had different reasons for pursuing constitutional reform, if Madison's theory was unimportant at the Convention, and if it was almost never evoked to explain and defend the Constitution during the ratification contest, then Madison's role as a guide to the original understanding of the Constitution must be substantially limited—at least if the original understanding is conceived as a *shared* understanding that accompanied ratification.[60]

More broadly, a new portrait of Madison's role in the formation and ratification of the Constitution emerges. In this portrait, Madison is seen as a brilliant and prescient constitutional theorist but a frustrated reformer. Always ahead of his contemporaries, he identified a score or so of "vices" in the existing system but emphasized ones that his contemporaries thought were relatively unimportant. He thus approached constitutional reform with different goals than those of his fellow Framers and with proposals—especially the universal veto—that were unsuitable to most of them. Moreover, Madison defended a constitution much different from the one that he had sought and with arguments that were not necessarily understood or well received. This portrait, which is only hinted at in most studies of James Madison, merits full development.[61]

Notes

1. Introduction to Alexander Hamilton, James Madison, and John Jay, *The Federalist,* ed. Jacob E. Cooke (Middletown, CT: Wesleyan University Press, 1961), xiii. All subsequent citations of the *Federalist* papers are to this edition.

2. *Federalist* No. 10, 56. Only a few statesmen or philosophers had defended the idea of an extended republic prior to the publication of Madison's theory. Hume's essay "The Idea of a Perfect Commonwealth" (1754) is apparently the first defense in the history of political thought of the contention that a republic can best be instituted in a large geographical area. In 1784 William Vans Murray, an American law student in England, had written an essay titled "Extent of Territory" based on Hume's essay. Madison had presented his theory of an extended republic in his June 6, 1787, speech at the Constitutional Convention and in his famous October 24, 1787, letter to Jefferson. The Federalist John Stevens had presented a challenge to the small republic thesis in two of his "Americanus" essays, published on November 2 and 30, 1787. Finally, Hamilton's *Federalist* No. 9 had appeared on November 21, 1787. See David Hume, *Essays: Moral, Political, and Literary,* ed. Eugene F. Miller (Indianapolis, IN: Liberty Classics, 1985), xiiin8; for Murray, see Theodore Draper, "Hume and Madison: The Secrets of Federalist Paper No. 10," *Encounter* 58 (February 1982): 41; for Stevens's "Americanus" essays challenging the small republic thesis, see "Americanus I" and "Americanus III," in *The Debates on the Constitution: Federalist and Anti-Federalist*

Speeches, Articles, and Letters during the Struggle over the Ratification, ed. Bernard Bailyn (New York: Library of America, 1993), 1:227–30, 437–41; *Federalist* No. 9, 50–65.

3. *Federalist* No. 14, 83.

4. "Essays of Brutus," October 18, 1787, in *The Complete Anti-Federalist,* ed. Herbert Storing (Chicago: University of Chicago Press, 1981), 2:368–72.

5. Ibid., 2:369–70.

6. For the possibility that Madison was responding directly to Brutus, see Emery G. Lee III, "Representation, Virtue, and Political Jealousy in the Brutus-Publius Dialogue," *Journal of Politics* 49 (November 1997): 1073–95; Lance Banning, *The Sacred Fire of Liberty: James Madison and the Founding of the Federal Republic* (Ithaca, NY: Cornell University Press, 1995), 202; Alexander Hamilton, James Madison, and John Jay, *The Federalist with Letters of Brutus,* ed. Terence Ball (Cambridge: Cambridge University Press, 2003), xxi–xxv; Terence Ball, "A Republic—If You Can Keep It," in *Conceptual Change and the Constitution,* ed. Terence Ball and J. G. A. Pocock (Lawrence: University Press of Kansas, 1988), 137–64.

7. *Federalist* No. 10, 58, 61.

8. Ibid., 62.

9. Ibid., 64, 57.

10. Jon Metcham, the managing editor of *Newsweek,* recently called *Federalist* No. 10 "American secular scripture" and invoked it in a discussion of religion in America on *Meet the Press,* Easter Sunday, April 16, 2006. The other quotation here is from Robert Dahl, *A Preface to Democratic Theory* (Chicago: University of Chicago Press, 1956), 5. See also the quotations in the next note.

11. Douglass Adair, who sought to rescue Madison's theory from Charles Beard's interpretation of it, characterized Madison's argument as a "complicated piece of speculative political philosophy" and his "most amazing political prophecy." See Douglass Adair, *Fame and the Founding Fathers: Essays by Douglass Adair,* ed. Trevor Colbourn (New York: W. W. Norton, 1974), 92, 97. Robert Dahl once said that "perhaps in no other political writing by an American is there a more compactly logical, almost mathematical, piece of theory than in Madison's *The Federalist* No. 10." He also called it "one of the most lucid and compact sets of political propositions ever set forth by an American" (*Preface to Democratic Theory,* 5, 15). Martin Diamond, who launched his remarkably successful academic career on his interpretation of *Federalist* No. 10, wrote that Madison's argument is "rightly regarded as the most important original political writing by an American." Diamond also wrote that "nothing is more important to an understanding of both the theoretical and practical issues in the founding of the American Republic than a full appreciation of Madison's stand on behalf of the very large republic." See "The Declaration and the Constitution: Liberty, Democracy, and the Founders" and "What the Framers Meant by Federalism" in *As Far as Republican Principles Will Admit: Essays by Martin Diamond,* ed. William A. Schambra (Washington, DC: AEI Press, 1992), 237, 102. Finally, Ralph Ketcham has written that "The Tenth *Federalist* Paper ranks as perhaps the most significant contribution to the theory of government ever written by an American." See "Notes on James Madison's Sources for the Tenth *Federalist* Paper," *Midwest Journal of Political Science* 1 (May 1957): 20. For additional praise of Madison's argument, see Samuel Kernell, "Introduction: James Madison and Political Science," in

James Madison: The Theory and Practice of Republican Government (Stanford, CA: Stanford University Press, 2003), 3, and the comments cited in Larry Kramer, "Madison's Audience," *Harvard Law Review* 112 (January 1999): 612–23.

12. Akhil Reed Amar, *America's Constitution: A Biography* (New York: Random House, 2005), 43.

13. Jack Rakove, "The Great Compromise: Ideas, Interests, and the Politics of Constitution Making," *William and Mary Quarterly,* 3rd ser., 44, no. 3 (1987): 427. Douglass Adair argued that the delegates at the Convention were "considerably impressed" with Madison's June 6 speech introducing the extended republic thesis. See *The Intellectual Origins of Jeffersonian Democracy: Republicanism, the Class Struggle, and the Virtuous Farmer* (Lanham, MD: Lexington, 2000), 120; Irving Brant said that Madison's June 6 speech was "the most significant speech of the convention—one into which he [Madison] threw his whole philosophy of government" and that the theory of the extended republic formed the "invisible core of the Constitution." Brant also argued that the extended republic theory was initially set forth as a means to persuade delegates that it was safe to elect at least one branch of the national government directly by the people. See Irving Brant, *James Madison: Father of the Constitution, 1787–1800* (Indianapolis, IN: Bobbs-Merrill, 1950), 43. Finally, William Lee Miller argues that Madison's theory, as he developed it in memoranda prepared before the Convention, was the source of several of his speeches and that it was eventually "incorporated in the underpinnings of the United States Constitution." See *The Business of May Next: James Madison and the Founding* (Charlottesville: University Press of Virginia, 1992), especially 22–33, 53–60; quotation at 28.

14. Amar, *America's Constitution,* 43. Douglass Adair observed that prior to 1913 and the publication of Charles Beard's *Economic Interpretation of the Constitution,* "practically no commentator on *The Federalist* or the Constitution, none of the biographers of Madison, had emphasized *Federalist* 10 as of special importance for understanding our 'more perfect union.'" Nevertheless, Amar and Kramer err when they suggest that Adair agreed with their conclusion that Madison's theory had virtually no impact on Madison's generation. It is, of course, possible that Madison's theory was important to his generation but ignored by nineteenth-century historians. This, indeed, was Adair's position. He argued forcefully that "Madison's theory as abstract speculative thought played a significant role in the writing and ratification of the United States Constitution" and attributed the lack of concern with Madison's theory to the attention that nineteenth-century historians paid to the "burning political issues" of their day, namely, the powers and structure of the federal Union and the relationship of the states to the national government. See Amar, *America's Constitution,* 523n95; Kramer, "Madison's Audience," 670n256; Adair, *Fame and the Founding Fathers,* 73–92, especially 75–80. Quotations from Adair are found on 75–76 and 77, respectively.

15. Kramer, "Madison's Audience," 616. Emphasis in original.

16. Throughout this essay, my subject is Madison's theory of an extended republic, not simply the argument of *Federalist* No. 10. The primary reason for this focus is that *Federalist* No. 10 is only one expression of Madison's theory, and, as I point out below, Madison's theory evolved over time.

17. See "Vices of the Political System of the United States," in *The Papers of James Madison,* ed. William T. Hutchinson et al. (Chicago: University of Chicago Press; Charlottesville: University Press of Virginia, 1962–91), 9:345–58 (hereafter cited as *Papers*).

18. Madison to Jefferson, October 24, 1787, *Papers,* 10:212. For similar statements, see also "Speech of June 6th, 1787," in *Notes of Debates in the Federal Convention of 1787 Reported by James Madison,* ed. Adrienne Koch (New York: W. W. Norton, 1987), 76; *Federalist* No. 10, 56–57.

19. The most influential versions of this thesis have been set forth by Gordon Wood and by the editors of the Madison Papers, especially Charles Hobson. See Gordon S. Wood, *The Creation of the American Republic, 1776–1787* (Chapel Hill: University of North Carolina Press, 1969), especially 463–75; "Editorial Note: Vices of the Political System of the United States," *Papers,* 9:345–48, and "Editorial Note: Madison to Thomas Jefferson, 24 October 1787," *Papers,* 10:205–6; Charles Hobson, "The Negative on State Laws: James Madison, the Constitution, and the Crisis of Republican Government," *William and Mary Quarterly,* 3rd ser., 36, no. 2 (1979): 215–35.

20. Martin Diamond, "What the Framers Meant by Federalism," in *Republican Principles,* 93–197; Martin Diamond, Winston Mills Fisk, and Herbert Garfinkel, *The Democratic Republic: An Introduction to American National Government* (Chicago: Rand McNally, 1966), 42–48.

21. Diamond, Fisk, and Garfinkel, *Democratic Republic,* 43.

22. Diamond, "What the Framers Meant," 100.

23. Rakove, "Great Compromise," pp. 434–35.

24. Ibid., 439, 444–45.

25. *Federalist* No. 1, 5.

26. Christopher Wolfe, "On Understanding the Constitutional Convention of 1787," *Journal of Politics* 39 (February 1977): 97–118. Wolfe, however, is willing to make this claim only about the role of the theory at the Convention. He stresses that Madison's theory was important in the ratification struggle (188). This interpretation is also shared by James H. Hutson, who calls for the emancipation of studies of the Convention from the assumption that Madison's theory was important there. See "Riddles of the Federal Constitutional Convention," *William and Mary Quarterly,* 3rd ser., 44, no. 3 (1987): 420–22.

27. Wolfe, "Understanding the Constitutional Convention," 104.

28. Ibid., 112, 113.

29. Michael Zuckert, "Federalism and the Founding: Toward a Reinterpretation of the Constitutional Convention," *Review of Politics* 48 (Spring 1968): 166–210, especially 187–97; Zuckert, "A System without Precedent: Federalism in the American Constitution," in *The Framing and Ratification of the Constitution,* ed. Leonard Levy and Dennis Mahoney (New York: Macmillan, 1986), 132–40, especially 142–49; Zuckert, "The Political Science of James Madison," in *History of American Political Thought,* ed. Bryan-Paul Frost and Jeffrey Skikkanga (Lanham, MD: Lexington Books, 2003), 163–65; Zuckert, "Toward a Corrective Federalism: The United States Constitution, Federalism and Rights," in *Federalism and Rights,* ed. Ellis Katz and G. Allan Tarr (Lanham, MD: Rowman and Littlefield, 2003), 78, 82–86.

30. For Hobson's contributions, see "Editorial Note: Vices of the Political System of the United States," in *Papers,* 9:347–48; "Editorial Note: Madison to Thomas Jefferson, 24 October 1787," in *Papers,* 10:205–6; Hobson, "Negative on State Laws," 215–35.

31. James Madison to George Washington, April 16, 1787, *Papers,* 9:384.

32. James Madison to Edmund Randolph, April 8, 1787, *Papers,* 9:370.

33. Zuckert's interpretation marks a conflation of the pluralist and impartial representation readings. His reading suggests that the interaction between interest groups will create impartial majorities in Congress. See Zuckert, "Political Science of James Madison," 164–65.

34. Ibid., 164.

35. Zuckert, "Federalism and the Founding," 187.

36. Ibid., 192.

37. Ibid., 191 (quoting Diamond, "What the Framers Meant," 104).

38. Kramer, "Madison's Audience," 651.

39. Ibid., 663.

40. Kramer's challenge to the traditional view that Madison's argument for an extended republic was a standard response to the Anti-Federalists' claims about the extended republic was foreshadowed in some brief comments that Herbert Storing made: "There are bits and pieces of this view of the extended republic in other Federalist writings; but it is nowhere referred to specifically by other Federalist writers, so far as I can discover, and there is little evidence that it was influential or even widely understood. This is not the place to solve the still perplexing problem of the influence and authority (which are not the same) of Madison's famous account of the large republic. It is perhaps not surprising that the great body of Federalists stayed closer to the surface and to traditional views." See "The 'Other' Federalists Papers: A Preliminary Sketch," in *Toward a More Perfect Union: The Writings of Herbert J. Storing,* ed. Joseph M. Bessette (Washington, DC: AEI Press, 1995), 100–101.

41. Kramer, "Madison's Audience," 669.

42. Ibid., 679.

43. Ibid., 623, 670.

44. On Madison's dissatisfaction with the judicial remedy for protecting rights within the states, see Michael Zuckert, "Judicial Review and the Incomplete Constitution: A Madisonian Perspective on the Supreme Court and the Idea of Constitutionalism," unpublished paper provided by the author.

45. See especially Madison's speech of June 30 at the Constitutional Convention, reprinted in *Notes of Debates,* 223–25.

46. U.S. Constitution, Section 1, Articles 2 and 10.

47. Miller, *Business of May Next,* 28.

48. The phrase "great national discussion" is from *Federalist* No. 1, 5.

49. Woody Holton, "'Divide et Impera': *Federalist 10* in a Wider Sphere," *William and Mary Quarterly,* 3rd ser., 62, no. 2 (2005): 177.

50. Bernard Bailyn, *The Ideological Origins of the American Revolution* (Cambridge, MA: Belknap, 1967; enlarged ed. 1992), 366, 368, 367. Stevens's "Americanus" essays I and III, which set forth his argument for an extended republic, are included in Bailyn, *Debates on the Constitution,* 1:227–30, 437–42.

51. The possibility also exists, however, that even Madison's argument for the salutary effects of a multiplicity of interest groups was not particularly novel. Madison's model was religious diversity, and the belief that a multiplicity of religious sects had promoted religious liberty had wide currency in the early republic. Madison apparently used to quote approvingly Voltaire's aphorism: "If one religion only were allowed in England, the government would possibly become arbitrary; if there were but two, the people would cut each other's throats; but as there are such a multitude, they all live happy and in peace." See Adrienne Koch, *Madison's "Advice to My Country"* (Princeton, NJ: Princeton University Press, 1966), 76; Irving Brant, *James Madison* (Indianapolis, IN: Bobbs-Merrill, 1941), 1:68.

52. Kramer, "Madison's Audience," 623, 670. Lance Banning's important scholarship on James Madison contains a variation of this same error of trying to diminish the role of the theory of the extended republic in Madison's political thought. Banning, in *The Sacred Fire of Liberty,* acknowledges that Madison's argument from *Federalist* No. 10 is "indispensable to understanding the concerns and hopes that generated the Virginia Resolutions and inspired James Madison's defense of the completed Constitution" (207). Nevertheless, Banning insists that "undue fascination" with it has led to both a distorted view of its place within and misunderstandings about the character of Madison's political thought. The theory of the extended republic, Banning suggests, provides a "brilliant preface" to the defense of the Constitution that Madison provided as Publius (205–6, 213), but is hardly the alpha and omega of his beliefs. Excessive attention to *Federalist* No. 10, Banning warns, has led scholars to believe that Madison was exclusively concerned in the mid-1780s with the threat of majority factions and that his only goal was to protect individual rights from this threat. It has also invariably led them to portray Madison as more of an advocate than he was for centralizing power in the national government, ignoring the centrality of federalism to his founding vision, suggesting that he hoped to expand the responsibilities taken on by the national government, and slighting his concern with the responsiveness of rulers and the necessity of controlling them. Finally, Banning opposes the "impartial representation" or "disinterested umpire" reading of Madison's theory and suggests that it is inseparably linked to the errors of a "Hamiltonian" misreading of Madison's political thought and goals (469–70, notes 52–54). Once he lost the universal negative, Banning argues, Madison did not expect the national government to act as a neutral umpire between the nation's many factions. See also Banning, "The Hamiltonian Madison: A Reconsideration," *Virginia Magazine of History and Biography* 92 (January 1984): 3–28.

53. See Alan Gibson, "Veneration and Vigilance: James Madison and Public Opinion, 1785–1800," *Review of Politics* 67 (Winter 2005): 5–36; Colleen Sheehan, "Madison v. Hamilton: The Battle over Republicanism and the Role of Public Opinion," *American Political Science Review* 98 (August 2004): 405–24.

54. See Alan Gibson, "Impartial Representation and the Extended Republic: Towards a Comprehensive and Balanced Interpretation of the Tenth *Federalist,*" *History of Political Thought* 12 (Summer 1991): 262–304.

55. In "Property," Madison wrote "that alone is a just government, which *impartially* secures to everyman, whatever is his *own*." In *Papers,* 14:266. Emphasis in original.

56. See Gibson, "Veneration and Vigilance"; Sheehan, "Madison v. Hamilton."

57. Gordon Wood, *Creation of the American Republic,* especially 467, 499–518.

58. These themes of meeting state building imperatives, making the United States viable in an international system of states, and preventing civil war and the creation of separate confederacies in the United States are brought out in several excellent studies that may well transform our understanding of the purposes of constitutional reform and the original meaning of the Constitution. See Max M. Edling, *A Revolution in Favor of Government: Origins of the U.S. Constitution and the Making of the American State* (Oxford: Oxford University Press, 2003); Peter Onuf and Nicholas Onuf, *Federal Union, Modern World: The Law of Nations in an Age of Revolution, 1776–1814* (Madison, WI: Madison House, 1993); David C. Hendrickson, *Peace Pact: The Lost World of the American Founding* (Lawrence: University Press of Kansas, 2003); Amar, *America's Constitution.*

59. The quoted phrase is Adrienne Koch's characterization of Madison's note-taking role at the Convention. See *Notes of Debates,* viii.

60. It is possible, of course, to argue that Madison's theory was the *best* response to Montesquieu's small republic theory, even if it was not the standard reply. Madison's observations that diversity unavoidably results when liberty is granted and that a multiplicity of interests grow up in all "civilized" societies suggest that the small republic thesis was unrealistic in any society and inapplicable to the American situation. More positively, Madison's claims about the virtues of a multiplicity of interests suggest that the homogeneity suggested by the small republic thesis is not only impossible to attain but also undesirable. Thus, considered based upon its philosophical veracity rather than its immediate historical impact, it may well be that Madison's theory merits the praise that it has received. Obviously, however, such a line of argumentation can establish only the *philosophical authority* of Madison's theory as a response to Montesquieu, not its importance at the Convention, in explaining the logic and structure of the Constitution, or as a guide to the original understanding of the Constitution.

61. Forrest McDonald has been one of the few leading founding scholars who has challenged the idea that Madison was the father of the Constitution. By McDonald's count, "Overall, of seventy-one specific proposals that Madison moved, seconded, or spoke unequivocally in regard to, he was on the losing side forty times." See *Novus Ordo Seculorum: The Intellectual Origins of the Constitution* (Lawrence: University Press of Kansas, 1985), 208–9.

GORDON P. HENDERSON

A Portrait of James Madison's Views on Citizenship and Leadership in Popular Government

James Madison's reputation as one of the more learned and philosophical of the framers of the Constitution is fairly well established. Despite questions about his mastery of the presidency, he is likewise known as an astute practitioner of politics who took great care not only with what he did but also with what he said and wrote.[1] Given these two character traits and the unique historical moment he shared with his contemporaries, it seems reasonable that he would have conceived of the constitutional system he advocated, defended, and utilized as a grand experiment.[2] The dependent variable in such an experiment would be, to paraphrase Lincoln, whether a popular government affording a maximum of liberty and equality could endure. The many familiar independent variables include the extent of the republic, separation of powers, checks and balances, federalism, and the many other institutional attributes of "Madisonian" democracy.[3]

This chapter focuses on two independent variables of behavior in this experiment: citizenship and leadership. Just as Madison and his fellows made certain assumptions about how the institutions they designed would promote the endurance of the American constitutional system, they also made assumptions about what citizens and leaders should and would do as they worked with and through those institutions. Madison's more familiar observations on these variables are that "the seeds of faction are thus sown in the nature of man" and the corollary that "enlightened statesmen will not always be at the helm." Although these statements illume his expectations, they do not do so with sufficient complexity.

Madison had a fairly complex view of, and perhaps somewhat radical expectations about, what citizens and leaders should and would do to preserve the constitutional system.[4] These expectations are relevant to twenty-first-century

America since the constitutional design remains much as it was in Madison's day. If the framers' expectations about practices of citizenship and leadership were as important to them as were their institutional expectations, then it is critical to know what the former expectations were. Furthermore, even a cursory review of contemporary American politics in a constitutional context reveals that significant political battles are being fought, won, and lost over institutional expectations in such areas as federalism, presidential prerogative, separation of power, and judicial review. Likewise, of course, there appears to be no end to energetic debate about the qualities necessary for good citizenship and leadership. The story of James Madison's thoughts on these subjects certainly provides a useful starting point. This chapter will focus on determining what the thoughtful Madison expected those qualities to be if the grand experiment were to work.

Madison's Citizens

In drawing his portrait of citizenship, Madison spoke, as it were, in three voices. The first is that of the *political scientist* who objectively surveys what is known from political history without reference to the peculiarities of the American situation or to the Constitution that is to govern it. As a political scientist, Madison offered observations on how citizens can be expected to behave under various scenarios and circumstances regardless of who they are. In this capacity, Madison essentially engaged in an Enlightenment study of human nature, or, in more modern parlance, political psychology,[5] in order to identify what to expect.

Madison's second voice is akin to that of the *cultural anthropologist*. In this capacity, he offered his observations on the character, habits, and expectations of Americans that bear relevance to political citizenship. Madison sometimes expressed his observations as a cultural anthropologist in hyperbolic prose consistent with the historical context and the polemic character of the texts in which he made them. Nevertheless, Madison's observations on particular qualities of American citizens constitute an important part of his overall portrait of citizenship. As these qualities present culture-specific opportunities and limitations on the republican experiment, it is as though he considers them to be intervening variables that complement his previous treatment of political psychology.

Madison's third voice can be characterized as that of the *political engineer*. In this role Madison discussed what citizens must and must not do if the constitutional system is to work. He based such observations in part, of course, on the possibilities and limitations of citizenship revealed in his empirical discussions of political psychology and American culture. He also based them, however, on the design of the constitutional system, its underlying objectives, and its operation at the micro-level. It is within the context of Madison's role as a political engineer that he provided his definition of good citizenship. In other words, while the constitutional system reflects and accommodates the verities of citizenship that Madison's first two voices describe, his third voice describes those behaviors necessitated by the constitutional design in light of, and sometimes despite, what can be expected.[6]

Political Scientist

Madison's political science, like all political philosophy, was shaped by political experience. Consequently, the major themes that he explicated as a political scientist grew from his own concerns and extensive experiences. Liberty was chief among these themes and closely related were the virtues of popular government in support of that liberty. The vices of popular government, most notably faction, constitute a third theme also related to the protection of liberty. The fourth theme, religion, and the fifth, a bill of rights, together allow Madison to address very specifically the principal virtues of liberty and its abuse.

Madison began his portrait of the citizen with liberty. In a famous passage from *Federalist* No. 10, Madison observed that liberty "is essential to political life," that is, to any political life at all. It is essential in the same sense that air is biologically essential to life.[7] In Madison's judgment, liberty is the *sine qua non* of political life; it is not simply desirable, or merely desirable to Americans. Consistent with Enlightenment thinking, liberty is universally essential. The citizens that Madison envisioned, then, require liberty to exist at all.

Liberty is essential to political life for Madison, and for the Enlightenment thinkers more generally, on both normative and functional grounds. Its normative value, of course, is individual self-fulfillment. This was expressed by Locke and paraphrased in the Declaration of Independence: liberty leaves the individual free to be ("life"), to do ("liberty"), and to create ("the pursuit of happiness" or "estate"). The functional value of liberty stems from the unique identity each individual acquires as such individuals live, act, and create. Without identity, not only does the individual lack self-fulfillment, but society itself also acquires a sameness that serves as a foundation for tyranny. Thus, individual liberty serves itself by distinguishing individuals. Although this gets untidy, as in Hobbes's description of the state of nature and Madison's of faction, the "self-subverting" quality of liberty, to paraphrase Michael Walzer,[8] inclines individuals within and among groups to establish personal identities and thereby to resist the homogenizing efforts of others. The personal and political value of liberty to individuals, then, lies in individual self-fulfillment guaranteed by self-identification.

The task of Madison's political science, then, was to adopt a governmental form capable of maximizing liberty to support the ideal citizen. That governmental form, of course, is popular government. While the popular form, because it involves the citizens in self-government, is most conducive to maximizing liberty, it is, of course, fraught with hazards threatening liberty. Madison thus preferred the republican over the pure democratic form.[9]

Madison's discussion of democratic and republican forms of governance allowed him to explore features of human behavior that constitute the core of the citizen. People will respond to their circumstances on the basis of what they think is their own good. As he puts it in "Vices of the Political System of the United States" (1787), individuals will not have "a prudent regard to their own good as involved in the general and permanent good of the community."[10] Madison described the problem succinctly in his October 1788 letter to Jefferson on the idea of a bill of rights:

> Wherever the real power in government lies, there is the danger of oppression. In our governments, the real power lies in the majority of the community, and the invasion of private rights is chiefly to be apprehended, not from acts of Government contrary to the sense of its constituents, but from acts in which the Government is the mere instrument of the major number of the constituents. . . . Wherever there is an interest and a power to do wrong, wrong will be done, and not less readily by a powerful & interested party than by a powerful and interested prince . . . [so that] in a popular government, the political and physical power may be considered as vested in the same hands, that is in a majority of the people, and consequently the tyrannical will of the sovereign is not to be controuled [*sic*] by the dread of an appeal to any other force within the community.[11]

Exercising their liberty, citizens will think first of themselves and only secondarily, if at all, of the rights and interests of their fellow citizens or of the community as a whole. This tendency is so powerful that although he observed in *Federalist* No. 49 that individual citizens are likely to suppress their differences for the greater good during crises, he noted in "Vices of the Political System" that even during the Revolutionary War, the states, at the behest of their citizens and politicians, fulfilled their "obligations to the union" only "imperfectly." As he indicated in *Federalist* No. 10, the problem is made even worse as the size of an interested group increases. Even when virtuous leaders raise the quality of public debate, "the example will never be followed by the multitude."[12]

Here, of course, Madison developed his well-known theory of faction. The differences of opinion, occupation, wealth, and interest that result from liberty manifest themselves in the formation of factions. Faction is "thus sown in the nature of man." Factional behavior will come naturally to citizens in both their public and private lives. If unchecked, it will have serious "adverse" consequences for the "rights of other citizens" and/or the "permanent and aggregate interests of the community."[13]

Importantly, Madison noted that "we well know that neither moral nor religious motives can be relied on as an adequate control." Indeed, as the number included in the faction increases, these potential restraints diminish in their influence. He observed darkly in "Vices of the Political System" that popular assemblies, having sworn an oath in very much religious terms, nevertheless take actions "against which their [individual] consciences would revolt if proposed to them under the like [religious oath], separately in their closets." And when religion is "kindled into an enthusiasm," so that one might expect its influence in restraining self-interested factions to increase, "its force like that of other passions, is increased by the sympathy of a multitude," so that it "will hardly be seen with pleasure at the helm of government."[14]

While religion as an influence of restraint on the citizen is thus limited, it actually takes on a more threatening quality. Writing to Thomas Jefferson in Paris to explain and justify the work of the Philadelphia Convention, Madison, apologizing for "this immoderate digression," observed that far from being a restraint, religion represents one of the greatest dangers. "Even in its coolest state, it has been much oftener a motive to repression than a restraint from it." Furthermore, in his 1785 *Memorial and Remonstrance* against a Virginia bill that would compensate "Teachers of Christian Religion," Madison contended that membership in "civil society," along with all of its rights and duties, is secondary to the individual's status as "subject of the Governor of the Universe." The state cannot, therefore, have any "cognizance" of the individual's religious conscience so that each may "render to the Creator such homage, and such only, as he believes to be acceptable to him." Finally, "fifteen centuries" of the "incorporation with civil policy" of Christianity have resulted in "pride and indolence in the Clergy; ignorance and servility in the laity; [and] in both superstition, bigotry, and persecution."[15] Religion occupies a realm completely separate from the polity, except as each individual's private views shape positions on policy.[16]

In concluding this discussion of Madison's political science of citizenship, it helps to recall an important observation he made about political psychology in accepting the idea of a bill of rights. To his friend Thomas Jefferson (1788), and later in his speech to the House of Representatives introducing the Bill of Rights (1789), he argued that while "paper barriers" may be "too weak to be worthy of attention" as a restraint on the majority's abuse of the government as an "instrument," a bill of rights may well have two advantageous effects. Foremost is that by presenting them in a "solemn manner" akin to a religious oath as described above, the "political truths" so declared will "become incorporated with the National Sentiment [and thereby] counteract the impulses of interest and passion." Second, where the government itself is the source of abuse, rather than an instrument of the majority, the community will appeal to its declared rights to promote a campaign against the abuse.[17] The Bill of Rights, then, would become part of the fundamental political knowledge of citizens that they will use to restrain themselves as well as the government, perhaps more effectively and responsibly than religion.

Madison's political science views of citizens can be summarized as follows. Citizens require liberty if they are to live in a civil (political) society. From the standpoint of the individual, this means nothing less than forging a personal identity through liberty: the freedom to live, to do, and to create. As a practical matter, the development of personal identities protects the individual from the conformist efforts of others while also fragmenting society. Popular government is the most effective means of maximizing the virtues while controlling the vices of liberty. Chief among the vices is the natural tendency of individuals with similar identities to combine into factions. The most dangerous of these is the majority, and increasingly so the larger it is. Neither religion nor morality will be an effective restraint on the factious, "oppressive" tendencies of citizens. Religion itself becomes a danger to both the individual and the community when it is legally entangled with government. Commitment to a bill of rights, akin to articles of religious faith, will serve to reinforce in the citizens the vigilance necessary for the preservation of their liberties by emphasizing the priority of personal self-fulfillment and the development of distinct personal identities.

Cultural Anthropologist

Madison's observation of the American people through the revolutionary and early republican years appears to have made him confident that the grand experiment would work. He saw among his fellow citizens a political maturity that was both lacking elsewhere and necessary to the success of the American experiment. He also saw, however, that Americans had some fairly significant expectations that government would have to meet. And, as implied in his more general discussion of the fatal flaw of popular government—factionalism—he also recognized the need for caution.

The chief characteristic that Madison identified as essential to the success of the American experiment was nationhood. Perhaps nowhere was he more eloquent than in *Federalist* No. 14: "Hearken not to the unnatural voice which tells you that the people of America, knit together as they are by so many cords of affection, can no longer live together as members of the same family; can no longer continue [as the] mutual guardians of their mutual happiness; can no longer be fellow citizens of one great, respectable, and flourishing empire. . . . The kindred blood which flows in the veins of American citizens, the mingled blood which they may have shed in defense of their sacred rights, consecrate[s] their union and excite[s] horror at the idea of their becoming aliens, rivals, enemies."[18] While he certainly tailored these hyperbolic words to appeal to an audience seemingly unwilling to sacrifice its parochial interests, they nevertheless clearly indicate that Madison considered the confederate alternative inappropriate to the American situation. He found the Americans to have been together long enough to have forged a national conscience; to have developed a mutual interdependence; to have shared at least one traumatic experience; and to have progressed far enough in the task of nation building that to turn back would be unthinkable.

Madison was confident, then, that there was a sufficiently national consciousness to allow for a national ratification of the Constitution. As he noted to George Washington, the people, and not merely the state governments, would have to ratify the new system if it were to attain "its proper validity and energy," since it would be making "inroads on the existing Constitutions of the states."[19] Applying his political science to the particular circumstances of the Americans, then, Madison found that in their exercise and bloody defense of their individual liberty, they had in fact acquired a national identity. This, in turn, consistent with his understanding of identity politics, allowed them to distinguish themselves from and defend against the encroachments of the other nations of the world.

In *Federalist* No. 43 Madison observed that once the Constitution was ratified, the states remaining in "dissent," while having no "political relation" with those that ratified, would continue their "moral relations" anyway. Madison acknowledged in several places and in several contexts that the states would remain a key feature of a more national republic. In the same letter to Washington, for instance, he noted that the attempt to abolish states and create a single national union would be "as inexpedient as it is unattainable." In *Federalist* No. 46 he nearly contradicted his appraisal of national sentiment cited above: "the first and most natural attachment of the people will be to the governments of their respective states." Even during the Revolutionary War, "the attention and attachment of the people," after the initial crisis, was "to their own particular governments," and certainly "the federal council was never the idol of popular favor." Further reassuring his readers that the state perspective would retain a major place in the new system, he observed that members of Congress would have a more "local spirit" than the state legislatures would have a national one. And finally, he likened the response of the people to encroachments by the federal on the state governments to their response to Great Britain: "A correspondence would be opened. Plans of resistance would be concerted. One spirit would animate and conduct the whole. The same combinations, in short, would result from an apprehension of the federal, as was produced by the dread of a foreign yoke."[20]

The political habits of Americans would not change merely because a new form of government had been adopted. Indeed, the "republican" form of government had been adopted precisely to be "reconcilable with the genius of the American people; [and] with the fundamental principles of the Revolution."[21] While thus far this would seem to be an advantage, and Madison certainly saw it that way, the persistence of certain other habits among the Americans was cause for concern. In *Federalist* No. 10, and indeed throughout the *Federalist,* Madison spoke in specific detail of the many horrors in policy brought about by factionalism. As noted above, he also expressed with some personal chagrin the degree to which the states refused to cooperate even during the most difficult moments of the war.

In his letter to Jefferson on the idea of a bill of rights, he bemoaned the coddling, so to speak, of liberty. While the common concern was with government abuse of power, Madison pointed out that lack of power could be just as dangerous. Government in some situations constantly accommodates itself by relaxing controls until "the abuses of liberty beget a sudden transition to an undue degree of power." Adding that this principle applied especially to "the existing governments of America," Madison concluded that "liberty [is] equally exposed to danger whether the Government have [*sic*] too much power or too little power." In his *National Gazette* essay of January 19, 1792, titled "Charters," Madison predicted that the Americans would be peculiarly motivated to "establish the efficacy of popular charters, in defending liberty against power, and power against licentiousness."[22]

Madison also wrote often in praise of the intelligence of the American people. While the manner in which he made these comments suggests rhetorical flourish, the frequency with which he did so suggests the conviction that the experiment would indeed require a relatively mature political wisdom among the citizenry.[23] In *Federalist* No. 37, for instance, he pronounced "with assurance that the people of this country, enlightened as they are with regard to the nature, and interested, as the great body of them are, in the effects of good government," will act to see that good government is achieved. Furthermore, he noted in his report on the Virginia Resolution defending the concept of interposition against those who feared it would be used unnecessarily that the "temperate consideration and candid judgment of the American public" would reserve such significant actions for only the most serious of situations.[24]

A second feature of the praise Madison had for the American public is what can best be characterized as courage. Americans know change is needed, he wrote in *Federalist* No. 38. In *Memorial and Remonstrance* (1785), he spoke with admiration of the "free men of America" who did not hesitate to take action before the British further solidified their power. In *Federalist* No. 14 he highlighted the combination of wisdom and action: "Is it not the glory of the people of America that, whilst they have paid a decent regard to the opinions of former times and other nations, they have not suffered a blind veneration for antiquity, for custom, or for names, to overrule the suggestions of their own good sense, the knowledge of their own situation, and the lessons of their own experience? To this manly spirit posterity will be indebted."[25]

The political culture of citizenship that Madison portrayed as unique to the American people appears to have left him cautiously optimistic. Even as he and

Jefferson became increasingly alarmed by the Hamiltonian tendencies of the late Washington and Adams administrations, he continued in his public writings to rely upon earlier themes to rally public opinion. Those themes include appeals to a national patriotism as well as continued loyalty to the states. Americans were intelligent and moderate in their consideration of great questions, or at least they can be if the misconstrued self-interest and/or conniving politicians did not lead them astray. Finally, when they recognized, after due consideration, the need for action, they boldly moved ahead without hesitation. In Madison's understanding, the American citizen identified with the United States on three levels: as a nation, as a state, and as an individual. The first two were meant to assure the liberty necessary to the third. When they failed at this, he was guardedly hopeful that their individual identity would prompt the exercise of what Jürgen Habermas called a "constitutional patriotism" to correct the wrong.[26]

Political Engineer

Madison's understandings of the character and requisites of citizenship for popular government and the confidence he had in their unique manifestations in America were the foundations upon which he built his advice to his fellow citizens. In this last voice, Madison emphasized what the good citizen should, and should not, be in order for the constitutional experiment to succeed.

In the first place, Madison observed, in the *National Gazette* essay titled "Charters" (1792), that the very complicated systems of federalism and the internal separations of power require that there be "a more than common reverence for the authority which is to preserve order thro' the whole." The first responsibility, then, is to protect the Constitution. The main engine of this protection is public opinion. "All power has been traced up to opinion," he declared in the same essay, so that even "the most arbitrary government is controuled [*sic*] where the public opinion is fixed." In *Federalist* No. 52 he asserted that the function of the scheme of representation in the House of Representatives was to protect liberty by assuring that "the government in general should have a common interest with the people." In the *National Gazette* essay titled "Government of the United States" (1792), he made the direct admonition that the Constitution itself is not sufficient to its own self-preservation: "The people who are the authors of this blessing, must also be its guardians. Their eyes must be ever ready to mark, their voice to pronounce, and their arm to repel or repair aggressions on the authority of their constitutions; the highest authority next to their own, because the immediate work of their own, and the most sacred part of their property, as recognizing and recording the title to every other."[27] The authority of the Constitution, as well as the limits it imposes on the government, were vital to the well-being of the people. But since the people created it, they were responsible for sustaining it.

In writings directed at two laws that Madison opposed as threats to the well-being of the republic, he described what citizens must do to make their public opinion felt sufficiently to correct the problem. In *Memorial and Remonstrance* (1785) he warned against complacency: "it is proper to take alarm at the first experiment on our liberties." This is the "first duty of citizens." He argued similarly in the Virginia Resolutions (1799) that citizens had a right and duty to act when laws, in this instance the Alien and Sedition Acts, "deeply and essentially [affect] the vital principles of their political system." The act of interposition must be in response to a case, "not of a light and transient nature, but of a nature dangerous to the great purposes for which the constitution was established." To assure that such extreme acts take place only when warranted, there must be free and open discussion during elections, and, in a criticism of the Sedition Act, a free press capable of conducting the discussion and providing vital information to enlighten the public.[28]

It is fitting to conclude this discussion of Madison's portrait of the good citizen with what is perhaps among the most vital decision-making functions of citizenship: the decision to go to war. In the *National Gazette* essay titled "Universal Peace" (1792), Madison argued that war can come about either by a government that wants it or a people that wants it. In the former case, where a government wishes to wage a war the public does not want, the public need only subordinate the will of the government to its own. This is accomplished when the government is "regenerated" through elections. And, again, these elections were to take place in the context of an informed and enlightened discussion.

When the public itself is the source of a will to war, and the government is attuned to it, the discussion must turn not, as it often does, on "occasional impressions, and inconsiderate pursuits." Rather, it will be necessary to subject "the will of the society to the reason of the society." He went on, then, to describe ways to assure this, specifically by making the generation that advocates war to bear its greatest burdens: "Were a nation to impose such restraints on itself, avarice would be sure to calculate the expences [*sic*] of ambition; in the equipoise of these passions, reason would be free to decide for the public good; and an ample reward would accrue to the state, first, from the avoidance of all its wars of folly, secondly, from the vigor of its unwasted resources for wars of necessity and defence."[29]

The qualities of citizens described by Madison were derived from his study of political history, the unique features of American political culture, and the citizenship requisites of the constitutional experiment he did so much to design. The Constitution itself was intended to facilitate popular government because only with the liberty it protects can the citizen have a genuine political life. And given the verities revealed by the history of political behavior, the constitutional design was intended to control them, especially the pernicious effects of faction. Madison was confident that Americans possessed a sufficiently national conscience combined with a commitment to the values stemming from the Revolution to make the system work. It was on the basis of that confidence that he recommended the kinds of political practices they would have to adopt if they were to succeed.

Madison's Leaders

Madison's writings in the 1790s expressing concerns about the direction the nation was going often took the form of pleas to his fellow citizens to recall the vital role they played in the political system. His words in the *National Gazette* essays and the *Report on the Virginia Resolution* suggest that he believed they had forgotten that role and that they needed only rise to action, as they had done in the past, to recover. As this and the foregoing discussion suggest, Madison gave priority of action and responsibility to the citizenry. The government was to be made to conform to the society. But in order for this to happen, the leadership in government needed certain qualities making them both able and willing to thus conform.[30] Citizens would, however, need to take the initiative.

Madison made clear in his *Memorial and Remonstrance* that lawmakers are subservient to society. Arguing that society has no business regulating religion, he continued: "still less can it [religion] be subject to [the authority] of the Legislative Body. The latter are but the creatures and viceregents of [society]. Their jurisdiction is both derivative and limited: it is limited with regard to the co-ordinate departments, more necessarily is it limited with regard to the constituents." Referring to legislators ("rulers") who encroach upon "the great barrier that defends the rights of the people" as "tyrants," he more damningly said that members of a public that permit this are themselves enslaved.[31]

In *Federalist* No. 48 Madison warned that in a representative system, the people must be most wary of the legislature. Its actions are masked by complexity, and its access to "the pockets of the people" makes it especially dangerous.[32] In "Vices of the Political System" he attributed to legislators three motives for seeking office: ambition, interest, and the public good, of which the latter is least and the second is most often in play.[33] When self-interest is the motive, the legislator is especially energetic in gaining and keeping office. When a majority of legislators with like interests can form a majority, they "join in a perfidious sacrifice" of the interest of their constituents so as better to serve their own. Elections might be thought to enable the public to rid themselves of this menace. But "base and selfish measures" are often "masked by pretexts of public good and apparent expediency." Other more "honest but unenlightened representatives" are then taken in by this masquerade and become its unwitting supporters.[34]

This harsh portrait of the legislator, of course, is a core reason for the constitutional design. The dependence on the people, especially in the lower house, helps meliorate legislative excesses. But the people are themselves subject to the danger of majority faction, for which both the extended republic of *Federalist* No. 10 and the internal auxiliary precautions of *Federalist* No. 51 are intended.[35] That is, if the electorate is ultimately to force the government to conform to society, and society can itself become oppressive, then restraints must be put in place at the nexus of public will and official action.

But Madison's aspirations for leadership were not limited to manipulating them to restrain themselves according to their self-interest. Although he observed in *Federalist* No. 10 that "enlightened statesmen will not always be at the helm," the small number of representatives in a republic can "refine and enlarge the public views." They are "a chosen body of citizens, whose wisdom may best discern the true interest of their country, and whose patriotism and love of justice will be least likely to sacrifice it to temporary or partial considerations."[36]

Madison's admiring references to his experience with the framers in 1787 are another indicator of the model of leadership he has in mind.[37] In *Federalist* No. 40 he characterizes them as "patriotic and respectable citizens" who themselves recognized the seriousness of the situation and the anxiety of the people. They did not adhere rigidly to the existing form of the Articles of Confederation and developed innovative approaches. By the same token, they were careful not to do too much.[38] Thus, leadership in the Madison mold must be able to balance the need for action against the need for caution and the public will against the public good.

Madison's Hopes for Success

James Madison's extensive involvement in the founding moments of the American political system makes him an ideal subject of studies that seek to identify the original expectations of the framers. Madison took an empirical approach to identifying the lessons of history about human political behavior as well as the unique features of the American political culture that would be relevant to the success of popular government in the United States. As for his expectations of leadership, he again combined the lessons of history with the specific qualities of those he had encountered in his own political experience.

Armed with the results of these studies, he set out in search of solutions to the plethora of problems confronting the United States after the Revolutionary War while remaining true to the principles for which he believed the war had been fought and to which the Americans were irrevocably committed. Although the resultant constitutional system was in many respects disappointingly different from his original design,[39] his explications of it in the *Federalist* and his assessments of it during its first decade provide much information on what he thought citizenship and leadership would have to be if the system were to be a success.

The portraits of citizenship and leadership that emerged in these writings are grounded in an unflinching characterization of individual human self-interest and its exacerbation in a "multitude." But since the young America to which Madison spoke was committed to the extension of the still-revolutionary idea of individual liberty, its costs in terms of conflict and self-serving politics were to be outweighed by the personal and political identities it fostered. These, however, would have to be arranged into a typically complex Enlightenment balance of countervailing forces. And because the American political system would be a democratic republic, the citizenry would bear responsibility for raising the standards for themselves, as well as for their leaders so as to assure the maintenance of the requisite balance. As he concluded in "Vices of the Political System" (1787), "An auxiliary desideratum for the melioration of the Republican form is such a process of elections as will most certainly extract from the mass of society the purest and noblest characters which it contains; such as will at once feel most strongly the proper motives to pursue the end of their appointment, and be most capable to devise the proper means of attaining it."[40] That is, excellent leadership would be critical, as would an excellent citizenry to find and install it in office. Madison hoped that the constitutional compromises he described and rationalized in *Federalist* No. 51 were not too far removed from the realities of human behavior, and the American political culture, they were intended to control and to inspire.[41]

Notes

1. Gary Rosen, in *American Compact: James Madison and the Problem of Founding* (Lawrence: University Press of Kansas, 1999), observes that while "every one of his significant works arose in response to some practical need . . . Madison was a self-consciously philosophical statesman and freely related the issues of his day to a wider theory of politics" (3). Likewise, Jack N. Rakove, in *James Madison and the Creation of the American Republic,* 3rd ed. (New York: Pearson Longman, 2007), notes that Madison had a remarkable "ability to apply bookish learning to real problems," such as "the frustrations he had encountered in both state and national politics" (57), that he described in "Vices." Needless to say, Douglass Adair's "'That Politics May Be Reduced to a Science': David Hume, James Madison, and the Tenth Federalist," in *Fame and the Founding Fathers: Essays by Douglass Adair,* ed. Trevor Colbourn (New York: W. W. Norton, 1974), and Garry Wills's *Explaining America: The Federalist* (Garden City, NY: Doubleday, 1981) also enhanced Madison's intellectual reputation.

2. Madison refers to "the experiment" in several places, most notably *Federalist* Nos. 10 and 39 and the *National Gazette* essay "Charters" (January 19, 1792). These and other works by Madison appear in *James Madison: Writings,* ed. Jack N. Rakove (New York: Library of America, 1999) (hereafter cited as *Writings*).

3. The term "Madisonian" is itself brought into question by Samuel Kernell, who argues that while the "factional competition and checks and balances" of *Federalist* No. 51 certainly do describe the Constitution, they do not describe Madison's own

theoretical views. For those, he continues, one must turn to the Virginia Plan and *Federalist* No. 10. See "The True Principles of Republican Government," in *James Madison: The Theory and Practice of Republican Government,* ed. Samuel Kernell (Stanford, CA: Stanford University Press, 2003), 120. A rather cynical view of the Madisonian principles espoused in *Federalist* No. 51 appears in Richard K. Matthews, *If Men Were Angels: James Madison and the Heartless Empire of Reason* (Lawrence: University Press of Kansas, 1995): the role of citizens is limited largely to voting, after which they are to return quietly to "search for meaning inside the iron cage of the private domain" (9). See Rosen, *American Compact,* 4, for a counterargument.

4. Recent efforts to unmask this complexity include David F. Epstein, *The Political Theory of* The Federalist (Chicago: University of Chicago Press, 1984), 6; Rosen, who sees the *Federalist* as reflecting Madison's belief that personal, political motivations are just as important as economic motivations in the expression of self-interest (see *American Compact*); Garrett Ward Sheldon, *The Political Philosophy of James Madison* (Baltimore: Johns Hopkins University Press, 2001), xiv–xv, who sees Madison's blend of liberalism and classical republicanism, nationalism, and federalism as an effort to strike a governing balance sufficient to control his "Christian realist view of man's weak, sinful nature"; and Randall Strahan, "Personal Motives, Constitutional Forms, and the Public Good: Madison on Political Leadership," in Kernell, *James Madison,* who explores Madison's conceptions of the "higher motives of the public good . . . as well as the lower motives of ambition, interest, and passion" (74) that shape the behavior of both leaders and citizens.

5. See, for instance, Rakove, *Madison and the Republic,* 4, 37–39; Strahan, "Personal Motives," 65–66.

6. See note 3 above.

7. *Writings,* 161.

8. Michael Walzer, "The Communitarian Critique of Liberalism," *Political Theory* 18, no. 1 (February 1990): 15.

9. *Writings,* 164.

10. Ibid., 77.

11. Ibid., 421.

12. Ibid., 288, 72–73, 164, 77.

13. Ibid., 161. Madison articulated his theory of faction in several other places as well. See, in *Writings,* letter to George Washington (April 16, 1787), 81–82; "Vices," 76–79; speech to the Constitutional Convention (June 6, 1787), 92–93; and letter to Thomas Jefferson (October 24, 1787), 150–51.

14. Ibid., 78; see also letter to Jefferson, October 24, 1787, ibid., 151.

15. Ibid., 151, 30–31.

16. See Rakove, *Madison and the Republic,* 38, on the Enlightenment quality of Madison's views on religion and politics.

17. James Madison to Thomas Jefferson, October 17, 1788, *Writings,* 421–22; speech, June 8, 1789, ibid., 446–47.

18. Ibid., 172.

19. Letter to George Washington, April 16, 1787, in *Writings,* 83; see also *Federalist* No. 46, ibid., 266.

20. Ibid., 251, 80, 266, 267, 268, 270.

21. Ibid., 211.

22. Ibid., 422, 503.

23. Rosen, in *American Compact,* observes that Madison himself is an excellent instance of the idea that, despite its realism, "liberalism . . . must look to certain human excellences if it is to create political regimes that can endure" (5).

24. *Writings,* 196, 614.

25. Ibid., 31, 172.

26. Jürgen Habermas, *The Inclusion of the Other: Studies in Political Theory,* ed. Ciari Cronin and Pablo De Greiff (Cambridge, MA: MIT Press, 1998).

27. *Writings,* 503, 300, 508. See also Habermas, *Inclusion of the Other.*

28. *Writings,* 31, 612, 642–58, quotation on 655.

29. Ibid., 506, 507.

30. See Rosen, *American Compact,* 5, and Strahan, "Personal Motives," 66.

31. *Writings,* 530, 30–31.

32. Ibid., 282–83.

33. See Strahan, "Personal Motives," 71–72.

34. *Writings,* 76.

35. See note 3 above.

36. *Writings,* 165.

37. It is worth quoting at length from the conclusion of what is now included as the preface to Madison's *Notes of Debates in the Federal Convention*: "I feel it a duty to express my profound & solemn conviction, derived from my intimate opportunity of observing & appreciating the views of the Convention, collectively & individually, that there never was an assembly of men, charged with a great & arduous trust, who were more pure in their motives, or more exclusively or anxiously devoted to the object committed them, than were the members of the Federal Convention of 1787" (ibid., 841–42).

38. Ibid., 223–25.

39. See note 3 above.

40. *Writings,* 79–80.

41. See note 3 above.

THREE

Madison and the Bill of Rights

RODNEY A. GRUNES

James Madison and Religious Freedom

Although the U.S. Supreme Court has accorded Thomas Jefferson a higher profile, no American founder contributed more than James Madison in developing the nation's ideas on freedom of conscience, the free exercise of religion, and the separation of church and state. What makes Madison truly unique was his continued intellectual growth on these issues, especially his willingness to concede in his postpresidential years that he had violated his own commitment to a "perfect separation" between government and religion, as he believed the establishment clause of the First Amendment required.[1]

The evolution of Madison's thoughts on religious freedom fell into three distinct periods: prepresidential, presidential, and postpresidential.[2] In the first of these, which culminated in Madison's role in the writing and adoption of the First Amendment of the U.S. Constitution, Madison articulated the idea that religious liberty is a God-given inalienable natural right that predates the formation of society. As such, the government has no power to establish a religion, advance all religions equally, or prefer one religion over another. Madison expressed these views most forcefully and elegantly in his *Memorial and Remonstrance against Religious Assessments,* which he penned in 1785. During the presidential period, Madison continued to adhere to many key formative principles, yet he was more willing to accommodate religion in the public square, especially to meet the practical political requirements of leading the nation during the War of 1812. Finally, in his postpresidential years, Madison reflected on the inconsistencies between his ideas on religious liberty and the policies he followed during his presidency. Perhaps mirroring change in his personal faith from an orthodox to a "Deistic form of Anglicanism,"[3] Madison conceded that he violated his own principles and the establishment clause of the First Amendment when he sought to accommodate religion as a wartime president. During this third period, especially in his *Detached Memoranda*, which he wrote sometime between 1817 and 1832, Madison embraced what constitutional scholars call the "strict separation" position between church and state.

James Madison's jurisprudential journey has had a major impact on American ideas on religious freedom. These views have also become part of the contemporary separationist-accommodationist debate in the U.S. Supreme Court involving the intentions of the framers and the meaning of the religion clauses of the First Amendment. As a primary contributor to the final wording of these clauses, one might expect that the Court would cite Madison as a major authority in its church-state decision making. For the most part, however, it has failed to do so.

Madison's Personal Faith

Part of the problem in evaluating and accepting Madison's evolving views on the meaning of the First Amendment religion clauses results from what historian Lance Banning calls the "puzzle" of Madison's private religious faith.[4] This "puzzle" comes from contradictions that were evident in his family and educational background and continued throughout his life. While his father was a vestryman and reared his son within the established church of Virginia, for his part Madison never identified himself as an Episcopalian. Though he never took full communion, he attended church regularly and, like his father, often invited ministers to his house. At age eleven, Madison's family sent him to an academy run by Donald Robertson. It was here that he learned Latin and was exposed to Enlightenment thought. Yet, concerned about the spread of Deism at William and Mary, the Madisons sent their son to Princeton (the College of New Jersey), an institution known for training American Presbyterian clergy. At Princeton Madison studied under its influential new president, the Reverend John Witherspoon, who provided his prize student with a solid grounding in Calvinist theology, eighteenth-century rationalism, the nature of politics, and, in the year following graduation, Hebrew and ethics. This background led to additional paradoxes. As Ralph Ketcham has noted, Madison reveled in Voltaire's "devastating jibes" at religion, maintained a deep personal attachment to the general aspects of Christianity and morality, identified with Enlightenment antagonism toward clericalism, offered cordiality to Jews, and opposed the ridicule of Catholics.[5] Perhaps Joseph Loconte summarizes these contradictions best when he notes that "Madison was certainly not the devout Christian that some conservatives make him out to be. Yet neither was he the Enlightenment skeptic of liberal imagination."[6]

To complicate matters further, Madison said very little about his personal faith after beginning his political career. Viewing his personal beliefs as a private concern, Madison rarely spoke or wrote about religious matters. In papers and letters that have survived, it appears that he moved away from the orthodox Christianity that was dominant in his early adult years and adopted ideas more consistent with "Liberal Christianity" (Unitarianism) and Deism. An illustrative example involves letters exchanged in 1825 with the Reverend Frederick Beasley, the provost of the University of Pennsylvania and an Episcopal minister, who had sought Madison's response to his writings on the nature of God. In addition to referring to "Nature's God," Madison responded by declaring that "the belief in a God All Powerful wise & good is so essential to the moral order of the World & to the happiness of man, that arguments which enforce it cannot be drawn from too many sources."[7] As David L. Holmes points out, Madison omits any reference to Jesus, the Bible, the church, or the Judeo-Christian tradition.[8]

The Prepresidential Years

Although his personal religious views evolved over time, Madison maintained a "lifelong zeal for religious freedom."[9] Consistent with Craig Grau's earlier chapter in this book, Ralph Ketcham has noted that "there is no principle in all of Madison's wide range of private opinions and long public career to which he held with greater vigor and tenacity than this one of religious liberty."[10] However, the harsh persecution that the established church in Virginia meted out to his friends and others for their dissenting views convinced Madison that he had to develop a broader secular basis for defending religious freedom. Ketcham observes that Madison did this by maintaining that "it was a fundamental human right of all men to believe, or not believe, whatever their conscience dictated."[11] Moreover, as political scientist Vincent Philip Muñoz notes, Madison went still further, arguing that since religious freedom is an inalienable human right that predates the social compact, the proper role of government was to remain "noncognizant of religion."[12] What makes this especially remarkable, of course, is that the prevailing view of the time was that state support of religion was necessary and desirable as a function of good government.

The development of Madison's more secular approach to protecting religious liberty is first evident in 1776 at Virginia's first constitutional convention. Here he took a strong leadership position in criticizing the language used in George Mason's proposed religious freedom provision for inclusion in a Virginia Declaration of Rights. Specifically, Madison objected to the use of the word "toleration" and perhaps the sectarian closing in the following proposal: "That religion, or the duty which we owe to our Creator, and the manner of discharging it, can be directed only by reason and conviction, not by force or violence; and therefore, that all men should enjoy the fullest toleration in the exercise of religion, according to the dictates of conscience, unpunished and unrestrained by the magistrate unless, under color of religion, any man disturb the peace, the happiness, or safety of society. And that it is the mutual duty of all to practice Christian forbearance, love, and charity towards each other." In Madison's view, mere toleration was not a strong enough basis for guaranteeing the free exercise of religion. Moreover, Mason's provision seemed to assume that government possessed the authority to determine how much to tolerate when religious liberty was an unalienable right of the people. However, Madison was unable to convince the convention to support his stronger and more sweeping substitute proposal for fear that it might eliminate the established church. Presented by Patrick Henry, Madison's substitute provided more sweeping language while retaining Mason's "exceptions" as it declared that "all men are equally entitled to the full and free exercise of [religion] according to the dictates of Conscience; and therefore no man or class of man ought, on account of religion, to be invested with peculiar emoluments or privileges; nor subject to any penalties or disabilities unless, under color of religion, any man disturb the peace, the happiness, or the safety of society." After the convention also rejected a second amendment, Madison finally succeeded in convincing the body to include his proposed language that "all men are equally entitled to the free exercise of religion, according to the dictates of conscience" in its final version for protecting religious liberty in Article XVI. The exceptions in both the Mason proposal and the Madison substitute were simply dropped.[13]

Scholars generally agree that changing the language of Article XVI was a major accomplishment in the development of religious liberty. In getting the convention to support his language, says Ketcham, "Madison had made possible complete liberty of belief or disbelief, and the utter separation of church and state."[14] Lance Banning goes still further, noting that "from that point forward, with unwavering consistency," Madison "envisioned total freedom of opinion, absolute equality for various denominations, and an end to the prevailing intermixture of the logically distinctive spheres of politics and religion, this world and the next."[15]

Despite the significance of the Virginia Declaration of Rights, historian Irving Brant is undoubtedly correct when he describes Madison's *Memorial and Remonstrance against Religious Assessments,* published anonymously in 1785, as "the most powerful defense of religious liberty ever written in America."[16] The *Memorial* was designed to mobilize political and religious opponents of Patrick Henry's property tax "Establishing a Provision for Teachers of the Christian Religion," a proposal that was originally designed to authorize government support for Christian ministers, churches, and worship. Amendments allowed each property owner, however, to specify which Christian denomination should receive the tax money, less 5 percent for state administration, to be used "for a Minister or Teacher of the Gospel, or the providing of places of divine worship." When taxpayers specified no denomination, the act directed the Virginia General Assembly to use the tax money "for the encouragement of seminaries of learning."

Aimed at persuading both public opinion and state legislators, Madison's *Memorial* consists of fifteen articles that taken together treat an established religion as an attack on liberty, equality, the rights of conscience, and the idea of republican government. Specifically, Articles 1–4 and 13–15 set forth and reiterate the philosophical and theological arguments against adoption of the assessment bill. Articles 6–7 and 9–12 offer pragmatic arguments of the bill's harm to religion, especially Christianity. Finally, Article 8 disputes the view that state support of religion supports the stability of civil society.[17]

The philosophical heart of Madison's *Memorial* is found in Article 1 where, borrowing liberally from the social contract ideas of John Locke in the *Second Treatise of Government* and his own contributions to Article XVI of the Virginia Declaration of Rights, he states:

> The Religion then of every man must be left to the conviction and conscience of every man; and it is the right of every man to exercise it as these may dictate. This right is in its nature an unalienable right. It is unalienable because the opinions of men depending only on evidence contemplated by their own minds, cannot follow the dictates of other men. . . . It is the duty of every man to render to the Creator such homage and such only as he believes acceptable to Him. This duty is precedent, both in order of time and in degree of obligation, to the claims of civil society. . . . We maintain, therefore, that in matters of religion, no man's right is abridged by the institution of Civil Society, and that religion is wholly exempt from its cognizance.[18]

For Madison, then, "the equal rights of every citizen to the free exercise of religion" and freedom of conscience are unalienable rights that existed prior to forming civil society. Separation of church and state guarantees protection of these rights and preserves the integrity of Christianity and other religions. In Madison's view, the state lacks all authority over religion and possesses no power to determine which religion is more legitimate than another. If the state can establish Christianity or a particular denomination as the official religion, explained Madison, it can just as easily establish another religion or sect at some later time. Madison argued that opposition to established religion should not be interpreted as hostility to religion. Rather, his intention was to strengthen Christianity and other religions. This can best be achieved, argued Madison, by strictly separating church and state while prohibiting the government from taking any "cognizance" of religion.[19]

Madison's commitment to equal rights for believers and nonbelievers is a central argument in the *Memorial*. Viewing religious faith as essentially a private matter, he forcefully argued that all men were entitled to their natural rights. In his words, "Whilst we assert for ourselves a freedom to embrace, to profess, and to observe the religion which we believe to be of divine origin, we cannot deny an equal freedom to those who minds have not yet yielded to the evidence which has convinced us. If this freedom be abused, it is an offence against God, not against man: To God, therefore, not to man, must an account of it be rendered."[20]

As Irving Brant has pointed out, Madison's arguments against the assessment bill also had an impact on the future of church-state jurisprudence. In addition to maintaining that any use of taxpayer funds constituted "an establishment of religion," he saw state-mandated contributions to religious institutions through taxes as a violation of an individual's religious liberty. Thus, "financial support of religion was unconstitutional if the basic law either forbade an establishment of religion or guaranteed the rights of conscience."[21]

Following the victory over the assessment bill, Madison turned his attention to passing Thomas Jefferson's Act for Establishing Religious Freedom. After its adoption with little opposition in 1785, Madison led a political coalition that successfully decriminalized heresy, guaranteed the free exercise of religion, prohibited religious taxes, and ended all religious tests for public office.[22]

Two years later, James Madison helped draft a new constitution for the United States in Philadelphia. Although there was concern that republican government required a virtuous populace, the debates generally omitted any reference to Christian doctrine or the need to form a new government that was consistent with God's will.[23] The thirty-six-year-old "father of the Constitution" shared this view when he wrote the following to Thomas Jefferson: "The inefficacy of this restraint [religion] on individuals is well known. The conduct of every popular assembly, acting on oath, the strongest of religious ties, shows that individuals join without remorse in acts against which their consciences would revolt, if proposed to them separately in their closets. When indeed Religion is kindled into enthusiasm, its force like that of other passions is increased by the sympathy of the multitude. But enthusiasm is only a temporary state of religion, and whilst it lasts will hardly be seen with pleasure at the helm. Even in its coolest state, it has been much oftener a motive to oppression than a restraint from it."[24] Article VI of the Constitution provided that "no religious test shall ever be required as a qualification to any office or public trust under the States." Though some critics viewed this as an open invitation to "Jews, Heathens, and Pagans of every kind,"[25] Madison defended this provision in *Federalist* No. 52 when he wrote that the U.S. Congress must be "open to merit of every description . . . without regard to . . . any profession of religious faith."[26]

Although Madison rejected the use of religion to restrain abuses of republican liberty in the nation and the states, he understood the need for some mechanism to protect individual rights. His experience with the assessment bill and Virginia's religious freedom statute, says historian Lance Banning, convinced Madison that only "a multiplicity of interests—and thus a large and diverse republic—[provided] the most effective safeguard for the rights of all."[27] As Madison himself explained in *Federalist* No. 51, "the security for civil rights must be the same as for religious rights. It consists in the one case in the multiplicity of interests and, in the other, in the multiplicity of sects."[28] Thus, an enlarged republic with a new constitution and pluralism would best guarantee the freedoms of every citizen.

Because of this viewpoint, James Madison did not initially support amending the new constitution to include a bill of rights. As he explained to the Virginia ratifying convention in 1788, the proposed constitution would protect the nation against the threat of factions and the national government had been given "no jurisdiction" over religion.[29] Moreover, ambitious government leaders representing a majority faction too often simply ignore protections listed in state bills of rights. As he stated in a letter to Thomas Jefferson:

> Repeated violations of these parchment barriers have been committed by overbearing majorities in every state. In Virginia I have seen the bill of rights violated in every instance where it has been opposed to a popular current. Notwithstanding the explicit provision contained in that instrument for the rights of conscience, it is well known that a religious establishment would have taken place if the legislative majority had found, as they expected, a majority of the people in favor of the measure. . . . Wherever the real power in a government lies, there is the danger of oppression. In our governments the real power lies in the majority of the community, and the invasion of private rights is chiefly to be apprehended, not from acts of government contrary to the sense of its constituents, but from acts in which the government is the mere instrument of the majority number of the constituents.[30]

Madison's sentiments echoed those of other Federalists. As Paul Finkelman has noted, they found that adding a bill of rights was unnecessary, useless, redundant, violative of republican constitutional principles, and potentially dangerous to the basic liberties of the people. The problem of dangerousness was especially troubling for Madison, who feared, for example, that New Englanders would "weaken" attempts to separate church and state and narrow "the rights of Conscience."[31]

However, Madison was a practical politician who was committed, above all else, to securing the ratification of the new constitution as well as heading off calls for a second convention to amend the new document. While he understood that the most common Anti-Federalist complaint was the absence of a bill of rights, Madison thought that another constitutional convention might very well undermine or change the Philadelphia document. Thus, by the time of the Virginia ratifying convention, he had adjusted his public position by indicating a willingness to consider adding a bill of rights, at least amendments that were "not objectionable, or unsafe," *after* ratification of the Constitution.[32]

This tactical concession to his opponents was made necessary by strong opposition to ratification, which included that from Baptists in his home area, Orange County, Virginia, who sought protection for religious liberty. According to Ralph Ketcham, this opposition convinced Madison to confer with John Leland, a Baptist preacher and old friend with whom he had worked for fifteen years in fighting "religious bigotry" in Virginia. In return for Leland's withdrawal of opposition to the Constitution and support of Madison's election to the Virginia ratifying convention, Madison agreed to support a bill of rights after ratification.[33]

Although Richard Labunski has recently argued that Madison changed from "initial opposition, to lukewarm acceptance . . . , to enthusiastic endorsement as a way of increasing support for the new Constitution,"[34] there is little evidence that Madison was ever "enthusiastic" about moving away from his original position. As Ketcham points out, Madison continued to maintain that the omission of a bill of rights was not "a material defect," but, in a letter to Thomas Jefferson, he was now willing to concede two modest advantages: "1. The political truths declared in that solemn manner, acquire by degrees the character of fundamental maxims of free government, and as they become incorporated with the national sentiment, counteract the impulses of interest and passion. 2. Altho' it be generally true . . . that the danger of oppression lies in the [self-] interested majorities of the people rather than in the usurped acts of the Government, yet there may be occasions on which the evil may spring from the latter sources; and, on such, a bill of rights will be a good ground for an appeal to the sense of the community."[35] Finkelman also supports this view. "While never actually opposed to the idea of rights," he explains, "in 1787–89 Madison was never convinced a bill of rights was either necessary or completely harmless."[36] Yet Finkelman concedes that a "reluctant" Madison made tactical changes in his position for pragmatic political reasons. Patrick Henry and his allies, for example, sought to defeat Madison's bid for a seat in the first Congress assembled under the Constitution by gerrymandering his congressional district so that it was "heavily antifederal" in composition. In addition, they spread rumors that Madison opposed a religious freedom amendment. This prompted Madison, as part of his political campaign, to make an "unequivocal pledge" to the Reverend George Eve, an influential Baptist minister, and others that he was willing to support and recommend to the states "provisions for all essential rights, particularly the rights of Conscience in the fullest latitude."[37]

On June 8, 1789, Representative James Madison made good on his campaign promise by proposing nineteen amendments, divided into nine articles, in the first session of the new Congress. Madison offered other tactical reasons for his support of a bill of rights, including helping persuade North Carolina and Rhode Island to enter the Union, lessening opposition to and disaffection with the new government, defeating calls for a second constitutional convention, and allowing the government to address controversial issues. On a more institutional level, Madison stated that he supported amendments because "it will be proper in itself, and highly politic, for the tranquility of the public mind, and the stability of the government, that we should [add] . . . a declaration of the rights of the people."[38]

As Ralph Ketcham has pointed out, Madison's chief institutional concern in proposing a bill of rights was to strengthen the power of the new national government in order to promote the public good.[39] This is especially evident with respect to his original proposal on religious liberty: "The civil rights of none shall be abridged on account of religious belief or worship, nor shall any national religion be established, nor shall the full and equal rights of conscience be in any manner, or any pretext infringed."[40] In Ketcham's view, prohibiting the government from infringing on civil rights or establishing a national religion demonstrated Madison's concern with protecting both the "processes of government" so that public business could be conducted "freely and fairly" and the individual's right to liberty of conscience. Ketcham also finds that this phrasing of the right of conscience is as clear and categorical as possible, avoiding the pitfall of inadequate and vague wording that had always been worrisome to Madison.[41]

This proposal, along with another that prohibited state governments from violating, among other fundamental liberties, "the equal rights of conscience," was sent to a House select committee that made slight changes in Madison's initial proposal but rejected his attempt to place limitations on the states. This rejection was a major defeat for Madison, who, according to Finkelman, was always more concerned with limiting the powers of the states than limiting the power of the new national government. Moreover, it was also one of the few amendments on which Madison was willing to speak "with great enthusiasm."[42]

By the time the full House of Representatives debated Madison's initial proposal, Fisher Ames of Massachusetts and Samuel Livermore of New Hampshire had made key amendments to the original proposal. Because the Senate adopted language that differed from the House version, a conference committee, which Madison headed, had to iron out the differences. The compromise language that emerged, "Congress shall make no law respecting an establishment of religion, or prohibiting the free exercise thereof," was incorporated into the final version of the First Amendment. While the actual words were not his, made no mention of the rights of conscience, and eliminated any linkage to the nature of government and the public good, Madison supported the amendment. Such support was consistent with his overall political objectives: increasing approval and limiting objections to the new Constitution. In addition, this language satisfied states' rights advocates who viewed the prohibition against establishing a religion as also prescribing congressional involvement with states' establishment of religion. As Ketcham explains, "though the freedom of religion clauses of the First Amendment placed sweeping restrictions on national laws about religious establishment and free exercise of conscience, they also were designed deliberately to let states proceed as they wished on such matters—something Madison opposed and had tried his best to prevent."[43] Thus, Donald L. Drakeman is only partially right when he says that it is reasonable to conclude that Madison's ideas on religious liberty "were simply enacted in language proposed by others."[44]

However, Madison's actions during this period were sometimes inconsistent with the eloquence of his statements on religious freedom. As a member of the House of Representatives, for example, Madison served on the joint committee that recommended the clergyman that became the first congressional chaplain. In his postpresidential years, Madison would find this practice to be unconstitutional.[45]

The Presidential Years

As president, James Madison made decisions both supporting and opposing a strict separation of church and state. For example, he twice vetoed legislation on grounds that it violated the establishment clause of the First Amendment. The first of these occurred in February 1811, when Madison vetoed a measure that incorporated the Protestant Episcopal church in Alexandria, which was then part of the District of Columbia and hence within the jurisdiction of the U.S. Congress. This bill contained rules for electing and removing ministers and for church support of the poor. The constitutional violation occurred, said Madison, because government possesses no authority over religion, and the power to grant a charter also implies the power to repeal or regulate. His veto message included a second reason that has particular contemporary salience for those promoting faith-based initiatives. According to Madison, "Because the bill vests in the said incorporated church an authority to provide for the support of the poor and the education of poor children of the same, an authority which, being altogether superfluous if the provision is to be the result of pious charity, would be a precedent for giving to religious societies as such a legal agency in carrying into effect a public and civic duty."[46] Shortly afterward, Madison vetoed a second measure, one that set aside five acres of government-owned property to a Baptist church in the Mississippi Territory. Madison argued that the establishment clause prohibited appropriating taxpayer funds "for the use and support of religious societies."[47] These actions are consistent with the philosophy that Madison expressed in the Virginia Declaration of Rights, the *Memorial and Remonstrance,* and his first inaugural address, where he again stated that religious functions and the right of conscience were "wisely exempted from civil jurisdiction."[48]

President Madison departed from these views and embraced a more accommodationist position during the War of 1812, when he issued four presidential proclamations declaring days of prayer and thanksgiving. Madison expressed some reluctance over this practice, since he began each with a disclaimer that

Congress had requested him to issue the proclamation, though Thomas Jefferson, his immediate predecessor, had resisted such requests. Illustrative of this ambivalence was Madison's first proclamation that stated, "Whereas the Congress of the United States by a joint resolution of the two houses, have signified that a day may be recommended to be observed by the people . . . to all those who shall be piously disposed [to pray]."[49] In addition to conditional language, these proclamations were nonsectarian in the sense that they used "Deistic" terminology and, as Madison noted at the time, were intended as recommendations rather than presidential commandments. In a passage quoted by Donald L. Drakeman, and in language reminiscent of his *Memorial and Remonstrance,* Madison explained, "If the public homage of a people can ever be worthy of the Holy and Omniscient Being to whom it is addressed, it must be that in which those who join in it are guided only by their free choice, by the impulse of their hearts and the dictates of their consciences." While the intentions behind these accommodationist proclamations may never be known, Drakeman persuasively argues that this use of "public religion" was probably motivated "to unite the divided country during the War of 1812 by focusing attention on the national covenant that superseded regional and political factionalism."[50]

Another departure from earlier views on the separation of church and state involved the appointment of legislative and military chaplains. Although he would maintain that there were constitutional problems with such appointments after leaving office, he made no such objections while serving as president. Indeed, Congressman Madison made no objection when they were first authorized. Nor did he object earlier when Thomas Jefferson asked him, on his behalf, to introduce into the Virginia legislature a "Bill for Appointing Days of Public Fasting and Thanksgiving," which mandated a divine service and sermon from every "minister of the gospel."[51]

The Postpresidential Years

Perhaps the most authoritative statement of James Madison's view of the relationship between church and state and the religion clauses of the First Amendment is found in what he called *Detached Memoranda.* Although part of this document appeared in the March 14, 1914, issue of *Harper's* magazine, it was not published in full until Elizabeth Fleet discovered it and subsequently published her findings in the October 1946 issue of the *William and Mary Quarterly.* She found this document while examining the papers and preparing to write a biography on William Cabell Rives, whom Congress had assigned to organize Madison's papers for publication.

Although Madison wrote his *Detached Memoranda* after leaving the presidency, the date of the actual writing is unknown. Gaillard Hunt, in his introduction to the *Harper's* article, dated it "before 1832." William Cabell Rives said it was written "subsequent to his retirement from the presidency in 1817." And Fleet indicates that it was written "within a few years after" Madison left the presidency.[52]

As presented by Elizabeth Fleet, Madison's *Detached Memoranda* covers thirty-two pages, but only nine of these, presented under the heading "Monopolies, Perpetuities, Corporations, Ecclesiastical Endowments," involve the relationship of government and religion. Madison addressed eight different issues, including ecclesiastical monopolies, incorporation of churches, grants of public lands to churches, tax exemptions for religious entities, the Deity in governmental documents, congressional chaplaincies, military chaplaincies, and religious proclamations by the government. Taken as a whole, the *Detached Memoranda* represents Madison's strongest statement that the establishment clause of the First Amendment intended to create a strict separation between church and state.

Ecclesiastical Monopolies

Madison began by warning against all perpetual monopolies, suggesting that they "are forbidden not only by the genius of free Govts, but by the imperfection of human foresight." His main concern is with ecclesiastical bodies that engage in the silent and "indefinite" accumulations of wealth. Citing European history, Madison pointed out that conflict often arose and a reformation took place because the church had amassed excessive wealth, sometimes amounting to more than half a nation's wealth. Applying this experience to the United States, Madison issued the following warning: "Are the U.S. duly awake to the tendency of the precedents they are establishing, in the multiplied incorporations of Religious Congregations with the faculty of acquiring & holding property real as well as personal? Do not many of these acts give this faculty, without limit either as to time or as to amount? And must not bodies, perpetual in their existence, and which may be always gaining without ever losing, speedily gain more than is useful, and in time more than is safe? Are there not already examples in the U.S. of ecclesiastical wealth equally beyond its object and the foresight of those who laid the foundation of it?"[53] Still, Madison made no objection to grants made in perpetuity of public lands, as long as they were made on the basis of impartiality and for a fair price.

Incorporation of Churches

Equally dangerous to "the separation between Religion and Govt in the Constitution," said Madison, is a request made to Congress to charter (incorporate) a church. Here he made reference to his veto of a bill that sought to incorporate the Episcopal Church in Alexandria. But the most "notable" example of encroachment by ecclesiastical bodies, says Madison, is the influence exerted by the established church in trying to convince Virginia lawmakers to levy a general assessment in support of Christian sects.

As Leo Pfeffer has pointed out, Madison's arguments did not convince Congress. It has granted numerous corporate charters to ecclesiastical bodies in Washington, DC, included Georgetown University, a Jesuit institution, in 1844; Catholic University in 1887; and American University, a Methodist institution, in 1893. However, the former president would have been most troubled by congressional action in 1896 when it again incorporated the Episcopal Church of the Diocese of Washington.[54]

Grants of Public Lands to Churches

Another example of "encroachment by Ecclesiastical Bodies" involves the making of grants of public lands to churches. Madison did not directly discuss this issue; rather, he asked the reader to examine his "negatives" on two vetoed bills, one of which was his veto of a bill granting land to a Baptist church in the Mississippi Territory. Though not included in the *Detached Memoranda,* President Madison's veto message included the following explanation: "Because the bill in reserving a certain parcel of land of the United States for the use of said Baptist Church compromises a principle and precedent for the appropriation of funds of the United States for the use and support of religious societies, contrary to this article of the Constitution which declares that 'Congress shall make no law Respecting a religious establishment.'"[55]

Tax Exemption for Religious Entities

Still another "encroachment" that Madison suggested in the *Detached Memoranda* concerns granting of tax exemptions to religious bodies. While he identified no specific examples of this violation of church-state separation, Madison provides the cryptic statement that he had "withheld his signature" from a measure (apparently an 1816 bill that exempted Bible societies from paying duties on plates) and that we should "see" the attempt in Kentucky "to exempt Houses of Worship from taxes."[56]

However, Madison did not explain what appear to be inconsistencies on the tax exemption issue. In 1813, for example, he signed a bill that authorized a refund for duties paid by religious societies on imported plates used for printing Bibles.[57] Three years later, he signed "A Bill for the Relief of the Baltimore and Massachusetts Bible Societies," which returned the duty paid on plates by the Baltimore society and refunded duties to the Massachusetts society for imported Bibles that were later exported.

There is also some confusion on the reference to Kentucky. Madison seems to imply that this was an unsuccessful effort; yet the state's governor actually signed legislation on January 21, 1816, that provided a tax exemption to houses of worship, seminaries, and land on which they are erected.[58]

The final "encroachment" Madison discussed in the *Detached Memoranda* was the use of religiously sectarian language in official documents. After briefly discussing the assessment bill, his response in the *Memorial and Remonstrance,* and Jefferson's Virginia Statute for Religious Freedom, Madison argues against the use of sectarian language. Referring specifically to the Jefferson statute, Madison writes the following:

> In the course of the opposition to the bill in the House of Delegates, which was warm and strenuous from some of the minority, an experiment was made on the reverence entertained for the name & sanctity of the Savior, by proposing to insert the words "Jesus Christ" after the words "our lord" in the preamble, the object of which, would have been; to imply a restriction of the liberty defined in the Bill, to those professing his religion. The amendment was discussed, and rejected. . . .
>
> The opponents of the amendment having turned the feeling as well as judgment of the House against it, by successfully contending that the better proof of reverence for that holy name would be not to profane it by making it a topic of legislative discussion, and particularly by making his religion the means of abridging the natural and equal rights of all men, in defiance of his own declaration that his Kingdom was not of this world. This view of the subject was much enforced by the circumstance that it was espoused by some members who were particularly distinguished by their reputed piety and Christian zeal.[59]

Although the Statute for Religious Freedom does contain some general but nonsectarian language, the "father of the Constitution" achieved complete success in Philadelphia when he helped write a document that makes no mention of "Jesus Christ," "the Lord" or even "God."

Congressional Chaplaincies

In the *Detached Memoranda,* Madison expressed a major policy reversal, a change of "role" if not a change of "mind,"[60] when he maintained that the appointment of chaplains in the U.S. House and Senate constituted a clear violation of equal rights and constitutional principles. In his view, "the Constitution . . . forbids everything like an establishment of a national religion." He included congressional chaplains in this category. As Madison explained, "The law appointing Chaplains establishes a religious worship for national representatives, to be performed by Ministers of religion, elected by a majority of them; and these are paid out of the national taxes." However, Madison did not refer to his own participation as a representative on the joint committee that, in 1789, first nominated candidates to be congressional chaplains. Nevertheless, in the Memoranda, he viewed this practice as an example of the majority forcing its religious principles on the consciences of lawmakers who belong to minority religions or whose traditions forbid participation. Madison continued,

> The establishment of the chaplainship to Cong[res]s is a palpable violation of equal rights, as well as of Constitutional principles: The tenets of the chaplains elected [by the majority] shut the door of worship ag[ain]st the members whose creeds & consciences forbid a participation in that of the majority. To say nothing of other sects, this is the case with that of Roman Catholics & Quakers who have always had members in one or both of the Legislative branches. Could a Catholic clergyman ever hope to be appointed a Chaplain? To say that his religious principles are obnoxious or that his sect is small, is to life the evil at once and exhibit in its naked deformity the doctrine that religious truth is to be tested by numbers, or that the major sects have a right to govern the minor.[61]

Although he fails to explain how it might work in practice, Madison approved the idea that congressional chaplains, paid for by voluntary contributions from the lawmakers acting as private citizens, would be permissible under the establishment clause of the First Amendment.

Madison expressed a similar view in an 1822 letter to Edward Livingston. After agreeing with Livingston that religion should be immune from "civil jurisdiction," Madison called the appointment of congressional chaplains and their payment from public funds a "deviation" from this principle. He reiterated the view that congressional supporters of this policy would have better demonstrated their piety by making voluntary contributions—"a pittance from their own pockets." Surprisingly, he maintained that Congress took this position without his "approbation," and since the policy was not likely to be reversed, Madison suggested that it would be best to apply the Constitution to more serious conflicts.[62]

Military Chaplaincies

Conceding that the motive was "laudable," the *Detached Memoranda* argued that it would be desirable to "disarm" chaplainships in the army and navy. In Madison's view, the religious liberty of soldiers would thrive best if religious organizations rather than the government would fund military chaplains: "If the spirit of armies be devout, the spirit out of the armies will never be less so; and a failure of religious instruction & exhortation from a voluntary source within or without, will rarely happen; and if such be not the spirit of armies, the official service of their Teachers are not likely to produce it. It is more likely to flow from the labours of a spontaneous zeal." However, Madison recognized that this approach would be more difficult with respect to navies and their more "insulated crews." In that case, he suggested that "a devout officer," presumably acting in his private capacity, might be able to offer as much as an "ordinary chaplain." Whatever the difficulty, says Madison, "it is safer to trust the consequences of right principle, than reasonings in support of a bad one."[63]

Religious Proclamations by the Government

The other major reversal from Madison's presidential years involves his position on religious proclamations by public officials. In the *Detached Memoranda,* he offered five reasons against recommending days of fasting and thanksgiving. The first reason is that the government should limit its activities to subjects over which it has authority. "An advisory Govt," states Madison, "is a contradiction in terms." Second, public officials cannot claim to have received authority from constituents to advise them on matters of religion and conscience. As Madison explained, "they cannot form an ecclesiastical Assembly, Convocation, Council, or Synod, and as such issue decrees or injunctions addressed to the faith and Consciences of the people." Public officials may, however, make recommendations in their individual, nongovernmental capacities. Third, Madison maintained that official proclamations "nourish the erroneous idea of a national religion." This can be dangerous, said Madison, as history demonstrated in the theocracies of the Jewish nation and the European nations that embraced Christianity. In his view, official proclamations would still be wrong even if all individuals subscribed to the same religion or creed. This is "doubly wrong" in a pluralistic society, noted Madison, where some religious sects often are "alienated widely from others." Fourth, Madison found official proclamations dangerous because they could result in "a conformity to the creed of the majority of a single sect." Moreover, conflict may arise either when using the general nondenominational "ruler of the Universe" language of President George Washington or the sectarian calling for "Christian worship" by President John Adams. Lastly, Madison warned that the issuing of official proclamations makes religious ideas subservient to political views, "to the scandal of religion, as well as the increase of party animosities."[64]

Although he is not entirely convincing, Madison again excused his issuing of proclamations for fasting and thanksgiving as a president who was merely following the request of Congress. He also noted that he deliberately couched these proclamations in a manner as "to deaden as much as possible any claim of political right to enjoin religious observances by resting these expressly on the voluntary compliance of individuals."[65]

Madison made these same points in his 1822 letter to Edward Livingston. Conceding that executive proclamations involved a "deviation" from the strict principle of separating church and state and that the Constitution protected "the equality of *all* religious sects," Madison said that he found it necessary to follow the precedents set by his predecessors. His main excuse, however, was that he sought neither compulsion nor enforcement of these executive pronouncements. As the former president explained, "I was always careful to make the Proclamations absolutely indiscriminate, and merely recommendatory; or rather mere *designations* of a day, on which all who thought proper might *unite* in consecrating it to religious purposes, according to their own faith & forms."[66]

James Madison and the Supreme Court

Joseph L. Loconte observes that James Madison "viewed religious liberty as the capstone upon which the edifice of democratic freedom depended."[67] Yet, for Madison, this "inalienable" right that predated society should not be subject to the give and take of practical politics. In his view, religious liberty was largely a private matter involving a personal relationship between an individual and his Creator. He presented this idea most forcefully in his *Memorial and Remonstrance,* when he argued that public officials should take no "cognizance" of religion.

With the ratification of the Constitution and the Bill of Rights, Madison's views took on new significance. In addition to contributing greatly to the final wording of the free exercise of religion and establishment clauses of the First Amendment, Madison sought, albeit unsuccessfully, to apply these limitations on the national government to the states and localities. Although his intentions and the application of his views continue to engender lively debate,[68] it seems clear that in the *Detached Memoranda* he had moved closer to the Jeffersonian view that survival of religious freedom required a strict separation between church and state. In this document he conceded that he had erred by not adhering to his own understanding of the religion clauses during his presidential years. Thus, on reflection in his postpresidential years, he regarded even ceremonial examples of "public religion" as unconstitutional violations of the First Amendment.

James Madison has had only a modest impact on Supreme Court decision making in cases involving the religion clauses of the First Amendment. His contributions may be seen in three areas: the incorporation of the religion clauses of the First Amendment, the reliance on Madison and his writings by the justices in their written opinions, and the adoption or rejection of Madison's positions, especially as presented in his *Detached Memoranda.*

Incorporation of Religion Clauses

Ironically, one of James Madison's most significant contributions to Supreme Court jurisprudence involved one of his proposals that the First Congress rejected. Concerned that some states lacked a bill of rights while others abused "inalienable" rights, Madison sought to prevent this in the bill of rights he proposed as amendments to the U.S. Constitution. His fifth article, which he deemed "the most valuable . . . in the whole list," read in part, "No state shall violate the equal rights of conscience, or the freedom of the press, or the trial by jury in criminal cases." Though the House passed this provision by an extraordinary majority, the Senate defeated the amendment.[69]

Although the First Congress did not adopt this proposal, Madison's desire to prevent states and localities from limiting fundamental rights became the law of the land when the Supreme Court "incorporated" the religion clauses of the First Amendment through the due process clause of the Fourteenth Amendment. In the 1940 case of *Cantwell v. Connecticut,* for example, members of the Jehovah's Witnesses were convicted for playing anti-Catholic records, distributing pamphlets, and soliciting without a license in violation of a local ordinance. In a unanimous decision, Justice Owen Roberts held that this violated the free exercise of religion. As he explained, "We hold that the statute, as applied to the appellants, deprives them of their liberty without due process of law in contravention of the Fourteenth Amendment. The fundamental concept of liberty embodied in that Amendment embraces the liberties guaranteed by the First Amendment. The First Amendment declares that Congress shall make no law . . . prohibiting the free exercise [of religion]. The Fourteenth Amendment has rendered the legislatures of the states as incompetent as Congress to enact such laws."[70] Seven years later, in *Everson v. Board of Education,* the Supreme Court applied this same reasoning to the establishment clause of the First Amendment. Although a majority of five justices upheld a Ewing Township, New Jersey, program that authorized reimbursing parents for transportation costs to bus their children to Catholic schools, all nine justices voted for incorporation. Relying in part on Madison's *Memorial and Remonstrance,* Justice Hugo Black said the following: "The meaning and scope of the First Amendment, preventing [an] establishment of religion or prohibiting the free exercise, thereof, in light of its history and the evils it was designed forever to suppress, have been elaborated by the decisions of this Court prior to the application of the First Amendment to the states by the Fourteenth. The broad meaning given the Amendment by these earlier cases has been accepted by this Court in its decisions concerning an individual's religious freedom. . . . There is every reason to give the same application and broad interpretation to the 'establishment of religion' clause."[71]

Reliance on Madison by Supreme Court Justices

Unlike the "wall of separation" metaphor of Thomas Jefferson, the Supreme Court has never adopted "perfect separation" or "Great Barrier" phraseology.[72] However, several of the justices have relied on Madison's ideas in major religious freedom cases. Justice Wiley Rutledge, for example, attached the entire *Memorial and Remonstrance* to his dissenting opinion in *Everson v. Board of Education.* In this opinion, he argued that Madison's views should be understood as being similar to

Jefferson's idea that the establishment clause erected a "wall of separation" between church and state. Most important, he approvingly noted that Madison "opposed every form and degree of official relation between religion and authority," including the use of public funds to assist "any or all exercises of religion."[73] Because of this, he was highly critical of the Court's majority, which claimed to be following Madison and Jefferson when it upheld the ordinance that authorized the reimbursement of expenses for transportation to religious schools.

David Reiss convincingly expressed the importance of the Rutledge dissent and his analysis of Madison's importance to the development of religious liberty. Reiss notes that this "is the first opinion to combine eloquent appeals for religious toleration with a recommendation to actually fortify the wall of separation between church and state. Rhetorically, it also marks the ascendance of Madison as the primary historical actor in the fight for religious toleration."[74]

Justice William Rehnquist fundamentally disagreed with this assessment of James Madison. In his dissent in the 1985 "moment of silence" case of *Wallace v. Jaffree,* Rehnquist first marginalized Madison's role in writing the First Amendment and then maintained that the former president supported the mixing of religion and politics as long as it was done on a nonpreferential basis. According to Rehnquist, Madison intended to do little more than prevent the establishment of a national religion or church; he did not see the establishment clause "as requiring neutrality on the part of government between religion and irreligion."[75] Because of this, Rehnquist continued, Madison would not have had any problem in upholding the Alabama law that set aside a moment of silence for "meditation and prayer" at the start of each school day.

Most scholars disagree with Rehnquist's view that James Madison was a nonpreferentialist.[76] Madison himself seemed to reject this view in his *Memorial and Remonstrance* when he argued that both believers and nonbelievers have equal natural rights and that "we cannot deny an equal freedom to those whose minds have not yet yielded to the evidence which has convinced us."[77]

In the 1992 graduation prayer case of *Lee v. Weisman,* Justice David Souter also rejected this interpretation. After carefully evaluating the historical record, especially the original draft of the First Amendment and the *Detached Memoranda,* Souter concluded that James Madison was a "strict separationist." In his concurring opinion, he agreed with the Court's majority that nonsectarian invocations and benedictions delivered by invited clergy at official public school ceremonies were coercive and thus were prohibited by the establishment clause. However, he also argued that the nonpreferentialist view of the establishment clause was too narrow and that to accept it would require the Court "to engage in comparative theology." "The Virginia statute for religious freedom, written by Jefferson and sponsored by Madison," explained Souter, "captured the separationist response [and] on balance, history neither contradicts nor warrants reconsideration of the settled principle that the Establishment Clause forbids support for religion in general no less than support for one religion or some."[78]

Justice Souter further developed his understanding of Madison's church-state jurisprudence in the 1995 case of *Rosenberger v. University of Virginia.* Here he relied on Madison in dissenting from the Court, which held that a student organization at a state university with an evangelical Christian editorial viewpoint was entitled to receive funding on the same basis as other more secular student groups. Specifically, Souter returned to *Memorial and Remonstrance* to argue that Madison would have opposed any government subsidy of religion. In his view, Madison clearly rejects the nonpreferentialist position in paragraph 3 of the *Memorial* when he maintains: "Who does not see that . . . the same authority which can force a citizen to contribute three pence only of his property for the support of any one establishment, may force him to conform to any other establishment in all cases whatsoever?"[79]

Justice Clarence Thomas challenged Souter's interpretation of Madison and *Memorial and Remonstrance* in *Rosenberger.* In his concurring opinion, Thomas argued that James Madison was a nonpreferentialist who favored "neutrality," opposing only the government's favoring of one religion over another. According to Thomas, Madison's protest of Patrick Henry's assessment bill in the *Memorial* was not over "allow[ing] religious groups to participate in a generally available government program, but because the bill singled out religious entities for special benefits."[80]

This debate over the meaning of Madison's establishment clause views has continued in recent cases involving the public display of the Ten Commandments. In *McCreary County v. American Civil Liberties Union* (2005), for example, the Supreme Court struck down as unconstitutional the display of gold-framed copies of the King James version of the Ten Commandments in county courthouses. Writing for the Court, Justice David Souter refused to expand what has become known as the historical and ceremonial exception to establishment clause jurisprudence.[81] Instead, relying on the *Memorial and Remonstrance* as well as on several postpresidential Madison letters, Souter argued that the "historical record" and precedent demand that the Court maintain a strict separation between church and state. He chided Justice Antonin Scalia and the dissenters for seizing on "inconsistencies" and, in an oblique reference to the *Detached Memoranda,* stated, "it is worth noting that Jefferson thought his actions were consistent with non-endorsement of religion and Madison regretted any backsliding he may have done."[82]

Two other justices cited James Madison as an authority in *McCreary.* In a concurring opinion, Justice Sandra Day O'Connor, quoting from *Memorial and Remonstrance,* stated that "our guiding principle has been James Madison's—that '[t]he Religion . . . of every man must be left to the conviction of every man.' . . . To that end, we have held that the guarantees of religious freedom protect citizens from religious incursions by the States as well as by the Federal Government." Justice Scalia took a different view in his dissent. Relying on the presidential Madison, especially his first inaugural address where he expressed confidence "in the guardianship and guidance of that Almighty Being whose power regulates the destiny of nations," Scalia argued that Madison was an accommodationist who did not oppose religious displays in the public square.[83]

Justice John Paul Stevens added his voice to the debate over James Madison's establishment clause views in *Van Orden v. Perry* (2005), a Ten Commandments case that the Court decided on the same day as *McCreary.* Here the Court upheld as constitutional the displaying of the Commandments along with other monuments commemorating the "people, ideals, and events that compose Texan identity" in a park surrounding the Texas state capitol. Dissenting from this view, Justice Stevens argues that Chief Justice Rehnquist (and Justice Scalia in McCreary) seriously misrepresented the positions of James Madison, Thomas Jefferson, and other Founders. With respect to Madison, Stevens calls attention to the *Detached Memoranda* and letters written to Edward Livingston (1822) and to Jaspar Adams (1833) to demonstrate that he was a strict separationist. "More than once," explained Stevens, "Madison . . . repudiated the views attributed him by many, stating unequivocally that with respect to government's involvement with religion, the '"tendency to a usurpation on one side, or the other, or to a corrupting coalition or alliance between them, will be best guarded against by an entire abstinence of the Government from interference, in any way whatever, beyond the necessity of preserving public order, & protecting each sect against trespasses on its legal rights by others."'"[84]

Despite these competing interpretations, only Justices Rutledge, Souter, and Stevens correctly identified James Madison as a "strict separationist," and only Justices Souter and Stevens based their judgments, in part, on the postpresidential Madison who wrote the *Detached Memoranda.* Irving Brant and Leo Pfeffer also rely on Madison's later views to arrive at similar conclusions.[85]

With respect to the free exercise of religion, no Supreme Court justice relied on James Madison's ideas until the 1997 case of *City of Boerne v. Flores.* Here, Justice Sandra Day O'Connor, relying on Michael McConnell's analysis of Madison's *Memorial and Remonstrance* in an influential *Harvard Law Review* article,[86] argued in favor of granting religious exemptions from generally applicable laws and requiring the government to demonstrate a "compelling" reason to justify restrictions on free exercise rights.[87] Since Madison is silent on free exercise of religion issues in the *Detached Memoranda,* political scientist Vincent Philip Muñoz may be on strong ground when he argues that the message of the *Memorial* is that because of the social compact framework, "the state must remain noncognizant of religion."[88] In the 2005 case of *Cutter v. Wilkinson,* Justice Clarence Thomas disagreed with this view in a case involving whether protecting the free exercise of religion rights of prison inmates under the Religious Land Use and Institutionalized Persons Act of 2000 violated the establishment clause of the First Amendment. In his concurring opinion, Thomas maintained that this clause never "codified Madison's . . . view that the Federal Government could not legislate regarding religion."[89]

Detached Memoranda *Positions and the Supreme Court*

Writing in 1988, Leo Pfeffer demonstrated that the Supreme Court generally upheld Madison's postpresidential views in establishment clause cases through the Burger Court period. However, more recent decisions of the Court seem to be significantly at variance with Madison's "strict separationist" position.

Although no Supreme Court decisions deal with ecclesiastical monopolies, Pfeffer maintains that cases where tax money is used for the secular education of children in religious schools fall within the "incorporation of churches" part of Madison's *Detached Memoranda.* In cases decided between 1971 and 1985, the Court generally maintained a "strict separationist" position, as it regularly struck down laws that authorized the use of taxpayer funds to finance even secular instruction in religious schools.[90] However, this began to change with the 1997 case of *Agostini v. Felton,* where the Court maintained that the establishment clause did not prohibit New York City from using tax funds to send public school teachers into parochial schools to provide remedial education to disadvantaged students.[91] The Court took this more accommodationist position one step further in *Zelman v. Simmons-Harris* (2002) when it upheld a school voucher program allowing taxpayer money to be diverted to the education of children in religious schools.[92]

With respect to "grants of public lands to churches," the Supreme Court chose to ignore Madison's opposition to this practice in the 1982 case of *Valley Forge Christian College v. Americans United for the Separation of Church and State.* Here the Court refused to reach the merits of a challenge to the government selling surplus land to a sectarian institution, maintaining that taxpayers had no standing to challenge the sale.[93]

Although Madison alluded to a veto of a bill involving "tax exemption of religious entities" in the *Detached Memoranda,* the Supreme Court chose to ignore this in the 1970 case of *Walz v. Tax Commission* when it upheld a state law granting a tax exemption to religious and other charitable organizations. Writing for the Court, Chief Justice Warren Burger referred instead to the 1813 bill that Madison signed authorizing a refund to religious societies for duties paid on imported plates used for printing Bibles.[94]

In the *Detached Memoranda* Madison demonstrated his opposition to referring to a specific deity in government documents. This opposition may be seen in his *Memorial and Remonstrance* where he challenged Patrick Henry's assessment bill for teachers of the Christian religion and his successful defeat of an amendment to insert a reference to "Jesus Christ" in Jefferson's Virginia Statute for Religious Freedom. However, in *Vidal v. Girard's Executors* (1843), the Supreme Court stated that "the Christian religion is part of the common law" of all the states.[95] The Court went one step further in *Church of Holy Trinity v. United States* (1892) when it declared in dicta that "this is a Christian nation."[96] And in the 1931 case of *United States v. Macintosh,* the Court maintained that "we are a Christian people . . . acknowledging with reverence the duty of obedience to the will of God."[97]

While the Supreme Court has not ruled directly on the legality of military chaplains, it has considered the constitutionality of legislative chaplaincies under the First Amendment. In *Marsh v. Chambers* (1983), the Court rejected Madison's position as expressed in the *Detached Memoranda* and upheld under its historical or ceremonial exception to establishment clause jurisprudence the Nebraska practice of beginning each legislative session with a prayer offered by a Presbyterian minister who was paid with taxpayer funds.

Finally, although the Supreme Court has not expressed its views on proclamations declaring days of prayer and thanksgiving, it has taken a stance that seems contrary to the postpresidential Madison position with respect to related issues involving national religious holidays. In *Lynch v. Donnelly* (1984), for example, the Court relied on the long history of the government taking cognizance of religion and public funding of holidays with religious significance to uphold as constitutional the use of public finds for a nativity scene display in Pawtucket, Rhode Island's annual Christmas display.[98] However, in the 1989 case of *Allegheny v. American Civil Liberties Union,* the Court found that the establishment clause had been violated by a nativity scene displayed in a county courthouse that had a banner declaring "Glory to God to the Highest!"[99]

"Many Madisons" and the First Amendment

As the varying interpretations by Supreme Court justices have demonstrated, it is fruitless to seek consistency in James Madison's views on religious freedom. Those views underwent changes and adjustments during three periods of his life: the prepresidential, presidential, and postpresidential years. Although there are common threads in all three periods, those justices and scholars interested in the philosophical basis of his views tend to focus on the prepresidential years. Others more concerned in demonstrating that Madison sought to accommodate religion in the public square emphasize the presidential years. Finally, those interested in Madison's First Amendment jurisprudence, especially his evolving views on the necessity of a strict separation of church and state, give most attention to the postpresidential years.

The existence of "many Madisons"[100] should not detract from his extraordinary contributions to the development of American ideas on religious liberty, freedom of conscience, and the separation of government and religion. Though some scholars dismiss his postpresidential thoughts as the incoherent ideas of an aging former leader,[101] the *Detached Memoranda* makes coherent arguments for the unconstitutionality of mixing religion and politics.

For Madison, maintaining what he termed "a perfect separation" between church and state involved more than questions of constitutionality. He saw that it brought major benefits for religion, government, and society. In an 1819 letter to Robert Walsh, for example, he returned to observations made in his *Memorial* that the civil government in Virginia was not weakened by removing "the prop of religious establishment" and that instead of perishing, Christianity and other religions have flourished. As he explained, "The Civil Govt. tho' bereft of everything like an associated hierarchy possesses the requisite stability and performs its functions with complete success; Whilst the number, the industry, and the morality of the Priesthood, & the devotion of the people have been manifestly increased by the total separation of the Church from the States."[102] Madison expressed a similar view in his 1822 letter to Edward Livingston, where he wrote that he was sure that "religion & Govt. will both exist in greater purity, the less they are mixed together."[103]

Clearly, James Madison's writings and public actions will continue to provide support for those who interpret the First Amendment as permitting public officials to accommodate religion and those who maintain that they promote a strict separation between church and state. However, there can be no argument over the significance of Madison's contributions. As Garry Wills has concluded, "As a champion of religious liberty, he is equal, perhaps superior, to Jefferson—and no one else is in the running. Even if he is to be considered merely as a writer, only Jefferson and Franklin were manifestly greater stylists. No man could do everything for the country—not even Washington. Madison did more than most, and did some things better than any. That is quite enough."[104]

Notes

1. Madison coined the term "perfect separation" in a letter to Edward Livingston on July 10, 1822. See Gaillard Hunt, ed., *The Writings of James Madison* (New York: G. P. Putnam's Sons, 1900–1910), 9:102 (hereafter cited as *Writings*).

2. Other scholars refer to the "many Madisons" or the "mixed legacy" of Madison. See Gary Rosen, *American Compact: James Madison and the Problem of Founding* (Lawrence: University Press of Kansas, 1999), 1–9; Stephen D. Smith, "Blooming Confusion: Madison's Mixed Legacy," *Indiana Law Review* 75 (Winter 2000): 61–75.

3. David L. Holmes, *The Faiths of the Founding Fathers* (New York: Oxford University Press, 2006), 97.

4. Lance Banning, "James Madison and the Statute for Religious Freedom and the Crisis of Republican Conviction," in *The Virginia Statute for Religious Freedom: Its*

Evolution and Consequences in American History, ed. Merrill D. Pederson and Robert C. Vaughn (New York: Cambridge University Press, 1988), 109.

5. Ralph L. Ketcham, "James Madison and Religion—A New Hypothesis," *Presbyterian Historical Society* 38 (June 1960): 76–77.

6. Joseph Loconte, "Faith and the Founding: The Influence of Religion on the Politics of James Madison," *Journal of Church and State* 40 (Autumn 2003): 700.

7. Letter from James Madison to Frederick Beach on November 20, 1825, in *Writings,* 9:229–31.

8. Holmes, *Faiths of the Founding Fathers,* 96.

9. Irving Brant, "Madison: On the Separation of Church and State," *William and Mary Quarterly,* 3rd ser., 3, no. 1 (1951): 5.

10. Ketcham, "Madison and Religion," 80–81.

11. Ralph Ketcham, *James Madison: A Biography* (Charlottesville: University Press of Virginia, 1990), 58.

12. Vincent Philip Muñoz, "James Madison's Principle of Religious Liberty," *American Political Science Review* 97 (February 2003): 20.

13. James Madison, *The Papers of James Madison,* ed. William T. Hutchinson et al., (Chicago: University of Chicago Press; Charlottesville: University Press of Virginia, 1962–91), 1:174, 175 (hereafter cited as *Papers*). See also Daniel L. Dreisbach, "Church-State Debate in the Virginia Legislature: From the Declaration of Rights to the Statute for Establishing Religious Freedom," in *Religion and Political Culture in Jefferson's Virginia,* ed. Garrett Ward Sheldon and Daniel L. Dreisbach (Lanham, MD: Rowman and Littlefield Publishers, 2000), 137–41.

14. Ketcham, *Madison,* 73.

15. Banning, "Madison and the Statute," 113.

16. Quoted in Loconte, "Faith and the Founding," 709.

17. Pamela Draus, ed., *The Past-Present: Selected Writings of Eva Braun* (Annapolis, MD: St. John's College Press, 1997), 213. For an analysis, see Ketcham, *Madison,* 163–64, and Gregory Schaff, *Franklin, Jefferson, and Madison: On Religion and the State* (Santa Fe, NM: CIAC Press, 2004), 168–82.

18. *Papers,* 8:299; Schaff, *Franklin, Jefferson and Madison,* 168–69.

19. Banning, "Madison and the Statute," 119–22.

20. Schaff, *Franklin, Jefferson, and Madison,* 172.

21. Brant, "Separation of Church and State," 11.

22. Loconte, "Faith and the Founding," 712.

23. Mark Douglas McGarvie, *One Nation under Law: America's Early Struggle to Separate Church and State* (DeKalb: Northern Illinois University Press, 2005), 49.

24. Madison, letter to Thomas Jefferson, October 24, 1787, *Writings,* 5:30–31.

25. McGarvie, *One Nation under Law,* 51.

26. James Madison, *The Federalist Papers* (New York: New American Library, 1961), 326 (hereafter cited as *Federalist*).

27. Banning, "Madison and the Statute," 128.

28. *Federalist,* 324.

29. Schaff, *Franklin, Jefferson, and Madison,* 195–96.

30. *Papers,* 11:296–97.

31. Paul Finkelman, "James Madison and the Bill of Rights: A Reluctant Paternity," in *The Supreme Court Review, 1990*, ed. Gerhard Casper, Dennis J. Hutchinson, and David Strauss (Chicago: University of Chicago Press, 1991), 309, 311–12.

32. Ibid., 327–28.

33. Ralph Ketcham, *Framed for Posterity: The Enduring Philosophy of the Constitution* (Lawrence: University Press of Kansas, 1993), 94. This book expands on an earlier lecture that Ketcham wrote, as found in "The Dilemma of Bills of Rights in Democratic Government," in *The Legacy of George Mason*, ed. Josephine F. Pacheco (Fairfax, VA: George Mason University Press, 1983).

34. Richard Labunski, *James Madison and the Struggle for the Bill of Rights* (New York: Oxford University Press, 2006), 161.

35. Ketcham, *Framed for Posterity*, 95, 96.

36. Finkelman, "Madison and the Bill of Rights," 346.

37. Ibid., 335, citing letter of Madison to George Eve, January 2, 1789, in *Papers*, 11:404–5.

38. Quoted in Ketcham, *Framed for Posterity*, 98.

39. Ibid., 99.

40. *Papers*, 12:201.

41. Ketcham, *Framed for Posterity*, 100.

42. Finkelman, "Madison and the Bill of Rights," 344.

43. Ketcham, *Framed for Posterity*, 103.

44. Donald L. Drakeman, "Religion and the Republic: James Madison and the First Amendment," *Journal of Church and State* 25 (Autumn 1983): 433. For a discussion of the history and politics of the religion clauses, see Robert A. Goldwin, *From Parchment to Power: How James Madison Used the Bill of Rights to Save the Constitution* (Washington, DC: AEI Press, 1997), and Lance Banning, *The Sacred Fire of Liberty: James Madison and the Founding of the Federal Republic* (Ithaca, NY: Cornell University Press, 1995), 265–90.

45. Drakeman, "Religion and the Republic," 441, and Donald L. Drakeman, "James Madison and the First Amendment Establishment of Religion Clause," in Sheldon and Dreisbach, *Religion and Political Culture*, 226. For a contrary interpretation, see Robert L. Cord, "Original Intent Jurisprudence and Madison's Detached Memoranda," *Benchmark* 3 (January-April 1987): 79.

46. James D. Richardson, ed., *Messages and Papers of the Presidents* (Washington, DC: Government Printing Office, 1897–1908), 1:490.

47. Saul K. Padover, *The Complete Madison* (New York: Harper and Brothers, 1953), 308.

48. Muñoz, "Madison's Principle of Religious Liberty," 28.

49. Ibid. For a discussion of the "nondenominational" language that Madison used, see Garry Wills, *James Madison* (New York: Times Books, 2002), 155–56.

50. Drakeman, "Religion and the Republic," 441, 443.

51. Ibid., 441.

52. Leo Pfeffer, "Madison's 'Detached Memoranda?' Then and Now," in Pederson and Vaughn, *Virginia Statute for Religious Freedom*, 285–87. Also see Elizabeth Fleet, "Madison's Detached Memoranda," *William and Mary Quarterly*, 3rd ser., 3 (October 1946): 534–36.

53. Fleet, "Madison's Detached Memoranda," 552, 557.

54. Pfeffer, "Madison's 'Detached Memoranda,'" 288.

55. Richardson, *Messages and Papers,* 1:490.

56. Fleet, "Madison's Detached Memoranda," 555.

57. 6 Stat. 116 (1813).

58. Pfeffer, "Madison's 'Detached Memoranda,'" 294–95.

59. Fleet, "Madison's Detached Memoranda," 556.

60. Pfeffer, "Madison's 'Detached Memoranda,'" 299.

61. Fleet, "Madison's Detached Memoranda," 558.

62. Letter to Livingston on July 10, 1832, *Writings,* 9:100.

63. Fleet, "Madison's Detached Memoranda," 560.

64. Ibid., 560, 561.

65. Ibid., 562.

66. Letter to Livingston on July 10, 1822, *Writings,* 9:101.

67. Loconte, "Faith and the Founding," 715.

68. Compare Robert Cord, *Separation of Church and State: Historical Fact and Current Fiction* (New York: Lambeth, 1982), with Douglas Laycock, "'Nonpreferential' Aid to Religion: A False Claim about Original Intent," *William and Mary Law Review* 27 (Summer 1986): 875–923.

69. Leonard W. Levy, *The Establishment Clause: Religion and the First Amendment,* 2nd ed. rev. (Chapel Hill: University of North Carolina Press, 1994), 105.

70. *Cantwell v. Connecticut,* 310 U.S. 296, 303 (1940).

71. *Everson v. Board of Education,* 330 U.S. 1, 14–15 (1947).

72. See Paul Weber, "James Madison and Religious Equality: The Perfect Separation," *Review of Politics* 44 (April 1982): 163–86.

73. *Everson,* 330 U.S. at 39.

74. David Reiss, "Jefferson and Madison as Icons in Judicial History: A Study of Religion Clause Jurisprudence," *Maryland Law Review* 61 (2002): 94, 125.

75. *Wallace v. Jaffree,* 472 U.S. 38, 98 (1985).

76. Compare Cord, "Original Intent Jurisprudence," with Brant, "Separation of Church and State."

77. *Memorial and Remonstrance,* quoted in Banning, *Madison and the Statute,* 120.

78. *Lee v. Weisman,* 505 U.S. 577, 615, 616 (1992).

79. *Rosenberger v. University of Virginia,* 515 U.S. 810, 868 (1995).

80. Ibid., 854–55.

81. See *Marsh v. Chambers,* 463 U.S. 783 (1983), and *Lynch v. Donnelly,* 465 U.S. 668 (1984).

82. *McCreary County v. American Civil Liberties Union,* 545 U.S. 844, 878n25 (2005).

83. Ibid., 882, 888.

84. *Van Orden v. Perry,* 1545 U.S. 677, 725 (2005).

85. Brant, "Separation of Church and State," 3; Pfeffer, "Madison's 'Detached Memoranda,'" 288.

86. Michael W. McConnell, "The Origins and Historical Understanding of the Free Exercise of Religion," *Harvard Law Review* 103 (May 1990): 1409–1517.

87. *City of Boerne v. Flores,* 521 U.S. 5907 (1997).

88. Muñoz, "Madison's Principle of Religious Liberty," 20.

89. *Cutter v. Wilkinson,* 544 U.S. 709, 730 (2005).

90. See *Grand Rapids School District v. Ball,* 473 U.S. 373 (1985), and *Aguilar v. Felton,* 473 U.S. 402 (1985).

91. *Agostini v. Felton,* 521 U.S. 203 (1997). The change in the Court's view was made possible by the switch of one vote as Justice Clarence Thomas, an "accommodationist," replaced Justice Thurgood Marshall, a "strict separationist," in 1991.

92. *Zelman v. Simmons-Harris,* 536 U.S. 639 (2002).

93. *Valley Forge Christian College v. Americans United for the Separation of Church and State,* 454 U.S. 464 (1982).

94. *Walz v. Tax Commission,* 397 U.S. 664 (1970).

95. *Vidal v. Girard's Executor,* 43 U.S. 127, 198 (1843).

96. *Church of Holy Trinity v. United States,* 143 U.S. 457, 469 (1892).

97. *United States v. Macintosh,* 283 U.S. 605, 624 (1931).

98. *Lynch v. Donnelly,* note 81 above.

99. *Allegheny v. American Civil Liberties Union,* 492 U.S. 573 (1989).

100. Rosen, *American Compact,* 1–9.

101. See Cord, "Original Intent Jurisprudence," 84.

102. Letter from James Madison to Robert Walsh on March 2, 1819, in *Writings,* 9:432.

103. Letter to Livingston on July 10, 1822, in *Writings,* 9:102.

104. Wills, *James Madison,* 164.

JOHN R. VILE

James Madison's *Report of 1800*

The First Amendment, Freedom of the Press, and the Common Law

As an earlier chapter of this book indicates, scholars often identify James Madison as the father of the U.S. Constitution,[1] but it is more accurate to identify him as the father of the Bill of Rights. More than any other individual, he took the lead in the First Congress to introduce these amendments and get them adopted.[2] When colleagues argued that more pressing matters were at hand,[3] Madison, who, as Rodney Grunes has shown in the previous chapter, was a relative latecomer to the cause, responded that the tasks of formulating and ratifying a bill of rights were essential to securing the support of the Anti-Federalists, who had expressed fear of the powers the new national government would exercise without such restraints.

One of Madison's few "failures" with regard to the composition of the Bill of Rights was his inability to get Congress to agree to an amendment to protect the right of conscience, freedom of the press, and trial by jury in criminal cases against state intervention.[4] In debates before the U.S. House of Representatives on August 17, 1789, Madison actually described this as "the most valuable amendment in the whole list." As he explained, "If there was any reason to restrain the Government of the United States from infringing upon these essential rights, it was equally necessary that they should be secured against the State Government. He thought that if they provided against the one, it was necessary to provide against the other."[5] Federal guardianship of the guarantees in the Bill of Rights against the states would have to await not only the adoption of the Fourteenth Amendment in 1868 but also a long series of Supreme Court decisions later using this amendment for this purpose.[6]

Background: The Alien and Sedition Acts

If one of Madison's chief concerns at the Constitutional Convention,[7] during ratification debates,[8] and in the First Congress (where he introduced the amendment to protect the right of conscience and freedom of the press against state action) centered on fears that states would abuse individual rights, he had shifted his focus by the end of the next decade to fears that the national government was doing so. In 1798, during the administration of President John Adams, when war threatened with France and members of both American parties viewed the motives of the other with suspicion, Federalists adopted the Alien and Sedition Acts. The latter made it a crime to criticize government officials.[9] David Jenkins has observed that "the ensuing public controversy over the Sedition Act represented the first serious debate over the original meaning of the First Amendment's press clause and was thus an important early juncture in American constitutional development."[10] Facts confirm Jenkins' assessment.

In the next two years, Federalists initiated fifteen libel prosecutions under this law and another three under state common law.[11] Madison, who was then serving in the Virginia state legislature, joined Vice President Thomas Jefferson (both of whom acted in secret) to draft the Virginia and Kentucky Resolutions,[12] which challenged the constitutionality of the new laws and urged states to "interpose" against them.[13] The resolution advanced a controversial view of states' rights that, as James H. Read's subsequent chapter in this volume demonstrates, became even more controversial when advocates of nullification and secession later attempted to appropriate it.

Madison's Report

After seven northeastern states responded unfavorably to the Virginia and Kentucky Resolutions,[14] Madison authored a defense of these resolutions for the Virginia legislature in a report issued in early 1800. Jefferson first proposed writing this report in August 1799. Madison, who headed the seven-member committee and drafted the report, apparently drew in part on an unpublished report that Edmund Randolph had written on the common law and on a pamphlet that St. George Tucker had authored titled "Letter to a Member of Congress; Respecting the Alien and Sedition Laws."[15] Adrienne Koch and Harry Ammon have said that there is no "more careful, precise and mature reiteration of the principles of self-government" anywhere in "American political literature."[16] Kurt Lash has used this report to understand Madison's view of the relationship between the national and state governments;[17] it is an equally useful source for examining Madison's view of freedom of speech and freedom of the press. Indeed, Robert Morgan identified the Virginia *Report of 1800* as "the one early document which in

Madison's opinion authentically interprets a part of the Constitution—the First amendment."[18] In arguing that Congress had exceeded its powers in adopting the Sedition Act, Madison answered the contention that Congress was exercising powers that it had inherited through common law. In responding to this notion, Madison argued that the First Amendment provisions upholding freedom of speech and freedom of the press extended protection beyond common law understandings of the subject.

Madison divided his argument into three parts. First, he argued that the Sedition Act was unconstitutional because it represented the exercise of a power that the Constitution had not delegated to Congress. Second, he argued that the law violated the First Amendment. Third, he argued that the law was especially threatening because it affected the right of publicly examining public men and public measures.

The Exercise of Powers Not Delegated by the Constitution

In challenging defenders of the law to show a constitutional provision that granted powers over the subjects of speech and press, Madison began by addressing the argument that the law was justified by "the common or unwritten law," which he further described as "a law of vast extent and complexity, and embracing almost every possible subject of legislation, both civil and criminal." Although Madison would soon indicate that he recognized that colonies and states had incorporated common law principles into their laws, he was intent on refuting the view that Congress might recognize such a law as part of "their united and national capacity." In refuting this notion, Madison examined the colonial period, the revolutionary period, the period under the Articles of Confederation, and the language of the Constitution itself. Madison acknowledged "that the common law, under different limitations, made a part of the colonial codes," but he said that it "was unknown to them as a law pervading and operating through the whole, as one society."[19] In the absence of a "common legislature" to adopt a "common will" or a "common magistracy" to enforce it, there was no national common law.

Nor did the Revolutionary War change this. Madison reviewed colonial arguments against parliamentary sovereignty, observing that, for some time, the colonists had recognized allegiance to "a common executive sovereign," albeit not to "any common legislative sovereign."[20] Although Madison did not specifically address whether there was a common judicial power during this time, he apparently thought not.

Madison had little trouble dismissing the idea that the Articles of Confederation had created a national common law. Shortly before citing Article II of that document, which vested sovereignty in the individual states, Madison observed that "this instrument does not contain a sentence or a syllable that can be tortured into a countenance of the idea that the parties to it were, with respect to the objects of the common law, to form one community. No such law is named, or implied, or alluded to, as being in force, or as brought into force by that compact."[21]

This brought Madison to the U.S. Constitution, which he had identified as "the oracle that must decide the important question." With a view to accommodating constitutional provisions relative to habeas corpus, ex post facto laws, and other legal technical terms, Madison began by admitting "that particular parts of the common law may have a sanction from the Constitution, so far as they are necessarily comprehended in the technical phrases which express the powers delegated to the government; and so far, also, as such other parts may be adopted by Congress, as necessary and proper for carrying into execution the powers expressly delegated."[22] Madison denied, however, that the Constitution went farther.

Federalists had relied on the provision in Article III, Section 2, granting judicial power in cases of "law and equity, arising under this Constitution, the laws of the United States, and treaties made, or which shall be made, under their authority" to advance the argument for such a broad scope. Proponents of a national common law attempted to link it to those cases not covered by U.S. laws and treaties. Madison observed that "never, perhaps was so broad a construction applied to a text so clearly unsusceptible of it." The phrase dealing with cases in law and equity may have been "a mere pheonasm or inadvertence," but Madison thought that it more likely referred either to cases, like those in Article I, Section 9, that limited state legislative powers, or to suits between citizens and foreigners or citizens of several states, which Article III vested in the courts. Madison further observed that the reference to "cases in law and equity" alluded to civil cases only: "Criminal cases in law and equity would be a language unknown to the law." Noting that the next paragraph of Article III vested the Supreme Court with appellate jurisdiction as to both law and fact, of "*all* the other cases," Madison argued that this necessarily excluded criminal cases involving juries "because the fact, in such cases, is not a subject of appeal."[23] Madison drew further support from the recently ratified Eleventh Amendment, which referred to "any suit in *law* or *equity,* commenced or prosecuted against one of the United States, by citizens of another state, or by citizens or subjects of any foreign power."[24] Since no one could bring criminal proceedings against a state, the terms must be limited to civil cases.

Madison was not finished. Even if one could read the Constitution as encompassing the common law, this would not justify the Sedition Act, which was "an act of legislative, and not of judicial power."[25] Madison further observed that the Constitution did not list the common law either in Article III, Section 3, or in the supremacy clause within Article VI.

Madison argued that incorporating the common law into American law would raise a host of practical questions. These would include such issues as which, if any, British statutes it included, to which time in British history it would apply, how it would be adapted to American circumstances, and the like.[26]

Madison said that if the Constitution established the common law, then Congress cannot alter it. Somewhat cleverly, perhaps too much so, he observed that Federalist proponents of the Sedition Act claimed that it was "a melioration of the common law" but that such melioration was not permissible if the common law were itself the law of the land.[27] More threateningly, if Congress did have the right to revise the law, then "the authority of Congress is coextensive with the objects of the common law," thus erasing all constitutional limits. If Congress has such a power, so must both the president and the courts. At the national level, where laws were still so few, an interpretation embodying the common law would effectively convert judges into legislators. Such power "would overwhelm the residuary sovereignty of the states, and, by one constructive operation, new-model the whole political fabric of the country."[28]

Having argued that the common law did not justify federal regulation of speech and press, Madison looked to specific constitutional provisions through which proponents had sought to justify such laws. It was improper to justify the law through the Preamble since it merely outlined the document's purposes and obtained its meaning from the provisions that followed.[29] The necessary and proper clause at the end of Article I, Section 8, provided no authority because it served not to grant "new powers to Congress" but to clarify powers already there. The Constitution granted Congress no express power over the press. The provision granting Congress the power "of suppressing insurrections" was too tangential. Congress could adopt laws "punishing" insurrection, which the executive and judiciary could enforce, but this did not include the power of limiting the press. Consistent with concerns he expressed when Federalists justified the establishment of a national bank,[30] Madison observed that "if the power to suppress insurrections includes the power to punish libels, or if the power to punish includes a power to prevent, by all the means that may have that tendency, such is the relation and influence among the most remote subjects of legislation, that a power over a very few would carry with it a power over all."[31]

The First Amendment as a Bar to the Sedition Act

Having argued that the Constitution granted Congress no power over the press, Madison proceeded to argue that the First Amendment positively forbade it from exercising such power. As in making his first argument, Madison again examined the common law. Madison summarized the arguments that proponents of the common law understanding had advanced: "1. That the 'freedom of the press' is to be determined by the meaning of these terms in the common law; 2. That the article supposes the power of the press to be in Congress, and prohibits them only from abridging the freedom allowed to it by the common law."[32] Arguing that his examination of the second proposition would show that the First Amendment denied Congress any power over the press, Madison nonetheless felt obligated to offer some observations related to the first proposition.

Madison thus acknowledged that British common law established the principle that freedom of the press consisted of "an exemption from all previous restraint on printed publications, by persons authorized to inspect or prohibit them." He argued that the American understanding of freedom of the press could not be limited to such a principle "since a law inflicting penalties on printed publications would have a similar effect with a law authorizing a previous restraint on them. It would seem a mockery to say that no laws should be passed preventing publications from being made, but that laws might be passed for punishing them in case they should be made."[33]

Madison sought to illustrate his point by highlighting "the essential differences" between "the British government and the American constitutions."[34] The British government, which Madison rather pointedly chose not to call a "constitution,"[35] was devoted to protecting the people from executive encroachments. Britons considered Parliament, as the people's representative, to be sovereign and "omnipotent." Accordingly, the only freedom that the British government secured was "an exemption of the press from previous restraint by licensers appointed by the king." By contrast, America enshrined "absolute sovereignty" in "the people, not the government," and "the legislature, no less than the executive, is under limitations of power." He continued, "Hence, in the United States, the great and essential rights of the people are secured against legislative as well as executive ambition. They are secured, not by laws paramount to prerogative, but by constitutions paramount to laws. This security of the freedom of the press requires that it should be exempt, not only from previous restraint of the executive, as in Great Britain but from legislative restraint also; and this exemption, to be effectual must be an exemption, not only from the previous inspection of licensers, but from the subsequent penalty of laws."[36]

Individuals who recognized the differences between the English and American systems might still insist that "the actual legal freedom of the press, under the common law, must determine the degree of freedom which is meant by the terms, and which is constitutionally secured against both previous and subsequent restraints." Here Madison appeared to make a concession that might well bring common law understandings in through the back door. Acknowledging the difficulty of determining "the proper boundary between the liberty and licentiousness of the press" (arguably itself a common law distinction), Madison still hoped to show that "the degree of rigor" accepted under British law was "inapplicable to, and not obligatory," in America.[37] Madison observed that "governments elective, limited, and responsible in all their branches, may well be supposed to require a greater freedom of animadversion, than might be tolerated" by a government, like Britain's, where the people operated on the principle that their hereditary king could do no wrong,[38] and where the legislature, which was largely hereditary, was held to be "infallible."[39]

At this point, Madison moved from considering theory to examining actual practices on both sides of the Atlantic.[40] Despite occasional prosecutions in Britain, "the freedom exercised by the press, and protected by public opinion, far exceeds the limits prescribed by the ordinary rules of law." In America, "in every state, probably, in the Union, the press has exerted a freedom in canvassing the merits and measures of public men, of every description, which has not been confined to the strict limits of the common law." In near biblical language, Madison observed that "on this footing the freedom of the press has stood; on this foundation it yet stands."[41]

Madison observed that the strongest supporters of the Sedition Act included those who were "in the habit of" making "unrestrained animadversions on the proceedings and functionaries of the state governments." He further denied, however, that his last remark should be "understood as claiming for the state governments an immunity greater than they have heretofore enjoyed."[42] Madison continued with an analogy that arguably remains one of the best explanations of why democratic societies continue to allow some questionable forms of speech.[43] Observing that "some degree of abuse is inseparable from the proper use of every thing," Madison said that states had decided to operate by the principle "that it is better to leave a few of its noxious branches to their luxuriant growth, than, by pruning them away, to injure the vigor of those yielding the proper fruits."[44] Although Madison did not say so, this analogy was so close to one that John Marshall, perhaps the leading Federalist opponent of the Sedition Act, had made in a letter to Charles Talleyrand dated April 3, 1793, that Madison almost surely adapted it from there. Seeking to explain why the United States had not suppressed negative reports in the press about France, Marshall opined that licentiousness may be a concomitant to freedom of the press: "Perhaps it is an evil inseparable from the good to which it is allied, perhaps is a shoot which cannot be stripped from the stalk, without wounding vitally the plant from which it is torn."[45] The "Address of the General Assembly to the People of the Commonwealth of Virginia" dated January 23, 1799, and once attributed to Madison,[46] had cited this statement, and even if Madison did not write it, he likely knew about it. Having utilized the analogy, Madison proceeded to attribute to the press "all the triumphs which have been gained by reason and humanity over error and oppression."[47] He observed that if acts like those of 1798 had been in effect during the Articles of Confederation, the United States might still be suffering under its "infirmities."

Madison had one more observation on the degree to which British law provided the parameters for common law within the United States. Noting that the

First Amendment contained protections for "the freedom of conscience, and of religion" as well as freedom of the press, he said that "it will never be admitted that the meaning of the former, in the common law of England, is to limit their meaning in the United States." Having thus denied that British common law could define the freedoms that the First Amendment protected, Madison proceeded to argue that the language of the amendment was designed to be "a positive denial to Congress of any power whatever on the subject."[48] He sought to prove this by reviewing the circumstances of its adoption, a task for which his service at the Constitutional Convention and his participation in ratifying debates uniquely suited him.

Madison observed that when Anti-Federalists had objected that Congress might suppress press freedoms, its defenders had responded that Congress could exercise only enumerated and incidental powers and that the press was not included among either. Madison was likely at least in part thinking about the *Federalist Papers.* In *Federalist* No. 42 Madison had defended the congressional power to define and punish piracies on the high seas.[49] Madison thus observed that "felony is a term of loose signification even in the common law of England; and of various import in the statute law of that kingdom. But neither the common nor the statute law of that, or of any other nation, ought to be a standard for the proceedings of this, unless previously made its own by legislative adoption."[50] In answering those who had feared that the new national government might suppress freedom of the press, Alexander Hamilton, who was now supporting the Alien and Sedition Acts, had further responded in *Federalist* No. 84: "Why declare that things shall not be done which there is no power to do? Why, for instance, should it be said that the liberty of the press shall not be restrained, when no power is given by which restrictions may be imposed? I will not contend that such a provision would confer a regulating power; but it is evident that it would furnish, to men disposed to usurp, a plausible pretense for claiming that power."[51] Madison observed that "it is painful to remark how much the arguments now employed in behalf of the Sedition Act, are at variance with the reasoning which then justified the Constitution, and invited its ratification."[52] Madison believed that states ratified the Constitution "in confidence that, as they might be proper, they [constitutional amendments] would be introduced in the form provided by the Constitution."[53]

The proposal that became the First Amendment subsequently provided against abridgement of freedom of the press. This amendment confirmed that "no power whatever over the press was supposed to be delegated by the Constitution, as it originally stood, and that the amendment was intended as a positive and absolute reservation of it." This purpose was confirmed by the accompanying language of these amendments, which referred to the provisions of the Bill of Rights as "declaratory and restrictive clauses." Madison seemed incredulous that individuals could first deny that the Constitution granted such power to Congress, next "explicitly declare" this denial in an amendment, and then reverse course and actually recognize such a power.[54]

This led to the obvious question: "Is the federal government . . . destitute of every authority for restraining the licentiousness of the press, and for shielding itself against the libelous attacks which may be made on those who administer it?" Madison's answer was unequivocal: "the federal government is destitute of all such authority."[55]

Given Congress's failure to adopt Madison's own proposed amendment to limit state powers over freedom of the press, does the absence of *federal* remedies mean the absence of *all* remedies? Madison's earlier analysis suggested that states had learned the wisdom of allowing some luxurious foliage rather than risk injuring fruit. Now, however, he focused on reasons to prohibit *federal* laws relative to libel:

> The peculiar magnitude of some of the powers necessarily committed to the federal government; the peculiar duration required for the functions of some of its departments; the peculiar distance of the seat of its proceedings from the great body of its constituents; and the peculiar difficulty of circulating an adequate knowledge of them through any other channel;—will not these considerations, some of other of which produced other exceptions from the powers of ordinary governments, altogether, account for the policy of binding the hands of the federal government from touching the channel which alone can give efficacy to its responsibility to its constituents and of leaving those who administer it to a remedy, for their injured reputations, under the same laws, and in the same tribunals, which protect their lives, their liberties, and their properties?[56]

Robert Morgan has argued that Madison was probably being deliberately ambiguous in formulating the last part of this passage, suggesting that federal officeholders whose reputations are impugned should seek redress "under the same laws, and in the same tribunals, which protect their lives, their liberties, and their properties."[57] The passage certainly suggests that Madison may have recognized that politicians might resort to libel actions in *state* courts, without necessarily *supporting* such a resort.

The "Address of the General Assembly to the People of the Commonwealth of Virginia" had argued that "every libelous writing or expression might receive its punishment in the State courts, from juries summoned by an officer, who does not receive his appointment from the President, and is under no influence to court the pleasure of Government whether it injured public officers or private citizens."[58] When scholars believed Madison had authored this address, they naturally attributed the same views to him.[59] However, the view that Madison authored the earlier address no longer prevails,[60] and it is thus uncertain that Madison was so committing himself to such state suits.[61]

Earlier in the report, Madison had said that state courts had granted more protection to the press than under English common law and that they had recognized that it was "better to leave a few of its noxious branches to their luxuriant growth, than, by pruning them away, to injure the vigor of those yielding the proper fruits."[62] Morgan, who believes that Madison took a more libertarian view of press freedom than did Thomas Jefferson, observes that Madison proposed a prefix to the Constitution granting the people the right to change their government when it was "adverse or inadequate" to its purposes, and Morgan does not believe that such speech would have been possible had state or federal libel laws prevailed.[63]

Whatever remedies Madison may or may not have believed were available at the state level, he ended this section of his report by reiterating that the issue of constitutional power turns on "the actual meaning of the instrument." In his view, it clearly excluded "power over the press . . . from the number of powers delegated to the federal government."[64]

The Special Danger of Libel Laws Directed to Protecting Public Officials

At least since the U.S. Supreme Court decision in *New York Times Co. v. Sullivan,* legal scholars have recognized that laws limiting criticism of public figures pose greater dangers to freedom of speech and press than those limiting libel of private persons.[65] A similar distinction serves as the basis for the third major division of Madison's report. Madison observed that the Sedition Act was especially alarming "because it is leveled against that right of freely examining public characters and measures, and of free communication among the people thereon, which has ever been justly deemed the only effectual guardian of every other right."[66]

After quoting the section of the Sedition Act providing penalties for those who criticized the president or members of Congress, Madison followed with six observations. First, the Constitution subjected members of the legislative and executive branches to election and the president to impeachment. Second, when officials failed to fulfill their trust, "they should be brought into contempt or disrepute, and incur the hatred of the people." Third, the only way for the people to know whether elected officials have violated their duties is "by a free examination thereof, and a free communication among the people thereon."[67] Fourth, if "the censorship of public opinion" were to work, it required that citizens be able "to discuss and promulgate" their views of public affairs freely.[68] Fifth, the Sedition Act covered the time period of both congressional and presidential elections. Sixth, it therefore subjected citizens to penalties for exercising the very freedoms that helped keep the government in check.[69]

Madison opined that if such restrictions became permanent, they would either "destroy our free system of government, or prepare a convulsion that might prove equally fatal to it."[70] By contrast, supporters of the law raised three defenses: it was limited to publications that were "false and malicious, and intended to defame"; authors were permitted to attempt to show the truth of their allegations; and the law limited the fines and prison terms that judges could impose. Acknowledging that some members of Congress might have concurred with the law in the belief that, without it, even harsher common law principles would control both the offense and its punishment, Madison denied that the defense of truth was an adequate guard against such legislation.

Madison raised four arguments. First, the common law placed the burden on defendants to prove the truth of their statements, rather than on the government to prove their untruth, and individuals often found it difficult to establish the truth of their assertions in court. Second, facts and opinions were difficult to separate, and "opinion, and inferences, and conjectural observations, cannot be subjects of that kind of proof which appertains to facts, before a court of law."[71] Third, the law's intention to stop defamation would have wider repercussions—what today's courts would identify as "a chilling effect."[72] Although he did not renew the analogy, Madison's arguments here were similar to his earlier analogy about the dangers of pruning:

> It is manifestly impossible to punish the intent to bring those who administer the government into disrepute or contempt, without striking at the right of freely discussing public characters and measures; because those who engage in such discussions must expect and intent to excite these unfavorable sentiments, so far as they may be thought to be deserved. To prohibit the intent to excite those unfavorable sentiments against those who administer the government, is equivalent to a prohibition of discussions having that tendency and effect; which, again, is equivalent to a protection of those who administer the government, if they should at any time deserve the contempt or hatred of the people, against being exposed to it, by free animadversions on their characters and conduct.[73]

Fourth, Madison highlighted the unequal impact of the Sedition Act, which would cause particular hardships in elections involving members of the government, against whom libel could be prosecuted, from challengers who "may be exposed to the contempt and hatred of the people without a violation of the act."[74]

Madison affirmed that both the Virginia Resolutions of 1798 and the statement Virginia adopted when it ratified the Constitution confirmed "that the liberty of conscience and freedom of the press were equally and completely exempted from all authority whatever of the United States." The defense of freedom of the press was important not only in its own right but also because it is so inextricably tied to freedom of conscience, which the same amendment protected. Madison made four connections between the two. First, since both rights "rest equally on the original ground of not being delegated by the Constitution, and consequently withheld from the government . . . any construction . . . that would attack the original security for the one, must have the like effect on the other." Second, both are delineated within the same amendment. Third, if one is interpreted through the common law, both are likely to be so interpreted. Fourth, any argument that would permit the abridgment of speech would also undermine the prohibitions on behalf of religion.[75]

Madison dedicated the last pages of his report to defending the propriety of the specific actions that Virginia had taken to defend the First Amendment. This chapter passes over these arguments because they deal more directly with Madison's views of federalism, which James Read treats later in this book, than with Madison's view of freedom of the press.

Influence and Further Analysis

Madison's report made the case both for extending broad protection to freedom of the press at the state level and for interpreting the original First Amendment as exempting the press from all congressional controls.[76] Madison's arguments, like those that Justice Hugo Black later advanced, are persuasive evidence that when the First Amendment said that "Congress shall make no law" abridging the freedom of the press, it really meant that Congress should not make any such law![77]

Madison's arguments gain their central strength from his appeal to original understandings of the central purpose of the First Amendment in affirming that Congress could not restrict freedom of speech and freedom of the press. Given the literal language of the First Amendment, however, the argument is convincing rather than absolutely compelling. The literal language of the First Amendment does not explicitly prohibit all abridgements of "the press" per se, merely of the "freedom of the press."[78] Hamilton and others could thus interpret the First Amendment simply to incorporate fundamental common law prohibitions against licensing and prior restraint into the document, along perhaps with Zenger-like innovations relative to jury participation in decision making and the ability to use truthfulness as a defense, without thinking that it therefore prohibited all regulation.[79]

If the founders designed the First Amendment absolutely to forbid federal legislation on freedom of the press, it is reasonable to conclude that the amendment also intended to prohibit Congress from adopting any laws respecting an establishment of religion, prohibiting the free exercise of religion, or abridging freedoms of speech or the right of peaceable assembly or petition.[80] However much some scholars have argued that Madison and other Republicans valued states rights over civil liberties,[81] Madison raised genuine concerns that if Congress is granted power over the press, it will also assume power over the subjects of other First Amendment rights.[82]

The issue of whether the authors and ratifiers of the Fourteenth Amendment designed it (as Justice Hugo Black argued)[83] to alter the relation of the nation and the states so as to apply all the provisions of the First Amendment and the rest of the Bill of Rights to the states is clearly beyond the scope of this chapter, but Madison's analysis, while it might have argued for such a position, arguably points to some problems with so doing in an absolutely literalistic way.[84] However broad such rights should be, it would be difficult to ban *all* state laws on the subjects unless one acts under the assumption that certain kinds of expressions—such as obscenity (at least that involving juveniles), libel, fighting words, and the like—are not exercises of speech or press at all. Such exceptions might themselves best be justified by appealing to common law understandings. Common law understandings were and are such a pervasive part of state laws that it is difficult to imagine that any amendment could, or should, completely ban their consideration.[85]

Leonard Levy believes that the framers may have intended for the First Amendment to reserve control of the press to the states, albeit states accepting British common law understandings of the subject, as modified in America by the Zenger case. Whereas Levy has argued that Madison and others were radically innovating when they advanced the "libertarian" interpretations of freedom of the press in the *Report of 1800* and elsewhere,[86] it seems just as reasonable to interpret their actions as simply applying an untested constitutional provision to new circumstances. Their arguments were no more innovative, and were arguably truer to the original intent of the First Amendment, than were those of the defenders of the Sedition Act.

In terms of influence, the U.S. Supreme Court eventually ruled in *United States v. Hudson and Goodwin* (1812)—ironically, in a libel prosecution that Republicans initiated against Federalists—that there was no federal criminal common law.[87] Interestingly, Justice Johnson largely ignored the substance of the meticulous arguments that Madison and others had raised and based his ruling on "public opinion," which Madison had undoubtedly influenced, and "the general acquiescence of legal men."[88] Given the vagaries of public opinion, Johnson would have constructed a stronger argument had he built upon those that Madison had advanced in his report.

While Madison thus partially prevailed at the national level, Federalist state judges and legal commentators often ended up incorporating the ideas that Hamilton and others had advanced in regard to common law. These judges and commentators exerted a powerful influence not only at the state level but also at the national level, in early twentieth-century cases involving subversive speech.[89]

Madison's greatest vindication probably came in the case of *New York Times Co. v. Sullivan,* when Justice William Brennan said that the great "lesson" to be drawn from the Sedition Act of 1798 was that "If neither factual error nor defamatory content suffices to remove the constitutional shield from criticism of official conduct, the combination of the two elements is no less inadequate." After reviewing Madison's report and other contemporary evidence, Brennan concluded that "although the Sedition Act was never tested in this Court, the attack upon its validity has carried the day in the court of history."[90]

Brennan, of course, further cited the Fourteenth Amendment and subsequent judicial interpretations to deny "that the constitutional limitations implicit in the history of the Sedition Act apply only to Congress and not to the States." Consistent with the difficulties of applying the same absolute prohibition to state as to federal libel laws, Brennan did not declare all state libel laws to be illegal, but he did create an "actual malice" standard that made it especially difficult for "public figures" to prove that they had been libeled.[91] This arguably came close to the idea that the Virginia Assembly had proposed the previous year when it suggested that individuals who thought they had been libeled should seek their vindication in state courts—where, however, standards appropriate to republican government would provide greater leeway for public criticism than Great Britain would have permitted. If, as seems likely, Madison's own views went even beyond those of the earlier report, the modern Supreme Court may still not have fully embraced his own libertarian views of the subject.

Notes

The author is pleased to acknowledge support for this project in the form of a summer grant from the Faculty Research and Creative Projects Committee at Middle Tennessee State University.

1. See John R. Vile, "James Madison and Constitutional Paternity," this volume. Madison's contributions to the Constitution included, but were not limited to, his participation in the Annapolis Convention that issued the call for the Convention, helping persuade George Washington to attend, attending the Convention and helping formulate and defend the Virginia Plan that set the initial agenda of the Constitutional Convention, taking the best notes of the Convention (not published until after his death), serving as one of the three authors of the *Federalist,* which defended the document, playing a key role in the Virginia ratifying convention, and then serving as a congressman, secretary of state, and president under the new system. Many of these achievements are considered in John R. Vile, *The Constitutional Convention of 1787: A Comprehensive Encyclopedia of America's Founding* (Santa Barbara, CA: ABC-CLIO, 2005), especially 427–38. For a book that focuses specifically on Madison's role at the Constitutional Convention, see William Lee Miller, *The Business of May Next: James Madison and the Founding* (Charlottesville: University Press of Virginia, 1992).

2. Excellent accounts of Madison's work for the Bill of Rights include Robert A. Goldwin's *From Parchment to Power: How James Madison Used the Bill of Rights to Save the Constitution* (Washington, DC: AEI Press, 1997); Richard Labunski, *James Madison and*

the Struggle for the Bill of Rights (New York: Oxford University Press, 2006); Paul Finkelman, "James Madison and the Bill of Rights: A Reluctant Paternity," in *The Supreme Court Review, 1990,* ed. Gerhard Casper, Dennis J. Hutchinson, and David Strauss (Chicago: University of Chicago Press, 1991), 301–47; and Ralph Ketcham, *Framed for Posterity: The Enduring Philosophy of the Constitution* (Lawrence: University Press of Kansas, 1993). Also see Ketcham's "The Dilemma of Bills of Rights in Democratic Government," in *The Legacy of George Mason,* ed. Josephine F. Pacheco (Fairfax, VA: George Mason University Press, 1983).

3. For relevant excerpts of debates in the First Congress that demonstrate Madison's persistence, see Philip B. Kurland and Ralph Lerner, eds., *The Founders' Constitution* (Chicago: University of Chicago Press, 1987), 5:20–40.

4. Madison's proposal, which he hoped to insert between the first and second clauses of Article I, Section 10, and which limits the powers of the states, would have provided that "No State shall violate the equal rights of conscience, or the freedom of the press, or the trial by jury in criminal cases." See ibid., 5:25. As will be made clear later in this chapter, Madison appeared to use the term "rights of conscience" as a shorthand for the rights protected by the two religion guarantees currently incorporated within the First Amendment. Another issue on which Madison did not prevail had to do with the placement of amendments. Madison wanted to integrate them into the existing constitutional text, but Congress followed the counsel of Connecticut's Roger Sherman and placed them at the end of the document instead. See John R. Vile, *The Encyclopedia of Constitutional Amendments, Proposed Amendments, and Amending Issues, 1789–2002,* 2nd ed. (Santa Barbara, CA: ABC-CLIO, 2003), 408.

5. Quoted in Kurland and Lerner, *Founders' Constitution,* 5:129.

6. This development is described in Henry J. Abraham and Barbara A. Perry's *Freedom and the Court: Civil Rights and Liberties in the United States,* 7th ed. (New York: Oxford University Press, 2003), 33–105.

7. In a "Preface to Debates in the Convention of 1787," which he wrote in his later years, Madison had observed that "in the internal administration of the States a violations [*sic*] of Contracts had become familiar in the form of depreciated paper made a legal tender, of property substituted for money, of Instalment laws, and of the occlusions of the Courts of Justice; although evident that all such interferences affected the rights of other States, relatively Creditor, as well as Citizens Creditors within the State." In *The Records of the Federal Convention of 1787,* ed. Max Farrand (New Haven, CT: Yale University Press, 1966), 3:548.

8. In *Federalist* No. 10 Madison had presented his view, which he had articulated at the Convention, that factions were much more likely to be oppressive in individual states than in an extended territory like that embraced by the nation as a whole. See Alexander Hamilton, James Madison, and John Jay, *The Federalist Papers* (New York: New American Library, 1961), 77–84 (hereafter cited as *Federalist*).

9. Both the laws tightening immigration and subjecting aliens to greater risk of deportation and the sedition laws were aimed at undercutting the Democratic-Republican opposition. This chapter focuses only on the Sedition Act, since it dealt directly with First Amendment freedoms. Section 2 of the Sedition Act provided in relevant part:

> That if any person shall write, print, author or publish, or shall cause or procure to be written, printed, uttered, or published, or shall knowingly and willingly assist or aid in writing, printing, uttering or publishing any false, scandalous and malicious writing or writings against the government of the United States, or either houses of the said Congress, or the said President, or bring them, or either of them, into contempt or disrepute; or to excite against them, or either of them, the hatred of the good people of the United States, or to stir up sedition within the United States, or to excite any unlawful combinations therein, for opposing or resisting any law of the United States, or any act of the President of the United States, done in pursuance of any such law, or of the powers in him vested by the constitution of the United States . . . then such person, being thereof convicted before any court of the United States having jurisdiction thereof, shall be punished by a fine not exceeding two thousand dollars, and by imprisonment not exceeding two years.

Found in James Morton Smith, *Freedom's Fetters: The Alien and Sedition Laws and American Civil Liberties* (Ithaca, NY: Cornell University Press, 1956), 441–42. Also see Smith's "The Sedition Law, Free Speech, and the American Political Process," *William and Mary Quarterly,* 3rd ser., 9 (October 1952): 497–511.

10. David Jenkins, "The Sedition Act of 1798 and the Incorporation of Seditious Libel into First Amendment Jurisprudence," *American Journal of Legal History* 45, no. 2 (2001): 154.

11. Norman L. Rosenberg, *Protecting the Best Men: An Interpretive History of the Law of Libel* (Chapel Hill: University of North Carolina Press, 1986), 87. Rosenberg observes that in a suit at common law, the Supreme Judicial Court of Massachusetts even applied the Blackstonian rule that "the greater the truth the greater the libel," and that New York courts refused to allow truth as a defense. He further observes that "only one acquittal was recorded under the Sedition Act or state common law between 1798 and 1800" (88).

12. The classic interpretation of this event remains the article by Adrienne Koch and Harry Ammon, "The Virginia and Kentucky Resolutions: An Episode in Jefferson's and Madison's Defense of Civil Liberties," *William and Mary Quarterly,* 3rd ser., 5 (April 1948): 145–76. See also Frank Maloy Anderson, "Contemporary Opinion of the Virginia and Kentucky Resolutions I," *American Historical Review* 5 (October 1899): 45–63, and "Contemporary Opinion of the Virginia and Kentucky Resolutions II," *American Historical Review* 5 (December 1899): 225–52; and K. R. Constantine Gutzman, "The Virginia and Kentucky Resolutions Reconsidered: 'An Appeal to the Real Laws of Our Country,'" *Journal of Southern History* 66 (August 2000): 473–96.

13. Scholars continue to debate the consistency of Madison's apparent nationalism at the Constitutional Convention and his later fears about national powers. One of the most articulate attempts at reconciling these views is presented by Lance Banning in *The Sacred Fire of Liberty: James Madison and the Founding of the Federal Republic* (Ithaca, NY: Cornell University Press, 1995). For the view that the Virginia Resolution reflected long-standing doctrine at the state level, see Gutzman, "Virginia and Kentucky Resolutions Reconsidered."

14. See Marvin Meyers, ed., *The Mind of the Founder: Sources of the Political Thought of James Madison* (New York: Bobbs-Merrill, 1973), 298.

15. For this and other background details of this report, see *The Papers of James Madison,* ed. William T. Hutchinson et al. (Chicago: University of Chicago Press; Charlottesville: University Press of Virginia, 1962–91), 17:303–7 (hereafter cited as *Papers*). For Randolph's notes on the common law, see 259–69.

16. Koch and Ammon, "Virginia and Kentucky Resolutions," 173.

17. Kurt T. Lash, "James Madison's Celebrated Report of 1800: The Transformation of the Tenth Amendment," *George Washington Law Review* 74 (February 2006): 165–200.

18. Robert J. Morgan, *James Madison on the Constitution and the Bill of Rights* (New York: Greenwood, 1988), 195.

19. Citations come from the accessible version in Meyers, *Mind of the Founder,* 315, 316.

20. Ibid., 317.

21. Ibid., 318.

22. Ibid., 316, 319. John Orth has observed in *How Many Judges Does It Take to Make a Supreme Court?* (Lawrence: University Press of Kansas, 2006) that "no sooner was the constitution reduced to writing than it became subject to the common-law process. The meanings of constitutional guarantees are developed, like statutes and the rules of the common law itself, from case to case" (72).

23. Meyers, *Mind of the Founder,* 319, 320.

24. This decision overturned the U.S. Supreme Court ruling in *Chisholm v. Georgia,* 2 Dall. (2 U.S.) 419 (1793).

25. Meyers, *Mind of the Founder,* 321.

26. Some, albeit not all, of these problems would also apply to the adoption of common law principles at the state level.

27. Because the common law is generally understood as a mechanism for adapting to ongoing change, this argument might be a bit too clever, but it certainly demonstrates the difficulty of attempting to constitutionalize such a diverse set of precedents.

28. Meyers, *Mind of the Founder,* 323–25.

29. Subsequent interpreters have agreed. Justice John Marshall Harlan I thus observed in *Jacobson v. Massachusetts* (197 U.S. 11, 22 [1905]) that "although that Preamble indicates the general purposes for which the people ordained and established the Constitution, it has never been regarded as the source of any substantive power conferred on the Government of the United States or on any of its Departments. Such powers embrace only those expressly granted in the body of the Constitution and such as may be implied from those so granted."

30. Gary Rosen has argued that Madison was less concerned about the establishment of the bank, which he, in fact, renewed during his second presidential administration, than he was about the implications of the broad constructions that were being used to justify it. See *American Compact: James Madison and the Problem of Founding* (Lawrence: University Press of Kansas, 1999), 150.

31. Meyers, *Mind of the Founder,* 328.

32. Ibid., 329.

33. Ibid. As Madison phrases this, it is not clear how this would be any less of a mockery in Great Britain than in the United States.

Fellow Republican Tunis Wortman made a similar argument when he asked, "Of what use is the liberty of doing that for which I am punishable afterwards? In the same sense it may be said that I have the liberty to perpetrate felony or murder, if I think proper to expose myself to the penalties annexed to those crimes." See Wortman's classic, *A Treatise Concerning Political Enquiry and the Liberty of the Press* (1800; Clark, NJ: Lawbook Exchange, 2003), 256.

34. Meyers, *Mind of the Founder,* 329. It is interesting that Madison uses the plural here, apparently referring not simply to the Constitution of 1787 but apparently also to state documents.

35. By contrasting the British "government" with American "constitutions," Madison highlighted the American view that the former was not truly "constitutional" because it was not written and superior to other acts of legislation.

36. Meyers, *Mind of the Founder,* 330. This argument appears to apply to libel laws within the states (all of which had developed a system of separated powers) as well as to laws that the national government might adopt.

37. Ibid., 331.

38. This assertion appears to be in tension with Madison's earlier claim that in Britain, the king could do no wrong.

39. Meyers, *Mind of the Founder,* 330.

40. Modern interpreters of the First Amendment in the United States have increasingly recognized that contemporary practice was often far more liberal than contemporary statements of the law. See, for example, Eric Burns, *Infamous Scribblers: The Founding Fathers and the Rowdy Beginnings of American Journalism* (New York: Public Affairs, 1996).

41. Meyers, *Mind of the Founder,* 332.

42. Ibid.

43. In addition to justifying liberal laws relative to libel, the analogy might also justify liberal laws relative to categories of speech such as blasphemy or obscenity.

44. Meyers, *Mind of the Founder,* 332.

45. Quoted in Gregg Costa, "John Marshall, the Sedition Act, and Free Speech in the Early Republic," *Texas Law Review* 77 (March 1999): 1011, 1024.

46. See Kurland and Lerner, *Founders' Constitution,* 5:140.

47. Meyers, *Mind of the Founder,* 332.

48. Ibid. Madison had raised a similar point in a letter to George Washington dated October 18, 1787. See Farrand, *Records,* 3:130. Edmund Randolph had observed that acceptance of common law crimes might allow Congress to initiate prosecutions for "Heresy and Witchcraft." See *Papers,* 17:267.

49. In so doing, he was being consistent with the position he had taken at the Constitutional Convention on August 17. In discussing a provision that would grant Congress the power "to declare the law and punishment of piracies and felonies," Madison advocated changing this to "define & punish." He explained, "Felony at common law is vague. It is also defective. One defect is supplied by Stat: of Anne as to running away with vessels which at common law was a breach of trust only. Be-

sides no foreign law should be a standard farther than is expressly adopted—If the laws of the States were to prevail on this subject, the citizens of different States would be subject to different punishments for the same offense at sea—There would be neither uniformity nor stability in the law—The proper remedy for all these difficulties was to vest the power proposed by the term 'define' in the Natl. legislature." See Farrand, *Records,* 2:315–16.

50. *Federalist,* 266. Morgan mentions this statement in *Madison on the Constitution,* 169. He further observes that the Seventh Amendment followed a Madison proposal to incorporate common law provisions for a jury and reasonably concludes that "it would appear that Congress agreed with Madison that, if common law rules or definitions were to be made authoritatively binding by the Constitution, it must be by specific, *express, and previous* adoption in the Constitution rather than by subsequent implication; or Congress must be authorized to adopt or adapt rules of the common law by statute" (171) (emphasis in original).

51. *Federalist,* 513–14. It is, of course, possible, if not likely, that Hamilton might have distinguished between restriction of the press and restriction of "liberty of the press." Under his view, laws such as the Sedition Act, which provided protections equal to, or greater than, those provided under English common law, did not, in fact, abridge true "liberty" of the press but only its abuse.

52. Meyers, *Mind of the Founder,* 334. Jack Rakove has convincingly demonstrated that Madison believed in interpreting "original intent" as much through the lens of those who ratified the Constitution as from the viewpoint of those who wrote it. Speaking to Congress in 1796, Madison, referring to the Constitutional Convention of 1787, thus observed that "the sense of that body could never be regarded as the oracular guide in expounding the Constitution. As the instrument came from them it was nothing more than the draft of a plan, nothing but a dead letter, until life and validity were breathed into it by the voice of the people, speaking through the several State Conventions. If we are to look, therefore, for the meaning of the instrument beyond the face of the instrument, we must look for it, not in the General Convention, which proposed, but in the State Conventions, which accepted and ratified the Constitution." See Rakove, *Original Meanings: Politics and Ideas in the Making of the Constitution* (New York: Alfred A. Knopf, 1996), 17–18. Also see Rosen, *American Compact,* 160. For recent treatments of the contributions that Madison and Hamilton made to the establishment of the Constitution, see Sheila S. Simon, *Odd Couple of the Constitution: James Madison and Alexander Hamilton* (Baltimore, MD: PublishAmerica, 2005), and Michael I. Meyerson, *Liberty's Blueprint: How Madison and Hamilton Wrote the Federalist Papers, Defined the Constitution, and Made Democracy Safe for the World* (New York: Basic Books, 2008).

53. Meyers, *Mind of the Founder,* 334.

54. Ibid., 335. Again, it seems worth noting that while Madison apparently thought the First Amendment precluded all regulation of the press, Hamilton and other Federalists might simply have thought that the amendment limited abridgement of the "freedom of the press." These varying interpretations certainly suggest that the task of phrasing constitutional language in terms that all will understand is difficult indeed.

55. Ibid., 336.

56. Ibid., 336.

57. Morgan, *Madison on the Constitution,* 179.

58. Quoted in Kurland and Lerner, *Founders' Constitution,* 5:139.

59. Drawing in part from Madison's earlier speech to the Virginia General Assembly, this is the interpretation that Walter Berns, whose view of the motives of southern Republicans is perhaps the least flattering of any contemporary interpretation (he believes they were chiefly interested in shielding the institution of slavery from criticism), offers in "Freedom of the Press and the Alien and Sedition Laws: A Reappraisal," *The Supreme Court Review 1970,* ed. Philip B. Kurland (Chicago: University of Chicago Press, 1971), 136. One difficulty with this interpretation is that it apparently was not shared by Judge (and later Chancellor) James Kent of New York. Writing in *People v. Croswell,* 3 Johns. Cas. 337, 393 (1804), a case in which he would have upheld a seditious libel conviction, Kent, who was a Federalist, associated Madison with the view that would have banned prosecutions at both the national and state level:

> I am far from intending that these authorities mean, by the freedom of the press, a press wholly beyond the reach of the law, for this would, be emphatically Pandora's box, the source of every evil. And yet the House of Delegates in Virginia, by their resolution of the 7th January, 1800, and which appears to have been intended for the benefit and instruction of the Union, came forward as the advocates of a press totally unshackled, and declare, in so many words, that 'the baneful tendency of the Sedition Act was but little diminished by the privilege of giving in evidence the truth of the matter contained in political writing.' They seem also to consider it as the exercise of a pernicious influence, and as striking at the root of free discussion, to punish, even for a false and malicious writing, published with intent to defame those who administer the government. If this doctrine was to prevail, the press would become a pest, and destroy the public morals. Against such a commentary upon the freedom of the American press, I beg leave to enter my protest.

60. Morgan, *Madison on the Constitution,* 178. The editors of *The Papers of James Madison* (see 17:199) have similarly decided not to include this report in his writings. Editor David B. Mattern confirmed in e-mail correspondence to the author, dated June 5, 2006, that no subsequent evidence has arisen since 1988 to indicate that Madison wrote the earlier address.

61. It is possible that Madison might have opposed criminal suits at both the state and national levels but that he would have permitted politicians to institute civil suits in the former.

62. Meyers, *Mind of the Founder,* 332.

63. Morgan, *Madison on the Constitution,* 181.

64. Meyers, *Mind of the Founder,* 337.

65. 376 U.S. 254 (1964). This case required public officials to demonstrate "actual malice" before they could win libel judgments in the courts.

66. Meyers, *Mind of the Founder,* 337.

67. Ibid., 338.

68. For the importance of this concept in Madison's thought, see Alan Gibson, "Veneration and Vigilance: James Madison and Public Opinion, 1785–1800," *Review of Politics* 67 (Winter 2005): 5–35.

69. Robert W. T. Martin observes that whereas Federalists tended to view office-holders as repositories of the public trust, Democratic-Republicans put greater focus on the power of the people to oversee their rulers. See *The Free and Open Press: The Founding of American Democratic Press Liberty, 1640–1800* (New York: New York University Press, 2001), 138–49.

70. Meyers, *Mind of the Founder,* 339.

71. Ibid., 340.

72. See entry in David Hudson, David Schultz, and John R. Vile, eds., *The Encyclopedia of the First Amendment* (Washington, DC: Congressional Quarterly, 2008).

73. Meyers, *Mind of the Founder,* 340.

74. Ibid., 341.

75. Ibid., 343–44. Madison's conflation of the establishment and free exercise clauses under the rubric of "the liberty of conscience" is fascinating in its own right. It might be one way of reconciling two clauses that judges and scholars sometimes view as being in tension with one another.

76. Zechariah Chafee, Jr., was among those who believed that the First Amendment was designed to eliminate British common law restrictions on freedom of speech and freedom of the press. See his *Free Speech in the United States* (Cambridge, MA: Harvard University Press, 1964), 19–20.

77. Black's view is sometimes referred to as "First Amendment absolutism." For further description, see Henry J. Abraham, "First Amendment Absolutism," in *The Oxford Companion to the Supreme Court of the United States,* ed. Kermit L. Hall (New York: Oxford University Press, 1992), 299–300. Even this interpretation, however, might allow some determination as to whether certain regulatory laws, those allocating broadcast licenses, for example, actually "abridge" or expand such freedom. Kurt T. Lash addresses this issue in "Power and the Subject of Religion," *Ohio State Law Journal* 59 (1998): 1089.

In *Associated Press v. United States,* 326 U.S. 1, 20 (1945), Justice Black upheld the application of the Sherman Anti-Trust Act to the Associated Press by saying, "It would be strange indeed, however, if the grave concern for freedom of the press which prompted adoption of the First Amendment should be read as a command that the government was without power to protect that freedom. The First Amendment, far from providing an argument against application of the Sherman Act, here provides powerful reasons to the contrary. That Amendment rests on the assumption that the widest possible dissemination of information from diverse and antagonistic sources is essential to the welfare of the public, that a free press is a condition of a free society." Such an interpretation might apply to related clauses. In discussing the establishment clause, Carl H. Esbeck thus observes that "[b]y the clause's terms, Congress is denied only the power to legislate 'respecting an establishment of religion,' thus leaving it free to more generally legislate 'respecting religion.'" See his "Dissent and Disestablishment: The Church-State Settlement in the Early American Republic," *Brigham Young University Law Review* (2004): 1577.

78. Morgan, *Madison on the Constitution,* interpreted Madison's actions as supporting the view that although the First Amendment prohibited Congress from adopting laws "*abridging*" First Amendment freedoms, he thought it was free "to *support* a free press should the members choose to do so in an appropriate way" (180).

79. The *Law and History Review* has three articles on common law understandings in the early republic. Kathryn Preyer, "Jurisdiction to Punish: Federal Authority, Federalism and the Common Law of Crimes in the Early Republic," *Law and History Review* 4 (Fall 1986): 223–65, and Robert C. Palmer, "The Federal Common Law of Crime," *Law and History Review* 4 (Fall 1986): 267–323, both argue that there were no federal common law crimes, whereas Stephen B. Presses, "The Supra-Constitution, the Courts, and the Federal Common Law of Crimes: Some Comments on Palmer and Preyer," *Law and History Review* 4 (Fall 1986): 325–35, disagrees.

80. In *Watson v. Jones,* 80 U.S. 679 (1872), the U.S. Supreme Court thus decided that U.S. courts would not exercise the power that British courts had exercised to judge the principles of faith that governed individual churches. After observing that "we can very well understand how the Lord Chancellor of England, who is, in his office, in a large sense, the head and representative of the Established Church, who controls very largely the church patronage, and whose judicial decision may be, and not infrequently is, invoked in cases of heresy and ecclesiastical contumacy, should feel, even in dealing with a dissenting church, but little delicacy in grappling with the most abstruse problems of theological controversy, or in constructing the instruments which those churches have adopted as their rules of government, or inquiring into their customs and usages," Justice Samuel Miller went on to proclaim, "In this country the full and free right to entertain any religious belief, to practice any religious principle and to teach any religious doctrine which does not violate the laws of morality and property, and which does not infringe personal rights, is conceded by all. The law knows no heresy, and is committed to the support of no dogma, the establishment of no sect" (728). In a number of nineteenth-century cases, however, state supreme courts ruled that obscenity could be prosecuted under the common law, even though such offenses had been primarily, if not exclusively, prosecuted in England in ecclesiastical courts. See, for example, *Commonwealth v. Sharpless,* 2 Serg. & Rawle 91 (Pa. 1815), and *Commonwealth v. Holmes,* 17 Mass. 336 (1821).

81. See especially Berns, "Freedom of the Press."

82. Justice George Sutherland took a very similar position in his dissenting opinion in *Associated Press v. National Labor Relations Board,* 301 U.S. 103 (1937), in which he would have allowed the Associated Press to discharge an employee for union membership and activities. Observing that some liberties, such as due process, were qualified, he argued that "those liberties enumerated in the First Amendment are guaranteed without qualification, the object and effect of which is to put them in a category apart and make them incapable of abridgment by any process of law. That this is inflexibly true of the clause in respect of religion and religious liberty cannot be doubted; and it is true of the other clauses save as they may be subject in some degree to rare and extreme exigencies such as, for example, a state of war" (135). Sutherland further argued that "the destruction or abridgment of a free press—which constitutes one of the most dependable avenues through which information of

public and governmental activities may be transmitted to the people—would be an event so evil in its consequences that the least approach toward that end should be halted at the threshold" (136). Concluding with the plea to "withstand all *beginnings* of encroachment," he observed that "the saddest epitaph which can be carved in memory of a vanished liberty is that it was lost because its possessors failed to stretch forth a saving hand while yet there was time" (141).

83. See, for example, his dissent in *Adamson v. California,* 332 U.S. 46 (1947).

84. Ironically, if Madison had succeeded in getting an amendment adopted limiting *state* control of the press, his arguments against such federal laws might not have been as persuasive.

85. James Madison effectively made this point in a letter to George Washington dated October 18, 1787. Madison was sharing his puzzlement over George Mason's criticism that the new Constitution did not secure the common law:

> What can he mean by saying that the Common law is not secured by the new Constitution, though it has been adopted by the State Constitutions. The Common law is nothing more than the unwritten law, and is left by all the Constitutions equally liable to legislative alterations. I am not sure that any notice is particularly taken of it in the Constitutions of the States. If there is, nothing more is provided than a general declaration that it shall continue along with other branches of law to be in force till legally changed. . . . What could the Convention have done? If they had in general terms declared the Common Law to be in force, they would have broken in upon the legal Code of every State in the most material points: they wd. have done more, they would have brought over from G[reat] B[ritain] a thousand heterogeneous & antirepublican doctrines, and even the *ecclesiastical Hierarchy itself,* for that is a part of the Common law. If they had undertaken a discrimination, they must have formed a digest of laws, instead of a Constitution.

Quoted in Farrand, *Records,* 3:130.

86. Leonard W. Levy, "Liberty and the First Amendment: 1790–1800," *American Historical Review* 68 (October 1961): 24.

87. 11 U.S. 32. Justice Johnson, however, did leave the door open to courts "to fine for contempt—imprison for contumacy—inforce [*sic*] the observance of order, &c." (34). In an earlier circuit court decision, *United States v. Worrall,* 2 Dall. (2 U.S.) 384 (C.C.D. Pa. 1798), Justice Samuel Chase had previously indicated that he also did not believe that federal courts had criminal common law jurisdiction. For subsequent confirmation of this, see Justice Clifford's dissent in *United States v. Cruikshank,* 92 U.S. 542, 595 (1876).

In *Swift v. Tyson,* 16 Pet. (41 U.S.) 1 (1842), Justice Joseph Story had asserted for a unanimous court that there was a national common law, separate from state laws, relative to commercial law. Speaking through Justice Louis Brandeis, another unanimous Supreme Court (8–0) overturned this decision in *Erie Railroad Co. v. Tompkins,* 304 U.S. 674 (1938). See Kermit L. Hall, *The Magic Mirror: Law in American History* (New York: Oxford University Press, 1989), 283–84.

88. 7 Cranch (11 U.S.) 32 (1812).

89. See Rosenberg, *Protecting the Best Men,* 101–29, and Jenkins, "Sedition Act of 1798," 197–213. *American Communications Assn. v. Douds,* 339 U.S. 382, 394 (1950), provides a good example of this influence. In upholding a law that required labor leaders to swear that they were not members of the Communist Party, Chief Justice Fred Vinson remarked, "Although the First Amendment provides that Congress shall make no law abridging the freedom of speech, press or assembly, it has long been established that those freedoms themselves are dependent upon the power of constitutional government to survive. If it is to survive it must have power to protect itself against unlawful conduct and, under some circumstances, against incitements to commit unlawful acts."

90. 376 U.S. 254, 273, 276 (1964). Anthony Lewis observes that "Brannan did something quite extraordinary. He held unconstitutional an act of Congress that had expired one hundred and sixty-three years before. He put the imprimatur of the Supreme Court—of the Constitution—on the arguments not only of Jefferson and Madison but of Gallatin and Nicholas and all the other Republicans who had resisted the Sedition Act. How little could they have expected that the drama of their resistance would be played out again, six generations later, in a constitutional decision of the Supreme Court." See *Make No Law: The* Sullivan *Case and the First Amendment* (New York: Random House, 1991), 145.

91. 376 U.S. 254, 276, 280 (1964). This standard required a plaintiff to prove that a libelous statement was made "with knowledge that it was false or with reckless disregard of whether it was false or not."

STEVEN P. BROWN

Mirroring Madison

The Historic and Continuing Influence of James Madison on the U.S. Supreme Court

As John Vile has demonstrated in an earlier chapter, scholars continue to discuss the appropriateness of designating James Madison as the father of the Constitution. But there can be no gainsaying his lasting influence on one of the most important institutions that the document created, namely, the U.S. Supreme Court.

This chapter considers the Court as a Madisonian mirror on three levels. At the first and most general level, the Court as it functions today—particularly in its use of judicial review—reflects Madison's own view that a powerful check on the legislative branch was necessary to prevent the tyranny of the majority, to which Congress was prone, as well as to maintain the proper relationship between the federal government and the states. A second and more direct reflection of Madison's influence is found in the Supreme Court's role as a protector of the rights and liberties of citizens against governmental abuse. Finally, the modern Supreme Court's First Amendment jurisprudence, particularly in regard to religious rights that are free of both governmental support *and* interference, as well as the "preferred position" of free speech, echoes Madison's own convictions on these subjects.

Madison, the Supreme Court, and Limiting Power

Scholars often cite the glaring weaknesses of the Articles of Confederation as the primary impetus for the convening of state delegates in Annapolis in September 1786 and in Philadelphia the following May. For Madison, who played a major role in organizing both conventions, the Articles were indeed problematic. However, he did not consider the Articles alone to be responsible for the growing disorder in the new country after the Revolution. The Articles' recognition of the near-absolute sovereignty of the states and its sole grant of national power to a unicameral Congress only confirmed a troubling trend.

For some ten years prior to the Convention, Madison had watched as most of the states concentrated governing power in their legislatures.[1] Executive and judicial officers in these states had few substantive responsibilities and were generally powerless to guard even these minor duties against legislative encroachment or interference. The absence of any real safeguard against legislative abuse within the states coupled with the well-known reluctance of the individual states to work together on regional or national measures for their common good did more than just endanger the fragile union. As historian Gordon Wood put it, such problems "threatened the revolutionary experiment in self-government" itself.[2]

In a letter that he wrote to George Washington one month before the Philadelphia convention, Madison outlined his vision of a new system of government, one that "may at once support a due supremacy of the national authority, and not exclude the local [or state] authorities wherever they can be subordinately useful." Among other things, he recommended that the national government be empowered with "a negative *in all cases whatsoever* on the legislative acts of the States. . . . Without this defensive power, every positive power that can be given on paper [to the national government] will be evaded and defeated. The States will continue to invade the National jurisdiction, to violate treaties and the law of nations and to harass each other with rival and spiteful measures dictated by mistaken views of interest." Such a negative on state legislation would affect more than just the external affairs of a state. Congress could also use it, he argued, to exert "controul on the internal vicissitudes of State policy, and the aggressions of interested majorities on the rights of minorities and of individuals." It would thus fall to the national government to be the "disinterested and dispassionate umpire in disputes between different passions and interests in the State."[3]

In short, as Madison envisioned it, the "national negative" would satisfy three critical needs of governance within the young country. First, it would subject the states to national law where national interests were at stake. Second, in exerting "controul on the internal vicissitudes of State policy," such a veto would also help balance power within those states where the legislature dominated the other branches of government. Third, it would permit the national government "to intervene *within* the states to defend rights against the threats that individuals faced within the very communities where they lived."[4]

Madison employed the Virginia Plan to introduce the idea of a "national negative" to the delegates at the Constitutional Convention. The plan called for a national legislature that could "negative all laws passed by the several States contravening in the opinion of the National Legislature the articles of Union."[5] In addition, he also proposed the adoption of a Council of Revision comprising the chief executive and several members of the judiciary to review acts of Congress and veto them if necessary. The Council would also review every state law before the application of the national negative against that law could become final.

Although many delegates agreed with Madison's basic argument for checks on congressional and state legislative action, they were unwilling to adopt the remedies he suggested. Opposition to his proposals arose predictably from delegates who saw the union of the executive and judicial branches in the Council of Revision as a violation of the separation of powers or who believed that a negative on state legislation in the hands of a national entity would intrude upon the powers of the states. The delegates did not, however, ignore Madison's concerns regarding legislative dominance and excessive state autonomy.

Instead of the Council of Revision, the Convention provided a check on national legislative power by giving to the executive alone a qualified veto over congressional action. To curb the states from striking out on their own against national interests, the Convention also adopted the "supremacy clause" of Article VI by which the Constitution became "the supreme Law of the Land; and the Judges in every State shall be bound thereby, any Thing in the Constitution or Laws of any State to the Contrary notwithstanding." Madison was bitterly disappointed by these substitutions and expressed his doubts in a letter to Jefferson soon after the Convention adjourned as to whether the Constitution thus written could adequately control the tendency of both the national legislature and the states to exceed their powers especially in "secur[ing] individuals against encroachments on their rights."[6]

Although the Convention did not adopt Madison's specific solutions, his observations of and concerns about legislative supremacy, unbridled state sovereignty, and individual rights led to the remedies he proposed in the Virginia Plan. Thus, in considering these resolutions, the delegates were reminded very early on in the Convention that even the popularly elected branch of government could be abusive of its citizens, mistaken in its legislation, or contemptuous in its attitude toward the national government.

Madison's contribution, however, lay not in the specific remedies he offered (since the delegates rejected them both) but in the principle upon which he based his "national negative" and Council of Revision. That principle called for empowering some entity within the new constitutional order to check the will of the legislatures and the states when they exceeded their authority. And while the delegates ultimately adopted other measures at that time, Madison's proposals nevertheless helped develop, according to Edwin S. Corwin, "a growing comprehension in the Convention of the *doctrine* of judicial review."[7]

Scholars have increasingly noted that American courts exercised judicial review long before the Supreme Court asserted it as a prerogative in *Marbury v.*

Madison (1803), the case that forever linked Madison's name to judicial review.[8] Recent research suggests that state and federal courts exercised judicial review as many as thirty-one times between the Philadelphia convention and the *Marbury* decision.[9] Historical antecedents aside, from Madison's perspective, it was perhaps inevitable that the Court would take on this role. The power to rein in Congress and the states was simply too great to entrust to one man alone, such as the president. And Madison's call for a national negative and Council of Revision to check legislative power clearly reflected his concern "that the real threats to rights in a republic lay not in the arbitrary acts of a government misruling its people but in the more disturbing possibility that popular majorities, acting *through* government, would willfully trample on the rights of individuals and minorities."[10]

That Madison agreed in principle, if not in practice for partisan reasons, with the Court's ruling in *Marbury* was further underscored when he offered his view of the Supreme Court many years later. In a letter to Nicolas Trist from 1831, Madison wrote, "With respect to the supremacy of the Judicial power on questions occurring in the course of its functions, . . . I have never ceased to think that this supremacy was a vital principle of the Constitution as it is a prominent feature of the text. A supremacy of the Constitution and laws of the Union, without a supremacy in the exposition and execution of them, would be as much a mockery as a scabbard put into the hand of a Soldier without a sword in it."[11] As clear as that statement is, however, it is important to note that Madison seemed to care less for the institution than for the purpose it served. He was obviously not the only one to acknowledge the impossibility of national unity unless the states yielded to the Constitution. And there were others who shared his concerns about legislative usurpation of powers and infringement upon minority rights. But he articulated better than most a vision of a national institution (such as his Council of Revision or Congress in possession of a national negative) to enforce the supremacy of the Constitution and guard against the tyranny of the majority. This explains why Madison, "unlike his friend Jefferson, eventually came to value the position of the Supreme Court in American political life."[12]

The modern Supreme Court mirrors Madison in several important respects with regard to judicial review. First, the Court has not hesitated to use its most important power to strike down government action that goes beyond the limits of state and federal authority. Second, and considered in more detail below, the Court has wielded its power of judicial review to protect the rights of minority interests whose views or beliefs have been outweighed by and thus left unprotected against the interests of the majority that controls the electoral branches of government. Although Madison initially offered a much different approach, he would not be displeased at the modern Court's use of judicial review in the name of good governance and minority rights.

In a letter to Henry Lee from 1834, Madison stated that his decision to run for Congress in 1789 instead of accepting an appointment in George Washington's first administration arose from his desire to "be of service in sustaining the Constitution against the party adverse to it."[13] Although Anti-Federalist sentiment was strong in several states, it was particularly acute in Virginia. Federalist proponents of the Constitution won the battle in June 1788, but only after the state ratifying convention agreed to forward to Congress some forty amendments. Emboldened by the same spirit that led an earlier group of Virginians to call for the reform of the Articles of Confederation, Anti-Federalists in the Virginia General Assembly vigorously lobbied the other states to convene a second convention to address the defects of the Constitution.

Led by Patrick Henry, Virginia's Anti-Federalists were particularly antagonistic toward James Madison. He came in a distant third in a three-man race when the legislature selected the first two Virginians to represent the state in the U.S. Senate. Henry opined to his associates on that occasion that Madison was "unworthy of the confidence of the people in the station of the senator" and that selecting him for this office would result "in producing rivulets of blood throughout the land."[14]

Once Madison indicated his intention to run for a seat in the first House of Representatives, Anti-Federalists in the General Assembly reacted by shaping his congressional district to include several areas where opposition to the Constitution ran strong. In addition, Henry personally recruited to run against Madison a young Anti-Federalist Revolutionary War hero, former delegate in the Continental Congress, and close personal friend of Madison named James Monroe. Even without the Anti-Federalist machine behind him, Monroe would have been a formidable candidate. But Madison believed that his chance of winning the election turned more on the rhetoric of Patrick Henry than on the person of James Monroe.

Having lost the battle for ratification in Virginia, Henry and other Anti-Federalists reshaped their arguments to suggest that Madison and others like him, if elected to Congress, would be unwilling to amend the Constitution to correct its problems. In a letter to George Washington one month before the election, Madison expressed his frustration that such mischaracterizations would doom his chances of winning the House seat: "It has been very industriously inculcated that I am dogmatically attached to the Constitution in every clause, syllable & letter, and therefore not a single amendment will be promoted by my vote, either from conviction or a spirit of accommodation. This is the report most likely to affect the election, and most difficult to be combated with success within the limited period."[15] On February 2, 1789, however, after having assured his district that he would entertain amendments, James Madison won his congressional district by a

336-vote margin. By the end of the month he was on his way to New York to take his seat in the First Congress.

Given the Constitutional Convention's rebuff of his own pet proposals for the Council of Revision and Congress's negative on state legislation, it was obvious that Madison was not among those whom he described in a letter to G. L. Turberville from November 1788 as thinking that "the Constitution lately adopted a faultless work." He readily admitted that there were "amendments which [he] wished it to have received before it issued from the place in which it was formed." Ever the pragmatist, however, Madison knew that entertaining amendments either in Philadelphia or at the state ratifying conventions would "throw the States into dangerous contentions, and . . . furnish the secret enemies of the Union with an opportunity of promoting its dissolution." But with the successful ratification of the Constitution, he went on to tell George Eve, an influential Baptist preacher, "Circumstances are now changed."[16]

Although the circumstances for amending the Constitution had changed to Madison's liking, two problems remained. First, some members of the First Congress were still hostile to the new Constitution, just as they had been before ratification. Second, other more supportive members remained very concerned about the need for greater protection of individual rights. Madison had no doubt that one or both groups would apply pressure to amend the Constitution. Thus, when Madison set out to attend the opening session of the First Congress, he was determined to play a key role in the amendment process for both personal and practical reasons. As Robert Goldwin has written, "He saw a bill of rights, *his* carefully constructed bill of rights, as the most effective solution. If he wrote the amendments, he could win the support of those who were still uneasy, without making any change at all in the constitutional structure. His primary objective was to keep the Constitution intact."[17]

On June 8, 1789, with apologies to his fellow House members for taking up their time when they had so much other important work to do, Madison introduced nine amendments containing some nineteen different proposals cobbled together from the more than two hundred amendments that the various state ratifying conventions had suggested. He admitted that his efforts stemmed, in part, from electoral promises that he had made to his own constituents. But he also acknowledged that opposition to the Constitution persisted throughout the country. He hoped that the amendments he would introduce would "extinguish from the bosom of every member of the community, any apprehensions that there are those among his countrymen who wish to deprive them of [their] liberty." More importantly, however, in returning to a theme he repeatedly stressed during the Philadelphia convention, he admitted that even the government established by the new Constitution might need a powerful check to keep it within its proper bounds: "I will candidly acknowledge, that, over and above all these considerations, I do conceive that the Constitution may be amended; that is to say, if all power is subject to abuse, that then it is possible the abuse of the powers of the General Government may be guarded against in a more secure manner than is now done. . . . We have in this way something to gain, and, if we proceed with caution, nothing to lose."[18] He then proceeded to introduce his amendments, which included the better part of what we now know as the Bill of Rights, as well as what would eventually become the Twenty-Seventh Amendment.

As significant as Madison's role was in introducing the Bill of Rights, his greater contribution lay in his insistence that Congress take up the amendments. More than a month would pass before the House assigned the amendments to a select committee for consideration and revision. He faced opposition from the Anti-Federalists who favored amendments that would have rendered greater structural changes to the Constitution. But he also incurred the displeasure of some of his Federalist supporters who thought the timing for such action was simply wrong. Nevertheless, the House was able to send seventeen articles to the Senate for its consideration by the end of August 1789. A month later, Congress sent twelve articles to the states, which ratified ten of them within the next two years.

The impact of Madison's efforts to introduce his amendments, coupled with his determination to make sure Congress considered them and sent to the states, cannot be exaggerated. The way he worded them was arguably even more important. "Bills of rights" in Madison's day could be understood only in the context of the state constitutions that included such provisions. Drafters generally placed these bills of rights at the beginning of their state constitutions where they, in effect, laid the foundation for all that was to follow. As Herbert Storing has argued, the wording was very different from that found in Madison's amendments, for those "state bills of rights were full of 'oughts' and general principles." That is, rather than listing specific guarantees of individual rights against governmental intrusion, early state bills of rights articulated the broad language of natural rights. As such, they provided an ideal or standard against "which a government can be judged and, when necessary, resisted."[19] And therein lay the problem.

Although Madison and his supporters in Congress undoubtedly agreed with the principles set forth in the state bills of rights, they were also concerned about the perpetuation of the government erected to protect those rights. Maintaining government at the expense of the people's rights was not acceptable, but neither was insisting on first principles and natural rights to the degree that they undermined the very government designed to protect them. Thus, "Madison drastically limited the kind of standard-setting, maxim-describing, teaching function of the bill of rights. . . . In the hands of Madison and the majority of the First Congress, the Bill of Rights became what it is today: not the broad principles establishing the ends and limits of government, not 'maxims' to be learned and looked up to by generations of Americans, not the statements of those first principles to which a healthy people should, according to the Virginia Declaration of Rights, frequently resort; but specific protections of traditional civil rights."[20] In rewording such rights, Madison ensured that the government would be secure enough to govern while not immune from change, and limited in its ability to abuse its people.

The modern Supreme Court mirrors Madison's approach to the Bill of Rights in three significant ways. First and foremost, the justices are chiefly interpreting Madison's amendments when they consider the constitutionality of governmental action. Although Madison did not originate any of the principles contained in the Bill of Rights, he overcame considerable opposition to introduce amendments so early in that first congressional session and subsequently ensured that Congress forwarded them to the states for ratification.

Second, although it would take some 140 years to do so, the Supreme Court eventually came to embrace Madison's own views about state governments infringing on individual rights. Echoing charges he leveled during the Constitutional Convention, Madison reminded his fellow House members that "the State Governments are as liable to attack these invaluable privileges as the General Government is, and therefore ought to be cautiously guarded against." Accordingly, he worded his fifth amendment to state specifically that "No State shall violate the equal rights of conscience, or the freedom of the press, or the trial by jury in criminal cases."[21] Such a restriction on the states garnered little support from his fellow Federalists. As for the Anti-Federalists in Congress whom Madison had tried to placate by offering amendments, this proposal "doubtless looked more like a musket shot than an olive branch."[22] Consequently, Congress stripped out the "no State shall" wording.

In the 1920s the Supreme Court began to question seriously whether the Constitution protected certain rights and liberties against local and state government infringement. Since John Marshall had first considered the issue in *Barron v. Baltimore* in 1833,[23] and in spite of the Fourteenth Amendment's specific ban on state action abridging the privileges and immunities of citizens or denying to them the equal protection of the laws, the Court had resisted arguments to make the guarantees of the Bill of Rights applicable against the states. In 1925, however, albeit in dictum only, Justice Edward Sanford announced in *Gitlow v. New York* that the First Amendment did in fact protect citizens against state infringement of their free speech and free press rights.[24] Over the next five decades the Court not only formally adopted Madison's "no State shall" approach to protecting rights via its incorporation doctrine but also extended it to virtually every guarantee listed in the Bill of Rights.

Third, the decisions of the modern Supreme Court largely reflect Madison's philosophy that there are few fully unfettered rights. Despite criticism, which was especially pointed during the Warren Court years, that the Supreme Court had either favored minority interests over the wishes of the greater community or gutted the power of government to protect the safety, health, welfare, and morals of its people in favor of individual rights, the modern Supreme Court has wisely never embraced the guarantees of the Bill of Rights as "first principles" upon which all else was predicated. For, "even rational and well-constituted governments need and deserve a presumption of legitimacy and permanence. A bill of rights that presses these first principles to the fore tends to deprive government of this presumption."[25]

Although the Court has rendered decisions that have sharply curtailed governmental intrusion into certain facets of American life, it has done so by calling into question the legitimacy of the intrusion, not the government. It is a Madisonian ideal that attempts to give to the people the fullest expression of their rights, without undermining the unique government that was established to protect those rights.

Madison, the Supreme Court, and the First Amendment

As mentioned above, Madison adopted a pro-amendment position in order to secure his election to the First Congress. This is not to suggest, however, that he determined the content of his amendments by political calculus alone. If anything, his desire to protect the Constitution by submitting his amendments before any others were proposed also gave him the opportunity to express, at least in part, his own thoughts on those rights and liberties most deserving of protection. Again, as mentioned before, little of the individual amendments originated with Madison. The order in which they were presented, however, did.

The first of the several amendments Madison placed before his fellow House members was a broad statement that he wished to prefix to the Constitution, which declared, in part, "that all power is originally vested in, and consequently derived from, the people."[26] His second and third amendments, the latter of which later became the Twenty-Seventh Amendment, dealt with the apportionment of House seats after the first census was taken and the altering of members' compensation, respectively.

The fourth amendment submitted by Madison, but the first one dealing with individual rights, was the longest of all of his proposals and included portions of what we now know as the First, Second, Third, Fourth, Fifth, Sixth, and Eighth Amendments. But it begins with the following:

> The civil rights of none shall be abridged on account of religious belief or worship, nor shall any national religion be established, nor shall the full and equal rights of conscience be in any manner, or on any pretext, infringed.

> The people shall not be deprived or abridged of their right to speak, to write, or to publish their sentiments; and the freedom of the press, as one of the great bulwarks of liberty, shall be inviolable.
>
> The people shall not be restrained from peaceably assembling and consulting for their common good; nor from applying to the Legislature by petitions, or remonstrances, for redress of grievances.[27]

Out of the many amendments that were proposed in the state ratifying conventions from which he had culled his list, Madison chose to list religion, speech, press, and assembly, the four bulwarks of the modern First Amendment, first. This did not surprise those who knew him.

Had Madison never become president—indeed, if he had never been a member of the Constitutional Convention—his name would still be remembered today because of his *Memorial and Remonstrance against Religious Assessments.* Madison wrote this short piece, which was published in the summer of 1785, in response to Patrick Henry's efforts to persuade the General Assembly to impose a tax on Virginians to "support teachers of the Christian religion." Madison's *Memorial and Remonstrance* set forth fifteen reasons for "remonstrating" against the proposed assessments. Among these was his contention that it was "a fundamental and undeniable truth, 'that religion or the duty which we owe to our Creator and the manner of discharging it, can be directed only by reason and conviction, not by force or violence.' The Religion then of every man must be left to the conviction and conscience of every man; and it is the right of every man to exercise it as these may dictate."[28] Madison's *Memorial and Remonstrance* was central to the defeat of the assessment bill. More importantly, it led directly to the 1786 passage of the Virginia Act for Establishing Religious Freedom, which Thomas Jefferson had drafted seven years earlier. Both men considered its enactment among their greatest accomplishments, and Jefferson included it as one of three accomplishments listed on his tombstone.

Of all the charges leveled against Madison during his 1789 House campaign, what distressed him most were reports that opponents were telling voters in his district that he had "ceased to be a friend to the rights of Conscience."[29] According to one of his biographers, "religious liberty stands out as the one subject upon which Madison took an extreme, absolute, undeviating position throughout his life." Although some observers have argued that Madison became much more skeptical of religion as he grew older, there is, nonetheless, "no evidence that [his] defense of religious liberty reflected any hostility to religion itself or to its social effects. On the contrary, he argued repeatedly that freedom of religion enhanced *both* its intrinsic vitality and its contribution to the common weal. He believed that attitudes and habits nourished by the churches could and did help importantly to improve republican government."[30]

As demonstrated in John Vile's previous essay on Madison's *Report of 1800*, Madison's commitment to the freedom of speech and freedom of the press was just as strong. Writing in response to the notorious Alien and Sedition Acts that Congress adopted during the Adams administration, Madison declared:

> Among those principles deemed sacred in America, among those sacred rights considered as forming the bulwark of their liberty, which the Government contemplates with awful reverence and would approach only with the most cautious circumspection, there is no one of which the importance is more deeply impressed on the public mind than the liberty of the press. That this *liberty* is often carried to excess; that it has sometimes degenerated into *licentiousness*, is seen and lamented, *but the remedy has not yet been discovered. Perhaps it is an evil inseparable from the good with which it is allied; perhaps it is a shoot which cannot be stripped from the stalk without wounding vitally the plant from which it is torn. However desirable those measures might be which might correct without enslaving the press, they have never yet been devised in America.*[31]

The modern Supreme Court has likewise recognized that free speech and freedom of the press—indeed, the entire First Amendment, as Justice Benjamin Cardozo characterized it—is "implicit in the concept of ordered liberty."[32] The trend in the Court's free speech and free press opinions since the 1930s has been to "unshackle the marketplace of ideas."[33] The manner in which it has done so, particularly with regard to unpopular speech, has been criticized by some as "liberty . . . carried to excess." But as Madison noted above, as well as more famously in his *Federalist* No. 10 "liberty is to air" analogy, the Court seems to have grasped the notion that the costs of overregulating the freedoms of speech and of the press are generally worse than the consequences from the spoken or printed word.

The modern Court has been less successful in establishing consistency in its religion decisions. It has followed a tortuous path in regard to religion and religious expression, erecting, in Justice Robert Jackson's famous words, "a legal 'wall of separation between church and state' as winding as the famous serpentine wall designed by Mr. Jefferson for the University he founded."[34] Such decisions have created a jurisprudential climate that has divided both the Court and the country, a consequence that Madison surely would have abhorred.

Madison and the Modern Supreme Court

The Constitution to which James Madison devoted so much of his time and talents has seen many changes in the 170 years that have passed since his death. States have ratified seventeen additional amendments since adopting the Bill of Rights. Some of these changed the structure of the original Constitution, as in altering the method for selecting senators and limiting presidential terms of office.

Other amendments were more rights-based, extending, for example, the equal protection of the law to African Americans and safeguarding their right to vote as well as that of women and eighteen-year-olds. Of arguably greater constitutional significance has been the interpretative changes of the Supreme Court. And in this sense, the Court's reflection of Madison may be a bit distorted.

Madison's political life was intertwined with questions of religion, speech, and government. He would agree with the modern Court's efforts to separate church and state, but he would be troubled by its inability to establish a solid and consistent foundation of precedent pertaining to religion and religious expression. He would probably be even more concerned about the all-or-nothing approach to the Court's church-state jurisprudence taken by interest groups that actively litigate in this area. He would find fault with Christian Right activists who seek the government's blessing on all things religious as well as with separationist groups who are unwilling to acknowledge religion's salutary effect on society.

Madison would have approved of the Court's incorporation doctrine. Whether he would have agreed with the unenumerated rights that the Court has also come to incorporate cannot be known, but he surely meant for the rights of the people to be secure against any encroachment by the local, state, or national governments.

Holding state governments accountable for constitutional violations is one thing; eroding state power is altogether different. Given those Court rulings that have allowed congressional power to expand virtually unabated from the New Deal era to the present (with a few notable exceptions during the Rehnquist Court), he would be forced to agree with the prediction of "Brutus," his Anti-Federalist critic in New York, who wrote in 1788, "Every adjudication of the supreme court, on any question that may arise upon the nature and extent of the general government, will affect the limits of state jurisdiction. In proportion as the former enlarge the exercise of their powers, will that of the latter be restricted."[35]

As noted earlier, Madison would also agree with the Court's wielding of judicial review as an effective tool for checking the power of the states and the other branches of government. But he would disapprove of judicial arrogance. The Supreme Court's broad pronouncement in *Cooper v. Aaron* that the *Marbury* decision "declared the basic principle that the federal judiciary is supreme in the exposition of the law of the Constitution" directly contradicts Madison's own views on the proper role of the judiciary.[36]

In 1788, commenting on Jefferson's draft of a proposed form of government for Virginia, Madison found merit in a proposal that would require the legislature to submit its bills to the executive and judicial departments before final passage.[37] Should either of those branches reject the bill, the legislature could simply remove the offending language to pass judicial scrutiny or override the veto and enact the law. But at that point, Madison recommended, "It should not be allowed the Judges or the Executive to pronounce a law thus enacted unconstitutional and invalid." He went on to lament the fact that neither the states nor the federal government had any procedure in place to deal with constitutional disagreements between branches: "In the State Constitutions and indeed in the Federal one also, no provision is made for the case of a disagreement in expounding them; and as the Courts are generally the last in making their decision, it results to them by refusing or not refusing to execute a law, to stamp it with its final character. This makes the Judiciary Department paramount in fact to the Legislature, which was never intended and can never be proper."[38] It is difficult to imagine the changes that might have occurred during the last forty years in interest group mobilization and litigation, the judicial nomination process, and the social fabric of our nation had the Supreme Court and its decisions not become, for whatever reason, "paramount in fact to the Legislature."

The "father of the Constitution" would doubtless find much about our government erected under that document to be strange and troubling if he were alive today. The vast power of the presidency, the professionalized nature of Congress, and the skewed balance of power that has enervated the state governments would all give him pause. But given his concerns about protecting the Constitution, the strength of the national government, and individual rights, he would find some comfort and some degree of familiarity in the modern Supreme Court.

Notes

1. Jack N. Rakove, *James Madison and the Creation of the American Republic,* 3rd ed. (New York: Pearson Longman, 2007), 50.

2. Gordon S. Wood, *Revolutionary Characters: What Made the Founders Different* (New York: Penguin, 2006), 157.

3. James Madison, *The Writings of James Madison,* ed. Gaillard Hunt (New York: G. P. Putnam's Sons, 1900–1910), 2:344–45, 346 (hereafter cited as *Writings*). Emphasis in original.

4. Jack N. Rakove, *Declaring Rights: A Brief History with Documents* (Boston: Bedford, 1998), 100.

5. *Writings,* 3:19.

6. Ibid., 5:27.

7. Edward S. Corwin, "The Progress of Constitutional Theory between the Declaration of Independence and the Meeting of the Philadelphia Convention," *American Historical Review* 30, no. 3 (April 1925): 536. Emphasis in original.

8. 1 Cranch (5 U.S.) 137 (1803).

9. William Michael Treanor, "Judicial Review before *Marbury,*" *Stanford Law Review* 58 (November 2005): 457.

10. Rakove, *Declaring Rights,* 148.

11. *Writings,* 9:476.

12. Wood, *Revolutionary Characters,* 163–64. In contrast to Jefferson, Madison was much more concerned about the dangers that might emerge from the legislative branch

than he was about the judiciary. And he consistently held to this view even after the Court affirmed and enlarged the powers of the national government in such cases as *McCulloch v. Maryland* (1819) and *Cohens v. Virginia* (1821). Shortly after the *Cohens* decision, Madison responded to a letter from his good friend Spencer Roane, whose public writings in a Richmond newspaper had excoriated John Marshall and the growing power of the Supreme Court. Madison confessed, "Whatever may be the latitude of Jurisdiction assumed by the Judicial Power of the U.S. it is less formidable to the reserved sovereignty of the States than the latitude of power which it has assigned to the National Legislature; and that encroachments by the latter are more to be apprehended" (*Writings,* 9:57).

13. *Writings,* 9:532.

14. Quoted in Irving Brant, *James Madison: Father of the Constitution, 1787–1800* (Indianapolis, IN: Bobbs-Merrill, 1950), 237.

15. *Writings,* 5:319–20.

16. Ibid., 5:298, 320.

17. Robert A. Goldwin, *From Parchment to Power: How James Madison Used the Bill of Rights to Save the Constitution* (Washington, DC: AEI Press, 1997), 73. Emphasis in original.

18. *Writings,* 5:374, 375.

19. Herbert J. Storing, "The Constitution and the Bill of Rights," in *How Does the Constitution Secure Rights?* ed. Robert A. Goldwin and William A. Schambra (Washington, DC: American Enterprise Institute, 1985), 30.

20. Ibid., 32.

21. *Writings,* 5:387, 378.

22. Akhil Reed Amar, *America's Constitution: A Biography* (New York: Random House, 2005), 320.

23. 32 U.S. 243 (1833).

24. 268 U.S. 652 (1925).

25. Storing, "Constitution," 32.

26. *Writings,* 5:376.

27. Ibid., 5:377.

28. Quoted in Philip B. Kurland and Ralph Lerner, *The Founders' Constitution* (Indianapolis, IN: Liberty Fund, 2000), 5:82.

29. *Writings,* 5:320.

30. Ralph Ketcham, *James Madison: A Biography* (Charlottesville: University Press of Virginia, 1990), 165, 167. See also Frank Lambert, *The Founding Fathers and the Place of Religion in America* (Princeton, NJ: Princeton University Press, 2003), 263.

31. *Writings,* 6:336. Emphasis in original.

32. *Palko v. Connecticut,* 302 U.S. 319, 325 (1937).

33. Daniel A. Farber, *The First Amendment* (New York: Foundation, 1998), 16.

34. *Illinois ex rel. McCollum v. Board of Education,* 333 U.S. 203, 238 (1948).

35. Ralph Ketcham, ed., *The Anti-Federalist Papers and the Constitutional Convention Debates* (New York: Mentor Books, 1986), 296.

36. 358 U.S. 1, 18 (1958).

37. In an 1818 letter to James Monroe, Madison again endorsed the "vest[ing] in the Judiciary Department [of] a qualified negative on Legislative *bills*. Such a Controul, restricted to Constitutional points, besides giving greater stability and system to the rules of expounding the Instrument, would have precluded the question of a Judiciary annulment of Legislative Acts" (*Writings*, 8:407).

38. Ibid., 5:294.

FOUR

Madison as a Party Leader

MARY STOCKWELL

Madison and Hamilton

The End of a Friendship

When Alexander Hamilton became the first secretary of the treasury under the Constitution in September 1789, he wrote a letter to a close friend of his who shared many of his ideas about the nation's economy. That man was James Madison, the most important leader in the newly elected House of Representatives of the Congress of the United States. Madison, in fact, had suggested to President George Washington that he name young Hamilton, then only thirty-two years of age, to this important post. As Madison had explained to Washington, Hamilton was "best qualified for that business" and was also "preferred by those who knew him personally."[1] For his part, Hamilton was well aware of the great responsibility that Madison had placed on his shoulders. It would be his job to find a way out of the enormous national debt that had built up as a result of the American Revolution. He later confessed that he took the job only because he believed Madison would be his staunchest supporter in the House of Representatives. Without their similarity in thinking, and without Madison's great "goodwill" toward him, Hamilton knew that the job of secretary of the treasury would be an impossible one.[2] He never suspected for one moment that the friend he was counting on for help would oppose every plan he had for the nation's economy. In the end, the battle between them would wreck Hamilton's own political career and send Madison, and his even dearer friend Thomas Jefferson, to the White House.

From the tone of the letter he sent to Madison on October 12, 1789, Hamilton seemed both excited and overwhelmed at the task at hand. "May I ask of your friendship," he wrote, "to put to paper and send me your thoughts on such objects as may have occurred to you for an addition to our revenue." Hamilton knew the problem was not so much in finding ways to raise revenue. There were many "objects" or ways to increase funds. Instead, the real problem would come from the many "prejudices" against "almost every object" or proposed method for raising those same funds. No matter what Hamilton might devise with the help of his friend Madison, he knew there would be opposition. But he also knew that the nation must come up with a solution to fix its financial woes quickly. He told Madison that he would have a complete plan ready for the upcoming session of Congress.[3]

Hamilton's *Report on Public Credit*

Hamilton went to work immediately on his *Report on Public Credit*. It would take him nearly three months of intense work to finish it in time for the opening of the next session of Congress in January 1790. He was inspired by the message he had received from the members of Congress, which asked him to shore up the nation's public credit. The reputation and good name of the United States depended on the ability of the country to pay its debts. The government must fulfill its obligations and so preserve the "honor and prosperity" of the nation under the new Constitution. Hamilton was convinced that he heard the sure and steady voice of his friend James Madison in these words.[4] From his many conversations with Madison, since they first met seven years before, he was certain that his ally in the House wished him to proceed in three important directions. First and foremost, the enormous debt of the United States must be "funded," meaning paid or leveraged in some way. Second, the current bondholders would have to be paid in this scheme. Any attempt to locate and reimburse the original bondholders would be impossible. Finally, the remaining state debts incurred during the Revolution must be "assumed" or paid by the national government.[5]

As Hamilton worked on his report, he saw himself continuing in a relationship he first developed with Madison when they both served together in Congress. Madison had come up to Philadelphia as a representative from Virginia in 1780, while Hamilton, fresh from his heroics at the battle of Yorktown, arrived as a delegate from New York in the fall of 1782. Immediately, Hamilton recognized that James Madison of Virginia was the head of a growing party of nationalists to which he himself belonged. Many of the young politicians in this group had little in common with the generation of politicians, such as Samuel Adams, for example, who dominated the proceedings. These men were nearly thirty years older than both Madison and Hamilton. They had come of age leading the fight against Great Britain that culminated in the Declaration of Independence in 1776. Their careers were tied to this event, and now in the following decade, they continued to espouse the same principles that had launched their careers. Above all else, they hated taxation and opposed it as an abuse of power by any government that used it. The rising debt of the nation did not frighten them as much as concentrated wealth and power did. They also blocked any attempt to strengthen the national government, fearing it would become as dangerous to freedom as the king and Parliament had once been.

Unlike this older generation of congressional leaders, Madison stood at the head of a group of younger politicians who saw the American Revolution not as the culmination of their careers but as the beginning. Their public lives were bound to the nation and its success, rather than to a local community or a state. Their political outlook had been shaped not in the colonial assemblies but in the Continental Army and the Confederation Congress. Many of them were frustrated in Philadelphia as they listened to the same arguments over and over against taking any measures to repair the ruined finances of the nation. The younger politicians were more worried about the damage that the growing debt and the inability to raise operating funds could do to the government and so to the nation. In their opinion, the older men who had launched the revolution were in danger of sinking the nation into ruin by clinging to principles that were now out of date. The Congress must raise money to support functions proper to an independent government and to leverage the debt, even if this meant levying taxes on the people.[6]

Hamilton always remembered that it was Madison who led the way in attempting to straighten out the finances of the United States in the early 1780s. While he was neither a dazzling writer nor a fiery orator, Madison commanded the respect of his peers by the sheer brilliance of his logic and the quiet persistence of his arguments. He was excellent at shaping policy behind the scenes, and he had a command of political theory and practical necessities that was nothing short of astounding. While he understood that states were wary of government grown too powerful, he was convinced that certain problems could be dealt with only at the national level. These included not just the Revolutionary War debt but also the army that had not been paid, the western territory that America had won only on paper, and the European powers that scoffed at American independence. As early as 1783, Madison also raised the issue of whether the government set up under the Articles of Confederation could meet the challenges facing his young nation. Every battle in Congress and between the states over how to pay the debt or solve any other problem invariably led to a debate on what the Articles of Confederation actually meant.[7]

In this political chaos, Madison and Hamilton joined forces over the issue they both believed was most pressing. Congress must first craft a financial plan for the nation and then be given the power to enforce it. The two young men made a powerful team. Hamilton was clearly the junior partner, while Madison was the leader. This can be seen in the resolutions both men worked on in February 1783 urging the older generation to face the economic problems of the present. Hamilton's version read as follows: "Resolved, that it is in the opinion of Congress that complete justice cannot be done to the creditors of the United States, nor restoration of public credit be effected, nor the future exigencies of the war provided for, but by the establishment of permanent and adequate funds to operate generally throughout the United States, to be collected by Congress."[8] The resolution was never introduced to Congress. Instead, a similar version written by Madison, which struck out the words "to be collected by Congress," was placed before the Congress. Even though Madison's version was milder than Hamilton's, it still went down to defeat.

All was not lost, however, for the team of Madison and Hamilton. On March 6, 1783, Madison introduced his *Report on Restoring Public Credit* to the Congress. The plan called for vesting power in the Congress to levy a 5 percent tariff on all imports. The tax would be collected by the individual states at the point of entry. The states would be allowed to appoint the collectors of these duties. The money could be held by the states until Congress requested the funds. An annual report would also be sent to the states describing how much had been collected. The tariff would be used over a period of twenty-five years to pay the interest and the principal on the debt from the war. All "reasonable expenses" incurred by the states in prosecuting the war would be assumed by the nation. After much debate and many revisions, Madison's Revenue Acts were finally approved by Congress on April 18, 1783. Hamilton later said that Madison had come up with the plan totally on his own. He had turned to no one for advice on it. While Hamilton disagreed with several specifics in the plan, he joined with fellow congressman Oliver Ellsworth in helping Madison write an address to the states in support of the proposal. According to the Articles of Confederation, the states would have to give their unanimous consent to Madison's plan if it was to become law. In order to win the support of all the states, Congress ordered the address to be published as a pamphlet.[9]

To this day, the "Address to the States," the writing of which was credited solely to James Madison, remains a powerful statement on the need for sound public credit in light of the ideals of the American Revolution. Madison gave his readers the grim facts and figures first. He said the debt of the United States amounted to $42,375,000. The annual interest on this debt was $2,415,956. The Revenue Acts proposed by Congress would at least be able to pay the interest on the debt. If the principal could not be paid, then new loans might be secured to pay the debt. A natural increase in commerce or possibly the sale of the "vacant territory" in the West might also provide funds that would be used to pay down the principal on the national debt.

After laying out the specific problems involved in leveraging the debt, Madison reminded his readers that the debt was owed to real people. It must be paid to the nation's allies as well as to its soldiers, "*that illustrious & patriotic band of fellow-citizens,* whose blood and whose bravery have defended the liberties of their country." It must also be paid to a "remaining class of creditors" who had "lent to the public the use of their funds," either directly as the original lenders or by receiving transfers from those same lenders. While Madison recognized that discriminating between the merits of all these creditors would be "a task equally unnecessary & invidious," somehow the debt must be paid for the good of the nation and the principles upon which the country was founded. "Let it be remembered finally that it has ever been the pride and boast of America," Madison explained in his conclusion, "that the rights for which she contended were the rights of human nature." God, the author of these rights, had poured out his blessings on the thirteen original colonies. Now the citizens of the United States held these same rights in "the greatest trust ever confided to a political society." If the United States succeeded, then people everywhere would benefit, but if the brave young nation failed, she would sink into tyranny, like the societies of old, and all humankind would suffer. If the thirteen states did not cease to fight among themselves, then they would have thrown off the tyranny of the king and Parliament only to replace it with the tyranny of the worst in human nature.[10]

While the two young friends shared many of the same ideas on government and finance, they were also bound together by the experience of one terrible day in the Congress that showed them the tyranny possible in human nature. In June 1783 they both peered through the windows of the Pennsylvania State House as a mob of angry soldiers gathered in front of the Congress. The men had never been paid for their services in the Continental Army, and so they had come to Philadelphia to demand justice. While at first there was no immediate danger from the crowd, Madison noticed that "spirituous drink from the tippling houses adjoining began to be liberally served out to the Soldiers."[11] Fearing the drunken mob might turn on them, and with no assurance from the local authorities that they would be protected, the Congress decided to leave Philadelphia and head to Princeton. The soldiers taunted the congressmen as they left the State House. Hamilton would always remember the angry faces turned toward him as he came down the steps and the bitter jeers thrown at him and his fellow congressmen. "The licentiousness of an army is to be dreaded in every government," he later wrote, "but in a republic it is to be more particularly restrained, and when directed against the civil authority to be checked with energy and punished with severity."[12]

The two friends parted company shortly after this incident. Hamilton left the Congress in late July, while Madison returned home to Virginia to straighten out his own finances. He was not long out of politics, however, and was soon elected to the Virginia Assembly in Richmond. Historians often focus on Madison's fight to win a complete separation of church and state at this time. However, a closer look at his actual activities in Virginia politics shows that he was an equally strong advocate of sound fiscal policies. Madison openly opposed the financial plans of

Governor Patrick Henry. One of the most brilliant leaders of the older generation of American politicians who had launched the revolution, Henry recommended that no taxes be collected in the state of Virginia in 1784. Madison fought a brave battle against this proposal and won payment of taxes in tobacco and other commodities rather than hard currency. He also told his fellow Virginians that they could not ignore provisions in the Treaty of Paris that required payments to Loyalists whose property had been confiscated during the American Revolution. Finally, and most importantly in the eyes of Hamilton, who kept an eye on his friend at a distance, Madison opposed any move toward the use of paper money, which he believed would only damage the economy further and sink Virginia, and so the nation, deeper and deeper into debt.

Like Hamilton, Madison was dedicated to the idea that government should promote and regulate trade. He proposed legislation that would dredge the James River and link it to major western rivers through the building of canals. He also made certain that representatives from Virginia sat alongside representatives from Maryland on the commission that would determine which state controlled the Potomac River. Madison caused his greatest sensation in the Virginia Assembly when he introduced a bill that allowed foreign ships to land only in Norfolk and Alexandria. He said this would reduce smuggling and make sure that duties were collected in an orderly manner. Despite the protests of Governor Henry, and even the concerns of his friend Thomas Jefferson, the bill passed once a few more Virginia cities were added to list of acceptable ports.[13]

Madison and Hamilton met again at the Annapolis Convention in September 1786. Virginia had called the convention to discuss problems with the Articles of Confederation. Under the Articles, the Congress had little authority to regulate commerce, an issue that had become increasingly important to George Washington, who was interested in building canals to link the Potomac, Monongahela, and Ohio rivers. As his actions in the Virginia Assembly had shown, James Madison was equally interested in canals that would link Virginia with the West. It would be impossible to begin such projects if the nation had no way of regulating business between the states. While Virginia had invited representatives from all thirteen states to come to Annapolis, only five states responded, including New York, which sent Alexander Hamilton. Even with this small representation, Madison joined forces once again with his friend Hamilton, as they had once done in their days together in the Congress, and led the way in calling for a revision of the Articles of Confederation to strengthen the power of the national government. Madison guided the younger Hamilton in the writing of the official call to the states for a convention in Philadelphia. Hamilton boldly proclaimed that "these States, to be happy, must have a stronger bond of Union and a confederation capable of drawing forth the resources of the country."[14] Madison's major change in Hamilton's proclamation was to tone down the attack on the current

Congress. He feared that the power of this body would be undermined before a new stronger system was in place.

At the Constitutional Convention, the two friends often disagreed over the best system of government to set up for their nation. Questions related to economic theory were rarely the main focus of the debates. But on July 26, 1787, when a discussion on the relationship between inequality and liberty took center stage, the two friends were allies once again. The issue arose during the debate over the length of terms for senators. Many feared that the Senate would become an aristocracy if the terms were too long. If the wealthy dominated the Senate, would liberty be destroyed? Madison became frustrated during the long debate over whether six-, seven-, or nine-year terms would better protect liberty. At one point, he reminded the delegates that they were deciding forever the fate of republican government. If for no other reason than that, they must determine how long a senator was to serve. The real issue in the debate was a practical one. The members of the Convention must create a stable political structure for their nation. Madison also said that inequality in property would always exist in a republic. It was not a threat to liberty but was in fact caused by liberty.

Speaking in support of his friend, Hamilton called himself as "zealous an advocate of liberty as any man whatever" and "trusted he should be as willing a martyr to it."[15] He agreed that the very fate of republican government was being decided in their hands. They must set as high a tone as possible for the new government. He also warned that they must not get sidetracked over the issue of liberty when they were actually deciding stability. Madison recorded Hamilton's arguments in his own notes: "He concurred also in the general observations of Mr. Madison on the subject. . . . It was certainly true that nothing like an equality of property existed; that an inequality would exist as long as liberty existed; and that it would unavoidably result from that very liberty itself."[16]

Once the Constitution was formally adopted on September 17, 1787, Hamilton and Madison worked more closely than ever to win its passage. They both knew that large states, like their own Virginia and New York, must back the Constitution or it would fail. They were certain that such a failure would mean the ultimate end of the United States of America, which would quickly dissolve into separate states. They threw themselves into the battle over ratification, which now began in earnest. The nation was soon divided between the Federalists who supported the Constitution and the Anti-Federalists who opposed it. Some of the bitterest opposition to the Constitution could be found in Hamilton's home state of New York. Like the other large states, New York had become a power in its own right under the Articles of Confederation. The state had grown rich by laying tariffs on goods imported from other states and nations. Many people in New York were in no mood to surrender their position to a more powerful national government.

Hamilton decided that a newspaper campaign would be the best way to persuade his state to support the Constitution. He first enlisted John Jay, a fellow New Yorker, to help him, but quickly turned to the man whose thinking was closest to his own, the brilliant James Madison.[17] All three decided to write essays defending the Constitution. In the end, Jay wrote only a handful of the eighty-five pieces, while Hamilton and Madison wrote the rest. These essays ran several times a week in four out of the five newspapers in New York throughout the spring of 1788. Collectively they became known as the *Federalist Papers.* Originally directed "To the People of the State of New York," they remain to this day the single greatest defense ever written of the Constitution and the government it brought to life. They are also a testament to just how similar Madison and Hamilton were in their understanding of political principles and in their hope for the future of their new nation at this time.

The first half of their essays attacked the weak national government created under the Articles of Confederation. Hamilton and Madison reminded their readers that the problems created by this weak government had led to the Constitutional Convention in Philadelphia. The Congress under the Articles of Confederation had few powers, while the individual states retained full sovereignty in almost every important political matter. The greatest flaw in the Articles of Confederation was the inability of the Congress to levy taxes. This meant that the national government could not raise an army or navy and thus could not provide for the common defense. Equally important, the Congress had little control over domestic or foreign trade since each state could set its own policies. If this weak government were allowed to continue, then the United States would soon be on the brink of foreign invasion, domestic unrest, and, most importantly, financial ruin.[18]

In the second half of the *Federalist,* Hamilton and Madison emphasized the strengths of the new government formed under the Constitution. Both men stated that experienced and competent men had written the Constitution in a spirit of compromise. The new government they had created would provide the nation with the best form of republican government possible, while at the same time it would prevent the worst abuses of uncontrolled democracy. They lauded the separation of powers between the legislative, executive, and judicial branches. Hamilton especially emphasized the fact that the bicameral national legislature would provide the checks and balances necessary for a stable government. The last part of the *Federalist* would have a profound effect on later interpreters of the Constitution, especially justices of the Supreme Court, who have consistently considered these documents as profoundly important as the Constitution itself.[19]

For the most part, the two friends wrote their articles separately. But in the case of *Federalist* Nos. 18, 19, and 20, they collaborated. These essays are miniature history lessons in which Madison and Hamilton, acting as the teachers of their young nation, described the failures of three other confederations in the past. They began with the story of the ancient Greek city-states. The Peloponnesian League was an attempt to link Greece together in a loose confederation where a council would pass laws for the benefit of all the city-states. Sadly, the jealousy of Sparta wrecked the league and made Rome's conquest of Greece inevitable. Madison and Hamilton were clearly directing a warning to the bickering states under the Articles of Confederation when they wrote, "By these arts, this union, the last hope of Greece, the last hope of ancient liberty, was torn into pieces." In the next article, the two friends told the story of the rivalries in medieval Europe that kept Germany from becoming a united and powerful nation. They explained how Germany was a place where emperors, princes, and states had battled against each other since the fall of Rome. Again as a warning to the thirteen American states, which refused to unite under the rule of a powerful national government, the two men explained that the "history of Germany is a history of wars." In the final article on which they collaborated, Madison and Hamilton described the United Netherlands as a confederacy "of a very remarkable texture" that nevertheless had been torn apart by petty jealousies from within and foreign invasions from without. "Experience is the oracle of truth," Madison and Hamilton concluded at the end of these three articles. Only a government like the one proposed in the Constitution could unite the states and prevent the descent into chaos that was inevitable in a confederation.[20]

Once the Constitution was adopted, Hamilton turned his attention to New York state politics, while Madison returned home and ran for a seat in the new House of Representatives. Patrick Henry so disliked him that he had redrawn the district lines hoping Madison would be defeated. Madison and his opponent, close friend James Monroe, went on a memorable debating circuit in the bitterly cold winter that left Madison's nose frostbitten and scarred for life. Madison won the election and headed to Philadelphia, where he organized the House and became a top advisor to President Washington. On the floor of the House of Representatives, he became a leading advocate of a strong secretary of the treasury. He argued that the secretary should have the power to prepare plans for improving the revenue and supporting the public credit. Some congressmen were worried that this was a dangerous precedent to set since it took the power to originate revenue bills away from the House. Madison disagreed, arguing that he saw no danger in the proposal. Surely, he explained, it was far more dangerous for the nation to lack well-formed plans for a sound financial future.[21]

Madison quickly became a champion of those who sought to fund the government of the United States properly. Instead of fighting taxation, he did his best to find a way both to sustain the new national government and handle the debt built up since the revolution. Madison believed that the tariff was the best way to raise funds in a country where local and national loyalties were so deeply divided. His idea met with stiff resistance as each section of the country fought for its own economic interests. Several northern states demanded protective tariffs to strengthen their own infant industries, while southern states called for low tariffs on the luxury items they imported in exchange for the cash crops they grew. Madison made a name for himself in the often bitter debates by always stressing the importance of the nation over the states. In the end, he won approval for the Tariff of 1789, which called for a 5 percent tax on most imports, although some duties ran as high as 50 percent. New Englanders especially grumbled that the Virginian and his supporters had pushed the duty on molasses up to 2½ cents a gallon.[22]

In November of that same year, Madison finally responded to Hamilton's request for advice on the report on public credit. After explaining that his delay in writing had been caused by an illness, Madison said that both the foreign and domestic debt must be paid. But since he had no firm ideas on the "modification of the public debt," he told Hamilton that he "ought perhaps to be silent." Even with such momentary self-doubt, Madison did make four specific suggestions. There should be an excise on home distilleries. He thought it could be crafted like the "Scotch Tax," which taxed home distilleries in Scotland based on their size. This tax would in turn necessitate an increase on duties on imported liquor. Madison also called for a land tax since it would be the most simple, certain, and equitable way to raise revenue. If Hamilton agreed, then Madison urged him to implement the land tax quickly before the states could object. His final suggestion was a stamp tax on proceedings of the federal court.[23]

The letter confirmed for Hamilton that he was following in the footsteps that his friend James Madison had laid down for him. In many respects, he saw the writing of the *Report on Public Credit* as the culmination of a joint endeavor that had brought the two men together from their days in the Congress through their fight for the ratification of the Constitution. Hamilton heartily agreed with Madison that the foreign and national debt must be paid. He calculated that the United States owed more than $11 million to foreign nations and more than $40 million to its own citizens. He argued that the foreign debt must be paid according to the exact terms of the original loan agreements. He recommended that the domestic debt be funded at par. This would be accomplished by calling in outstanding government securities and issuing new bonds of the same value in their place. The national government would also assume the remaining debts of the individual states and pay them off under similar terms. Finally, a sinking fund would be established to guarantee payment of both the interest and principal of the national debt. Hamilton recommended that the foreign debt be paid by taking out new loans overseas. This would prevent a serious cash drain from the American economy. The domestic debt could be funded through an increase in duties on imports and tonnage. More money could be raised by placing new duties on imported wines, distilled spirits, tea, and coffee.[24]

Madison's Response to Hamilton's Report

Alexander Hamilton was stunned when his friend James Madison, author of the "Address to the States," came to him just days before the debate on the report was about to begin to tell him that he would oppose it on several key points. He now favored "discrimination," a policy that would pay the original owners of government securities as well as the current ones. Madison said it was unfair that the patriotic people who bought the securities would get nothing while greedy speculators who had purchased those same securities would make a killing. He also opposed the assumption of state debts by the national government since Virginia and most of the other southern states had already paid off their debts. He demanded that Hamilton go back and recalculate state debts as of 1783. Hamilton was in shock since these two positions meant that Madison had completely reversed the stands he had taken on these matters since the early 1780s. In deference to his longtime political ally, whose intellect and honesty he so respected, Hamilton tried to work out a scheme where both ideas would be possible. But he finally became convinced that neither was workable. There was simply no way to track down all the owners of the securities. Similarly, it was unheard of to repay a debt that was already paid. Hamilton convinced most representatives in Congress of the "inexpediency" of discrimination. The House defeated Madison's call for discrimination by a vote of 36 to 13 but remained deadlocked over the assumption of state debts by the national government, voting the measure down by 31 to 29.[25]

Hamilton's Perspective on His Rift with Madison

This is the point in the story where most historians join sides with Madison and eventually Jefferson against Hamilton. Looking ahead and seeing Hamilton as the future mastermind of the Federalist Party, they cannot admit that at this moment in time the secretary of the treasury was not the leader of a faction. Instead, he was a man who was dumbfounded at the actions of his friend and political ally. From Hamilton's point of view, Madison seemed to have abandoned overnight the positions he had steadily supported for nearly a decade. As he struggled to work out a compromise with his friend and so the Congress, Hamilton also seemed unaware of just how much Madison was influenced by his even closer friend, Thomas Jefferson, who had returned from France in December 1789 to assume his new role as Washington's secretary of state.

The fact that Hamilton did not understand the dynamics at work in the relationship between the two Virginians can be seen in a story Jefferson told years later in his "Anas." Though some historians doubt how accurate the story actually is, the tale that Jefferson tells makes sense if viewed within the context of Hamilton's friendship with Madison. Jefferson long remembered an afternoon when he approached President Washington's home in Philadelphia. He saw Hamilton looking somewhat overwrought, walking back and forth on the path in front of the house. He was obviously waiting for Jefferson and took hold of him, refusing to let him go until he unburdened himself about the impasse in the Congress over funding and assumption. Hamilton was convinced that the very fabric of the nation would come undone if the measures did not pass and the nation sank further into debt. As Jefferson tells it, before he knew what was happening, Hamilton had arranged a dinner later that evening with Madison. At that dinner, Hamilton won the approval of the Virginians for funding and assumption in exchange for moving the nation's capital to the Potomac River. The story clearly shows that Hamilton was confused by Madison's opposition and so turned to Jefferson to win his support. There was no sense in Hamilton's actions that he considered Madison's opposition a break in their alliance or their friendship. He remained convinced that somehow a compromise could be worked out and personal harmony restored. He also did not seem to suspect just how much Jefferson disagreed with him and despised him.[26]

Hamilton and Madison Split on the Tariff and Bank

At the same time that he submitted his *Report on Public Credit,* Hamilton also submitted his first recommendations to Congress regarding the tariff. Once again, it was Madison who rose to oppose the tariff in the House of Representatives. Hamilton had reported that the nation needed nearly $3 million to pay for government operating expenses as well as the interest on foreign and domestic debts. He suggested an increase in duties on imported wines, distilled spirits, tea, and coffee along with an excise tax on domestic spirits. Madison had recommended a similar excise tax on domestic spirits in 1783. But now, with a majority of his fellow congressmen bitterly opposed to the excise tax on domestic spirits, Madison crafted a bill that only increased duties on imports. The Tariff of 1790 quickly passed both the House and Senate and became law in September 1790. The bill essentially raised duties on all articles specified in the Tariff of 1789 by 50 percent. Higher duties were also placed on all manufactured goods.[27]

Overcoming his dismay that Madison had again opposed him, Hamilton was relieved that funding and assumption had passed along with a new tariff bill. He even considered the tariff an enlightened one since Madison had included a protective element in it to support manufacturing. Hamilton had just begun work on his *Report on Manufactures,* which would include Madison's idea on protective tariffs along with Washington's call to promote manufacturing as part of the national defense. As he worked on these issues, he also turned to his *Report on the Bank,* which was delivered to Congress in December 1790. He was convinced that the nation needed such a bank to increase the amount of capital in the country that could in turn be invested in trade and industry. The bank could also loan money to the government during national emergencies. If the bank were founded, the United States would join the ranks of the other great commercial nations of the world. In the end, Hamilton proposed that Congress charter the Bank of the United States for twenty-year periods that were renewable. The government would issue $10 million of stock at a cost of $400 per share. The national government would own 20 percent of the stock, while the remaining 80 percent would be sold to private investors. A twenty-five-member board of directors would govern the bank. Each director must be a citizen of the United States and would also hold stock in the bank. Five of the directors would be appointed by the government. The directors would in turn choose the governor of the bank.[28]

Once he delivered his report, Hamilton was thankful that the plan for the Bank of the United States passed the Senate without even a roll call vote. When the bill was introduced in the House, he hoped that Madison would find no flaw in the proposal but would instead support the measure. However, Madison did find a flaw in the bill's constitutionality. In a bitter debate with Congressman Fisher Ames of Massachusetts, a supporter of Hamilton, Madison attacked the bank as unconstitutional. While he was not against banks on principle, he was against this specific charter for a national bank since nowhere in the Constitution was such a power granted. It did not fall under the power of the government to tax and could not be seen as a part of the "necessary and proper" clause. Any benefit that might come to the nation from the bank could be achieved by other means clearly allowed in the Constitution, such as taxation, loans from individuals, or other banks. Despite Madison's opposition, the bill passed the House and headed to President Washington for signing. But Washington hesitated and asked his secretary of state and his secretary of the treasury to write reports on the constitutionality of the matter. Jefferson restated many of Madison's ideas, while Hamilton argued that the "necessary and proper" clause of the Constitution allowed for the creation of the bank. He used Madison's own description of the same clause in his *Federalist* No. 44 to bolster his argument. Madison had expressed his absolute faith in the "necessary and proper" clause just three years before by writing, "Few parts of the Constitution have been assailed with more intemperance than this; yet on a fair investigation of it, no part can appear more completely invulnerable. Without the substance of this power, the whole Constitution would be a dead letter." Agreeing with Hamilton, Washington signed the bank bill into law on February 24, 1791.[29]

Hamilton's *Report on Manufactures*

Hamilton was only slowly coming to realize that every proposal he made to Congress would cause an immediate reaction from Madison, even if the measures he proposed were originally called for by Madison. He saw this most clearly when he finally introduced his *Report on Manufactures* to the Congress in December 1791. In the report, Hamilton made thirty specific recommendations, primarily on raising tariffs to promote American manufacturing. The Congress took up Hamilton's recommendations during the debate over the Tariff of 1792. Washington had asked Congress to raise more money for the protection of the western frontier. A confederation of Ohio tribes had defeated an American army led by General Arthur St. Clair in November 1791. A new army must be sent west to defeat the tribes and open Ohio for settlement. Hamilton reported to Congress that $525,950 must be raised to equip the new army. This money could come from three possible sources. First, interest in the Bank of the United States could be sold. Second, the money could be loaned. Finally, taxes could be raised. Hamilton recommended the third option and asked Congress to increase import duties in the Tariff of 1792. While the new tariff began as an emergency revenue measure, it would also allow Hamilton to incorporate many of the recommendations made in his *Report on Manufactures.* Madison once again opposed Hamilton's plans, not because of the protective tariffs involved but because the report called for "bounties" to be paid by the government for new enterprises. Madison said this went beyond the powers delegated to Congress in the Constitution. After a bruising session in the House, a tariff bill was finally passed in May 1792 with the Congress incorporating twenty-six of Hamilton's thirty original recommendations from his *Report on Manufactures.*[30]

It was in the tough battle over the Tariff of 1792 that Hamilton finally decided that a "faction," led by Madison with the cooperation of Jefferson, was at work in his struggle with his old friend. During the previous year, a newspaper called the *National Gazette* began operation in the city of Philadelphia. The paper openly attacked Hamilton as an elitist, a monarchist, and a plutocrat, while it praised Jefferson practically as a demigod. Hamilton learned that a man named Philip Freneau was the editor of the paper. It did not take the secretary of the treasury long to discover that Freneau was an employee of the State Department and had been brought to Philadelphia by Thomas Jefferson just three days after the bank bill was passed. The pieces suddenly fell into place for Hamilton, who concluded that the wholesale assault on his policies had been as much the work of Jefferson as Madison. The classic battle between Hamilton and the Federalists on the one hand and Jefferson and the Democratic-Republicans on the other had begun. From the moment he made the connection between Freneau and the *National Gazette* in 1792 until his death in a duel at the hands of Aaron Burr in 1804, Hamilton opposed Jefferson, and along with him his former friend Madison, on every political issue of the day, including most notably the French Revolution, American neutrality, and Jay's Treaty.

In 1795 Hamilton resigned his post as the secretary of the treasury, saying he could not afford to support a wife and his many children on his small government salary. In his remaining years, he often brooded on what had gone wrong during his brief term of service to his country. "Am I a fool, a romantic Quixote," he asked his friend Rufus King, "or is there a constitutional defect in the American mind?"[31] He had started out with the certain hope that he could place the United States on a firm financial footing with the support of James Madison. But almost immediately upon the start of his service as secretary of the treasury, Hamilton found his old friend blocking his path at every turn. He would always look back at this time with bitterness and blame Thomas Jefferson for ruining his friendship and so his political alliance with James Madison. Jefferson, he believed, had returned from France with a polluted view of government as an evil entity that must be crushed at every turn. Jefferson, in turn, had polluted the brightest mind in America, James Madison, against the power of government. While he was angry at Madison, thinking he was not as honest and simple a person as he once believed, Hamilton never attacked him with quite the same fury as he did Jefferson. Some small flicker of their friendship seemed to remain alive in him and he preferred to think of Madison as misguided.[32]

Perspectives on the Hamilton-Madison Rift

Like any other human relationship, the end of the friendship between Hamilton and Madison must be viewed from many different perspectives. First and foremost, the brilliance of Hamilton's *Report on Public Credit* must be taken into consideration. This profound document remains a difficult read for even the most dedicated scholars of the early republic. Once presented to Congress, it shifted the dynamics of the relationship between the two men. Since the day when they had first met, Madison, not Hamilton, had been recognized as the greatest proponent of economic reform in the nation. But now James Madison found himself outpaced by an even more adept economic thinker. Although he had argued for a policy-making secretary of the treasury, Madison was up in arms when the man he recommended did just what he had asked him to do. The former leader suddenly found himself thrust into the background. Similarly, Jefferson, who had been overseas during the struggle to write and ratify the Constitution, returned to a United States that was greatly changed. He, too, was no longer considered the most brilliant man in the nation. That position had surely passed to the secretary of the treasury.

The friendship also ended because positions that James Madison took when he was in Congress looked different once those same positions were presented to him by another branch of the government. Madison and Hamilton were no longer standing side by side in the Congress but on opposite corners of a triangle of power that they had helped create. Like chess pieces in a great political game, Madison had remained in the legislative branch while Hamilton had moved to the executive. Suddenly, Madison could view his former opinions from a different perspective and so see consequences in them that he had never seen before. When Hamilton laid his *Report on Public Credit* before the Congress, Madison suddenly saw the potential danger of the financial system that he had long recommended. If the nation created such a system, then the wealthiest citizens might take advantage of it. They could control the finances of the nation and so direct its politics. Surely it was happening already in Hamilton's own Treasury Department. In contrast, it took Hamilton longer to understand that a shift in power had occurred. Along with Madison, he had been the most relentless critic of the government under the Articles of Confederation while in Congress. But now standing in the executive corner of the Constitution's triangle of power, opposition from the legislature appeared troublesome and even dangerous. Hamilton in the executive branch now saw Madison's opposition in the legislature as an obstructionist tendency that could tear the fragile republic apart. He was certain that, in a desperate bid for power, his opponents would say anything to win votes, only to abandon those same positions once elected. Men as intelligent as Jefferson and Madison could use their brilliance to become demagogues.

Lastly, the conflict between these two former friends must be seen as a power struggle made possible by the very government that both men fought so hard to create. The Constitution made an enormous amount of political power available to ambitious men. They could use that power for the good of the nation as they saw fit. That former friends could become mortal enemies as they reached for this power was an unintended consequence of the Constitution. Because the Constitution worked, Madison and Hamilton became enemies. The end of the friendship between these two men revealed still one more consequence of the Constitution that neither man had foreseen. It made possible the rise of political parties that kept the conflict between them alive without destroying the republic they both loved so well.

Notes

1. Alexander Hamilton to James Madison, October 12, 1789, in *The Papers of Alexander Hamilton,* ed. Harold C. Syrett (New York: Columbia University Press, 1961–87), 5:39 (hereafter cited as *PAH*).

2. Irving Brant, *James Madison: Father of the Constitution, 1787–1800* (Indianapolis, IN: Bobbs-Merrill, 1950), 281; Alexander Hamilton to Edward Carrington, May 26, 1782, in *Alexander Hamilton: Writings,* ed. Joanne B. Freeman (New York: Library of America, 2001), 736 (hereafter cited as *Hamilton Writings*).

3. Hamilton to Madison, October 12, 1789, *PAH,* 5:39.

4. Hamilton, *Report on Public Credit, Hamilton Writings,* 531.

5. Hamilton to Carrington, May 26, 1782, *Hamilton Writings,* 737.

6. Ralph Ketcham, *James Madison: A Biography* (New York: Macmillan, 1971), 117–18.

7. Martin Meyers, ed., *The Mind of the Founder: Sources of the Political Thought of James Madison* (Hanover, NH: University Press of New England, 1981), 17–18; a clear statement on Madison's views on the national debt and the Articles of Confederation in 1783 can be found in his "Speech in the Continental Congress on Revenue," in *James Madison: Writings,* ed. Jack Rakove (New York: Library of America, 1999), 17–20.

8. Hamilton, "Continental Congress Motion on the Establishment of Permanent Funds, February 12, 1783," *PAH,* 3:252–53.

9. James Madison, *Report on Restoring Public Credit, March 6, 1783,* in *The Papers of James Madison,* ed. William T. Hutchinson et al., 17 vols. (Chicago: University of Chicago Press; Charlottesville: University Press of Virginia, 1962–91), 6:311–16; although Hamilton remembered that Madison had written the report totally on his own, Hamilton's "Notes on a Plan for Providing for the Debt of the United States, January-April 1783" was found among Madison's papers, indicating that there was collaboration between the two friends on this important matter; see ibid., 6:248–49 for Hamilton's notes.

10. Perhaps because the work sounds so much like Hamilton, Madison's stirring "Address to the States" rarely makes it into collections of his writings; however, "Address to the States, by the United States in Congress Assembled" can be found in its entirety in Meyers, *Mind of the Founder,* 23–32, quotations at 31 and 32, emphasis in original. A page of the original pamphlet can also be seen in volume 6 of *Papers of James Madison.*

11. Ketcham, *James Madison,* 142.

12. Alexander Hamilton to John Dickinson, September 25–30, 1783, *PAH,* 3:451.

13. Irving Brant, *James Madison: The Nationalist* (Indianapolis: Bobbs-Merrill, 1950), 317, 361–62; historians should carefully review volume 8 of *Papers of James Madison* to gain a fuller understanding of Madison as more than a champion of church and state separation at this time; for examples in volume 8, see Madison's "Bill Restricting Foreign Vessels to Certain Virginia Ports, June 8, 1784," 64–66; "Resolutions Supporting Virginia Members of a Potomac River Commission, June 28, 1784," 89–90; "Bill Providing Funds for a James River Canal, December 18, 1784," 192–94.

14. Quote is taken from Hamilton's "Vindication of Congress," in *Alexander Hamilton and the Founding of the Nation,* ed. Richard Morris (New York: Dial, 1957), 87–88; for the call for the Constitutional Convention to the legislatures of Virginia, Delaware, Pennsylvania, New Jersey, and New York, see Hamilton, "Address of the Annapolis Convention, September 14, 1786," *Hamilton Writings,* 142–45.

15. James Madison, *Notes of Debates in the Federal Convention of 1787 Reported by James Madison,* ed. Adrienne Koch (New York: W. W. Norton, 1987), 196.

16. James Madison, "Notes in Convention, Tuesday, June 26," in *The Constitutional Convention: A Narrative History from the Notes of James Madison,* ed. Edward J. Larson and Michael L. Winship (New York: Modern Library, 2005), 56–59.

17. Hamilton to James Madison, May 19, 1788, *Hamilton Writings,* 418–19.

18. Alexander Hamilton, James Madison, and John Jay, *The Federalist Papers* (New York: New American Library, 1961), 33–255.

19. Ibid., 255–527.

20. Ibid., quotations at 128, 130, and 138.

21. *Annals of Congress,* 1st Cong., 1st sess. May 20, 384–98 and June 25, 1789, 616–31.

22. Ty M. Reese, "Tariff of 1789," in *Encyclopedia of Tariffs and Trade in U.S. History,* ed. Cynthia Clark Northrup and Elaine C. Prange Turney (Westport, CT: Greenwood, 2003), 1:357.

23. James Madison to Alexander Hamilton, November 19, 1789, *PAH,* 6:525–27.

24. Hamilton, *Report on Public Credit, PAH,* 6:65–168.

25. Hamilton to Carrington, *Hamilton Writings,* 736–37; Freeman, "Chronology," in *Hamilton Writings,* 1042.

26. Thomas Jefferson, "The Anas," in *The Writings of Thomas Jefferson* (Washington, DC: Thomas Jefferson Memorial Association of the United States, 1903), 269–80.

27. Mary Stockwell, "The Tariff of 1790," in Northrup and Turney, *Encyclopedia of Tariffs and Trade,* 1:357.

28. Hamilton, *Report on the Bank, PAH,* 6:67–106.

29. Brant, *James Madison,* 327–33; *Federalist* No. 44, 225–32.

30. Hamilton, *Report on Manufactures, PAH,* 10:291–302; Mary Stockwell, "Tariff of 1792," in Northrup and Turney, *Encyclopedia of Tariffs and Trade,* 1:357–58.

31. Alexander Hamilton to Rufus King, February 21, 1795, *PAH,* 18:278–79.

32. Hamilton to Carrington, *Hamilton Writings,* 736–51.

STEFANO LUCONI

James Madison and Impeachment

Theory and Practice

Origins of the Impeachment Mechanism

In medieval England the House of Commons developed impeachment as a legal procedure to aid in its struggle to curb the absolutistic excesses of the monarchy.[1] Although the Commons could not directly hold the sovereigns accountable for their orders, it could hold the ministers who carried them out liable for misconduct, corruption, neglect of duty, and other crimes. The Commons could ascribe misdeeds and detested measures to royal officeholders, who became liable for giving "bad advice" as well, a code expression for advocating policies that Parliament opposed. Therefore, in the face of the postulated inviolability of the sovereigns, the Commons progressively transformed impeachment from an instrument to chastise breaches of the law by single officeholders into its preferred method for asserting its independence from, and control of, its executive counterpart. Consequently, as Bryce Lyon has remarked, "impeachment was the first effective means devised to control the crown" in medieval England.[2] Indeed, after the introduction of a parliamentary regime in the late seventeenth century, which made royal ministers directly responsible to the House of Commons, the practice of impeachment underwent a remarkable decline.[3] As a matter of fact, no public officer has been impeached or subjected to impeachment proceedings since the acquittal of Lord Melville, the First Lord of the Admiralty, who was accused of misappropriating funds in 1805.[4]

The use of impeachment in British North America mirrored in part the transformations it underwent in England. The earliest colonial example of a legal action that resembled the impeachment procedure occurred in 1635 when John Harvey, the royal governor of Virginia, was removed from office on charges of misfeasance and was sent to England for judgment.[5] Notwithstanding claims of the governor's abuse of power, Harvey's refusal to share his powers with the Council of Burgesses made a significant contribution to his discharge.[6] Actually, in the course of the seventeenth century, impeachment became the means by which representative assemblies asserted their independence from their respective governors and the latter's officeholders. In the decades that preceded the War of Independence, impeachment turned into a tool to express claims against British imperial rule.[7]

Discussions of Impeachment at the Constitutional Convention and Ratifying Conventions

The extent to which the British precedents influenced the elaboration of the impeachment provisions in the federal Constitution is controversial.[8] Nonetheless, the delegates to the Philadelphia Convention were aware that the impeachment proceedings had a remarkable potential for political use and misuse. Such a risk was especially clear to James Madison. Indeed, when fellow Virginian George Mason suggested at the Convention that "maladministration" should be included among the impeachable offenses for the president, Madison objected that such a "vague term" would "be equivalent to a tenure during the pleasure of the Senate." As a result, the delegates replaced the expression with the less disputable and more legally strict "high crimes & misdemeanors against the State."[9]

In 1785 Madison held that a combination of representatives from the executive, judiciary, and legislative branches made up the best court for impeachment.[10] At the Constitutional Convention, in order to safeguard the independence of the president from Congress, he preferred the Supreme Court, or another tribunal, to the Senate alone for the trial and opposed the proposal that impeached presidents be suspended from office until acquittal. Although his former suggestion was defeated, a majority of the Convention agreed on his latter stand and prevented additional opportunities for Congress to paralyze the chief executive's agenda by means of mere impeachment without conviction.[11]

Yet not even the final formulation of the impeachment clause was exempt from politicization. Commenting on the jurisdiction of impeachable crimes in *Federalist* No. 65, Alexander Hamilton clearly pointed out that such offenses "are of a nature which may with peculiar property be denominated *political,* as they relate chiefly to injuries done immediately to the society itself." In this context, Hamilton undoubtedly used the adjective "political" in its Greek etymological meaning, namely, with reference to the government of the republic. Although "political" did not necessarily signify "partisan" in Hamilton's eyes, he was unable to rule out factionary degenerations in the resort to impeachment. As he subsequently remarked in the same article, in the prosecution of impeachable crimes "there will always be the greatest danger that the decision will be regulated more by the comparative strength of parties than by the real demonstration of innocence or guilt."[12] Other voices also pointed to the politicizing of the impeachment process. For instance, arguing against the ratification of the Constitution, Arthur Lee of Virginia relayed his concerns that the mere displeasure of, or opposition to, the Senate would result in the impeachment of executive officers.[13]

Hamilton, who did not attend the Constitutional Convention during the debate on impeachment,[14] was so concerned with the politicization of such legal proceedings that he revived Madison's suggestion and contemplated an amendment to establish a less partisan court than the Senate alone. He therefore devised a larger body for the trial of impeachments that would include "the Senate, the Judges of the Supreme court of the United States and the first or senior judge for the time being of the highest court of general and ordinary common law jurisdiction in each state."[15] After Hamilton dropped his plan, one of his staunchest supporters in Congress, Egbert Benson of New York State, introduced a similar amendment in March 1791, but to no avail. Congress delayed the examination of the proposed amendment until its subsequent session, which took no further action.[16] In his 1788 remarks about the constitution of Virginia, Madison himself restated his own preference for a court of impeachment that was not limited to legislators.[17]

Although Madison endeavored to preclude the resort to impeachment as a tool of political warfare, he regarded this procedure as a viable instrument to punish illegal acts and decisions. For instance, while rejecting George Mason's objection to the chief executive's power of pardoning at the Virginia ratifying convention, Madison reassured the delegates that "if the President be connected in any suspicious matter, with any person, and there be ground to believe he will shelter him, the House of Representatives can impeach him; they can remove him if found guilty." Likewise, on the same occasion, when he outlined the treaty power provisions of the Constitution and argued that the president could not dodge the consent of the majority of the Senate, he added that "were the President to commit anything so atrocious as to summon only a few States [namely, senators]" he would be impeached for a "misdemeanor."[18]

Madison's Beliefs about the Scope of Impeachment

According to Madison, the punishment or prevention of abuses by means of impeachment should not be confined to the president only. During one of the 124 times he took the floor of the House of Representatives in the first session of the First Congress, he pointed out that "it is very possible that an officer who may not incur the displeasure of the President may be guilty of actions that ought to forfeit his place. The power of this House may reach him by means of an impeachment, and he may be removed even against the will of the President." In his view, an extensive interpretation of the impeachment provision afforded a necessary balance for the president's power of appointment and was "intended as a supplemental security for the good behavior of the public officers."[19] His words, therefore, echoed the original function of impeachment in medieval England as a means to remove evil favorites within the context of the separation of powers.

Yet, in Madison's opinion, extensive impeachment did not mean universal impeachment. Article II, Section 4, of the Constitution provides for dismissal "from office on impeachment" with reference to "the president, vice president and all civil officers of the United States." It did not seem, therefore, that this clause could be applied to other elected federal officials such as congressmen. Indeed, Madison argued in 1798 that "removal & disqualification, the punishments within the impeachment jurisdiction, were *chiefly* intended for offences in the Executive line."[20]

The Blount Impeachment

Unlike his previous theoretical statements, Madison made the latter assertion in connection with the proceedings against Senator William Blount of Tennessee and his alleged scheme to seize Spanish Florida and Louisiana in cooperation with Great Britain and her Indian allies.[21] On July 7, 1797, the House impeached Blount and, the following day, the Senate expelled him almost unanimously (twenty-five votes to one) on the grounds that his involvement in the conspiracy was "a high misdemeanor inconsistent with his public trust and duty as a Senator."[22] Blount's trial dragged on until January 11, 1799. The main controversy was not about Blount's participation in the intrigue, as his role in the plot had already been demonstrated and censured. Disagreement rested with whether a senator was a "civil officer" and belonged to the only category of U.S. citizens other than the president, the vice president, and the federal judges who were amenable to impeachment according to the Constitution. In addition, even if a senator were considered a "civil officer," it was unclear whether the Senate could also impeach someone who no longer held the office of senator, since it had already expelled Blount.[23] Madison thought not. After the House appointed the managers for Blount's impeachment, he feared that "a majority there as well as in the Senate are ready to go as far as the controul [*sic*] of their Constituents will permit."[24] The Senate eventually shared Madison's view. By fourteen votes to eleven, it decided that Blount was not a "civil officer" and dismissed the case for lack of jurisdiction.[25]

Blount was a former Federalist turned Republican, and the proceedings against him had had a partisan connotation from the very beginning. Federalist president John Adams had called congressional attention to Blount's misdeeds and provided the documentation to impeach him.[26] The Senate rejected a motion to defer consideration of the Blount case until the subsequent session nineteen votes to seven, with all its Federalist members voting against it. At the same time, the House—where the Federalists held a 58 to 48 majority—decided to impeach Blount upon pressures from such a staunch Federalist as Samuel Sitgreaves of Pennsylvania. Overcoming the arguments of Republicans John Nicholas of Virginia and Albert Gallatin of Pennsylvania, Sitgreaves assured his colleagues that he had positive legal opinions that a senator was amenable to the impeachment process. All eleven managers who prosecuted Blount on behalf of the House were Federalists. The one Republican elected, Abraham Baldwin, immediately resigned because of the few votes he had received and was replaced by another Federalist.[27]

Many Federalists who advocated Blount's conviction suggested that impeachable offenses should include not only crimes but misconduct as well. They also held that the impeachment procedure should not be limited to government officers. James A. Bayard of Delaware well epitomized this position. He not only argued that a senator was a "civil officer" as defined by the Constitution. He went beyond Blount's specific case and further elaborated on the scope and range of impeachment. In rejecting the call of Blount's counselors for a jury trial, Bayard pointed out that "impeachment is a proceeding purely of a political nature." He also added that the Constitution "has not described the persons who shall be the objects of impeachment nor defined the cases to which the remedy shall be confined." In his view, "where the Constitution has given us terms which it does not explain . . . we must have recourse to the common law," according to which "all the King's subjects are liable to be impeached." He therefore concluded that all U.S. citizens were amenable to this procedure. Indeed, Bayard emphatically argued for the application of impeachment, even of individuals who did not hold public offices: "Let us suppose, that a citizen not in office, but possessed of extensive influence . . . should conspire with the disaffected of our own country, or with foreign intriguers, by illegal artifice, corruption, or force, to place himself in the Presidential Chair, . . . in such a case, what punishment would be more likely to quell a spirit of that description, than absolute and perpetual disqualification for any office of trust, honor, or profit, under the Government; and what punishment could be better calculated to secure the peace and safety of the State from the repetition of the same offense?"[28]

The principle of universal impeachment would have provided a two-thirds majority of the Senate a means to prevent any person from holding public office for political reasons. The Federalists' obvious targets were their Republican opponents. The intent of Bayard's tirade did not sound different from Federalist Harrison Gray Otis's defense of the Alien and Sedition Acts, the controversial measures by which his party endeavored to suppress the Republican opposition, on the ground of the "necessity of purifying the country from the sources of pollution."[29] It is hardly by chance that Republicans such as Henry Tazewell of Virginia insisted on giving Blount a jury trial. Such a request would have shifted the proceedings from political ground to criminal prosecution, but the Senate rejected Tazewell's motion to that effect twenty-six votes to three.[30] All three supporters were Republicans. Furthermore, no lesser a person than Vice President Thomas Jefferson made available to Tazewell the legal references and notes to make his case.[31]

Maintaining that the plight of Republicans was at stake in the outcome of Blount's impeachment would sound far-fetched. However, the change in Jefferson's attitude toward the case exemplifies the increasing importance of its outcome in the Republican eyes. In July 1797 the vice president was so unconcerned about the proceedings of Blount's expulsion that he felt free to go back to Virginia during the debate and leave the president pro tempore of the Senate in charge.[32] Conversely, his subsequent behind-the-scenes endeavors to save Blount during the trial demonstrated that Jefferson had become aware of the broad political repercussions of this impeachment case for the future of the Republicans themselves in the face of possible political retaliation by the Federalists. As he wrote to Madison in early 1798, after returning to Philadelphia to preside over the Senate during the decision-making portion of Blount's trial, he saw "nothing in the mode of proceedings by impeachment, but the most formidable weapon for the purpose of a dominant faction that ever was contrived. It would be the most effectual one for getting rid of any man whom they consider as dangerous to their views, and I do not know that we could count on one third on an emergency."[33] Tazewell himself, who had already come out against the Alien and Sedition Acts, made a point of going to Philadelphia to attend the short session on impeachment, despite a serious illness that caused his death two weeks after Blount's acquittal.[34]

Proposals to Impeach Hamilton

Although Madison had drafted the 1798 Virginia Resolution against the Alien and Sedition Acts,[35] it is unlikely that partisanship accounted for his stand on Blount's trial. Madison seemed far more afraid of the devastating impact that the exploitation of impeachment within partisan conflicts could have on the political system of the recently established republic. Indeed, a few years earlier, despite what he considered to be malfeasance in office, he had refrained from calling for such a procedure, even though the defendant was both a presidential appointee and a Federalist. In 1793 Jefferson and Madison led a campaign to have Hamilton replaced as secretary of the treasury on the grounds that he had misapplied public funds for the total amount of $549,278.19, but they did not endeavor to resort to impeachment. They hardly even called for Hamilton's removal from office in the hope that congressional censure would be enough to persuade President George Washington to fire him.[36] The draft of a resolution that Jefferson wrote with

Madison's alleged help confined itself to urging Washington to dismiss Hamilton.[37] Furthermore, the two Republican leaders let U.S. representative William Branch Giles of Virginia, who actually introduced the final request for removal, drop it after listing Hamilton's alleged misdeeds.[38] In any case, Madison never attempted to launch any formal impeachment proceedings, although he believed that Hamilton was guilty, and Giles was to become one of the staunchest advocates of the political use of this procedure after the turn of the century.[39] Federalist Fisher Ames contended that "Madison has become a desperate party leader, and I am not sure of his stopping at any ordinary point of extremity."[40] Yet such supposed extremism did not involve resorting to impeachment for partisan purposes.

In 1793 Republicans had too few members in Congress to succeed in launching formal impeachment proceedings against Hamilton. Yet Madison stuck to his own reluctance to rely on such a procedure even after his party had gained a majority of the seats and had embraced impeachment as a viable means of partisan warfare. The 1800 elections marked the turning point. On this occasion, not only did Jefferson win the White House, but the Republicans also obtained 69 seats in the House, as opposed to the Federalists' 36, and secured control of the Senate for the first time, with 18 seats over the Federalists' 13.[41]

Impeachment of Federal Judges

After his defeat in the 1800 race for the White House, lame-duck president John Adams endeavored to make the judiciary into a Federalist bailiwick in order to balance the power the Republicans gained by winning control of the remaining two branches of government. Therefore, in the last few days of his term, he selected only Federalist judges to fill the positions on the bench of a new system of circuit courts that the outgoing Congress had established with the Judiciary Act of 1801. The Republican majority of the Seventh Congress proceeded to repeal this law in less than a year after Jefferson's inauguration.[42] Sixteen Federalist judges lost their seats and the remaining ones may have felt intimidated. According to Federalist senator William Plumer of New Hampshire, the Republicans aimed at the "destruction of the independence of the judicial department."[43]

Indeed, a radical wing of the party was not satisfied with the repeal of the 1801 Judiciary Act alone. It wished to pursue a more partisan course and remove all the Federalist judges from the federal bench. This scheme would have not only insulated Republican policies from review by federal judges but also allowed the Republican Party to secure a larger share of the winner's spoils by turning the judicial offices into patronage positions. William Branch Giles of Virginia, for instance, wrote to Jefferson that "a pretty general purgation of office has been one of the benefits expected by the friends of the new order of things and although an indiscriminate privation of office, merely for a difference in political sentiment might not be expected, yet it is expected, and confidently, that obnoxious men will be ousted."[44] When Jefferson suggested moderation toward the Federalists in his reply and let his correspondent know that he would refrain from "shocking their feelings by unnecessary acts of severity," Giles called for "an absolute repeal of the whole judiciary system, terminating the present offices."[45]

These radical views reached a climax when Edmund Pendleton proposed a number of constitutional amendments resulting in "subjecting the judges to removal by the concurring vote of both houses of Congress."[46] According to John Randolph of Virginia, "the clause in the Constitution granting to the judges their offices *during good behavior* was intended merely to guard them against *executive removals,* and not at all to restrain the two Houses of Congress, on whose representation the President ought to remove them."[47]

Adopting a constitutional amendment was a time-consuming procedure. Impeachment seemed a more direct and expeditious route to oust the most politicized Federalist judges. On February 3, 1803, President Jefferson forwarded to the House of Representatives evidence against one of them, John Pickering, showing that the judge was a hopelessly insane drunkard who had misconducted himself on the bench.[48]

Pickering's behavior as chief justice of New Hampshire's Superior Court had aroused complaints since the early 1790s, when this theretofore distinguished jurist revealed the initial symptoms of madness. In 1795, unable to persuade him to give up his position, his friends convinced Washington to appoint him to the federal court for the district of New Hampshire in the hope that he would handle its lighter caseload more easily. Pickering's mental state further degenerated in the following years. But it was only in 1803 that his impeachment became a viable option. The last straw was Pickering's verdict in *United States v. Eliza* (1802), in which he found for a Federalist claimant against the Republican prosecutor and the Jefferson administration in a case of the seizure of a ship, the *Eliza,* and her cargo for violation of revenue laws. The political interpretation of his ruling resulted in political retaliation. Only then did the judge's habitual intoxication with alcohol become an offense.[49]

The House impeached Pickering by a vote of forty-five to eight for presiding while he was intoxicated and for ruling in *United States v. Eliza* contrary to the statute.[50] The balloting was along partisan lines, as all the opponents of the procedure were Federalists. The Senate similarly voted along strict partisan lines to convict Pickering in 1804. Nineteen Republicans found him guilty and seven Federalists acquitted him.[51]

Madison, whom Jefferson had appointed secretary of state, took issue with the introduction of the spoils system within the federal administration. When the president yielded to the radical faction of the Republican Party, he reportedly even threatened to resign from the cabinet in protest.[52] Not surprisingly, therefore, he did not share his fellow Republicans' zeal in their crusade against Pickering and kept a very low profile during the proceedings. Although Madison had argued at the Constitutional Convention that "some provision should be made for defending the Community against the incapacity,"[53] the Constitution in the end did not list insanity among the impeachable offenses. Furthermore, since the Federalists tried to exploit lunacy as a bar in law to Pickering's trial, the Republican managers made a point of ignoring the judge's madness for fears that he could not be convicted and removed on the grounds of derangement.[54]

Nor did Madison join the Republicans' subsequent campaign against Supreme Court justice Samuel Chase. As Peter Charles Hoffer and N. E. H. Hull have remarked, Pickering's case was a "dress rehearsal" for the impeachment of the Federalist justices of the Supreme Court.[55] Indeed, the same day the Senate convicted Pickering, the House impeached Chase.[56] Although the latter was the Republicans' most immediate target, conventional wisdom had it that the eventual goal at least of the more radical wing of the party was to remove Chief Justice John Marshall.[57] The aim was to shape the Supreme Court in order to make its political orientation reflect the partisan alignment of the country. It is hardly by chance that Chase's impeachment, in which Randolph played a prominent role as the leading manager, was promoted in the aftermath of the controversial *Marbury v. Madison* (1803) decision in which the Supreme Court for the first time ruled a federal law unconstitutional and rebuked the Jefferson administration for failing to perform its duty. Actually, during the proceedings against Chase in the Senate, Giles contended that "impeachment is nothing more than an inquiry, by the two Houses of Congress, whether the office of any public man might not be better filled by another." He also added, with an indirect reference to *Marbury v. Madison,* "if the Judges of the Supreme Court should dare, *as they had done,* to declare an act of Congress unconstitutional, or to send a mandamus to the Secretary of State, *as they had done,* it was the undoubted right of the House of Representatives to impeach them, and of the Senate to remove them, for giving such opinion, however honest or sincere they may have been in entertaining them."[58] Marshall himself feared for the survival of judges' independence upon receipt of the article of impeachment against Chase.[59]

Chase was a staunch Federalist whose partisan conduct on the bench and ruthless enforcement of the Sedition Act against the critics of the Adams administration were notorious.[60] It was, however, mainly a political statement that elicited Republican rage at the judge. On May 3, 1803, while instructing a federal grand jury in Baltimore, Chase delivered a harsh attack on the Jefferson administration. In particular, he charged the Republican government with driving the country toward "mobocracy" because it had undermined the independence of judges by repealing the 1801 Judiciary Act and contended that all men should enjoy equal rights including universal suffrage.[61]

The procedure against Chase mirrored the politicking of the previous two impeachment cases. But the outcome was different. Unlike Blount, who was expelled from the Senate, and Pickering, who was removed from office, Chase was acquitted.[62] If the Senate had voted along partisan lines, with twenty-five Republicans and nine Federalists casting their votes, Chase would have been convicted. Indeed, all nine Federalists voted for dismissal. But the Republicans split, and some of them sided with the Federalists in the vote on the articles of impeachment.[63]

After Chase's acquittal, Randolph rushed back to the House of Representatives and introduced the amendment Pendleton had already proposed less than two years earlier to grant Congress the power to dismiss federal judges.[64] If Congress had ratified the measure, it would have made the judiciary subject to the majority party. But it was the last hurrah for the advocates of a politicization of the judiciary. Not only was consideration on Randolph's proposal postponed to the subsequent session of Congress but also, as Senator Plumer observed, the "[Jefferson] Administration disapproved of this violent measure."[65]

Randolph's mismanagement of the case contributed to Chase's acquittal.[66] Yet there were other reasons for that ruling. Most prominent among the latter was the decline in Republican radicalism since the beginning of the procedure against the associate justice. The impeachment of Pickering and Chase was part of a larger political conflict that opposed not only the Republicans and the Federalists but also radicals and moderates within Jefferson's party. The success of the latter faction affected the outcome of Chase's trial. In particular, the chief advocate of Chase's conviction and leader of the radical Republicans, Randolph, eventually broke with the Jefferson administration on key issues such as its complex compromise on the Yazoo land fraud case in Georgia. Since he identified himself with the impeachment process, Chase's exoneration was also an expedient means of discrediting Randolph and curbing his political influence, which did not displease Jefferson's stalwarts or the president himself.[67] As Federalist Rufus King of Massachusetts pointed out only a few weeks before the vote, "We have heard a rude and disorderly debate in the H. of R. concerning the Georgia claim; & some persons have conjectured that a serious division would arise among the Democrats—nay, that it already exists and that Judge Chase's best hope of acquittal proceeds from it."[68]

Madison was definitely among the beneficiaries of Randolph's loss of prestige resulting from Chase's acquittal. Virginian radicals were maneuvering to prevent the Republican Party from slating Madison for the presidency in 1808.[69] In addition, Randolph, and to a much lesser extent Giles, harshly criticized the controversial Yazoo compromise in vehement attacks that involved Secretary of State Madison as a member of the federal-state commission that had devised it.[70] It is, therefore, unsurprising that Madison was among the moderate Republicans who tried to win the favor of Vice President Aaron Burr, who presided at the Chase trial in his capacity as president of the Senate, although the latter had become a sort of political outcast after killing Hamilton in a duel in 1804. Madison's efforts to cultivate Burr did not go unnoticed. As Plumer maliciously remarked, "the Secretary of State, Mr. Madison, formally the intimate friend of General Hamilton, has taken its murderer into his carriage and . . . accompanied him on a visit to . . . the French minister."[71]

Madison was officially uncommitted on the outcome of Chase's impeachment. For instance, he wrote to Hugh Henry Brackenridge, "As to the heads of Departments approving or disapproving the acquittal of Judge Chase, they did not I believe intermeddle during the trial with a subject exclusively belonging to another department, and now that the constitutional decision has taken place, it would be evidently improper for themselves to pronounce for public use their opinion of the issue, however little disposed they may be to reserve, beyond the rules of official decorum."[72] In private, however, he could not refrain from rejoicing over the political blow to Randolph and his radical allies. John Quincy Adams remarked that he "had some conversation on the subject with Mr. Madison, who appeared much diverted at the petulance of the managers on their disappointment."[73]

Impeachment in Later Years

Although Madison derived political benefits from Chase's exoneration, his moderate approach to impeachment was basically also a defense of the Constitution against the extremism of radicals such as Giles and Randolph, who intended to politicize this procedure and turn it into an instrument of partisan warfare. He had already foreseen this potential outcome at the Constitutional Convention and operated in order to prevent it. His role, however, was more trenchant at the moment of the theoretical debate than when the constitutional provisions came to be enforced.

In any case, Chase's acquittal ended the Republican resort to impeachment as a political instrument. Two years later, when Giles urged Jefferson to adopt a more belligerent strategy against the alleged attempt of the Supreme Court to interfere with the inquiry into Burr's conspiracy, the president himself ruled out impeachment as an effective tool and argued that such a procedure was "a farce which will not be tried again."[74] As Jefferson further pointed out in his retirement years, Chase's proceedings had demonstrated to judges that "impeachment is an impracticable thing, a mere scare-crow."[75]

No impeachment was initiated during the Madison administration to cleanse the judiciary.[76] Following in his predecessor's footsteps, in order to counter Marshall's influence and overturn the Federalist majority on the Supreme Court, President Madison confined himself to filling vacancies by appointing judges whom he believed to be staunch Republicans.[77] This goal was virtually achieved in 1812, when the Senate confirmed Madison's nomination of Joseph Story, a former Republican congressman and speaker of the Massachusetts House of Representatives, to replace Federalist William Cushing, notwithstanding the objections of Jefferson, who called Story a "pseudo-Republican."[78] Although Story sided with Marshall in numerous cases, as Jefferson had feared, impeachment was no longer a viable means against the associate justice.[79]

Actually, after Chase's trial, resort to this legal procedure was discontinued for a quarter century until 1830, when the House impeached—but the Senate eventually acquitted—Judge James Hawkins Peck of Missouri. Politics was not involved this time, as Peck was charged with acting in a vindictive manner in convicting a lawyer of contempt in a case involving land grants. That Congress had concerned itself with Peck for almost four years, namely, since late 1826, before impeaching him further demonstrates how careful legislators became in the use of impeachment after Chase's exoneration.[80]

Notes

Research for this essay was made possible by a Batten Fellowship of the Robert H. Smith International Center for Jefferson Studies, Thomas Jefferson Foundation, Charlottesville.

1. William Holdsworth, *A History of English Law* (London: Methuen, 1956), 379–85.

2. Bryce Lyon, *A Constitutional and Legal History of Medieval England* (New York: Harper, 1960), 559.

3. George Burton Adams, *Constitutional History of England* (New York: Holt, 1921), 371–73.

4. Ivory Jennings, *Parliament* (New York: Cambridge University Press, 1957), 397.

5. Richard Ernest Jenkins, *The First Administration of Sir John Harvey, Royal Governor of Virginia, 1630–1635* (master's thesis, University of Virginia, 1967), 71–98.

6. Warren M. Billings, John E. Selby, and Thad W. Tate, *Colonial Virginia: A History* (White Plains, NY: KTO, 1986), 48, 70.

7. Peter Charles Hoffer and N. E. H. Hull, *Impeachment in America, 1635–1805* (New Haven, CT: Yale University Press, 1984), 15–56.

8. Raoul Berger, *Impeachment: The Constitutional Problems* (Cambridge, MA: Harvard University Press, 1973), 4–5, 89, 98–99, 122, 217–18; Hoffer and Hull, *Impeachment in America*, 266–70.

9. James Madison, *Notes of Debates in the Federal Convention of 1787*, ed. Adrienne Koch (New York: Norton, 1987), 605.

10. James Madison to John Brown, August 23, 1785, in *Letters and Other Writings of James Madison*, ed. Philip R. Fendall (Philadelphia: Lippincott, 1867), 1:180.

11. Madison, *Notes of Debates*, 605–6, 635.

12. Alexander Hamilton, James Madison, and John Jay, *The Federalist Papers*, ed. Clinton Rossiter (New York: New American Library, 1961), 396–97.

13. Cincinnatus [Arthur Lee], "Reply to Wilson's Speech, November 29, 1787," in *The Debate on the Constitution: Federalist and Antifederalist Speeches, Articles, and Letters*

during the Struggle over Ratification, ed. Bernard Bailyn (New York: Library of America, 1993), 1:114.

14. John C. Miller, *Alexander Hamilton: Portrait in Paradox* (New York: Harper, 1959), 176–78.

15. Alexander Hamilton, "New York Ratifying Convention: Amendments to the Constitution," July 15, 1788, in *The Papers of Alexander Hamilton,* ed. Harold C. Syrett (New York: Columbia University Press, 1962), 5:168.

16. *Annals of Congress,* 2nd Cong., 1st sess., 1977.

17. James Madison, "Observations of the 'Draught of a Constitution for Virginia,'" n.d. [ca. October 14, 1788], in *The Papers of James Madison,* ed. William T. Hutchinson et al. (Chicago: University of Chicago Press; Charlottesville: University Press of Virginia, 1977), 11:291–92 (hereafter cited as *Papers*).

18. Jonathan Elliott, ed., *The Debates in the Several State Conventions on the Adoption of the Federal Constitution* (New York: Lenox Hill, 1974), 3:498, 500.

19. *Annals of Congress,* 1st Cong., 1st sess., 372.

20. James Madison to Thomas Jefferson, March 4, 1798, *Papers,* 17:89.

21. Eleanore Bushnell, *Crimes, Follies, and Misfortunes: The Federal Impeachment Trials* (Urbana: University of Illinois Press, 1992), 25–41; Bucker F. Melton, *The First Impeachment: The Constitution's Framers and the Case of Senator William Blount* (Macon, GA: Mercer University Press, 1998), 60–262.

22. *Annals of Congress,* 5th Cong., 1st sess., 33–34, 44.

23. Melton, *First Impeachment,* 209–25.

24. James Madison to Thomas Jefferson, n.d. [ca. February 18, 1798], *Papers,* 17:82.

25. *Annals of Congress,* 5th Cong., 3rd sess., 2318–19.

26. Ralph Adams Brown, *The Presidency of John Adams* (Lawrence: University Press of Kansas, 1975), 140.

27. *Annals of Congress,* 5th Cong., 1st sess. 41, 448–59; ibid., 5th Cong., 2nd sess., 498, 953–55, 957.

28. Ibid., 5th Cong., 2nd sess., 2251, 2253, 2254. For Bayard's role in Blount's case, see also Morton Borden, *The Federalism of James A. Bayard* (New York: Columbia University Press, 1955), 47–61.

29. Susan Dunn, *Jefferson's Second Revolution: The Election Crisis of 1800 and the Triumph of Republicanism* (Boston: Houghton Mifflin, 2004), 109.

30. *Annals of Congress,* 5th Cong., 1st sess., 508.

31. Thomas Jefferson to Henry Tazewell, January 27, 1798, in *The Papers of Thomas Jefferson,* ed. Barbara B. Oberg (Princeton, NJ: Princeton University Press, 2003), 30:58–61.

32. "Itinerary and Chronology of Thomas Jefferson, 1795–1801," in *The Writings of Thomas Jefferson,* ed. Paul Leicester Ford (New York: Putnam's, 1896), 7:xxiv.

33. Thomas Jefferson to James Madison, February 15, 1798, *Papers of Thomas Jefferson,* 30:111.

34. Norma Lois Peterson, *Littleton Walter Tazewell* (Charlottesville: University Press of Virginia, 1982), 14–15.

35. Adrienne Koch, *Jefferson and Madison: The Great Collaboration* (New York: Knopf, 1950), 184–87.

36. Claude G. Bowers, *Jefferson and Hamilton: The Struggle for Democracy in America* (Boston: Houghton Mifflin, 1953), 197–203; Eugene R. Sheridan, "Thomas Jefferson and the Giles Resolutions," *William and Mary Quarterly, 3rd ser.,* 49, no. 4 (1992): 589–608; Ron Chernow, *Alexander Hamilton* (New York: Penguin, 2004), 424–28.

37. Thomas Jefferson, "Resolutions on the Secretary of the Treasury," February 27, 1793, in *The Papers of Thomas Jefferson,* ed. John Catanzariti (Princeton, NJ: Princeton University Press, 1992), 25:292–96. For Jefferson's authorship and Madison's involvement, see "Editorial Note," ibid., 280–92.

38. *Journal of the House of Representatives,* 2nd Cong., 1st sess., 147–48.

39. James Madison, "Resolutions Censuring the Secretary of the Treasury," March 1, 1793, *Papers,* 14:455–68; Dice Robins Anderson, *William Branch Giles: A Study in the Politics of Virginia and the Nation from 1790 to 1830* (Menasha, WI: George Banta, 1914), 95–97.

40. Quoted in Sidney Howard Gay, *James Madison* (Boston: Houghton Mifflin, 1912), 192.

41. John Ferling, *Adams vs. Jefferson: The Tumultuous Election of 1800* (New York: Oxford University Press, 2004), 171.

42. Richard E. Ellis, *The Jeffersonian Crisis: Courts and Politics in the Young Republic* (New York: Oxford University Press, 1971), 45–51.

43. William Plumer, *William Plumer's Memorandum of Proceedings in the United States Senate, 1803–1807,* ed. Everett S. Brown (New York: Macmillan, 1923), 101.

44. William Branch Giles to Thomas Jefferson, March 16, 1801, in *Thomas Jefferson Papers,* microfilm edition, reel 23, Library of Congress, Washington, DC.

45. Thomas Jefferson to William Branch Giles, March 23, 1801, *Writings of Thomas Jefferson,* 8:26; Giles to Jefferson, June 1, 1802, *Jefferson Papers,* reel 23.

46. Edmund Pendleton, "The Danger Not Over," October 20, 1801, in *The Letters and Papers of Edmund Pendleton, 1734–1803,* ed. David John Mays (Charlottesville: University Press of Virginia, 1967), 2:698.

47. Timothy Pickering to George Cabot, January 29, 1804, in Henry Cabot Lodge, *Life and Letters of George Cabot* (Boston: Little, Brown, 1877), 338. Emphasis in original.

48. *Message from the President of the United States, Enclosing Sundry Documents, Relative to John Pickering, District Judge of the District of New Hampshire* (Washington, DC: Duane, 1803).

49. Lynn W. Turner, "The Impeachment of John Pickering," *American Historical Review* 54, no. 3 (1949): 485–507; Ellis, *Jeffersonian Crisis,* 69–75; Frank Thompson and Daniel H. Pollitt, "Impeachment of Federal Judges: An Historical Overview," *North Carolina Law Review* 49, no. 1 (1970): 95–97; Hoffer and Hull, *Impeachment in America,* 207–17; Bushnell, *Crimes, Follies, and Misfortunes,* 43–55.

50. *Annals of Congress,* 7th Cong., 1st sess., 642; "House of Representatives," *National Intelligencer* 7 (March 7, 1803): 3.

51. *Annals of Congress,* 8th Cong., 1st sess., 366–67; "Impeachment," *National Intelligencer* 8 (March 14, 1804): 3.

52. Ellis, *Jeffersonian Crisis,* 38.

53. Madison, *Notes of Debates,* 332.

54. Plumer, *Memorandum,* 155–69; John Quincy Adams, *Memoirs of John Quincy Adams,* ed. Charles Francis Adams (Philadelphia: Lippincott, 1874), 2:299.

55. Hoffer and Hull, *Impeachment in America,* 206–7.

56. "Judge Chase Impeached," *National Intelligencer* 6 (March 14, 1802): 3.

57. Albert J. Beveridge, *The Life of John Marshall* (Boston: Houghton Mifflin, 1919), 4:160–62; Gerald W. Johnson, *Randolph of Roanoke: A Political Fantastic* (New York: Minton, Balch, 1929), 141; Bruce Ackerman, *The Failure of the Founding Fathers: Jefferson, Marshall, and the Rise of Presidential Democracy* (Cambridge, MA: Belknap, 2005), 199, 214–15.

58. John Quincy Adams, *Memoirs,* 1:321–22. Emphasis in original.

59. John Marshall to James M. Marshall, April 1, 1804, in *The Papers of John Marshall,* ed. Charles F. Hobson (Chapel Hill: University of North Carolina Press, 1990), 6:278.

60. Jane Shaffer Elsmere, *Justice Samuel Chase* (Muncie, IN: Janevar, 1980), 15, 31–33, 56–57, 86–89, 92–136.

61. *Trial of Samuel Chase, an Associate Justice of the Supreme Court of the United States,* (Washington, DC: Samuel H. Smith, 1805), 2:v–viii.

62. Ellis, *Jeffersonian Crisis,* 76–82, 96–102; Thompson and Pollitt, "Impeachment of Federal Judges," 97–100; Herbert A. Johnson, "Impeachment and Politics," *South Atlantic Quarterly* 63, no. 4 (1964): 552–63; Hoffer and Hull, *Impeachment in America,* 228–55; Bushnell, *Crimes, Follies, and Misfortunes,* 57–88.

63. *Annals of Congress,* 8th Cong., 1st sess., 665–69; *Trial of Samuel Chase,* 2:493; "Judgment Pronounced on the Impeachment Against Samuel Chase," *National Intelligencer* 9 (March 4, 1805): 3; Plumer, *Memorandum,* 309–10.

64. Russell Kirk, *John Randolph of Roanoke: A Study in American Politics* (Indianapolis, IN: Liberty Fund, 1997), 209.

65. Plumer, *Memorandum,* 311.

66. Alexander B. Lacy, Jr., *Jefferson and Congress: Congressional Method and Politics, 1801–1809* (Ph.D. diss., University of Virginia, 1963), 263; Leonard Baker, *John Marshall: A Life in Law* (New York: Macmillan, 1974), 430–31; Hoffer and Hull, *Impeachment in America,* 252. For an account sympathetic toward Randolph, see William Cabell Bruce, *John Randolph of Roanoke, 1773–1833* (New York: Putnam's, 1922), 206.

67. Ellis, *Jeffersonian Crisis,* 83–95, 103–5; William H. Rehnquist, *Grand Inquests: The Historic Impeachments of Justice Samuel Chase and President Andrew Johnson* (New York: Morrow, 1992), 110–13.

68. Rufus King to Timothy Pickering, February 18, 1805, in *The Life and Correspondence of Rufus King,* ed. Charles R. King (New York: Putnam's, 1897), 4:440.

69. Ellis, *Jeffersonian Crisis,* 87.

70. Irving Brant, *James Madison: Secretary of State, 1800–1809* (Indianapolis: Bobbs-Merrill, 1953), 230–40.

71. Baker, *John Marshall,* 426–27; Ellis, *Jeffersonian Crisis,* 92; Plumer, *Memorandum,* 203–4.

72. James Madison to Hugh Henry Brackenridge, May 29, 1805, *James Madison Papers,* microfilm edition, series 1, General Correspondence, reel 8, Library of Congress.

73. John Quincy Adams, *Memoirs,* 1:365.

74. William Branch Giles to Thomas Jefferson, April 6, 1807, *Jefferson Papers,* reel 38; Jefferson to Giles, April 20, 1807, *Writings of Thomas Jefferson,* 9:46.

75. Thomas Jefferson to Thomas Richie, December 25, 1820, *Writings of Thomas Jefferson,* 10:171.

76. Irving Brant, *James Madison: The President, 1809–1812* (Indianapolis: Bobbs-Merrill, 1956).

77. Ackerman, *Failure of the Founding Fathers,* 224.

78. Thomas Jefferson to Henry Dearborn, July 16, 1810, in *The Writings of Thomas Jefferson,* ed. Andrew A. Lipscomb (Washington, DC: Thomas Jefferson Memorial Association, 1907), 12:399.

79. R. Kent Newmyer, *Supreme Court Justice Joseph Story: Statesman of the Old Republic* (Chapel Hill: University of North Carolina Press, 1985).

80. John F. Reinhardt, "The Impeachment Proceedings Against Judge James Hawkins Peck," *University of Kansas City Law Review* 12 (1943–44): 106–18; Thompson and Pollitt, "Impeachment of Federal Judges," 101–2; Bushnell, *Crimes, Follies, and Misfortunes,* 91–113.

JOHN ALLPHIN MOORE, JR.

James Madison, David Hume, and Modern Political Parties

A reading of the *Federalist* (particularly James Madison's Nos. 10 and 51) and of helpful counsels from David Hume reveals that certain framers of the U.S. Constitution had developed a model of a large, centralized, multifarious country, so beset by assorted interests that modes of cooperation among otherwise disparate groups would prove to be the only way to conduct public business. Despite the conventional wisdom that the American founders opposed political parties (there is no mention of parties in the Constitution), it is arguable that the theoretical fashioning of a republican "empire"[1] anticipated the formation of a party system, a system some political scientists believe is essential to the effective workings of a modern democratic state.

The political scientists' insinuation may resonate with even clearer tone when we consider one of the more pressing international concerns at the turn of the millennium—crafting whole and reasonably peaceful political entities from diverse populations in the same geographical area. The history of internal tumult in newly independent nations around the globe suggests that the task is not easy. Separated by ethnicity, religious differences, national aspirations, economic rivalries, and sometimes even language, inhabitants in these and other realms have been beset by devastating civil wars that too often attract outside, and unwelcome, intrusions. The American founders, mindful of analogous dysfunction from their reading of history, and wary of perceptible differences among their countrymen, worried about keeping their new nation together and at times imagined political enemies as dangerous promoters of disunion.

To add to the mix, one of the lessons of history in the two centuries since the American Revolution is that unity among rebels while gaining freedom from a colonial master is less difficult to sustain than keeping the liberated country unified and peaceful after independence has been achieved. Too often, a winning clique establishes a one-party, even repressive, regime and looks upon any potential "legitimate" opposition as traitorous, leaving civil war as the probable tool to voice disagreement. In his Pulitzer Prize–winning book of vignettes on the "Founding Brothers," Joseph Ellis posited as his overarching theme this very apprehension among the first generation. He argued that key decisions that leaders made at the commencement of the country—including Congress's determination to avoid dealing with the issue of slavery—sought to avert having acrimonious controversies descend into a confrontational and disorderly melee. Ellis documented that "the American Revolution did not 'devour its own children' and lead to blood-soaked scenes at the guillotine or the firing-squad wall. . . . The revolutionary generation found a way to contain the explosive energies of the debate in the form of an ongoing argument or dialogue that was eventually institutionalized and rendered safe by the creation of political parties."[2]

Accordingly, this essay invites fresh contemplation on the role and place of political parties in the founders' intellectual terrain. It suggests more convergence of the earlier view with the modern one than tradition recommends.

Current Recognitions of the Need for Political Parties

Late nineteenth-century historian Edward Stanwood issued the modern students' judgment: "The existence of a free government without a division into parties is an impossibility."[3] Hence many scholars believe that a party system, especially a two-party system, actually makes it possible for government, particularly in a large, varied society such as the United States, to work. Such a system forces divergent interests and views to coalesce and compromise on a common party program or legislative proposal. This may be the only reasonable way to get anything done in a legislature where so many, sometimes seemingly incompatible, points of view might otherwise work against a governing majority. Likewise, in seeking to win a presidential election, a party must appeal to as many regions, economic interests, and creedal inclinations as possible in order to attract a majority of the popular and electoral vote. Thus, a coincidental blessing, particularly of a two-party system, is that it directs political debate to the ideological center, furthering unity and moderation. Some scholars argue that if parties can apply their practices across extended geographic areas they might—by drawing committed party members from throughout the nation—help deflect sectional clashes. That is, parties might remedy the modern political problem of governing ethnically, religiously, ideologically, and economically mixed populations.[4] Finally, the political environment must accept an election result that brings the out party into power and causes the defeated, formerly dominant party to leave office, believing that if it can then amass its own sufficiently capacious coalition, it has a reasonable chance of winning future elections and returning to power. Such an event first happened in the American election of 1800, and by the 1830s the practice became, with the aberrant exception of the 1860 election, standard in U.S. politics.

Current Views of the Founders and Political Parties

Alongside this explanation of the virtues of a two-party system is the scholarly insistence that the founders of the American republic abhorred parties and wished to erase their influence from politics. The late Austin Ranney, former president of the American Political Science Association, maintained that "as most of the Framers saw it, competing political organizations are inherently subversive of good government and the national interest." Ranney titled one of his articles "Political Parties and Article VIII of the Constitution" (there was no Article VIII), submitting that since parties are indeed crucial to the effective workings of democracy, later generations understandably corrected an oversight of the founders.[5] Samuel H. Beer, Harvard political scientist, has declared that Madison's "pejorative view of party" accorded with "received opinion of his time,"[6] but he missed the more favorable and modern view of political parties as not only inevitable but also desirable in systems of self-government. In a well-received study on "The American Revolution of 1800," now three decades old, Daniel Sisson disapproved of any conclusion that the election of 1800 demonstrated the calculated formation and establishment of a modern political party arrangement; the founders, according to Sisson, championed a "classical" outlook, "necessitating only one faction in power and abhorring the existence of an 'opposition.'"[7] The most eminent historian of the founding period from the present generation, Gordon Wood, has articulated the conventional view: "No one thought that the emergence of parties was a good thing; indeed, far from building a party system in the 1790s, the nation's leaders struggled to prevent one from developing."[8]

And yet Stanley Elkins and Eric McKitrick, in an immense, prize-winning study of the Federal period, designated a section of their book "Madison Revises *The Federalist*" to imply a "highly significant modification of theory" in Madison's convictions, from viewing parties as "disruptive, subversive, and wicked" in 1787–88 to his altered opinion of the 1790s, when challenging his erstwhile collaborator Hamilton and devising the first modern political party. Among the results, Elkins and McKitrick opine, were "certain shocking new elements of political practice"—the new party system.[9]

These scholarly sentiments reflect a widely supported supposition that the founding generation can best be understood as "republican," rather than as "modern" or "liberal," in intention. While the term "republicanism" has been burdened with considerable meaning, its power as an analytical tool rests with the masterful work of, among others, J. G. A. Pocock[10] and his contemporaries in American studies such as Professors Wood,[11] Elkins, and McKitrick, cited above. These scholars see the founders as inheritors of the ideological debates between England's "Court" and "Country" that had been taking place from at least the late seventeenth century. Court politicians, associated with commerce, banking, cities, and interest-pursuing aspects of the modern world were challenged by an older Whig "Country" group, motivated by a desire to return to a more upright past by promoting the common purpose and opposing the corruption of the new political and financial arrangements surrounding the Court. These Country rivals found their backdrop in what Pocock called the "Machiavellian Moment," by which he meant the surfacing of a political language during and after the Renaissance determined to refurbish classical notions of civic virtue. "Virtue" and "republicanism," words widely used in the late eighteenth century, seemed to militate against the apparent "passions" and "interests" so characteristic of factions, parties, and, indeed, modern commercial and political life. The conversation, insist the proponents of the republican theory of the founding, made its way across the ocean from the British mother country to the colonies and to the new nation. The civic republican side of this conversation then became the basis of early American political thought.[12]

Students of politics—some influenced by the civic republicanism theories discussed above—find that, at least until Madison's theoretical breakthrough sometime long after 1787, eighteenth-century thinkers saw parties and factions as virtually synonymous. And factions, or parties, were evil because they mobilized self-interested, malignant, even heinous groupings, intent upon disrupting the political order, and causing instability, anarchy, even, eventually, tyranny. Thus, a traditional interpretation of Madison's *Federalist* Nos. 10 and 51 is that he designed them to inform serious readers how to check, indeed "break," factions and avoid parties.[13] Only later, according to some more recent commentaries, did Madison, under the pressure of urgent political challenge, reverse himself and begin the intellectual journey to approving political parties.[14] Other scholars, as we have seen, are disinclined even to make this concession to Madison and other founders. Thus, the current affirmation that parties are indispensable to democracy coincides with a fashionable assumption that the founders, whose lives and actions predated modern political history, missed this now obvious but essential point.[15]

Reconsideration of Traditional Views

This latter-day premise needs rethinking. We must revisit and reconsider the advice of the founding generation. The attitude toward "rights" represents a useful commencement in this exercise. How can we account for Publius's initial resistance to a written Bill of Rights? And what does this resistance tell us about the emergence of a party system?

Both Hamilton and Madison, outwardly supportive of rights in what might be called the Lockean sense—that is, the conceit that individual rights belonged to a person from nature preliminary to the formation of society or government—knew well that a *statement* of rights was insufficient for assuring their protection; there are clearly historical examples where statements of rights in state and national constitutions proved toothless in practice. Hamilton, in *Federalist* Nos. 84 and 85, argued that the Constitution itself was the best guarantee of rights, and Madison, in letters to Jefferson and in the *Federalist,* argued against "parchment barriers" (No. 48) and in favor of "auxiliary precautions" rather than mere statements to assure rights (No. 51).

Madison's preparatory studies for Nos. 10 and 51 are contained in a paper on "The Vices of the Political System of the United States," which parallels some of Hume's notions and sheds light on Madison's ideas on rights. In these observations of April 1787, penned before the Constitutional Convention, and well before the writing of the *Federalist,* Madison agonized about a passionate majority perpetrating "unjust violations of the rights and interests of the minority, or of individuals." He dismissed the proposition that religion would provide a sufficient restraint by observing that in the name of religion, "individuals join without remorse in acts, against which their consciences would revolt if proposed to them under the like sanction, separately in their closets." When religion was "kindled into enthusiasm," it was even more dangerous, making religion "a motive to oppression."[16] These remarks are similar to Hume's charge that "parties of religion are more furious and enraged than the most cruel factions" in modern times, and his warning that "enthusiasm" was politically dangerous.[17] And religious factions were but the most obvious of the menacing factions that jeopardized rights.

Madison faced the question of how a modern state builder could protect rights within states containing a multiplicity of different and sometimes conflicting interests or "factions," including religious factions. This is the setting for Madison's theoretical breakthrough. Contrary to conventional wisdom, this breakthrough preceded the rivalry of the 1790s.

In his careful and shrewd study of the *Federalist,* David Epstein only hints that Madison intended different meanings for "faction" and "party."[18] He may well be right. We know that by the early 1790s Madison had begun to provide newspapers with detailed justifications for the formation of competing political parties.[19] Of these essays, the most significant was the contribution of January 23, 1792, written for the *National Gazette:* "In every political society, parties are unavoidable. A difference of interests, real or supposed, is the most natural and fruitful source of them. The great object should be to combat the evil . . . by [among other things] establishing a political equality among all . . . [and] by making one party a check on the other, so far as the existence of parties cannot be prevented, nor their views accommodated. If this is not the language of reason, it is that of *republicanism*. . . . In all political societies, different interests and parties arise out of the nature of things, and the great art of politicians lies in making them checks and balances to each other."[20]

Influences of David Hume

Madison's remarks here were no revision of his earlier views in the *Federalist;* they were, rather, an extension of his arguments in Nos. 10 and 51, in which he revealed an influence from David Hume.[21] Notably, the late Douglass Adair once described Hume's influence on Madison as "a parallel march of ideas"[22] and concluded that "Hume's book [the political essays] was open on the table beside him" as he composed *Federalist* No. 10.[23] Madison's biographer Ralph Ketcham notes that Madison, during the late winter of 1786 and early spring of 1787, when he was in New York for the congressional session, had likely read Hume's essay "Idea of a Perfect Commonwealth."[24] Indeed, this is precisely the time when Madison was composing his notes on "The Vices of the Political System of the United States," notes that would inform several of his *Federalist* essays. In "Idea of a Perfect Commonwealth," Hume had proposed that a republic could in fact exist in a large, empire-sized country.[25] The claim was contrary to the accepted position, articulated by Montesquieu, that a republic could exist only in a small, homogeneous, and rather parochial area. A Greek *polis* provided the example. Citizens shared common ethnicity, language, and religion. Each citizen participated in the governing of the community; for the republic to be sustained, citizens had to be virtuous. Virtue, said Montesquieu, was the mainspring of a republic. Because virtue—a loving commitment to the common purpose—was unlikely, if not impossible, in a large country with various interests and different kinds of people, an empire could not be republican.[26] Hamilton and Madison each used the *Federalist* to describe the new country with its new Constitution as both an "empire" *and* a "republic." Understandably, they preferred Hume's position to Montesquieu's.

In addition, Hume had argued that parties are, at the least, a necessary evil and as inevitable as are factions, in any society. It is important to bear in mind Madison's 1792 statement above while surveying the Scotsman's ideas about political parties. They could not be destroyed, Hume believed, without destroying liberty itself. At least in England, he found that "parties themselves will always subsist."[27] Although "parties are seldom found pure and unmixed . . . a party may be denominated either personal or real . . . [that is] founded on personal friendship or animosity . . . or . . . on some real difference of sentiment or interest." Hume advised that while "the influence of faction is directly contrary to that of laws [and that] Factions subvert government . . . [nonetheless] to exclude faction from a free government, is very difficult, if not altogether impracticable . . . [and] to abolish all distinctions of party may not be practicable, perhaps not desirable, in a free government."[28] The key for Hume is revealed in the statement that "the only dangerous parties are such as entertain opposite views with regard to the essentials of government."[29] For Hume, as for Madison and Hamilton, political differences must not be "*about* the constitution" but "*within* the constitution."[30]

As David Miller has pointed out, when Hume discussed the opposing "Court" and "Country" political alignments in England in his *History* and essays, he always urged them to moderate their arguments.[31] Miller cites the following passage from "That Politics May Be Reduced to a Science": "Would men be moderate and consistent, their claims might be admitted; at least might be examined. The *country-party* might still assert, that our constitution, though excellent, will admit of mal-administration to a certain degree; and therefore, if the minister be bad, it is proper to oppose him with a *suitable* degree if zeal. And, on the other hand, the *court-party* may be allowed, upon the supposition that the minister were good, to defend, and with *some* zeal too, his administration. I would only persuade men not to contend, as if they were fighting *pro aris et focis,* and change a good constitution into a bad one, by the violence of their factions." Elsewhere in the same essay, Hume proclaims: "I shall always be more fond of promoting moderation than zeal."[32] That is, he explicated, like a modern political scientist, one possible value of a two-party system: its moderating influence. Hume's conjectural ideal commonwealth thus contained an official opposition designed to criticize and check the policies of the government.[33]

Madison's Articulation of the Problem

Madison elaborated on these Humean counsels both in explaining the rise of parties in the new republic (as demonstrated above) and in his Nos. 10 and 51 of the *Federalist.* Although scholars have mined the latter for many years, it is important to reconsider them as the possible theoretical foundation for what was to become the American two-party system.

There is no better starting point than the celebrated No. 10.[34] Madison starts the essay promising that the new constitution will provide a political union capable of breaking and controlling "the violence of faction." He then defines faction as an aggregation of citizens, either a minority or majority, who convene and act together out of some common "impulse of passion" or "interest"; Hume, who wrote extensively on "passion," "interest," and "faction," saw factions as deriving either from "affection" or "interest."[35] Such factions, said Madison, act against the rights of other citizens or against the common good of the full community. How can the mischief of faction be removed? By two methods, explains Madison: remove the causes or control the effects of faction. As to the first solution, the only ways to remove the causes would be either to destroy liberty or to give every citizen the same opinions. But liberty is to faction "what air is to fire, an aliment[36] without which it instantly expires." To abolish liberty because it fuels faction would be as foolish as abolishing air because it nourishes fire. To be precise, liberty is as fundamental to politics as air is to life. And, second, it is impossible to force on each citizen the same opinion, because the "diversity in the faculties of men," which government is obligated to protect and sustain, along with fallible reason and self-interest, which inhere in the "nature of man,"[37] means that free human beings will develop different opinions. In fact, contrary opinions arise regarding religion, government, and "many other points." Some of these differences derive from "unequal distribution of property."[38] That is, property holders and those without property have different and distinct interests. Additionally, there are creditors and debtors, "a landed interest, a manufacturing interest, a mercantile interest, a moneyed interest," and many more interests that surface in "*civilized*" nations [emphasis added]. How a political society balances and manages these various, disparate, and potentially disruptive interests is the "principal task" of government. Parties *and* factions—Madison inserts each word separately and discretely—will inevitably be involved in this endeavor. In addition, the undertaking must be accomplished while securing the "public good," "private rights," and "popular government." The *Federalist* directs its inquiries to understanding and explaining how to do this.[39]

In No. 51 Madison continues the inquiry and tenders an answer.[40] Here he reminds readers of his evidence in No. 10 that "different interests necessarily exist in different classes of citizens." He then underscores the danger of a "majority" united by a common "interest" arising in order to do serious damage to the rights of the minority. As in No. 10, he offers optional resolutions, emulating Hume, who frequently used the same numerical-option method: either creating a "will of the community independent of the majority—that is, of the society itself" (a "general will"?)—or "*comprehending* [emphasis added] in the society so many separate descriptions of citizens" that no "unjust" majority could ever arise. It is this second method, assures Madison, that will characterize the United States with its new constitution. "The society itself will be broken into so many parts, interests and classes of citizens, that the rights of individuals, or of the minority, will be in little danger. . . . In a free government the security for *civil rights* [emphasis added] must be the same as that for religious rights. It consists in the one case in the multiplicity of interests, and in the other in the multiplicity of sects." Such balance, Madison believed, would be more supportive of rights—that is, civil rights as well as religious rights—than would be a "parchment barrier." Hamilton would agree, as he said in Nos. 84 and 85.

By explaining the plural character of American society, accenting checks and balances, and forwarding the consequent inference to "comprehend" various ill-assorted interests into working coalitions, these legendary ruminations seem to supply tenable grounds for later rationalizations (including Madison's) for the formation of political parties. Of course, Madison worried throughout his career and during his retirement about parties' excessive partisanship and the unbending zeal by which they might disrupt the union. In addition to the bitter divisiveness of the 1790s, the political crisis surrounding the War of 1812 was particularly stressful for the fourth president, as Federalists in New England (and even elsewhere in the country) defied his war policies.[41] Nonetheless, he was instrumental in creating the first political party in the nation's history and is even credited by biographer Irving Brant with having introduced the phrase "Republican Party."[42] Over the course of a long life during which the two-party system ripened into a modern form, Madison discussed parties in at least two ways: one from his own partisan point of view—acclaiming the Democratic-Republican Party and criticizing its opponents[43]—and, sometimes in the same utterance, meditating on the natural tendency in free societies for parties to exist. In the essay where he announced the emergence of the Republican Party (in September 1792), he explained that parties were "natural to most political societies [and] likely to be of some duration in ours."[44] He often returned to the essential analysis that first appeared in the 1792 essays. In 1824 he wrote, "Besides the occasional and transient subjects on which parties are formed, they seem to have a permanent foundation in the variance of political opinions in free States, and of occupations and interests in all civilized States."[45]

Balance and the Two-Party System

Recapitulating to this point: Madison (and Hamilton) sought to explain how a large country, one the size of an "empire," could retain a republican character. In so doing, they strayed from Montesquieu's fashionable and "celebrated" contention that such a fusion was not viable.[46] As they cogitated on this challenge, they read Hume.[47] Hume proved satisfying because he asserted that a republic *could* exist in a large territory. Moreover, in Hume's *Essays* Madison found welcome wisdom regarding the possibilities of having a highly diverse population live peaceably together. Hume revealed the promise of competitive political parties in this endeavor. This does not mean that Madison replicated in strict template all the details of Hume's thought on these matters.[48] After all, the founders were dealing with unique and pressing issues that confronted them some two decades after the final edition of the *Essays* was published. Madison applied and adopted Hume's insights in order to craft a rather novel political science, appropriate to the needs of the new nation.

Yet, returning to a first look at *Federalist* No. 51, readers may discover a mottled and perplexing political science. Indeed, a heterogeneous society of so many different kinds of people with immensely differing interests, disallowing other interests from doing what they passionately want to do, would seem to forebode a political community in constant rigidity, unable to do anything—good or bad. Perhaps individual rights would be protected, but could anything else be done? Could the country, for example, ever come together to educate its children or defend itself against attack? On numerous other occasions in the *Federalist,* the authors make plain the unequivocal need for energy and efficiency.[49] Indeed, the framers designed the Constitution to produce unity and decisiveness in a nation they perceived as divided and paralyzed.

The key to understanding this apparent paradox is to grasp the eighteenth-century—almost Newtonian—notion of balance; when Hume wrote that "the *balance of power* is a secret in politics, fully known only to the present age,"[50] he anticipated Madison's elaboration of checks and balances. But Madison also spoke of the inevitability of difference, of faction, of multiple interests. He urged the "comprehension" of assorted, different, often passionate, groups in such a way as to restrain their worst features and control their effects. Like Hume, Madison said (in the January 23, 1792, quotation cited earlier) that "the great art of politicians lies in making [parties] checks and balances to each other." He insisted that, as a consequence, republicanism and popular government could be made modern and natural. And he said that "justice is the end of government. It is the end of civil society."[51] In fact, Madison was describing a "civilized" nation as contrasted to an uncivilized nation.[52] Madison's system was to work—or work better than other systems—because it detached, then balanced in a civil symmetry, interests, political function, and administrative territory. The most difficult task was to refine out of differing interests and opinions policies that would be wise and in the common purpose. In such a diverse country with no definable majority, this could be done only if several competing interests, or factions, compromised and coalesced (Madison used the word "comprehend"; Hume extolled the "tendency to a coalition," which afforded "the most agreeable prospect of future happiness"[53]) to form an alliance, as in the legislature, to get something done. But because each faction would have to restrain its most passionate desires, or its most outlandish demands, the rights of the coalition partners would tend to be protected.

Contemporary political scientists would point out that the resultant moderation should likewise provide more plausible security for the rights of those out of power and help persuade them to craft their own ample coalition, in the hopes of gaining political power. The consequences for the entire nation would be precisely what modern scholars suggest are the benefits of a two-party system: the elimination of violence and the resolution of conflict among contending elements of society, weak ideological passion, and a tendency toward unification of the country. In order to win elections and ultimately to govern, parties must appeal to as many geographic, ideological, ethnic, economic, and class interests as possible. Contemporary scholars thus argue that a two-party system provides modern democracies the means to govern and tends to keep the country united and moderate, unlikely to follow extremist factions in veering off into foolish directions.[54]

But this recent assessment is only apparently recent; before a *conception* of the modern party organization had developed, before a *language* had identified the modern party structure, and before the competitive two-party system surfaced as a historical fact in the United States, Madison (aided by his reading of Hume) had elaborated a theoretical basis for what would become that system, of which he was one of the foremost initiators. This review of his writings shows that his actions were not deviations from his earlier musings but were the fruition of his political science.

Notes

1. Both Hamilton and Madison used the term. See, for example, Hamilton in No. 1 and Madison in No. 14 of *The Federalist Papers* (New York: Mentor, 1961), 33 and 104.

2. Joseph J. Ellis, *Founding Brothers: The Revolutionary Generation* (New York: Knopf, 2001), 15.

3. Edward Stanwood, *A History of the Presidency from 1788–1897* (Boston: Houghton Mifflin, 1898), 123. Perhaps the more famous statement came from E. E. Schattschneider a generation later: "Modern democracy is unthinkable save in terms of political parties." See Schattschneider, *Party Government* (New York: Rinehart, 1942), 1.

4. In addition to the citations of Stanwood and Schattschneider above, see the anthology edited by Russell J. Dalton and Martin P. Wattenberg, *Parties without Partisans: Political Change in Advanced Industrial Democracies* (Oxford: Oxford University Press, 2000), particularly the introduction, which repeats several of the assumed values of a party system while discussing challenges to the system in our own day. Scholars often assert that a developing country must accept "democracy," which invariably includes a "multiparty system," in order to be accepted as a functioning modern nation-state.

5. Austin Ranney, "Political Parties and Article VIII of the Constitution," in *A Grand Experiment: The Constitution at 200; Essays from the Douglass Adair Symposia,* ed. John Allphin Moore, Jr., and John E. Murphy (Wilmington, DE: Scholarly Resources, 1987), 57–68.

6. Samuel H. Beer, *To Make a Nation: The Rediscovery of American Federalism* (Cambridge, MA: Harvard University Press, 1993), 258–59.

7. Daniel Sisson, *The American Revolution of 1800* (New York: Knopf, 1974), 25. Sisson titled chapter 2 of his book "The Idea of a Non-Party State."

8. Gordon S. Wood, *Revolutionary Characters: What Made the Founders Different* (New York: Penguin, 2006), 55.

9. Stanley Elkins and Eric McKitrick, *The Age of Federalism* (New York: Oxford University Press, 1993), 263.

10. See especially *The Machiavellian Moment: Florentine Political Thought and the Atlantic Republican Tradition* (Princeton, NJ: Princeton University Press, 1975). For

Pocock's discussion of Hume, see 493–509; for his coverage of eighteenth-century America, see chapter 15, 506–52.

11. See Gordon S. Wood, *The Creation of the American Republic, 1776–1787* (Chapel Hill: University of North Carolina Press, 1969), and his Pulitzer Prize–winning *The Radicalism of the American Revolution* (New York: Knopf, 1992).

12. Pocock averred in *Machiavellian Moment* that "the dread of modernity itself" (509) had been transplanted to America. Of course, there has always been the counterargument that thinkers and actors in the United States at its inception, instead of being republican in the sense described above in the text, were uniquely "liberal," that is, individualistic, entrepreneurial, and devoid of the political arguments and socially inequitable patterns of the Old World. See Louis Hartz, *The Liberal Tradition in America* (New York: Harcourt, 1955), for an early and influential statement of this theme, and, for a more nuanced rendition, Joyce Oldham Appleby, *Capitalism and a New Social Order: The Republican Vision of the 1790s* (New York: New York University Press, 1984), and *Liberalism and Republicanism in the Historical Imagination* (Cambridge, MA: Harvard University Press, 1992). Gary Rosen has also designated Madison, at least, as a liberal, one with distinct ideas about how to implement liberal nostrums in a way that would assure the public good. See *American Compact: James Madison and the Problem of Founding* (Lawrence: University Press of Kansas, 1999). Back at the other end of the argument, Garrett Ward Sheldon has reasserted the republican stance by contending that Madison's Calvinist worldview drove him toward civic republicanism. See *The Political Philosophy of James Madison* (Baltimore, MD: Johns Hopkins University Press, 2001).

13. See Wood, *Radicalism,* 253–55.

14. This, as noted above, is the thesis of Elkins and McKitrick. See *Age of Federalism,* 263–70.

15. Richard Hofstadter took an in-between position in his classic historical narrative of the origin and development of the American party system, *The Idea of a Party System: The Rise of Legitimate Opposition in the United States, 1780–1840* (Berkeley: University of California Press, 1969): "[A]lmost as soon as their national government was in operation, [the founders] found it necessary to establish parties. . . . The new Constitution which they had so ingeniously drawn up could never have been made to work" without the innovation of political parties (viii).

16. James Madison, "Vices of the Political System of the United States," April 1787, in *The Papers of James Madison,* ed. William T. Hutchinson et al. (Chicago: University of Chicago Press; Charlottesville: University Press of Virginia, 1962–91), 9:355–56.

17. David Hume, "Of Parties in General" and "Of Superstition and Enthusiasm," in *Essays Moral, Political and Literary,* ed. Eugene F. Miller, rev. ed. (Indianapolis, IN: Liberty Classics, 1985), 63, 74. "Enthusiasm" carried a commonly understood meaning in the eighteenth century; according to the *Oxford English Dictionary:* "Fancied inspiration; a vain confidence of divine favour or misdirected religious emotion, extravagance of religious speculation." The *OED* cites eighteenth-century theologian and scientist Joseph Priestly's use of the word as: "Enthusiasm [makes us] imagine that we are the peculiar favorites of the divine being." Of course, as the essay's title suggests, Hume worried as well about "superstition," which he saw as "a blind and terrified credulity."

18. David Epstein, *The Political Theory of* The Federalist (Chicago: University of Chicago Press, 1984), 211. Richard Hofstader, who often conflated the words "party" and "faction" in the utterances of early Americans, nonetheless noted that Samuel Johnson's famous dictionary defined "party" in less clearly invidious terms than it did "faction." See *Idea of a Party System,* 11.

19. See, for example, "The Union. Who Are Its Real Friends?" March 31, 1792, and "A Candid State of Parties," September 22, 1792, *Papers,* 14:274–75, 370–72. These are examples of several "editorial" comments provided by Madison to the *National Gazette.* Other examples can be found elsewhere in volume 14.

20. "Parties," January 23, 1792, *Papers,* 14:197–98.

21. Douglass Adair, "'That Politics May Be Reduced to a Science': David Hume, James Madison and the Tenth Federalist," and "'Experience Must Be Our Only Guide': History, Democratic Theory, and the United States Constitution," in *Fame and the Founding Fathers,* ed. Trevor Colbourn (New York: Norton, 1974), 75–123. Hume's influence on the founders is often asserted; see, for example, relevant passages in Garry Wills, *Explaining America: The Federalist* (New York: Doubleday, 1981), Forrest McDonald, *Alexander Hamilton: A Biography* (New York: Norton, 1979), and Elkins and McKitrick, *Age of Federalism.* Gary Rosen has written, "That Hume influenced [Madison's] ideas on faction, representation, and the extended sphere is beyond dispute." See *American Compact,* 107. Drew McCoy, in his lucid exploration of Madison's ongoing thinking about the difficulties of maintaining a republic, noted that "Hume's influence on Madison now appears indisputable." McCoy found Madison's thoughts frequently paralleling Hume's. See *The Last of the Fathers: James Madison and the Republican Legacy* (Cambridge: Cambridge University Press, 1989), 43n7, 48–49, 55, 59. Also see Mark G. Spencer, *David Hume and Eighteenth-Century America* (Rochester, NY: Rochester University Press, 2005), especially chapter 6. Interestingly, Hofstadter referred to parallel "Madisonian" and "Humean" views of *parties* and even suggested that at times Jefferson shared the "Hume-Madison view." See *Idea of a Party System,* 24–27. Finally, it is worth recalling Jefferson's dexterous explanation of Hume's influence on America's founders: "Every one knows that judicious matter and charms of style have rendered Hume's history the manual of every student. I remember well the enthusiasm with which I devoured it when young, and the length of time, the research and reflection which were necessary to eradicate the poison it had instilled into my mind." Letter to Colonel William Duane, August 12, 1820, in *The Life and Selected Writings of Thomas Jefferson,* ed. Adrienne Koch and William Peden (New York: Random House, 1944), 605–6. Madison, equally charmed, saw the poison as elixir.

22. This quotation, from Adair's long-unpublished but frequently studied Ph.D. dissertation, *The Intellectual Origins of Jefferson Democracy* (Yale University, 1943), 261, can now be found in the published version edited by Mark E. Yellin, *The Intellectual Origins of Jeffersonian Democracy: Republicanism, the Class Struggle, and the Virtuous Farmer* (New York: Lexington, 2000). For Adair's full argument, see 130–39. Frederick G. Whelan defends Adair's essential contention; see his *Order and Artifice in Hume's Political Philosophy* (Princeton, NJ: Princeton University Press, 1985), 342.

To be sure, there is support, but also there are several demurs from Adair's claim. For a variety of opinions, see Edmund S. Morgan, "Safety in Numbers: Madison,

Hume and the Tenth Federalist," *Huntington Library Quarterly* 49 (Spring 1986): 95–112; Theodore Draper, "Hume and Madison: The Secrets of Federalist Paper No. 10," *Encounter* 58 (February 1982): 34–47; and Marvin Meyers, "Reflection and Choice: Beyond the Sum of the Differences," in *The Mind of the Founder,* ed. Marvin Meyers, rev. ed. (Hanover, NH: University Press of New England, 1981), xi–xlvii. I agree with Meyers that the founders took ideas from several thinkers and developed their own distinctive political philosophy. Still, Meyers's dismissal of Adair's thesis by suggesting that Hume, in the essay "Idea of a Perfect Commonwealth," did not touch upon the "number and diversity of social economic interests" (xxviii) as did Madison in No. 10 is an imperfect critique, because Hume *did* comment on such diversity of interests—in a discussion of factions—in the essay "Of Parties in General," which Madison almost certainly read. See Hume's remarks (*Essays,* 54–64) and the discussion in John B. Stewart, *The Moral and Political Philosophy of David Hume* (New York: Columbia University Press, 1963), 201–3. As would be expected, this paper argues for the accuracy of Adair's observation.

23. Adair, "Politics Reduced to Science," 105n18. The first reference to Hume in the *Madison Papers* is a letter from Madison's college friend William Bradford, dated October 13, 1772, which paraphrases a selection from *An Enquiry Concerning Human Understanding:* "Human nature is the same in every age if we make allowance for the difference of customs and Education, so that we learn to know ourselves by studying the opinions and passions of others." See *Papers,* 1:73. While a representative in the Continental Congress, Madison served on a committee issuing a report on books to be collected for the use of Congress, and the two Hume entries he placed in this extensive bibliography were the *History of England* and the political essays, likely the two Hume works most familiar to Madison and others of the founding generation. See the book list dated January 24, 1783, *Papers,* 6:80–87.

24. Ralph Ketcham, *James Madison: A Biography* (Charlottesville: University Press of Virginia, 1990), 186–87.

25. David Hume, "Idea of a Perfect Commonwealth," *Essays,* 512–29. A salient paragraph in Hume's complex proposal reads: "Let GREAT BRITAIN and IRELAND, or any territory of equal extent, be divided into 100 counties, and each county into 100 parishes. . . . If [the commonwealth] be of *greater extent,* it were better to enlarge the parishes, or throw more parishes into a county, than increase the number of counties" (516, emphasis added). "Commonwealth" and "republic" were virtually synonymous in the eighteenth century, referring to a type of government based on the consent of the people. The English "commonwealth" of 1649–60 has been described as a republic. Several U.S. states, guaranteed a "republican form of government" in Article IV, Section 4, of the Constitution, called themselves "commonwealths" (Massachusetts, Pennsylvania, Virginia, and Kentucky).

26. See Hamilton's *Federalist* No. 9, 73. Montesquieu, *De l'esprit des lois,* édition de R. Derathe (Paris: Garnier, 1973), 3:25–35. The original French edition was published in 1748. The first English translation, by Thomas Nugent, appeared in 1750. Madison and Hamilton were quite familiar with Montesquieu's main arguments, and they were both at pains in the *Federalist* to explain how the Americans had solved problems the "celebrated" French philosopher had described. Indeed, Montesquieu's name appears

twelve times in the *Federalist,* more than any other thinker. See Nos. 9, 43, 47, and 78. Thomas S. Engeman, Edward J. Erler, and Thomas B. Hofeller, eds., *The Federalist Concordance* (Chicago: University of Chicago Press, 1988).

27. Hume, "The Parties of Great Britain," *Essays,* 65.

28. Hume, "Of Parties in General," *Essays,* 56, 55; "Of the Populousness of Ancient Nations," *Essays,* 407; and "Of the Coalition of Parties," *Essays,* 493.

29. Hume, "Of the Coalition of Parties," *Essays,* 493.

30. These are the words of Knud Haakonssen, "The Structure of Hume's Political Theory," in *The Cambridge Companion to Hume,* ed. David Fate Norton (New York: Cambridge University Press, 1993), 205.

31. David Miller, *Philosophy and Ideology in Hume's Political Thought* (Oxford: Clarendon, 1981), 176–77. Miller, like Frederick Whelan in *Order and Artifice,* argues that Hume's philosophy, originating in his *Treatise of Human Nature,* is logically relevant to, and consistent with, his political thought. Contrariwise, Duncan Forbes, in *Hume's Philosophical Politics* (Cambridge: Cambridge University Press, 1975), finds little relevant connection between Hume's philosophy and his political ideas.

32. Hume, "That Politics May Be Reduced to a Science," *Essays,* 30–31, 27. Emphasis in original.

33. Hume, "Idea of a Perfect Commonwealth," 519–20. Frederick Whelan explains that "Hume as a political scientist devoted much attention to the origins of political parties and to the function of parties in the British Constitution, regarding them as a natural and largely beneficial phenomenon in a free government" (*Order and Artifice,* 326). There is coverage of parties in Hume's *History of England* (1778; Indianapolis, IN: Liberty Classics, 1983), particularly in the last volume. Here, too, Hume sees and has some approval of what we might call a "two-party" system. See, for example, 6:375–76.

34. *Federalist* No. 10, 77–84.

35. "Of Parties in General," 59.

36. The word "aliment" can be found in Hume's "Of Parties in General," 58. According to Adair, it was an uncommon and rarely used word in the eighteenth century; thus, its appearance here, Adair believed, helped underscore the Hume-Madison connection. See Adair's "Politics Reduced to Science," 104–5.

37. Hume's critique of classical political theory for unrealistically emphasizing community virtue and unified purpose while ignoring human nature and being unaware of divisive passions among citizens and of the spirit of faction undoubtedly affected Madison. For Hume's unfavorable assessment of classical political thought, see "Of the Populousness of Ancient Nations," 407–8; noteworthy for the present study, Hume asserted that the ancients, rather than promoting moderation among differing factions, simply followed the practice of having the victorious faction or party "butcher all of the opposite party who fell into their hands, and banish such as had been so fortunate as to escape their fury" (407). Because of such statements, Thomas Pangle has argued that Hume's views of human nature as set forth in his political essays helped undermine the idea of "virtuous" "classical republicanism" and set the stage for the triumph of modern liberalism in the thinking of the American founders. See "Human Nature and the Constitution," in *Confronting the Constitution,*

ed. Allan Bloom (Washington: AEI Press, 1987), 18–21. The relevant section of Pangle's essay is titled "Hume's Attack on Classical Republicanism." James Moore accentuated this same theme, writing that "the classical republican tradition comes to an end with the political science of Hume." See "Hume's Political Science and the Classical Republican Tradition," *Canadian Journal of Political Science* 10 (December 1977): 810. This essay endorses Pangle's and Moore's interpretation.

38. This is the section of No. 10 that must have leapt out at Charles Beard. Madison, however, saw a "civilized" political society containing a "multiplicity" of interests (and opinions), not just property divisions.

39. According to Albert O. Hirschman, the new emphasis in the eighteenth century (a new emphasis from the attraction to science) was, as Hume insisted, to look at human beings as they really were, not as they ought to be. Thus, passions, which are part of human nature, were to be harnessed, not repressed, and in being harnessed provide for the general welfare. Hirschman calls this the "Principle of the Countervailing Passion," which he sees as derivative of Hume's notions of balancing passions. See Hirschman, *The Passions and the Interests: Political Arguments for Capitalism before Its Triumph* (Princeton, NJ: Princeton University Press, 1977), 14–26.

40. *Federalist* No. 51, 320–25.

41. Ketcham, *Madison,* 536–38, and Roger H. Brown, "The Republic in Peril, 1812: Party Loyalty and War," in *After the Constitution: Party Conflict in the New Republic,* ed. Lance Banning (Belmont, CA: Wadsworth, 1989), 397–410.

42. Irving Brant, *James Madison: Father of the Constitution, 1787–1800* (Indianapolis, IN: Bobbs-Merrill, 1950), 348. Brant was referring to the essay "A Candid State of Parties," September 22, 1792, in which, the biographer says, Madison conferred the "political christening" on the phrase "Republican Party." *Papers,* 14:372.

43. In a letter to William Eustis dated May 22, 1823, he wrote: "The people are now able everywhere to compare the principles and policy of those who have borne the name of Republicans or Democrats, with the career of the adverse party; and to see and feel that the former are as much in harmony with the spirit of the nation and the genius of the Gov't as the latter was at variance with both." In *Writings of James Madison,* ed. Gaillard Hunt (New York: G. P. Putnam's Sons, 1900–1910), 9:135.

44. *Papers,* 14:371.

45. Madison, letter to Henry Lee, June 25, 1824, *Writings,* 9:190. The fine, Humean pitch of this communication may be discerned in the following words that appear later in the same letter: "The Constitution itself . . . must be an unfailing source of party distinctions. . . . There is nevertheless sufficient scope for combating the spirit of party, as far as it may not be necessary to fan the flame of liberty, in efforts to divert it from the more noxious channels; to moderate its violence, especially in the ascendant party; to elucidate the policy which harmonizes jealous interest; and that particularly to give to the Constitution that just construction, which with the aid of time and habit, may put an end to the more dangerous schisms otherwise growing out of it." One may juxtapose this statement regarding parties with the Hume quotations on pages 355 and 356 above and with Hume's ideas on "time" and "habit"; for the latter, see *A Treatise of Human Nature,* ed. Ernest C. Mossner (1739–40; London: Penguin, 1969), 1:ii; *An Enquiry Concerning Human Understanding* (1748; Amherst, MA: Prometheus,

1988), sections 4–7; and "On the Origins of Government," *Essays,* 39, where the Scotsman wrote that "habit soon consolidates what other principles of human nature had imperfectly founded."

46. This is the way Madison scholar Jack Rakove has put it:

> In his analysis [of the problems confronting the new nation], Madison sought to demonstrate how an entirely different set of assumptions could reaffirm the American commitment to republican government. In so doing, however, his deepest concern was to prove that a national republic would protect minority interest and individual rights against the danger of a "factious majority": a majority which, while claiming to embody the popular will, actually preferred its own interests to the public good. . . . Experience taught that neither "a prudent regard" for the general good nor "respect for character" nor even religion could deter an impassioned or interested majority from pursuing "unjust violations for the rights and interests of the minority, or of individuals."

See *James Madison and the Creation of the American People* (Glenview, IL: Scott Foresman, 2002), 48. Hume understood this challenge and addressed it in writings read by Madison and likely by Hamilton. While Madison was a perfectly capable political thinker (and certainly a good student), Hume's essays provided Madison the suggestive fodder to help him develop the "entirely different set of assumptions" Rakove knows the American founder sought.

47. A more careful scrutiny of the *Federalist* essays than can be accommodated by this chapter reveals a considerable attraction to Hume's arguments, particularly in the *Essays* and the *History*. One example not featured here is the influence Hume exerted on Madison's No. 49. See particularly McCoy, *Last of the Fathers,* 43–49. For this line of reasoning, I am also indebted to Nora Ming-Ming Ho, author of "David Hume, James Madison, and *The Federalist*" (senior thesis, California State Polytechnic University, Pomona, 1998).

48. This needs to be said in response to Edmund Morgan, who dismissed Adair's thesis with a detailed examination of the essay "Idea of a Perfect Commonwealth" and who insists that Hume's aims therein were in some regards opposite of, or unrelated to, Madison's in the late 1780s. See "Safety in Numbers," *Huntington Library Quarterly* 49 (Spring 1986): 95–112. The present chapter, obviously, argues that Madison read much more than this single essay and found in Hume's full corpus stimulating ideas for addressing vital concerns.

49. See, for example, Madison in *Federalist* No. 37, 226, and Hamilton in *Federalist* No. 70, 423.

50. Hume, "Of Civil Liberty," *Essays,* 93.

51. Madison, *Federalist* No. 51, 324. Hume saw government as having "no other object or purpose but the distribution of justice." See "The Origin of Government," *Essays,* 37–38.

52. See *Federalist* No. 10, 79. To "civilize" was an English rendering of a French verb derived from the Latin root for "civil," "civic," and "city," suggesting, thus, an enriched and just relationship of citizens to one another and a citizenry that is cosmopolitan,

not provincial; varied, not homogeneous; and living in a highly developed society. The word "civilize" was in use in English by the seventeenth century.

"Civic" comes from the Latin *civicus,* that is, "citizen"; by the sixteenth century, according to the *Oxford English Dictionary,* it was a word "pertaining to a city." "City" is from the Latin *civitas,* again meaning "citizen," and "civil" is from the Latin *civilis,* also "citizen." The French permutation "to civilize" meant "to bring out of barbarism [and up to] the standards of behaviour and the tastes of a highly developed society; to enlighten, refine and educate." See relevant entries in the *Oxford English Dictionary.*

53. Hume, "Of the Coalition of Parties," 494.

54. This rendition of the value of parties is widely broadcast; see Austin Ranney, "Article VIII"; John A Moore, Jr., and Myron Roberts, "The Art of Politics: Parties and Elections," chapter 9 in *The Pursuit of Happiness: Government and Politics in America,* 5th ed. (New York: Macmillan, 1992); and John F. Bibby and L. Sandy Maisel, *Two Parties or More? The American Party System* (Boulder, CO: Westview, 2003).

FIVE

Madison as President

BYRON W. DAYNES AND MARK P. HOPKINS

James Madison

Brilliant Theorist, Failed Tactician

Thoughtful people who discuss James Madison today are more likely to focus on his association with the Constitution than on his painful years as the fourth president of the United States. In fact, when confronting these two "James Madisons"—the constitutional master thinker and the two-term president—the question that immediately comes to mind is how this brilliant contributor to the Constitution could have been considered a less-than-successful president. In somewhat different terms, how could this man who helped create the model document for democracies worldwide have so poorly mismanaged the presidency—the very office he helped create?

Evidence would suggest that his contemporaries also puzzled about this apparent contradiction. Early records assert that while citizens highly respected Madison's contributions as a leading constitutional thinker,[1] both Federalists and disgruntled Jeffersonian Republicans questioned his performance as president.

Examining what took place during his two terms in office seems the only way to put this man in a proper political and historical perspective. Certainly the most influential of the early works on Madison is Henry Adams's history of Madison's two administrations, which stresses his ineptitude during the War of 1812 and suggests what Madison should have done differently rather than presenting an impartial understanding of the events that took place.[2] Garry Wills, in his book on James Madison, recognizes Madison's failures as president yet also seeks to understand the cause of the crises that faced him, many of which were not of Madison's own creation. Accordingly, Wills concludes that Madison was a "shrewd constitutionalist" yet a "hapless commander in chief."[3] Other scholars of the presidency, such as James Barber, classify Madison in like manner. According to Barber's classification, Madison was a "passive-positive" president—one who was compliant, receptive, and other-directed yet failed to take charge or be innovative in the presidency.[4]

Comparative rankings of the U.S. presidents reflect the consensus that Madison had some major failings as president and consistently evaluate him as "average." Both the 1948 and 1962 surveys by Arthur Schlesinger, Sr., so rated Madison, placing him as fourteenth and twelfth among other presidents, respectively.[5] The 1982 *Chicago Tribune* poll ranked Madison as seventeenth among presidents, while the 1982 Murray-Blessing poll ranked him as fourteenth.[6] More recent surveys reflect even greater disappointment in Madison's presidency. For example, the 1996 poll by Arthur Schlesinger, Jr., ranked Madison as seventeenth, classifying him as the first among "average" presidents.[7] Similarly, Madison was ranked sixteenth in the *Chicago Sun-Times* survey and eighteenth in the 2000 C-Span poll.[8] Hence, in seven surveys taken between 1948 and 2000, Madison's rankings are relatively consistent as compared to other presidents.

Madison's contributions to the creation of the American presidency were less consequential than those of such nationalists as James Wilson and Alexander Hamilton, both of whom advocated a strong presidency for the American political system. Madison chiefly emphasized the need for a "balance of powers"[9] between the executive and the legislative branches, which encouraged him to support a strong Congress and a weaker executive. Ironically, the very principles of republican government that Madison espoused may have contributed to his weaker presidency. Had Madison exhibited more decisive leadership, and had he exercised the same prerogative power as George Washington did in some of the uncertain situations that faced the first president, James Madison would likely have been considered a more successful president today. But given this dilemma, the authors of this chapter posit that despite Madison's role in the creation of the American presidency and American government in general, the crisis conditions he faced—some of his own making, but others beyond his control—resulted in his own weakened presidency.

Methods

Madison's performance as president can be categorized according to the following five presidential roles:

1. *Opinion/Party Leader*—a combined role suggesting a president's relationship to party and public opinion;
2. *Legislative Leader*—a role indicating a president's relationship to Congress;

3. *Chief Executive*—a role involving a president's relationships with cabinet, administrative staff, and bureaucracy;

4. *Chief Diplomat*—a role that examines a president's relationship to other nations; and

5. *Commander in Chief*—a role referring to a president as the nation's highest military leader.

These roles are not equally powerful. Under normal circumstances, for example, a president acting as commander in chief is in a more powerful position than a president who has assumed the role of opinion/party leader. A president using his commander in chief role has access to more legal authority, can have an increased dominance in decision making, is increasingly protected from interfering organized interests, and has greater ability to rally the nation behind him in a crisis. These five roles may thus be arranged on a power continuum with commander in chief ranked as the most powerful presidential role, followed by chief diplomat, chief executive, and legislative leader, with opinion/party leader being the president's weakest role.[10]

The Roles

Opinion/Party Leader

This composite role suggests the direct relationship the president has with the people through the political party and public opinion. This role is generally the president's weakest. The president's effective use of this role depends on individual skill rather than on the resources or substantial authority available to him. Thus, few presidents have dominated their surroundings in this role, and Madison was no exception.

Madison lacked the strong public presence and charisma to lead effectively as president. Though his support during his presidency varied with the events of the War of 1812, he struggled to influence public opinion. For example, an observer during Madison's first inaugural address reported that the president appeared "extremely pale and trembled excessively when he first began to speak."[11] Moreover, historians of Madison's presidency corroborate that view, suggesting that the president lacked "people skills" and certainly did not have a "charismatic personality." Further, his physical appearance did not suggest a person exerting strong leadership.[12] Madison suffered in comparison to the strapping physical presence of George Washington; he was about five feet four inches tall, slightly built, and troubled by serious illness most of his life.[13] Madison's illnesses often got in the way of his ability to lead. He related one instance in a letter to James

Monroe dated March 21, 1808, where his health was particularly troublesome to the situation at hand: "I have found the task extremely laborious, and being infirm in health, and otherwise hard pressed on important subjects, I have been obliged to let it devolve in a good measure on others."[14] Leonard D. White, a noted scholar of the period, indicated that the reason James Madison might have been a successful democratic theorist but an unsuccessful president was that he had a "weak personality" but possessed a "superior intellect." White adds that Madison would probably have made a more competent president of the University of Virginia than of the United States.[15] As U.S. president, Madison lacked the strong public presence of his predecessor, Thomas Jefferson, and as a result, he continually struggled to fill the void left by the third president.

While Madison gave few public speeches, he held regular White House socials for the public and was somewhat successful in easing some of the political tensions between Federalists and Republicans through this social contact.[16]

Socials. Prior to Madison's presidency, Jefferson had avoided social activities because his adherence to strict Republican beliefs led him to avoid ceremony, and because the passing of his wife deprived him of an adequate hostess. However, as Madison entered the presidency, First Lady Dolley Madison played a crucial role in maintaining contact with the people and elected officials through her "drawing-room socials," which she held every Wednesday evening.[17] The Madisons also made it a point to keep the White House doors open to the entire citizenry, not just the powerful elites. Of those that attended, Mary Latrobe, a family friend, describes these socials held in the Madisons' drawing room: "Mrs. Madison gives drawing rooms every Wednesday. The first one was very numerously attended by none but respectable people. The Second, La la [persons of middle-class standing] . . . the last by a perfect rabble of beards and boots."[18]

Dolley Madison began her public socials following her husband's presidential inaugural ceremonies. The Madisons were also the first presidential couple to hold an inaugural ball, an activity that became another way of reaching out to the public. James and Dolley Madison made every possible effort not to give the impression of opulence at the White House and were thus careful in both their dress and the decor selected for the White House.[19] Dolley Madison's charm and charisma as hostess endeared her to politicians as well as to the public at large.

Travels. While Madison's socials had a positive effect on public opinion, the president did very little traveling to influence public opinion during his two terms. He did, however, visit his generals in the field on specific occasions to oversee military operations and make recommendations. But even during these visits, he seldom took the chance to make public appearances and speak in favor of the war, as table 12.1 makes clear.

Table 12.1

Presidential Tours and Other Popular Communication of the First Six Presidents

President	*N of Tours*	*N of Speeches on Tour (est.)*	*N of Other Speeches*	*Total Speeches (est.)*	*Average N of Speeches per Year (est.)*
Washington	2	20	5	25	3
J. Adams	0	0	6	6	1
Jefferson	0	0	3	3	5
Madison	0	0	0	0	0
Monroe	2	40	0	42	5
J. Q. Adams	0	0	5	5	1

Source: Jeffrey K. Tulis, *The Rhetorical Presidency* (Princeton, NJ: Princeton University Press, 1987), 64.

Speeches. Madison failed to use the full potential of his role as opinion/party leader in that he limited himself to giving speeches primarily to Congress rather than to members of the public. Madison followed Jefferson's model and rarely spoke directly to the public; instead, he relied on proclamations as his mode of communicating with the people. According to Jeffrey K. Tulis, Madison did not engage in any popular rhetoric, not even to rouse the spirits of the soldiers and citizenry during the war or to defend his policies.[20]

The Press. Madison's relations with the press were similar to what they had been during Jefferson's presidency—essentially, tense and negative. Publications representing New England Federalists and strict Jeffersonian Republicans were especially critical. In response to Madison's restraints on commerce, several newspapers and pamphlets depicted the president as arraigning power to himself like a dictator. For example, John Lowell, a Federalist, embodied New England's general sentiment when he wrote the anti-war pamphlet titled "Mr. Madison's War," in which he accused Madison of manipulating and pushing the nation to war.[21] Although the charges were false, the *Federal Republican* also accused Madison of "arrogating to himself the power of commencing war, without the authority of Congress." The *New York Evening Post* characterized Madison's manner of writing as "smoother than oil" and yet with a "drawn sword in his hand." Responding to accusations that Madison's reimposition of the commercial restraints was wicked and foolish, the same paper proclaimed the president "too weak to be wicked."[22] Rather than answering most of these charges directly, Madison simply continued forward and was careful not to disclose anything that would provoke additional outbursts in the press.

Where Madison was strong in this role was in his dealings with the Democratic-Republican Party, where his efforts helped contribute to the ultimate demise of the Federalist Party by the 1830s. Despite his contributions to the Democratic-Republican cause, James Madison could not always depend on his own party to give him the needed support for his leadership. The primary problem lay with the southern old-line Republicans who had favored James Monroe in the 1808 presidential election. In the ensuing Republican presidential nomination, Monroe supporters were so embittered that they boycotted the caucus, thus ensuring Madison an overwhelming victory.[23] Monroe felt estranged from the Republican Party not only because he disagreed with Madison on certain issues but also because Jefferson had favored Madison to be his successor.[24] Though Monroe refused an earlier invitation by Madison, in 1811 he conceded to serve in his cabinet as secretary of state[25] and later, 1814–15, served concurrently as secretary of war. When Monroe became a part of the administration, he brought greater unity to the Republican Party and encouraged the passage of some of Madison's programs in Congress.[26]

Legislative Leader

As legislative leader Madison had trouble securing support for his programs, suggesting his weakness in this role. This became evident as he attempted to restrict commerce. Before Madison became president, Jefferson had signed the Embargo Act of 1807, which restricted foreign trade and encountered stiff Federalist resistance. In response to this widespread opposition, the Embargo Act was replaced on March 1, 1809, with the Non-Intercourse Act, which reopened all overseas shipping except that with France and Britain. Upon entering office, Madison continued to enforce the Non-Intercourse Act but was unable to attract sustaining support for it. Heavily influenced by the advice of his secretary of the treasury, Albert Gallatin, Madison called for more rigid enforcements of coastal trade, where most of the violations of the embargo had occurred.[27] Although Jefferson urged Madison to hold firm to these trade restrictions,[28] New England Federalists, who had vested interests in foreign commerce, criticized them. As a result of Madison's restrictions on trade, the press spuriously depicted Madison as being too dependent on Jefferson, even to the extent of calling him Jefferson's "monkey on a leash."[29] More importantly, the Non-Intercourse Act led to serious turmoil in New England.[30] In response to this opposition, Madison encouraged the Congress to pass a lesser act, known as Macon's Bill Number 2, on May 1, 1810, to supersede the Non-Intercourse Act. This act removed all restraints on shipping but provided for their restoration should free commerce prove unworkable.[31]

But tensions with Britain continued to grow. Opposing factions in his own party and opposition from New England left Madison unable to convince the Congress to continue negotiations with Britain that might avoid war. In frustration, Madison turned the decision for declaring war over to the Congress, which supported his earlier belief that "the executive has no right, in any case, to decide the question, whether there is or is not cause for declaring war."[32]

In so placing the responsibility to declare war on Congress and failing to provide decisive leadership himself, the nation was poorly prepared for military operations. As president, Madison seemed content to make recommendations and passively devolve responsibility on the Congress. Regarding the lack of military officers, for example, Madison vaguely urged Congress to provide the need for possible war: "Towards an accomplishment of this important work, I recommend for the consideration of Congress, the expediency of instituting a system, which shall, in the first instance, call into the field, at the public expence, and for a given time, certain portions of the commissioned and noncommissioned officers."[33]

In continuing to stress the Republican principle of "balance of powers,"[34] Madison encouraged a Congress that would never allow for anything but a weakened presidency. Moreover, the president did not feel the need to apologize for his position. Robert Allen Rutland described Madison as deemphasizing the importance of the military, in favor of preserving individual liberty. Although Congress wanted war, it proved reluctant to finance military operations. According to Rutland, Republican opposition to taxes harmed funding of the war.[35] Madison himself had stated, "I cannot undertake to lay my finger on that article of the Constitution which granted a right to Congress of expending, on the objects of benevolence, the money of their constituents."[36] In effect, adherence to Republican principles harmed the war effort.[37] The Republican Congress was reluctant to provide funds for military equipment.[38] New England Federalists also obstructed the raising of forces. As Madison stated, "The seditious opposition in Mass[achusetts] & Con[necticut] with the intrigues elsewhere insidiously co-operating with it, have so clogged the wheels of the war, that I fear the campaign will not accomplish the object of it."[39] Madison's inability to persuade Congress to support general military operations placed him in a weakened position to bargain and negotiate with Britain.

Chief Executive

As chief executive, Madison witnessed instability in his own administration in the frequent changes in personnel within his cabinet. With continuing dissent, the Senate scrutinized each of Madison's proposed appointments, limiting the many choices he might have made for his cabinet. As a result, Madison ended up accepting one of the weakest cabinets in American history. Many of the major department secretaries either came to oppose Madison's policies or demonstrated incompetence. Ralph Ketcham observed that Madison was involved in crisis of both "severe political difficulties and surrounded by less-than-ideal colleagues" facing "the climactic years of the Napoleonic Wars." Feeling that he needed to retain key members of Jefferson's cabinet to ensure a stabilized environment, he had to fill the remaining vacancies with men that Congress would approve. As a result, Madison appointed many men who were poorly qualified or even disloyal, as is evidenced in the State, War, and Navy departments. Yet even then, Madison's cabinet was not wholly useless, as he did have a few exceptional cabinet members such as Albert Gallatin and, later, James Monroe, who served in Madison's second term. The composition of Madison's cabinet can be largely attributed to party infighting and Madison's inability to resolve sectional tensions. For example, Madison was unable to convince the Congress to move treasury secretary Albert Gallatin, whom Madison had retained from the Jefferson cabinet, to the State Department. Rather, because of his inability to lead his party effectively and resolve conflict, Madison had to settle for "affable but incompetent Robert Smith" at State.[40]

Robert Smith proved so troublesome that the president had to intervene personally on several occasions.[41] Smith opposed the administration's position on trade with France, for example, and compromised the war efforts against Britain by undercutting public as well as congressional confidence in the administration. Madison did take matters into his own hands and dismissed Smith in 1811, replacing him with fellow Virginian James Monroe as secretary of state.[42] Smith, however, did not stop harassing the administration. Rather, he published a book, *Robert Smith's Address to the People of the United States,* continuing to criticize Madison for failing to heed his warning and for allowing Napoleon to take advantage of the United States.[43]

In addition to disloyalty and incompetence in the State Department, Madison faced a similar situation in the War and Navy departments. In the words of contemporary John Randolph, everyone in Washington, with the exception of the president, viewed the secretaries of war and navy as "incapable of discharging the duties of their office."[44] Again demonstrating poor judgment influenced by "sectional politics," Madison made ill-advised choices in selecting persons for these two cabinet positions. Because the Federalists in Congress and Republicans from New England would not serve because of their opposition to the war effort, the pool of potential candidates for office was somewhat limited. But Madison tried to appease these critics by appointing as his first secretary of war the slow and inefficient William Eustis. Eustis had no real military experience and resigned on December 3, 1812, after supporting some near disastrous campaigns during the fall of that year. Madison then replaced Eustis with John Armstrong, a man Madison never fully trusted. Similarly, Madison appointed Paul Hamilton, a Republican from South Carolina, as navy secretary despite his lack of naval experience. Although Hamilton was quite successful in the early months of the war, he blamed Madison for its failures and accused him of betrayal. Hamilton resigned on December 31, 1812, under extreme congressional criticism for the failures of the war.[45]

Madison appointed other cabinet officers who were qualified but failed to perform their responsibilities for other reasons. For example, Madison retained Jefferson's attorney general, Caesar A. Rodney—a competent Republican from Delaware. Though Rodney was qualified for this position, he continued his own private law practice in Wilmington, keeping him away from Washington for weeks and months at a time and causing him severely to neglect his duties.[46]

To compound Madison's problems, the president's management style made him very reluctant to fire officeholders who were not fulfilling their responsibilities.[47] John Armstrong, as secretary of war, serves as an example. After failing to carry out many of Madison's war plans, Madison finally confronted Armstrong and indicated, as he shows in this memo, that "I had always treated him with friendliness and confidence and that as there was but a short distance before me to the end of my public career, my great wish, next to leaving my country in a state of peace and prosperity, was to have preserved harmony and avoid changes, and that I had accordingly as he well knew acquiesced in many things, to which no other consideration would have reconciled me."[48] Friendship, in other words, often prevented Madison from calling his subordinates to account for their actions. This made it difficult to maintain an efficient cabinet.

While Madison called few cabinet meetings,[49] he held enough regular meetings to discuss and define policy, but even here Madison was usually at odds with particular cabinet members and preferred tolerating, rather than settling, these differences. Thus, the president usually dealt with serious problems only after they became unavoidable. J. C. A. Stagg suggested that rather than anticipating problem areas within his administration, Madison reacted to events; Stagg even called him "an inept manager of men," one who a contemporary, Jonathan Roberts, claimed was unable to "hook men to his heart as his predecessor could."[50] Madison preferred either to take additional responsibility upon himself or to delegate it to other cabinet members. For example, when John Armstrong finally resigned, Madison asked James Monroe to assume the responsibilities of both secretary of war and secretary of state rather than bring someone else into the cabinet. Madison faced a further problem, one not anticipated in the Constitution, when his vice president, Elbridge Gerry, died in 1814.[51]

Madison's opponents criticized the instability of his cabinet. John Randolph, for one, excoriated Robert Smith, secretary of state, for being "notoriously incompetent" and described John Armstrong as a "speculative parricide," while also denouncing several generals of the army as incompetent. Fellow Republicans also criticized Madison for appointing men from Congress to his cabinet, accusing these congressmen of changing from being "agents of the people" to "tools of the executive."[52] Table 12.2 illustrates the frequency of change and instability within Madison's administration.

Contemporary scholars of Madison's administration have been no kinder to him than earlier critics. Charles F. Faber and Richard B. Faber, for example, ranked Madison twenty-third among presidents for his administrative skills.[53] Similarly, the 2000 C-Span poll gave Madison a low ranking for his administrative skills, placing him at eighteenth among presidents. The *Chicago Sun-Times* survey similarly ranked Madison low for political leadership, giving him 2.99 points out of 5 points.[54]

Table 12.2
Madison's Cabinet

Office	*Secretary*	*Service Dates*
Secretary of State	Robert Smith	1809–11
	James Monroe	1811–17
Secretary of the Treasury	Albert Gallatin*	1809–14
	George W. Campbell	1814
	Alexander J. Dallas	1814–16
	William H. Crawford	1816–17
Secretary of War	William Eustis	1809–13
	John Armstrong	1813–14
	James Monroe	1814–15
	William H. Crawford	1815–16
Attorney General	Caesar A. Rodney*	1809–11
	William Pinkney	1811–14
	Richard Rush	1814–17
Secretary of the Navy	Paul Hamilton	1809–12
	William Jones	1813–14
	B.W. Crowninshield	1815–17

**Indicates a holdover from the Jefferson administration*

Source: William A. Degregorio, *The Complete Book of U.S. Presidents, 5th ed.* (New York: Gramercy Books, 2001), 64–65.

Chief Diplomat

Madison was no more successful as chief diplomat. He failed to win French support or that of other nations to strengthen America's hand in opposing Britain during the war. Madison, like Jefferson, generally favored the French. He trusted that Napoleon would honor the U.S. request for fair trade and commerce and would no longer seize U.S. ships if the United States would promise not to trade with Britain, but France did not fulfill its part of the agreement as it continued to seize "large numbers of American vessels that had entered the ports of the French empire and its satellites." Moreover, once they seized these vessels, France refused to return them and instead continued to sell them, citing "municipal regulations" to justify its action. In reacting to this situation, the president's Federalist and Republican opponents harshly criticized Madison, alleging that France had duped him. Despite this, Madison went ahead and proclaimed a position of nonintercourse against Britain on November 2, 1810, limiting all trade between the two countries. J. C. A. Stagg identifies this action as one of the most controversial decisions of Madison's career.[55]

Madison was also unable to force Britain to trade freely and fairly with the United States. Since he was convinced that Britain relied on the United States for "necessaries"[56]—resources and commodities—he believed that he could get Britain to honor his demands for free trade by severing ties with Britain. But this was not to be. Madison's threats of war also failed to encourage fair commerce.[57]

To Madison's credit as chief diplomat, he did stand up to the British, clearly articulating the conditions that Britain would have to meet before the United States would rescind its commerce restrictions. Henry Adams described these conditions. Madison expected Britain to: (1) release American seamen from their ships, (2) end the impressments of seamen from American ships, and (3) discontinue its naval blockades.[58] Yet America's demands went unmet. James Monroe, in a letter to Madison, prior to his appointment as secretary of state, made it clear that he did not desire war with Britain: "I was sincerely of the opinion . . . that it was for the interest of our country, to make an accommodation with England, the great maritime power, even on moderate terms, rather than hazard war, or any other alternative." Monroe then added, "If you are disposed to accept my services under these circumstances and with this explanation, I shall be ready to render them, whenever it may suit you to require them."[59]

But Madison was politically astute enough to accept Monroe's offer of services, recognizing that if the pressures continued to increase, it would be only a matter of time before America was forced into war. When Britain failed to meet the final U.S. demands, a majority of War Hawks in Congress—among them the Speaker of the House, Henry Clay, as well as other policy makers such as Richard M. Johnson, John C. Calhoun, George M. Troup, and John A. Harper[60]—continued the war pressures. In fact, Speaker Clay made matters worse for the president by ensuring that the War Hawks would have a firm hold on Congress by appointing ardent supporters of the war to the most important congressional committees.[61] By a strong majority, the House voted to support America's first declared war, as table 12.3 shows. Although the western and southern states supported the war, the New England Federalists fiercely opposed it. Some Federalists cynically called the war "Mr. Madison's War," much as Harry Truman's critics later labeled the "police action" in Korea, as "Truman's war."[62] Neither Madison nor Truman saw war as their first choice, but they thought their situations gave them few other alternatives.

Despite Congress's continued support for war, congressional leaders wanted Madison to be the one to first urge a policy of war, taking the pressure away from Congress.[63] And so Madison agreed to deliver a rather lengthy speech to Congress on June 1, 1812, "recommending" the option of war.[64] As Donald R. Hickey observed, this speech turned out to be more of a suggestion that Congress "consider the question of war" rather than an actual call for it.[65]

Thus, as chief diplomat, Madison was relatively ineffective in handling the concerns resulting from Britain's belligerence. Throughout his negotiations with Britain, Madison recognized Congress as the primary branch in foreign affairs since it was the only institution that could declare war. This fact alone weakened

Table 12.3

Vote on the War of 1812, June 4, 1812

State	*Yes*	*No*	*Not Voting*	*Total*
Connecticut	0	7	0	7
Delaware	0	1	0	1
Georgia	3	0	1	4
Kentucky	5	0	1	6
Louisiana	0	0	1	1
Maryland	6	3	0	9
Massachusetts	6	8	3	17
New Hampshire	3	2	0	5
New Jersey	2	4	0	6
New York	3	11	3	17
North Carolina	6	3	3	12
Ohio	1	0	0	1
Pennsylvania	16	2	0	18
Rhode Island	0	2	0	2
South Carolina	8	0	0	8
Tennessee	3	0	0	3
Vermont	3	1	0	4
Virginia	14	5	3	22
Totals:	79	43	15	143

Source: Derived from Reginald Horsman, *The Causes of the War of 1812* (Philadelphia: University of Pennsylvania Press, 1962), 293.

Madison's ability to engage in diplomacy effectively. In a discussion with British minister Augustus J. Foster after Congress had declared war, Madison "expressed his sincere desire to see the causes of the war removed." But when asked if an immediate armistice might prevent war, Madison answered that it would depend on Congress and whether it was in session at the time.[66] Again, Madison refused to take assertive responsibility as chief diplomat, instead relying on congressional action. Britain also had tried to remedy situations when it agreed, shortly before the United States formally declared war, to repeal the naval laws that were chiefly responsible for the conflict. Because communication was slow in arriving at the White House, however, Madison did not receive notice of Britain's decision until after the war had begun.[67]

Commander in Chief

As commander in chief, Madison was both directly responsible for or, at the very least, somewhat involved in several of the war defeats. Garry Wills blames these on "poor generalship, military cowardice, and insubordination."[68] Again, Madison's failure to act decisively, his poor judgment in choosing military officers and cabinet personnel, and his inability to convince Congress to fund a military force sufficient to confront Britain made failure in this conflict almost a certainty.

War also showed Madison to be a poor military strategist, since he found himself relying too much on congressional advice, which often proved detrimental to the success of the war. Throughout the course of the war, Congress was dominated by the War Hawks,[69] many of whom desired to use the war to achieve territorial expansion. These expansionists, under the leadership of Henry Clay, even wanted to conquer Canada.[70] Canada's heavy trade with Britain and its subjugation to British rule made it an attractive target; the War Hawks also thought that Canada's annexation would force Britain to acquiesce to American demands. James Monroe thus observed that advocates of invading Canada viewed this action "not as an object of the war but as a means of bringing it [the war] to a satisfactory conclusion."[71] Fears of Britain allying with Indians hostile to encroaching settlers further compounded the need to confront Canada.

With pressure from Congress and the growing threat from confederating Indian tribes, Madison ordered the invasion of Canada. His orders included invading Canada at Detroit and carrying out the rest of the attack at Niagara, after which forces would push toward Montreal and conquer it as well.[72] But these efforts failed, and Madison took the blame because of faulty military strategy. In a private letter to William Wirt he indicated, "whatever blame may be justly chargeable on the Executive, I will, in the confidence with which we both write, intimate the plan for giving effect to the war, originally entertained by that branch of the Government."[73]

Not only was the invasion of Canada strategically unsound, but it was also implemented by incompetent generals who mishandled military operations. Madison chose General William Hull, an unfit and aged general, to invade Canada at Detroit; he soon surrendered to an inferior force of British and Indians without resistance.[74] Madison's general at Niagara, Henry Dearborn, was overly cautious and, faced with deficient numbers of troops and supplies, ultimately turned back from battle.[75] The few successes in the war came in the form of early naval victories. The *Essex,* the *Constitution,* and other U.S. ships won decisive victories against British naval vessels, which, unfortunately, encouraged Britain to rely on a naval blockade that lasted nearly for the duration of the war.[76]

Meanwhile, Madison unwisely left the security of the District of Columbia in the hands of Secretary of War John Armstrong and General William H. Winder. As the president knew more about the defense of the capital city than did Armstrong, Madison anticipated an attack on the capital and suggested taking steps to ensure its defense. Armstrong, however, opposed these efforts and refused to take active measures to protect the city, arguing that it was improbable that the British would attack the capital.[77] In responding to Armstrong's hesitancy, Madison appointed an inexperienced and inept general, William H. Winder, to defend the city. While Winder wanted to mobilize the militia immediately to protect the capital, Armstrong argued instead that the militia fought best on the spur of the moment.[78] Both Secretary of State Robert Smith and Armstrong disliked Madison's policies, which offered Armstrong further incentive to oppose the president. In addition, Armstrong may have had presidential ambitions in mind, which would further have discouraged him from being too supportive of the president.[79] But as Ralph Ketcham purports, Madison was ultimately to blame for his poor judgment in entrusting the city's defenses to a "petulant, insubordinate secretary of war, John Armstrong, and to a blundering general, William H. Winder."[80]

The resulting battle of Bladensburg, which saw the White House and Capitol burn,[81] was a major disaster for the United States. Though additional militia forces from Maryland were called on for help, the undisciplined troops were unable to prevail.[82] Madison himself even arrived on the scene with a pair of borrowed dueling pistols, but he gave advice, rather than military orders, to the troops. Seeing he was of little use there, he soon returned to the safety of Washington. In Washington, Madison unsuccessfully attempted to stabilize the situation in the District by asking James Monroe to become acting general—along with his other duties—putting him in charge of the defense of the city.[83]

This evidence forms a solid basis for the conventional wisdom that the War of 1812 was "one of the worst humiliations in American history."[84] The British burned the White House, the Capitol, and many other government buildings, causing the president, his family, and his staff to flee temporarily. Madison tried to put the best face on such humiliations by stressing the limited victories at sea and in New Orleans. He was certainly not the last president to try to put a favorable spin on war disaster for public and Congress.

Positive Contributions of Madison's Presidency

In looking at James Madison's tenure as president, it is reasonable to ask what, if any, lasting contributions he made to the development and understanding of that institution. His positive contributions fall chiefly in five areas: (1) religious liberty; (2) civil liberties; (3) party loyalty; (4) national security; and (5) presidential success.

Religious Liberty

Madison emphasized the separation of church and state throughout his presidency, and in so doing he returned to the nondenominational practice set by George Washington. This focus on separation has become so accepted today that many people consider it to be a central part of the Constitution. As Rodney Grunes's earlier essay explains, Madison phrased proclamations of prayer and fasting in Deistic language and as congressional recommendations rather than as presidential mandates. He further disallowed a tax exemption for churches. He also showed his support for separation in exercising his veto three times to prevent state assistance to churches looking for governmental funding to assist them in building church structures and procuring religious supplies.[85]

Civil Liberties

Madison's scrupulous focus on constitutionality resulted in increased protection for civil liberties that elevated citizen's rights to a level unsurpassed by his predecessors. Madison, as the "father of the Constitution," placed particular emphasis on protecting the Bill of Rights. Beyond his insistence on separation of church and state, for example, the president continued to stress the dangers of maintaining a standing army in times of peace. As he stated, "the means of defence against foreign danger, have been always the instruments of tyranny at home."[86] Although his administration was the first to witness a declared war, in another instance Madison indicated that "of all the enemies to public liberty, war is perhaps, the most dreaded." At the conclusion of the War of 1812, Madison proudly pointed out that during his tenure in office, the war had been won without compromising American civil liberties.[87]

To protect civil liberties did not mean that Madison necessarily compromised his Republican focus on the need for the "balance of powers" principle.[88] This was too deeply ingrained in the Democratic-Republican Party and in the character of the American people. Madison thought he was able to both protect civil liberties and maintain this balance.

Leadership of the Democratic-Republican Party

Madison was certainly a loyal Republican in every sense of the word, as Republicanism framed much of his thinking, but, like Jefferson, Madison had a sense of "practical politics" and could set aside adherence to party principle if circumstances dictated otherwise. Although Henry Adams argued that the demands of war forced Madison to discard Republican principles in favor of Federalist principles,[89] Madison's actions are better explained as a willingness to adapt Republican principles to the demands of waging war and the ensuing rapid expansion in industry and population during the postwar era. While the Federalists had emphasized economic trade, technology, centralization, and other modern ideas associated with the British credit system,[90] Madison responded to modernity through modification of Republican principles. The success of the navy following the War of 1812, for example, showed Americans that one could maintain a maritime force without endangering civil liberties. And Madison also set aside his earlier antagonism toward the national bank that Alexander Hamilton and George Washington had so earnestly encouraged. Madison saw its establishment and maintenance as the best way to ensure needed funds to conduct the war. Again, this illustrated Madison's adaptability to realities of the political situation at hand.

So what does the War of 1812 teach regarding invasion of the American home front? It seems to suggest that democratic government and the protection of civil liberties may not easily lend themselves to effective military engagement against foreign powers. Under the limits of the Constitution, war power is delegated into so many hands that it makes effective military actions difficult. As the Pearl Harbor and 9/11 attacks indicate, checks and limits of decentralized government and the need for maintaining an open society may sometimes make democracy difficult to defend. Madison's legacy might also suggest that the preservation of liberty and securing impenetrable borders are not easily compatible. Rather, limits on military authority and restraints on the concentration of power are the costs that citizens must pay to protect civil liberties.

Was Madison a Failure?

Did Madison's involvement in the War of 1812 constitute presidential failure? Not completely. His inability to generate support for his war programs, his incapability to respond adequately to the threats of war, and his failure to select more competent generals and cabinet officials, culminating in the burning of Washington, all reflected leadership failures.

Yet Madison's popularity at the end of his second term was relatively high,[91] and trade and industry advanced rapidly. America's burgeoning population was quickly expanding, extending to the West, and the nation had a new spirit of unity and confidence. The War of 1812 proved for the first time that America was able to declare war and stand up to one of the major powers. Indeed, Americans could now boast that Andrew Jackson was a better military leader than the Duke of Wellington. The War of 1812 also settled once and for all the question of independence from Britain and in so doing at last protected the rights of Americans at sea, which were very important for Madison as president. The war created a spirit of shared patriotism, of "Americanism," which helped unite the nation and cautiously advanced it into the period of prosperity.

As Madison adhered to the constitutional structure of a dominant Congress and weakened executive, however, he became frustrated with the constitutional limits on the executive in times of war. The delays and inability to act to meet the demands of war eventually convinced Madison that that the construction of the executive department was "the worst part of a bad Constitution."[92] Madison eventually came to see that a limited executive under the constitutional system bore a striking similarity to the war leadership experienced by Americans under the Articles of Confederation where no separate executive existed.

To return to presidential ratings, it is difficult to rate Madison much higher than "average" given the difficulty he had governing. Madison's strength of mind exhibited during the formation of government, his sensitivity to the evils of concentrated power, and his penetrating understanding of democratic government, revealed in the *Federalist Papers* and elsewhere, needed to be accompanied by a style of governing he did not often exhibit.

Madison further showed how increasingly difficult it was for a president to govern because he lacked the sort of personality and assertiveness to reach out, or appear to reach out, to the public and Congress. It is the strong presidents—the active-positivists, in James David Barber's term,[93] presidents with personal energy, direction, and a positive attitude under the most trying of circumstances, such as Franklin D. Roosevelt, John Kennedy, and Ronald Reagan—who typically have the easiest time governing, reaching out to the citizenry, demanding allegiance from subordinates and party members, securing respect from the Congress, and, most importantly, preserving civil liberties for every American. This definition clearly does not apply to Madison. Nor did he exhibit the governing skill that Richard Neustadt felt essential for presidential strength, namely, the ability to bargain with established powerful interests.[94]

Madison was able to compensate for some of his weakness in working with the first lady, allowing Dolley Madison to exert her particular charm and magnetism in softening some of the conflict and political tensions that surrounded her husband. And while this helped him reach out to segments of the political system and to the people, it could not fully compensate for his weak style of leadership, his misjudgments in the selection of subordinates, his difficulty working with others, and his lack of charisma.

Madison's personal beliefs also at times impeded the effective execution of his responsibilities as president. While he wanted to force Britain into a free trade agreement, for example, his mistaken faith in a trade embargo only worsened relations with Britain and his own constituents.

The most successful presidents effectively respond to crisis by either shaping or implementing popular will. Unfortunately, Madison ineffectively handled the central crisis he faced and showed poor judgment in many of the decisions he made. For this reason alone, Madison as president could not be rated higher than "average." His role in creating republican government, rather than his services as president, proved to be his central legacy.

Notes

1. Lance Banning, *The Sacred Fire of Liberty* (Ithaca, NY: Cornell University Press, 1995), 112–13.

2. Henry Adams, *History of the United States of America during the Administrations of James Madison* 2 vols. (1889–91; New York: Literary Classics of the United States, 1986).

3. Garry Wills, *James Madison* (New York: Times Books, 2002), 2.

4. James David Barber, *The Presidential Character* (Englewood Cliffs, NJ: Prentice Hall, 1992), 11.

5. Arthur Schlesinger, Sr., "The U.S. Presidents," *Life,* November 1, 1948, 65; "Our Presidents: A Rating by 75 Historians," *New York Times Magazine,* July 29, 1962, 12.

6. Robert K. Murray and Tim H. Blessing, "The Presidential Performance Study: A Progress Report," *Journal of American History* 70, no. 3 (1983): 535–55; *Chicago Tribune Magazine,* January 10, 1982, 8–13, 15, 18.

7. Arthur M. Schlesinger, Jr., "Rating the Presidents: Washington to Clinton," *Political Science Quarterly* 112, no. 2 (1997): 179–90.

8. University C-Span Survey of Presidential Leadership, March-December 1999, http://www.americanpresidents.org/survey/historians/04.asp; *Chicago Sun-Times Survey on the American Presidency* (Chicago: Chicago Sun-Times, 2000).

9. James Madison, "Saturday, July 21, 1787. In Convention," in *Notes of Debates in the Federal Convention of 1787 Reported by James Madison,* ed. Adrienne Koch (New York: W. W. Norton, 1987), 340.

10. Raymond Tatolovich and Byron W. Daynes, *Power in the United States* (Monterey, CA: Brooks/Cole, 1984).

11. Quoted in Robert Allen Rutland, *The Presidency of James Madison* (Lawrence: University Press of Kansas, 1990), 20.

12. F. C. Blahut, "Madison: America's Most Underrated President," http://www.americanfreepress.net/Books/20_James_Madison_Book_Review.htm; Walter R. Borneman, *1812: The War That Forged a Nation* (New York: HarperCollins, 2004), 41; Henry F. Graff, *The Presidents* (New York: Charles Scribner's Sons, 1996), 60.

13. Early writings record Madison's height as being between five feet four inches and five feet six inches. However, most records report that admirers and defenders of Madison usually added inches to his actual height. Furthermore, people reported that Dolley, who was five feet six inches, noticeably dwarfed her husband, which would most likely indicate that his height was five feet four inches. Conover Hunt Jones, *Dolley and the "Great Little Madison"* (Washington, DC: American Institute of Architects Foundation, 1977), 13.

14. James Madison to James Monroe, March 21, 1808, in *Letters and Other Writings of James Madison: Fourth President of the United States* (Philadelphia: J. B. Lippincott, 1865), 2:423.

15. Leonard D. White, *Jeffersonians* (New York: Free Press, 1951), 36.

16. David B. Mattern and Holly C. Shulman, eds., *The Selected Letters of Dolley Payne Madison* (Charlottesville: University Press of Virginia, 2003), 92.

17. Ibid., 94.

18. Talbot Hamlin, *Benjamin Henry Latrobe* (New York: Oxford University Press, 1955), 311. The term "la-la," according to the *Oxford English Dictionary Online* means "'so-so,' not so good as it might be, poor." See http://dictionary.oed.com/cgi/entry/50129131?query_type=word&queryword=la-la&first=1&max_to_show=10&sort_type=alpha&result_place=1&search_id=jnEs-3czDa9-5869&hilite=50129131.

19. Mattern and Shulman, *Selected Letters of Dolley Payne Madison,* 93.

20. Jeffrey K. Tulis, *The Rhetorical Presidency* (Princeton, NJ: Princeton University Press, 1987), 67.

21. Ralph Ketcham, *James Madison: A Biography* (Charlottesville: University Press of Virginia, 1990), 537.

22. Quotations in the paragraph drawn from Irving Brant, *James Madison: The President* (New York: Bobbs-Merrill, 1956), 226–28.

23. William A. DeGregorio, *The Complete Book of U.S. Presidents,* 5th ed. (New York: Gramercy Books, 2001), 61.

24. Ibid.

25. Ibid., 64.

26. Adams, *History,* 2:589–91.

27. Ernest Sutherland Bates, *The Story of Congress, 1789–1935* (New York: Harper and Brothers, 1936), 77–78.

28. Adams, *History,* 1:114–15.

29. Rutland, *Presidency of Madison,* 4.

30. This culminated in the Hartford Convention in December 15, 1814, which called for limiting the central government even to the point of secession on the part of New England. J. C. A. Stagg, *Mr. Madison's War* (Princeton, NJ: Princeton University Press, 1983), 472–73.

31. Roger H. Brown, *The Republic in Peril: 1812* (New York: Columbia University Press, 1964), 22.

32. Helvidius No. 4, in *The Pacificus-Helvidius Debates of 1793–1794,* ed. Morton J. Frisch (Indianapolis: Liberty Fund, 2007), 87.

33. *The Papers of James Madison: Presidential Series,* ed. J. C. A. Stagg, Jeanne Kerr Cross, and Susan Holbrook Perdue (Charlottesville: University Press of Virginia, 1996), 3:53.

34. "Saturday, July 21, 1787. In Convention," in Madison, *Notes of Debates,* 340.

35. Rutland, *Presidency of Madison,* 137, 107.

36. *Annals of Congress,* 3rd Cong., 1st sess., 170.

37. Rutland, *Presidency of Madison,* 107.

38. Stagg, *Mr. Madison's War,* 153.

39. James Madison to Thomas Jefferson, August 17, 1812, in *The Writings of James Madison, Comprising His Public Papers and Private Correspondence, Including His Numerous Letters and Documents Now for the First Time Printed,* ed. Gaillard Hunt (New York: G. P. Putnam's Sons, 1900–1908), 8:210–11.

40. Ralph Ketcham, "James Madison," in *The Presidents: A Reference History,* ed. Henry F. Graff, 2nd ed. (New York: Charles Scribner's Sons, 1997), 64.

41. "Madison, Francis James Jackson, and Robert Smith: 9 October–11 November 1809: Editorial Note," in *The Papers of James Madison: Presidential Series,* ed. J. C. A. Stagg, Jeanne Kerr Cross, and Susan Holbrook Perdue (Charlottesville: University Press of Virginia, 1992), 2:10–11.

42. Frank N. Magill and John L. Loos, *The American Presidents* (Pasadena, CA: Salem, 1986), 87.

43. Preface to volume 3, *The Papers of James Madison: Presidential Series,* ed. J. C. A. Stagg, Jeanne Kerr Cross, and Susan Holbrook Perdue (Charlottesville: University Press of Virginia, 1996), 3:xxxii.

44. Ketcham, *Madison,* 521.

45. Wills, *James Madison,* 117–18, 63.

46. Ketcham, *Madison,* 482.

47. Charles F. Faber and Richard B. Faber, *The American Presidents Ranked by Performance* (Jefferson, NC: McFarland, 2000), 52.

48. Jack N. Rakove, ed., *James Madison: Writings* (New York: Library of America, 1999), 706.

49. Wills, *James Madison,* 65.

50. Stagg, *Mr. Madison's War,* 506–7.

51. DeGregorio, *U.S. Presidents,* 63.

52. "From Cassius," June 29, 1810, in *Papers: Presidential Series,* 2: 394.

53. Faber and Faber, *Presidents Ranked by Performance,* 23.

54. See note 8 above.

55. Stagg, *Mr. Madison's War,* 55, 56.

56. Ibid., 14.

57. Ketcham, *Madison,* 512–13.

58. Adams, *History,* 2:594–95.

59. James Monroe to James Madison, March 23, 1811, in *The Papers of James Madison: presidential series,* ed. J. C. A. Stagg, Jeanne Kerr Cross, and Susan Holbrook Perdue (Charlottesville: University Press of Virginia, 1996), 3:230.

60. Donald R. Hickey, *The War of 1812* (Urbana: University of Illinois Press, 1989), 30.

61. Ketcham, *Madison,* 512–13.

62. Melvin I. Urofsky, *The American Presidency* (New York: Garland, 2000), 54; Arnold A. Offner, *Another Such Victory: President Truman and the Cold War, 1945–1953* (Stanford, CA: Stanford University Press, 2002), 377.

63. Hickey, *War of 1812,* 44.

64. James Madison to Congress, June 1, 1812 in *The Papers of James Madison: Presidential Series,* ed. J. C. A. Stagg, Jeanne Kerr Cross, and Susan Holbrook Perdue (Charlottesville: University Press of Virginia, 1999), 4:437.

65. Hickey, *War of 1812,* 44.

66. Irving Brant, *James Madison: Commander in Chief* (New York: Bobbs-Merrill, 1961), 33.

67. Rutland, *Presidency of Madison,* 99, 100, 104.

68. Wills, *James Madison,* 2.

69. White, *Jeffersonians,* 37.

70. Adams, *History,* 1:134.

71. Brant, *Commander in Chief,* 18.

72. Ketcham, *Madison,* 534.

73. Madison, *Letters and Other Writings,* 2:574.

74. DeGregorio, *U.S. Presidents,* 65.

75. Ketcham, *Madison,* 539.

76. DeGregorio. *U.S. Presidents,* 66.

77. White, *Jeffersonians,* 220; Borneman, *1812,* 222; Anthony S. Pitch, *The Burning of Washington* (Annapolis, MD: Naval Institute Press, 1998), 19.

78. C. Edward Skeen, *John Armstrong, Jr., 1758–1843* (Syracuse, NY: Syracuse University Press, 1981), 190.

79. Borneman, *1812,* 223.

80. Ralph Ketcham, "Madison, James," *Encyclopedia Americana,* http://ap.grolier.com/article?assetid=0256610-00&templatename=/article/article.html.

81. John McElroy diary, August 24, 1814, Maryland Province Archives, Special Collections, Georgetown University Library.

82. Hickey, *War of 1812,* 197–98.

83. Walter Lord, *The Dawn's Early Light* (New York: W. W. Norton, 1972), 107, 117, 124; Irving Brant, *The Fourth President: A Life of James Madison* (Indianapolis: Bobbs-Merrill, 1970), 572; Wills, *James Madison,* 139.

84. Philip B. Kunhardt, Jr., Philip B. Kunhardt III, and Peter W. Kunhardt, *The American President* (New York: Riverhead Books, 1999), 200–207.

85. Wills, *James Madison,* 155–56.

86. "Friday, June 29, 1787. In Convention," in Madison, *Notes of Debates,* 214.

87. James Madison to the Republican Members of the Legislature of Massachusetts, March 7, 1815, in *Letters and Other Writings,* 2:599.

88. "Saturday, July 21, 1787. In Convention," in Madison, *Notes of Debates,* 340.

89. Henry Adams suggested that by the end of the war, Madison had adopted the presidency of George Washington as his model. Madison came to accept a national bank, made provisions for continued national defense, refused to reduce the navy's size, and recommended legislation to further economic prosperity. See Adams, *History,* 2:1239–41, 1253–54.

90. Wills, *James Madison,* 154–55.

91. Lyle Emerson Nelson, *American Presidents* (Armonk, NY: M. E. Sharpe, 2004), 133.

92. James Madison to Caleb Wallace, August 23, 1785, in *The Papers of James Madison,* ed. Robert Rutland, William M. E. Rachel, Barbara D. Ripel, and Fredrika J. Teute (Chicago: University of Chicago Press, 1973), 8:352.

93. Barber, *Presidential Character,* 266–99, 341–85.

94. Richard E. Neustadt, *Presidential Power and the Modern Presidents: The Politics of Leadership from Roosevelt to Reagan* (New York: Free Press, 1990), 40, 150.

SAMUEL B. HOFF

The Legislative Messages of the Madison Administration

The legislative messages of America's presidents have gained renewed attention in recent years. That is appropriate, given that such communication is necessary in order to achieve a complete and balanced understanding of a president's administration and to evaluate its success accurately. Indeed, presidential messages to Congress furnish insight into an administration's priorities and policies. Further, they provide evidence of the state of relations between the executive and legislative branches of American national government. These messages likewise reveal the beliefs, values, and philosophy of the president, of the people who serve in the administration, and often of the nation as a whole.

This chapter presents a comprehensive overview of the legislative messages of America's fourth president, James Madison. It does so in four stages. It begins with a summary of his background prior to his tenure in the presidential office. It next explains Madison's orientation to Congress. It then analyzes several types of messages using content analysis, descriptive statistics, and a comparative approach. Finally, the essay evaluates the impact of these messages for President Madison's overall legacy and for his place among American chief executives.

Background Prior to the Presidency

James Madison was born in Port Conway, Virginia, on March 16, 1751, and was the eldest son of James Madison, Sr., and Nelly Conway. He grew up on his family's plantation, named Montpelier, which remained his home and refuge throughout his life. Educated by a mentor until he was sixteen, Madison later enrolled at the College of New Jersey—now Princeton—and graduated in just two years. As David

Nordquest's earlier chapter explained, Madison's formal education imbued him with knowledge of philosophy, languages, and religion in particular. Although he studied law after college, he did not intend to pursue it as a career and never was admitted to the bar.[1]

James Madison's physical stature and personality were not those typically associated with an elected official. At adulthood, he stood five feet four inches tall and weighed just one hundred pounds. He was generally shy and reserved, and he was openly nervous around strangers. He spoke in a hushed voice that contemporaries often described as weak. Yet his formal training in debate and his willingness to listen to all sides of an argument were characteristics that benefited him and that others regarded positively.[2]

Madison's political positions prior to being elected president were perhaps the most impressive of any person of his era. He began his career as a member of the Orange County, Virginia, Committee of Safety in 1774. During the first year of the revolution against Britain in 1775, Madison served as a colonel in the Orange County militia. In 1776 he was a delegate to the Virginia Convention, which drafted guidelines for a state government and for the rights of citizens. That same year, he began the first of three stints as a member of the Virginia House of Delegates. He gained executive experience in 1778–79 as a member of the Virginia Council of State, the multiperson body with which the governor had to share power.[3]

At the national level, Madison served in the Continental Congress and the legislature under the Articles of Confederation. He was a delegate to the Annapolis Convention, the 1786 meeting that issued a call for the Constitutional Convention of the following year. Madison's unparalleled role in authoring and advocating the Constitution and the Bill of Rights led to his dual titles as "father" of each.

During the administration of George Washington, Madison served as a member of the U.S. House of Representatives from Virginia. In addition to his contribution to the passage of the Bill of Rights, Madison was involved in several legislative deliberations affecting the early development of the presidency. These included the establishment of the first three cabinet departments, the debate over the parameters of presidential removal power, and even how to address the chief executive.[4] At least one source credits Madison with actually coining the title "Mr. President."[5]

After the pivotal 1800 presidential election, when Thomas Jefferson's Democratic-Republican Party swept the Federalists aside, Madison served as secretary of state. He helped the Jefferson administration secure the Louisiana Purchase and confront attacks on American ships by the Barbary states and European powers.[6]

In the election of 1808, James Madison defeated Charles Pinckney of South Carolina by an electoral vote margin of 122 to 47. He won twelve of seventeen states in the Union at that time, mostly in the South and West. He was inaugurated on March 4, 1809.[7]

According to Ralph Ketcham, Madison's inaugural address "restated conventional republican principles but gave no hint of new directions which the government might take."[8] Yet Madison's background, his personality, and immediate political events converged to create an approach to Congress that helped determine the number and content of his legislative messages.

James Madison's personality type led him to be generally agreeable among those with whom he interacted, according to Steven Rubenzer and Thomas Faschingbauer. They further label Madison as among the "philosophes," whose traits likewise include conscientiousness and openness to ideas. Madison and the other chief executives who are classified as philosophes were not impulsive or prone to emotional outbursts.[9]

A second explanation for President Madison's approach to Congress is the impact that Jefferson holdovers had on his cabinet and therefore on communication with the legislature. As illustrated by table 12.2 in the previous chapter, over his eight years in office, Madison had two secretaries of state, four secretaries of the treasury, four secretaries of war, three attorney generals, and three secretaries of the navy.[10] Partly as a result of this unprecedented turnover, Madison held fewer cabinet meetings than previous presidents.[11] South Carolina congressman John C. Calhoun noted that Madison could not control those around him effectively and permitted "division in his cabinet."[12]

James Madison's approach to Congress was also a product of the Republican Party that he led. Michael Riccards finds that Republican beliefs—such as "its parsimonious vision of government, its antimilitary ethos, its faith in a barely enlightened common people, its insistence on decentralization of public institutions, and its disregard of a national bank and national financial structures"—led to the War of 1812.[13] Madison enjoyed a Republican majority in Congress for his entire time in office. However, the number of Republicans in the House had declined by twenty-two members at the outset of his first term.[14] In his second bid for office, Madison's electoral tally exceeded that of his initial election, but the margin of victory was smaller, as was the number of states he won.[15] Stephen Skowronek attributes this change to sharp decline of support for Republican policies that took place in the New England states.[16]

A final influence on James Madison's relations with Congress was the immediate political situation, which required that the president focus more attention on foreign affairs than domestic policy. This trend continued throughout most of Madison's tenure as president. It should be noted that some policies such as the Embargo Act were inherited from the previous administration, while others such as the Non-Intercourse Act and Macon's Bill Number 2 were fashioned amid growing hostility from external powers. That acrimony led to war with Great Britain in 1812.[17]

Examination of Madison's Legislative Messages

This section examines the content of various types of legislative messages by President Madison and analyzes their significance. Jeffrey Tulis holds that James Madison established a form of rhetoric that was not only common among early nineteenth-century presidents but also consistent with the beliefs of the party to which the chief executive belonged.[18] Philip Abbott counts Madison as one of the early presidents whose messages are "recognized for making major contributions to American political philosophy."[19]

Inaugural and Annual Messages

Madison's two inaugural messages are starkly different in length and content; this is a direct result of the impact of the War of 1812 on his second such message. The 1809 inaugural is just five paragraphs in length. Madison referred to peace and friendly intercourse, but likewise to internal improvements, increasing revenue, and to paying off debts. Alternatively, the 1813 inaugural, at eleven paragraphs, is twice as long as the 1809 speech. This message justified the war with Britain and pointedly criticized the enemy for its lack of humanity in fighting the war. Madison stated that to "render the war short and its success sure, animated and systemic exertions alone are necessary, and the success of our arms now may long preserve our country from the necessity of another resort to them."[20]

Madison sent his Annual Messages to Congress in written form. These messages, like others transmitted to the legislature during the era, "were institutional devices suited to the demands of separation of powers and the president's role as a co-partner in a deliberative process."[21]

Rather unlike his previous Annual Messages, President Madison's eighth Annual Message—which some scholars call his Farewell Address—returned to his prepresidential utterances on the purpose of government. He stated his hope that the American government would pursue the public good; watch over the freedoms of speech, press, and religion; maintain public faith; avoid intrusions into other nations; do justice to other nations and require justice from them; and create laws that diminish the likelihood of war. Madison offered the following thanks to the public at large: "The period of my retiring from public service being at little distance, I shall find no occasion more proper than the present for expressing to my fellow-citizens my deep sense of the continued confidence and kind support which I have received from them."[22]

Special Messages to Congress

Table 13.1 lists the number of special messages that presidents serving from 1789 to 1897 sent to one or both chambers of Congress.[23] Three trends are immediately derivable from the frequency with which President Madison employed this type of message. First, James Madison issued a total of 130 special messages to

Congress during his initial term in office, the most for a president serving up to that time. His overall total of 202 special messages transmitted to Congress during his eight years in office falls between the 200 such messages that President George Washington sent and the 212 that President Thomas Jefferson issued.

A second evident trend emanates from President Madison's issuance of special messages to the House of Representatives during his first term. As table 13.1 depicts, President Madison sent thirty such messages to the House, which was double the number that any of his predecessors sent during a full term in office. His frequent communication with the House of Representatives was no doubt a consequence of his familiarity with that body based on his previous political experience. As this author has demonstrated in an earlier study, it may have also been a reaction to having a constant party majority in the House.[24] Following Madison's example, every ensuing chief executive from James Monroe through Grover Cleveland issued a double-digit number of special messages to the House of Representatives.

A third trend evident from an examination of table 13.1 is the drop in the number of President Madison's special messages to Congress during his second term. Indeed, the total number of such messages fell from 130 in Madison's first term in office to 72 during his second term. Generally, that proves true for every two-term president who followed Madison during the nineteenth century except James Monroe. One rationale for this divergence is that President Madison found other types of messages such as proclamations (see below) through which to communicate during his second term.

Presidential requests to declare war on a hostile nation are unique among special messages sent to Congress. James Madison sent his war message to both chambers on June 1, 1812. It followed years of disagreement with England over trade issues, British impressment of American seamen and seizure of American ships, and a British alliance with Native Americans in the western region of the United States. Madison's request for a declaration of war chided the British for their "progressive usurpations" and "accumulating wrongs."[25] Congress voted to approve a declaration of war against Britain with a 19–13 vote in the Senate and a 79–49 vote in the House.[26] The margin of approval for the War of 1812 remains the smallest among all congressional declarations of war in U.S. history.[27] According to Garrett Sheldon, Madison regarded the war with Britain as "wholly within the jurisdiction of the federal central government and that of the executive branch as well."[28]

Proclamations

Proclamations were one of the major forms of popular communication in the nineteenth century. Tulis postulates that the "central rhetorical appeal of any proclamation will be the authority of the president (or of the government as a whole) rather than factors peculiar to the president's persuasive abilities." Yet he holds that the majority of proclamations in the nineteenth century were "horta-

Table 13.1

Frequency of Special Messages Sent to Congress by Term, 1789–1897

President	*To House*	*To Senate*	*To Both Chambers*
Washington	2	41	61
Washington	5	22	69
J. Adams	10	29	45
Jefferson	16	25	53
Jefferson	14	33	71
Madison	**30**	**37**	**63**
Madison	**15**	**26**	**31**
Monroe	38	55	26
Monroe	97	66	34
J. Q. Adams	67	65	40
Jackson	41	87	40
Jackson	43	71	42
Van Buren	77	85	42
Tyler	77	123	21
Polk	43	115	23
Fillmore	31	130	36
Pierce	56	168	47
Buchanan	41	102	21
Lincoln	28	126	69
A. Johnson	133	181	49
Grant	53	123	37
Grant	40	46	38
Hayes	31	66	28
Arthur	74	105	228
Cleveland I	31	95	118
B. Harrison	11	29	113
Cleveland II	21	57	39
Totals	1,125	2,108	1,484

Source: Compiled by the author from data available in James D. Richardson, ed., *Messages and Papers of the Presidents* (New York: Bureau of National Literature, 1897).

tory and declaratory, like Washington's Thanksgiving Proclamation."[29] James Madison's use of the presidential proclamation as a vehicle for messages to both Congress and the public was unique in its contradiction of the aforementioned trends. Table 13.2 provides a yearly summary of the number of proclamations issued by the Madison administration. This yearly count leads to several observations. First, James Madison issued one or more proclamations in every year of his tenure. His total of twenty-two proclamations exceeded that of any of his predecessors and the combined total of those of John Adams and Thomas Jefferson.[30] Second, the number of proclamations that Madison issued was highest during the four-year period encompassed by the War of 1812 (1812–15) and was higher in Madison's second term as president than in his first term. Madison may have turned to the proclamation as an additional, alternative way to contact Congress later in his tenure.

Table 13.2

Number of Vetoes by Year

Year	*Vetoes*
1809	2
1810	2
1811	1
1812	4
1813	1
1814	5
1815	5
1816	1
1817	1

Source: Data drawn from Gregory Harness, *Presidential Vetoes, 1789–1988* (Washington, DC: Government Printing Office, 1992).

A second manner in which James Madison's proclamations diverged from the type normally released by chief executives in the nineteenth century was that the topics were substantive, not symbolic. A content analysis of the proclamations reveals six main topics:

- One initiated the War of 1812, and one recognized the peace treaty that ended it.
- Four proclamations called for a day of prayer during the War of 1812.
- Four proclamations dealt with pardons emanating from the War of 1812, of which three were aimed at army deserters and one at a foreigner who was captured during the war.
- Three proclamations were requests for a special session of Congress, all war-related.
- Three proclamations essentially served as warnings to various groups: one warned external powers not to detain neutral ships; another cautioned Louisiana citizens not to pick a fight with neighboring Spain; and another prohibited the illegal taking of public land.
- One proclamation was issued following Britain's 1814 attack on Washington during the War of 1812.[31]

Veto Messages

President Madison and Congress did agree on much during Madison's two terms in office. A summary of major acts and treaties reveals that the Eleventh Congress (1809–10) enacted three; the Twelfth Congress (1811–12) enacted fifteen, the Thirteenth Congress (1813–14) enacted ten, and the Fourteenth Congress (1815–16) enacted eleven.[32]

When President Madison and the legislature disagreed on principle, policies, or priorities, Madison wielded the veto. Table 13.3 depicts presidential veto use from 1789 to 1865.[33] The findings from Madison's utilization of the veto again point to the path-breaking nature of his legislative messages. President Madison vetoed five bills by regular means during his two terms in office, a figure not exceeded until the administration of John Tyler. During his first term, President Madison vetoed three bills, including two that would have used public funds or land to establish churches and one that would have led to penalties against absent or disabled District Court judges.

During his second term, President Madison vetoed bills dealing with the proposed Bank of the United States and with using surplus finds funds from the Bank to pay for internal improvements. Listing four reasons for his Bank veto in January 1815, Madison later that year supported the Bank's rechartering, possibly as a way to defray the estimated $120 million cost of the War of 1812.[34] Madison issued his final veto on the penultimate day of his second term. He rejected an internal improvement bill due to his philosophy of classical republicanism.[35] According to Robert Rutland, "a massive program of road and canal building was too much of a constitutional stretch for this Framer of the Constitution."[36]

Table 13.3 likewise shows that James Madison was the first American president to implement the pocket veto, using it twice overall. In 1812 Madison rejected a bill that would have established a uniform rule for naturalization. In 1816 he used a pocket veto to void a bill that would have permitted free importation of Bible stereotype plates,[37] ostensibly due to concerns over a conflict with the establishment clause of the First Amendment.

Table 13.3

Presidential Veto Use, 1789–1865

President	*Regular Vetoes*	*Pocket Vetoes*	*All Vetoes*	*Overrides*
Washington	2	0	2	0
J. Adams	0	0	0	0
Jefferson	0	0	0	0
Madison	**5**	**2**	**7**	**0**
Monroe	1	0	1	0
J. Q. Adams	0	0	0	0
Jackson	5	7	1	0
Van Buren	0	1	1	0
W. Harrison	0	0	0	0
Tyler	6	4	1	1
Polk	2	1	3	0
Taylor	0	0	0	0
Fillmore	0	0	0	0
Pierce	9	0	9	5
Buchanan	4	3	7	1
Lincoln	2	5	7	0

Source: Data drawn from Gregory Harness, *Presidential Vetoes, 1789–1988* (Washington, DC: Government Printing Office, 1992).

All of President Madison's regular vetoes were sustained. His total number of vetoes issued—seven—was not exceeded until Andrew Jackson's administration. Robert Spitzer labels James Madison as the "first president to use the veto with vigor," though he also contends that Madison was "still working within the veto logic established by Washington."[38] The information presented here places Madison in a class apart from his predecessors in how he employed the veto. Madison deserves credit for moving justifications for vetoes away from purely constitutional objections and toward pending legislation.

Evaluating Madison's Messages and His Presidency

Some called James Madison a "puppet" of Thomas Jefferson, his immediate presidential predecessor. Conversely, Irving Brant asserts that while Jefferson may have been more prescient about the need for a bill of rights, "Madison was infinitely superior to Jefferson in the application of those guarantees to specific circumstances."[39] For Thomas Bailey and Garry Wills, James Madison's final year in office was greatly helped by the successful conclusion to the War of 1812.[40] Ralph Ketcham holds that Madison's "only real war aim and the crowning achievement of his public life" was to "vindicate the republican concept of government."[41]

The several types of legislative messages that President Madison used certainly portrayed his purpose as described by Ketcham. Madison demonstrated his recognition of reserved powers for his office as well as the checks that the president has on other branches. Madison, whose niche previously seemed to be in Congress, proved his executive mettle through his adept and unprecedented legislative messages.

An assessment of James Madison's contribution to the American presidency leads to several conclusions. First, Madison's steady demeanor during the dark days of the War of 1812 upheld the tradition of staying cool in a crisis.[42] He was the first of several presidents reelected during a major war, certainly in part due to effective utilization of legislative messages. Second, Madison's political party—which was divided for most of his time in the presidency—remained dominant for another eight years after he retired. Indeed, Whitney and Whitney observe that Madison took James Monroe's victory in the 1816 presidential election "as a personal tribute."[43]

Perhaps the final word on James Madison should come from members of the legislative branch. Senator Henry Clay believed that James Madison "rendered more important services to his country than any other man, Washington only excepted." Congressman Daniel Webster stated that James Madison had "as much to do as any man in framing the Constitution, and as much to do as any man in administering it."[44] Madison, one of five presidents to take his oath of office in the House chamber,[45] would have appreciated those legislators' sentiments.

Notes

1. William A. DeGregorio, *The Complete Book of U.S. Presidents: From George Washington to George W. Bush* (New York: Gramercy Books, 2001).

2. Ibid.

3. David C. Whitney and Robin Vaughn Whitney, *The American Presidents* (Pleasantville, NY: Reader's Digest Association, 2001).

4. Ibid.

5. Lu Ann Paletta and Fred L. Worth, *The World Almanac of Presidential Facts* (New York: Pharos Books, 1988).

6. DeGregorio, *U.S. Presidents.*

7. Ibid.

8. Ralph Ketcham, *James Madison: A Biography* (Charlottesville: University Press of Virginia, 1990), 474.

9. Steven J. Rubenzer and Thomas R. Faschingbauer, *Personality, Character, and Leadership in the White House: Psychologists Assess the Presidents* (Washington, DC: Brassey's, 2004).

10. Whitney and Whitney, *American Presidents.*

11. Garry Wills, *James Madison* (New York: Times Books, 2002).

12. Quoted in DeGregorio, *U.S. Presidents,* 69.

13. Michael P. Riccards, *The Ferocious Engine of Democracy: A History of the American Presidency* (Lanham, MD: Madison, 1995), 1:80.

14. As figured from the chart "Political Control of Congress," in Whitney and Whitney, *American Presidents.*

15. DeGregorio, *U.S. Presidents.*

16. Stephen Skowronek, *The Politics Presidents Make: Leadership from John Adams to George Bush* (Cambridge, MA: Belknap, 1993).

17. Gorton Carruth, ed., *The Encyclopedia of American Facts and Dates* (New York: Harper and Row, 1987).

18. Jeffrey K. Tulis, *The Rhetorical Presidency* (Princeton, NJ: Princeton University Press, 1987).

19. Philip Abbott, *The Exemplary Presidency: Franklin D. Roosevelt and the American Political Tradition* (Amherst: University of Massachusetts Press, 1990).

20. Quoted in James D. Richardson, ed., *Messages and Papers of the Presidents* (New York: Bureau of National Literature, 1897), 2:511.

21. Tulis, *Rhetorical Presidency,* 55.

22. Quoted in Richardson, *Messages and Papers,* 2:564.

23. Compiled by Samuel B. Hoff, "The Legislative Messages of the Lincoln Administration," in *Abraham Lincoln: Contemporary: An American Legacy,* ed. Frank J. Williams and William D. Pederson (Campbell, CA: Savas Woodbury, 1995).

24. Samuel B. Hoff, "Electoral and Party Influence on Presidential Messages, 1789–1897," paper presented at the Annual Meeting of the Northeastern Political Science Association, Philadelphia, PA, 1983.

25. Quoted in Richardson, *Messages and Papers,* 2:489.

26. A. J. Langguth, *Union 1812: The Americans Who Fought the Second War of Independence* (New York: Simon and Schuster, 2006).

27. Robert A. Doughty et al., *American Military History and the Evolution of Warfare in the Western World* (Lexington, MA: D. C. Heath, 1996).

28. Garrett Ward Sheldon, *The Political Philosophy of James Madison* (Baltimore, MD: Johns Hopkins University Press, 2001), 105.

29. Tulis, *Rhetorical Presidency,* 52–53.

30. Hoff, "Legislative Messages of Lincoln."

31. Compiled from proclamations found in Richardson, *Messages and Papers,* vols. 1 and 2.

32. Stephen W. Stathis, *Landmark Legislation, 1774–2002* (Washington, DC: CQ Press, 2003).

33. Compiled from data found in Gregory Harness, *Presidential Vetoes, 1789–1988* (Washington, DC: Government Printing Office, 1992).

34. *Encyclopedia of the American Presidency,* ed. Leonard W. Levy and Louis Fisher (New York: Simon and Schuster, 1994), s.v. "Madison, James."

35. Sheldon, *Political Philosophy of James Madison.*

36. "Madison, James," *Encyclopedia of the American Presidency,* 3:1002.

37. Harness, *Presidential Vetoes, 1789–1988.*

38. Robert Spitzer, *The Presidential Veto: Touchstone of the American Presidency* (Albany: State University of New York Press, 1988), 30–31.

39. Irving Brant, *The Fourth President: A Life of James Madison* (Indianapolis, IN: Bobbs-Merrill, 1970), 644.

40. Thomas A. Bailey, *Presidential Greatness: The Image and the Man from George Washington to the Present* (New York: Appleton-Century, 1969); Wills, *James Madison.*

41. Ralph Ketcham, "James Madison," in *The Presidents: A Reference History,* ed. Henry Graff (New York: Simon and Schuster, 1997), 71.

42. Wills, *James Madison.*

43. Whitney and Whitney, *American Presidents,* 43.

44. Quotations from DeGregorio, *U.S. Presidents,* 68.

45. Tim Taylor, ed., *The Book of Presidents* (New York: Arno, 1972).

HENRY J. ABRAHAM

President James Madison's Appointments to the U.S. Supreme Court

In an earlier chapter, Steven P. Brown documented the tremendous contributions that James Madison made to the formation of the U.S. Supreme Court as an institution. As the fourth U.S. president, however, James Madison had only two opportunities to fill vacancies on the highest tribunal in the land.

Fate had provided far more attractive opportunities for appointments to all three of Madison's predecessors. Washington, who began with a clean slate, was able to nominate a stunning fourteen justices, of whom twelve were confirmed and eleven served. John Adams had three, four if one counts the second appointment of John Jay as chief justice in 1800, which the Senate approved, but which Jay, who had never enjoyed his first stint, from 1789 until 1795, enthusiastically declined.[1] Jay's decision not to accept had fortuitously opened the door for President Adams's supreme contribution to the judicial process, namely, the appointment of the great John Marshall as chief justice in 1801. Jefferson appointed three, William Johnson, Brockholst Livingston, and Thomas Todd, all theoretically Jeffersonian in political embrace. But of that trio, only Johnson provided at least marginal satisfaction to our third president, in balancing out the nationalistic Court headed by Marshall, to whom Jefferson, his cousin, always referred as "that gloomy malignity."

Madison's Presidency

As Byron Daynes and Mark Hopkins have demonstrated in a previous chapter, Jefferson's successor, James Madison, who came to the presidency in 1809, did not find the office very congenial. Justly regarded as the "father of the Constitution" because of his seminal work in bringing that document into existence between 1787 and 1789, and, after an initial disinclination, formulating and embracing the amendments that became the Bill of Rights, he ultimately played a crucial role in persuading Congress to adopt that hallowed codicil to the Constitution.[2] Withal, the "great little Madison," as he was often called by his contemporaries, a first-rate statesman and diplomat and a superb intellect, neither liked the political process nor possessed an aptitude for it. He proved the maxim that great statesmen are by no means great—or even good—politicians. He was essentially uncomfortable in the presidency and proved to be indecisive and inept in the very area he had been deemed an expert: foreign affairs. Moreover, he failed where Jefferson had been so strong: in his relationship with, and his ability to manage, Congress. But he did give the country Joseph Story, the "American Blackstone"—second only to John Marshall in influence and power on the high bench in the first third of the nineteenth century and one of the truly great justices to grace the Supreme Court.

It was midway in Madison's first term that two vacancies occurred on the Court. The last two surviving Washington appointees, Justices William Cushing and Samuel Chase (the latter had barely survived impeachment in 1805), had died in the fall of 1810 and mid-1811, respectively. Jefferson's party looked forward to their replacements with great expectations, for here was the first chance to turn the Federalist majority on the bench into a minority. All knowing eyes were on Madison, who was bombarded with advice from many Democratic-Republican quarters—most notably from Jefferson. Publicly espousing the two cardinal Jeffersonian criteria of party loyalty and geography, Madison began his search soon after Cushing's death, but his search would not end until November 1811.

Failed Appointments

To fill Cushing's seat, Madison first turned to Jefferson's able attorney general from 1801 to 1804, Levi Lincoln of Massachusetts, whose dedication to Democratic-Republicanism was beyond question and for whom Jefferson strongly lobbied. Madison had been alerted that the candidate might well decline for reasons of age or health—he was sixty-two and plagued by very poor eyesight—but Jefferson continued to press for the nomination, and in October 1810 the president asked Lincoln to accept it. Late in November Lincoln responded negatively; yet Madison chose to disregard the refusal and formally nominated him on January 2, 1811. The Senate confirmed him with enthusiasm on the following day and sent his commission to him forthwith. But Lincoln, in effect now facing blindness, felt he had to persist in his decision—much as he would have relished becoming a thorn in Marshall's side.

Madison waited a month then nominated another proved and prominent New England Democratic-Republican leader, Alexander Wolcott of Connecticut. An attorney of little distinction, Wolcott had long served as U.S. collector of customs, making himself obnoxious to the Federalists through what they regarded as his extreme partisanship both in and out of office. The Senate rejected him decisively, 9 to 24. Within ten days the president had selected another candidate—again a Democratic-Republican, but one who had begun to show a measure of political independence—his minister to Russia, John Quincy Adams. The latter was then eminently acceptable to both political parties, and the Senate confirmed him unanimously as soon as the nomination reached it. His parents, John and Abigail Adams, who had urged his acceptance, were overjoyed. But to their consternation and that of Madison—who sensed a future political rival—John Quincy Adams declined the appointment. He pleaded insufficient legal acumen—he had a distinct distaste for the law and the bench, both of which he viewed as "taxing and dull"—and quite frankly acknowledged too much political ambition to accept such a post. Madison now resolved to sit back and wait. It was not until seven months later, in mid-November 1811, that he sent to the Senate the controversial name of Joseph Story of Massachusetts, passing over Jefferson's hard-pushed candidacy of his former postmaster general, Gideon Granger of Connecticut.

Madison's Appointment of Joseph Story

What finally prompted Madison's selection of Story is unclear, although Story's uncle, Isaac Story, was a longtime friend of the president. What is clear is that Jefferson and almost the entire Democratic-Republican leadership opposed the just-turned thirty-two-year-old legal whiz—a nineteen-year-old Harvard graduate in 1798—a personal friend of John Marshall who had given every indication of leaning toward Federalism. He also had refused to support Jefferson's controversial Embargo Act of 1807. All of this bothered Madison considerably less than Jefferson—indeed, the president was much more inclined to look sympathetically at some aspects of Federalist policy than was Jefferson, although the latter was a pronouncedly more adamant Anti-Federalist out of office than he was in office. It is often easier to be a dogmatic critic than a dogmatic fashioner of policy. Story's nomination sent Jefferson into a rage. He pronounced him a "pseudo-Republican," a "political chameleon," an "independent political schemer."[3] Jefferson particularly feared Story's personal admiration for the chief justice and for his propertarian views. He would see some of his worst fears confirmed shortly.

The Senate was not especially enchanted with the Story nomination, either, but its members were ready to end the impasse that had caused the vacancy of one Supreme Court seat for more than a year and another for several months. The country, too, had tired of what looked like an appointment charade, and there was general relief when the Senate quickly and without a record roll call confirmed the controversial young New Englander on November 18, 1811, three days after

Madison had sent his name over. At a mere thirty-two, he would be the youngest appointee ever to attain the Court (William Johnson having been a month and a half older when he preceded Story in 1804).[4] Story's record stands to this day.

Joseph Story's appointment proved to be one of the most fortuitous in the history of the Court and the country. Both in terms of intellectual leadership and jurisprudential commitment, he was an outstanding justice. Standing with Marshall for almost a quarter of a century, and continuing for another decade after Marshall's death until his own in 1845, Story was arguably perhaps even more determined than Marshall to further the national posture in the face of mounting storm signals to the Union. Obviously, Story—who strongly disliked both Jefferson and Andrew Jackson—was neither a democrat nor a confirmed majoritarian, and thus he personified the intellectual antithesis of the Democratic-Republican creed, not withstanding his formal party affiliation. Yet the role this towering common law jurist played in the stabilization of the republic and in its growth and security was second only to Marshall's. He left lasting monuments to constitutionalism, nationalism, and legal scholarship. These included his famed lectures at the Harvard School of Law, where he served as Dane Professor while a member of the Court; his cosponsorship with Chancellor James Kent of New York of the American equity system; his work on copyrights and patents; and his elucidation of property, trust, partnership, insurance, commercial, and maritime law.

Unlike Story's dalliances with poetry, his seminal *Commentaries on the Constitution of the United States,* published in 1833, repeatedly republished since, and still available in abridged form, remains an indispensable work in the study of constitutional law and history. Story's treatises went through seventy-one editions, and he continues to hold the record for being the most frequently published Supreme Court justice to date. Story announced his retirement as of the end of the 1844–45 term. Worn out and concerned about what he regarded as the declining quality and influence of his beloved tribunal, Story proposed to devote his full time to his Harvard Law School professorship, but in September 1845 he died, shortly before he was to leave the bench. He had served magnificently for almost thirty-four years, and all published lists ranking and rating the performance of Supreme Court justices have bestowed the status of "great" upon Joseph Story.[5]

Madison's Appointment of Gabriel Duvall

On the same day the Senate confirmed Joseph Story, it had already approved the nomination of fifty-eight-year-old Gabriel Duvall of Maryland, a faithful Democratic-Republican, to fill the vacancy caused by the death of his fellow Marylander Samuel Chase. Of considerably less stature and surrounded by infinitely less controversy than Story, Duvall nonetheless proved to be a competent if unexciting jurist—even called a leading candidate for the title of "the most insignificant justice" by one commentator[6]—fulfilling Madison's expectations on grounds of both political compatibility and legal acumen. He had served with distinction on his state's highest court for six years and in 1802 had become comptroller of the treasury in the Jefferson and (subsequently) Madison administrations. Looking every inch the legendary jurist, he spent more than twenty-three quiet years on the bench—during which time he penned only eighteen or nineteen opinions—resigning at eighty-two, almost totally deaf.

Duvall could always be counted upon to be a faithful supporter of Chief Justice John Marshall's jurisprudence of national hegemony, often at the disadvantage of the states. The legendary chief had no problems with Justice Duvall's votes. Only once did the latter leave the Marshall reservation in a case questioning national governmental power in interpreting constitutional authority, here the contract clause, in the famous Marshall-authored 1819 decision of *Dartmouth College v. Woodward*.[7] Duvall was the sole dissenter—but he wrote no opinion. The chief carried the day five to one.

The Years That Followed

During the six remaining years of his presidency, Madison had no further opportunities to make a Supreme Court appointment. This period commenced what remains the longest no-vacancy stretch in the history of the Court, twelve years, closely followed by the eleven and a half years of the Rehnquist Court, from 1994 to 2005. In fact, no vacancy arose until 1823 when Justice Henry Livingston died at age sixty-six after sixteen years of service—enabling James Monroe, Madison's successor, to make his one and only appointment. Monroe, a president of above-average ability and performance, encountered difficulties with Congress similar to those encountered by his friend and colleague Madison. Yet he was a better administrator, and he knew how to pick excellent associates, especially in the foreign policy field. Monroe was a good Democratic-Republican, but he was even less committed to party doctrine than was Madison, and it was widely doubted that he would be more than casually concerned with a nominee's party loyalty.

Madison may not have been a strong president *qua* president—none of the students of the presidency ranked his performance higher than "average."[8] But the "father of the Constitution" was not only its major framer; he advanced its future with the brilliant essays he contributed to its adoption in *The Federalist,* joined by Hamilton and Jay. And he gave his country the great Joseph Story. Serene and wistful, James Madison retired to his beloved Montpelier with Dolley in 1817.

Justice Duvall died in 1835, the year before Madison did. Andrew Jackson, who succeeded John Quincy Adams as president, initially nominated Roger Taney to succeed him. After the Senate rejected this nomination, Jackson succeeded in elevating Taney to the chief justice position that had opened with John Marshall's death and put Philip Barbour in Duvall's seat. Story continued on the court about ten more years, after which James K. Polk replaced him with Levi Woodbury.

Notes

1. Jay had characterized the Court as a thoroughly "inauspicious" body that did little work, had dissatisfied members, and lacked popular esteem and understanding. Jay so thoroughly disliked his job as the institution's first chief justice that he not only spent one year of his brief six-year tenure in England on a diplomatic mission, but also ran twice for governor of New York. When he succeeded on the second try, he gleefully resigned from the Court.

In a letter to Adams dated January 2, 1801, Jay reported that he "left the bench perfectly convinced that under a system so defective it would not obtain the energy, weight, and dignity which are essential to its affording due support to the national government, nor acquire the public confidence and respect which, as the last resort of the justice of the nation, it should possess." Quoted in John V. Orth, *How Many Judges Does It Take to Make a Supreme Court? And Other Essays on the Law and the Constitution* (Lawrence: University Press of Kansas, 2006), 42, citing Albert J. Beveridge, *The Life of John Marshall* (Boston: Houghton Mifflin,1919), 3:55.

2. See, among others, Richard Labunski, *James Madison and the Struggle for the Bill of Rights* (Oxford: Oxford University Press, 2006).

3. R. Kent Newmyer, "A Note on the Whig Politics of Justice Joseph Story," *Mississippi Valley Historical Review* 48 (December 1961): 482.

4. William O. Douglas, who was forty-one when Franklin Roosevelt appointed him in 1939, would be the next youngest more than a century and a quarter later. Story's record stands as of this writing and is not likely to be overturned. Indeed, only sixteen have attained the Court by the age of forty-five, and just four in the twentieth century: William O. Douglas, Potter Stewart, Byron White, and Clarence Thomas.

5. See appendix A in Henry J. Abraham's *Justices, Presidents, and Senators: A History of the U.S. Supreme Court Appointments from Washington to Clinton,* 5th ed. (Lanham, MD: Rowman and Littlefield, 2008).

6. David B. Currie, "The Most Insignificant Justice: A Preliminary Inquiry," *University of Chicago Law Review* 50 (Spring 1983): 466–80. Judge Frank H. Easterbrook was tempted to follow suit but decided that Justices Todd, Clifford, and McKinley were even more "insignificant," with Todd as the champion. Ibid., 480.

7. 4 Wheat. (17 U.S.) 518 (1819).

8. See Abraham, *Justices, Presidents, and Senators.*

SIX

Madison as Elder Statesman

JAMES H. READ

Madison's Response to Nullification

James Madison was the last surviving founding-era figure of significant authority able to bear living witness to the intentions and understandings of those who framed and ratified the Constitution.[1] Thomas Jefferson and John Adams, neither of whom had any direct role in framing the Constitution, had died in 1826; most other key figures had long since passed from the scene. During the crucial years of the nullification controversy from 1828 to 1833, Madison was not only still alive but intellectually sharp, still writing and corresponding, and closely following events despite his advanced age.

American constitutional argumentation in the 1830s employed the putative intentions and understandings of the framers as a common argumentative strategy, in a way not dramatically different from that which individuals employ today. Once the actual participants and witnesses to some great event have departed, succeeding generations must rely on written documents and conflicting traditions of interpretation to keep alive the memory and authority of the event. In his Springfield Lyceum Address of 1838, Abraham Lincoln spoke of the founding as "a legacy bequeathed us, by a once hardy, brave, and patriotic, but now lamented and departed race of ancestors."[2] Americans still frequently invoke the legacy of these "lamented and departed" ancestors in constitutional disputes. Americans can, for instance, safely argue that "if James Madison were alive today he would support such-and-such a constitutional position" because there is no chance of the *real* James Madison appearing and disputing such use of his authority.

But that is exactly what the elderly James Madison did during the nullification controversy, and his entry into the debates makes this moment in American history especially fascinating. Madison's participation in the nullification debate dramatized the very different way in which Madison and the "second-generation" statesman John C. Calhoun (1782–1850) thought about and used the language of the Constitution, and indeed how they conceived of republican government itself.[3] Madison certainly responded to nullification, and to the nullifiers' own use of Madison's Virginia Resolutions and Jefferson's Kentucky Resolutions of 1798, much differently than Calhoun and his followers did.

The South Carolina nullifiers' immediate target was the protective tariff of 1828, which they considered both unconstitutional and economically detrimental to southern planters, but they also foresaw threats to slavery from a too-powerful federal government.[4] The first comprehensive statement of the nullification theory came in the *South Carolina Exposition* of 1828, which Calhoun (at that time vice president of the United States) secretly authored; he did not publicly acknowledge his authorship of the doctrine until his Fort Hill Address of 1831. Calhoun argued in the *Exposition* that each individual state possessed the right to declare an act of federal legislation "null and void within the limits of the state"; this nullification would not only bind the citizens of the nullifying state but also suspend the operation of the federal law itself.[5] Thus a national tariff law, or any questionable act of legislation, would have to not only achieve a majority in both houses of the U.S. Congress but also be supported, or at least not actively opposed, by a majority within any individual state. In what was in effect a reversal of the constitutional amending process, Calhoun further argued that if three-quarters of the other states, in conventions called for the purpose, affirmatively rejected a single state's nullification of the law, the nullifying state would either have to rescind its nullification or secede from the Union; the other states were constitutionally obliged to allow the secession. Calhoun argued that Madison's Virginia Resolutions of 1798 and his *Report of 1800*, which further explain those resolutions, were, together with Jefferson's Kentucky Resolutions of 1798, key precedents for the doctrine of nullification.

In a series of publicly circulated letters written in the early 1830s, Madison fiercely denied that the Constitution allowed for nullification and insisted that the Virginia Resolutions properly understood gave no support to the doctrine. Calhoun subsequently claimed that Madison was betraying his earlier principles. A careful examination of Madison's Virginia Resolutions, along with his *Report of 1800* explaining and justifying those resolutions, sustains Madison's claim that the Virginia Resolutions did not endorse any constitutional right of single-state nullification. However, Madison could not easily deny that the Kentucky Resolutions—especially Jefferson's more radical, recently unearthed draft of those resolutions—did lend support to nullification. The nullifiers had in fact found the one point at which Madison and Jefferson, despite their personal friendship and political partnership, most differed, and these nullifiers succeeded in widening that gulf after Jefferson's death.

The argument between Madison and Calhoun went beyond simply interpreting constitutional language. Underlying the constitutional dispute was a fundamental difference over the nature of majority rule and the proper relation between majorities and minorities in a well-governed republic. Both Madison and Calhoun sought ways to protect the minority from an oppressive majority. But for Madison majority rule remained the foundational principle of republican government. He always insisted that he sought, as in *Federalist* No. 10, "a republican remedy to the diseases most incident to republican government."[6] By "republican remedy" Madison meant one that checked the abuses of majority rule while still preserving majority rule itself as the fundamental principle of republican government. Well-designed institutions and constitutional guarantees could make the majority act slowly and deliberately rather than hastily and passionately, but, in the long run, the majority still prevailed. Calhoun, by contrast, sought ways to put the rights and interests of the minority permanently out of reach of the majority, however deliberate and slow-moving. Calhoun believed that it was possible to found a political order on consensus (a jury model of decision making) instead of either majority or minority rule. Only those laws and decisions to which *no* significant economic or geographical interest objected were legitimate.

For his part, Madison did not admire any model of political decision making requiring unanimity. That was exactly the weakness of the Articles of Confederation, under which a single state could block any significant action. He saw the doctrine of nullification as a formula for either anarchy or minority domination, and thus as a betrayal of the fundamental principle of republican government.

Madison Differs with Calhoun's View of the Meaning of the Virginia and Kentucky Resolutions

Calhoun's original term for what came to be called nullification was "interposition," a term derived from Madison's Virginia Resolutions of 1798, which spoke of the right and duty of the states "to interpose for arresting the progress of the evil." The "evil" for Madison, as for Jefferson, was the Alien and Sedition Acts and, more generally, a "deliberate, palpable, and dangerous exercise" by the federal government of powers not granted by the Constitution.[7] Calhoun in the *Exposition* referred to "this right of interposition, thus solemnly asserted by the State of Virginia" in the Virginia Resolutions of 1798 and called it "the fundamental principle of our system."[8] Calhoun later came to accept and employ the term "nullification," which he borrowed from the words "nullification of the act is the rightful remedy" in Jefferson's draft of the Kentucky Resolutions. But it is ironic that Calhoun's original preferred term "interposition" derived from Madison, who soon publicly denounced both the doctrine itself and the invocation of his name in connection with it.

Madison's name did not carry as much political weight in Calhoun's time as Jefferson's did. Jefferson's birthday was commemorated throughout the United States; Madison's was not. Jefferson was a demigod while Madison remained human. Yet as the last surviving leader of the founding generation, and one who self-consciously preserved the political legacy of his generation, it was difficult to ignore Madison's authority and his arguments. During the nullification controversy, when South Carolina vainly sought support from other southern states, one of Calhoun's correspondents from Georgia informed him that "it is not believed among us that a State can annul an act of Congress within her boundary and remain in the confederacy. . . . Mr. Madison's recent exposition of [the Virginia Resolutions of 1798] is highly approved of here."[9]

In the *Exposition* (1828) and the Fort Hill Address (1831) Calhoun had interchangeably invoked as precedents for nullification the Kentucky Resolutions of 1798, which Jefferson had authored, the Virginia Resolutions of 1798, which Madison had authored, and the *Report of 1800,* Madison's extensive explanation and defense of the Virginia Resolutions and their opposition to the Alien and Sedition Acts, which is treated earlier in this volume. At least initially, Calhoun referred to "the principles of '98" without distinguishing between the Virginia and Kentucky Resolutions or between the constitutional thought of Madison and Jefferson. If anything, Calhoun relied more heavily in the *Exposition* on Madison's language than on Jefferson's. He quoted from Madison's Virginia Resolutions to the effect that "in cases of a deliberate, palpable, and dangerous exercise of other powers, not granted by the said compact, the States, who are parties thereto, have the right, and are in duty bound to interpose to arrest the evil, and for maintaining, within their respective limits, the authorities, rights, and liberties appertaining to them."[10] This left as an open question what Madison specifically meant by "interpose" and how in practice Madison expected states to challenge unconstitutional acts by the federal government.

Madison's initial entry into the tariff/nullification controversy came in 1828, before Calhoun had written the *Exposition* and before the constitutional question of nullification took center stage. At this point the issue was the more routine question of whether a tariff intended primarily for protection was constitutional. Madison expressed the "confident opinion" that the power in Congress "to impose a tariff for the encouragement of Manufactures" was "among the powers vested in that Body." When the Constitution was drafted and ratified, Madison argued, all sides understood that the phrase "to regulate trade" included encouragement of manufactures. Such was the universal practice of commercial nations at the time, and both those who supported and those who opposed the Constitution agreed that it would transfer to Congress the power to encourage manufactures. The first session of Congress, and every succeeding Congress for the next forty years, had acquiesced in this power, thereby adding the force of cumulative precedent to original understanding. Madison emphasized that his intention was to address only the constitutionality of encouraging manufactures, not the "justice and general good" of such a policy, "for which members of Congress are responsible to their constituents."[11]

Madison's concerns soon turned to the more critical question of a constitutional right of nullification. Madison claimed that this doctrine was fundamentally at variance with the Constitution and the obligations of the compact upon which it is based as well as with the Virginia Resolutions of 1798, which Madison himself had drafted. In an 1830 letter to Edward Everett, Madison responded to Everett's request for his opinion of "the nullifying doctrine" and "the proceedings of the Virginia Legislature in '98, as appealed to in behalf of that doctrine." Calhoun's authorship of the *Exposition* was not public knowledge at the time, but Madison may have already suspected Calhoun's involvement: "The distinguished names & high authorities which appear to have asserted and given a practical scope to this doctrine, entitle it to a respect which it might be difficult otherwise to feel for it."[12]

The point immediately at issue between Madison and Calhoun was whether the Virginia Resolutions of 1798 endorsed the right of a single state to nullify acts of the federal government that such a state judged to be unconstitutional. Calhoun interpreted "interpose" to mean single-state nullification. Madison denied that the Virginia Resolutions of 1798 contained "any reference whatever to a constitutional right in an individual State to arrest by force the operation of a law of the U.S." and instead called upon other states "*concurrently* and co-operatively" to remedy the obnoxious laws through "measures known to the Constitution, particularly the ordinary controul [*sic*] of the people and Legislatures of the States over the Govt. of the U.S."[13] The Virginia Resolutions declared the unconstitutionality of the laws but did not claim the right of a single state to *act* unilaterally on that judgment; they appealed to other states to participate in a collective remedy. In short, Madison had intended in the Virginia Resolutions not to thwart permanently the will of a national majority but to build a national majority to overturn the obnoxious laws in some constitutional manner.

Madison believed that giving each individual state a right, not only to declare the unconstitutionality of a federal law, but to act unilaterally on that judgment unless and until overturned by three-quarters of the other states, which is what Calhoun's doctrine of nullification entailed, would mean giving to the minority the power to impose the law upon the majority and thus "overturn the first principle of free

Govt." To give each individual state the right to be final judge of the Constitution "could not fail to make the Constitution and laws of the United States different in different States . . . & speedily put an end to the Union itself." If nullification meant merely that a single state declared the unconstitutionality of a law and then appealed to three-fourths of the other states to sustain its judgment, "the decision to be without effect during the appeal," then it would be unobjectionable in principle but would add nothing to the regular constitutional provisions for amendment. But South Carolina and Calhoun claimed that a single state's judgment affirmatively overruled the law of the United States unless and until overruled by three-fourths of the states. Such a doctrine, Madison says, "puts it in the power of the smallest fraction over ¼ of the U.S. . . . to give the law and even the Const[itution] to 17 States."[14]

Madison denied that there was any valid analogy between the reciprocal checks among the three branches of the national government established by the Constitution and the claim of a single state to nullify decisions of the national government. "In the case of disputes between independent parts of the same Govt., neither part being able to communicate its will necessarily brings about an accommodation." This is fundamentally different from "disputes between a state Govt. and the Govt. of the U[nited] States . . . each party possessing . . . an organized Govt. . . . and having each a physical force to support its pretensions."[15] Put another way, Madison denied that nullification would merely be a "negative" power like a presidential veto or judicial review; instead, nullification would constitute a "positive" power to act in unjust and dangerous ways. Calhoun, in contrast, treated nullification as a valid extension of the principle embodied in separation of powers at the national level.

Madison could not deny the possibility of "an undue preponderance" of power in the national government at the expense of "the rights and powers of the States in their individual capacities." In rejecting nullification Madison had to propose some other remedy. The first resort was the ordinary political process. Madison, like Jefferson, was confident that the Alien and Sedition Acts were "passed in contravention to the opinions and feelings of the community" and for that reason fell at the first election; this would not be of much reassurance to an entrenched minority interest that has the "opinions and feelings of the community" against it, which was Calhoun's central problem. The next resort was to amend the Constitution. If every constitutional resort failed, there remained the natural right of revolution.[16]

In the *Exposition* Calhoun had argued for a state's constitutional right of secession should three-fourths of the other states affirmatively override its nullification of federal law. Madison, in contrast, argued that the only way to justify the remedy of secession was as a resort to the natural right of revolution—not as a constitutional right. He mentioned receiving some South Carolina papers that refer to secession as a constitutional right. "If one state can at will withdraw from the others, the others can at will withdraw from her, and turn her, nolentem volentem, out of the union. Until of late, there is not a State that would have abhorred such a doctrine more than South Carolina, or more dreaded an application of it to herself. The same can be said of the doctrine of nullification which she now preaches as the only faith by which the Union can be saved."[17] Madison thought that both secession without permission of the other states and single-state nullification of a national law violated the compact at the foundation of the Constitution and the Union. Madison, like Calhoun, used the term "compact" to refer to the Union, but the two had very different understandings of the nature of that compact and the rights and duties it entailed.

A fair reading of the Virginia Resolutions, and of Madison's *Report of 1800* that explained and justified those resolutions, sustains Madison's later denial that they support single-state nullification. Despite Calhoun's invocation of the *Report of 1800* as precedent for nullification, the closing section of the report is clearly incompatible with Calhoun's doctrine of nullification. Madison's report affirms a state's right "of declaring the alien and sedition acts to be unconstitutional," of "communicating the declaration to other states," and of inviting other states to "concu[r] in making a like declaration, supported too by the numerous applications flowing immediately from the people." The object of such a declaration would be to lead states to make "a direct representation to Congress, with a view to rescinding the two offensive acts" or, by a two-thirds majority of states, to "propose an explanatory amendment to the constitution."[18] Madison, in other words, allowed a single state to make a verbal declaration that a federal law is unconstitutional, but he nowhere endorsed the right of a single state affirmatively and unilaterally to act on this declaration. All a single state could constitutionally do was sound the alarm and encourage other states to join it in overturning the obnoxious acts through constitutionally prescribed processes. What Madison said in 1830–31 in his response to nullification was in fact fully consistent with what he had said in 1800.

The Gap between Madison and Jefferson

Madison still had one major problem, however: Jefferson's Kentucky Resolutions did seem to support single-state nullification. Madison and Jefferson had disagreed over exactly this issue back in 1798, when they drafted the Virginia and Kentucky Resolutions.[19] By the time of the nullification crisis Jefferson was dead and could no longer explain his meaning. The Virginia Resolutions always referred to "States" in the plural, Madison explains, but "the Kentucky Resolutions, being less guarded have been more easily perverted. . . . Allowances . . . ought to be made for a habit in Mr. Jefferson as in others of great genius of expressing in strong and round terms, impressions of the moment."[20] Madison also pointed out that the nullifiers invoked Jefferson's record only when it supported their case and ignored him "whenever his authority is ever so clearly and emphatically against them." Jefferson, for example, had supported "the powers of the old Congress [under the Articles of Convention] to coerce delinquent states."[21] Madison hoped to demonstrate that if Jefferson were still alive, he would be on Madison's side, not that of the nullifiers; but, under the circumstances, the best he could do with Jefferson's Kentucky Resolutions was limit the damage.

Madison consistently maintained that the federal Constitution established a union that was neither wholly "national" nor wholly "federal" but a combination of the two. He made this argument in *Federalist* No. 39 and again in 1830 in his reply to the nullifiers. The American people were, for certain purposes, a single national political community and, for other purposes, a multiplicity of political communities. The existence—for certain purposes—of a single, sovereign American people did not require consolidating all political power in the national government at the expense of the states. It meant that the American people could deliberately choose how much power to vest in each level of government. "The Constitution was proposed to the people of the States as a *whole,* and unanimously adopted by the States as a *whole.*"[22] In cases of disputes about where to draw the line between national and state authority, some tribunal that represents the American people as a whole—not a single state—must settle the dispute. When he received a transcript of Calhoun's speech on the Force Bill, where Calhoun denied that there existed any American "nation" or any "American people" in the singular, Madison remarked to Virginia senator William Cabell Rives (the latter fresh from his Force Bill debate with Calhoun), "What can be more preposterous than to say that the States as united, are in no respect or degree, a Nation . . . and at the same time, to say that the States separately are completely nations & sovereigns; although they can neither speak nor harken to any other nation?"[23]

In his posthumously published "Advice to My Country," Madison urged "that the Union of the States be cherished and perpetuated" and warned against both the open enemy to the Union, who should be regarded as "a Pandora with her box opened," and "the disguised one" who should be regarded "as the Serpent creeping with his deadly wiles into Paradise."[24] Madison did not name these open and disguised enemies. He made clear, however, that the effect of Calhoun's doctrine of nullification would be to "speedily put an end to the Union itself." Calhoun for his part continually insisted that his own purpose was to save the Union, not destroy it. This combination of facts leaves little doubt as to how the elderly Madison categorized Calhoun.

Calhoun's Response

Calhoun found Madison's 1830 retrospective on the Virginia Resolutions unconvincing. He hinted that Madison's intellectual powers were failing, although there is not the slightest evidence of this.[25] In his 1833 debate with Senator Rives, who as already mentioned was corresponding with Madison during this period, and whose interpretation of the Virginia Resolutions accords with Madison's, Calhoun accused Rives of degrading the Virginia Resolutions "by explaining away their meaning and efficacy." If the Virginia Resolutions merely asserted the right to overturn abuses of federal power via ordinary political processes, it was too weak a remedy; moreover, it would have been "egregious trifling" to declare so solemnly "what no one had ever denied."[26] Calhoun's reply to Rives is in substance a reply to Madison.

But Calhoun appears subsequently to have realized that there were significant differences between Madison's understanding of American federalism and his own. He continued to speak as though the Virginia Resolutions supported his doctrine of nullification—ignoring Madison's own explanation of their meaning—but he sharply criticized what Madison said elsewhere about federalism, especially in *Federalist* No. 39.

Calhoun completely rejected the possibility of anything "partly national" and "partly federal." It was all or nothing. In the *Discourse on the Constitution* (1850) explicitly criticizing Madison's *Federalist* No. 39, Calhoun asked: "What can be more contradictious" than "a government partly federal and partly national?"[27] Either each individual state is unquestionably sovereign, and as sovereign retains the right of final judgment, or sovereignty lies in a "consolidated" federal government, and states are reduced to the equivalent of counties. "We might just as well speak of half a square, or half of a triangle, as of half a sovereignty."[28] If one is unwilling to vest all political power in the national government—and Calhoun judged that his contemporaries would be unwilling to do this—the only alternative was complete state sovereignty.

The Differing Perspectives

Both Madison and Calhoun were concerned with the danger of tyrannical majorities under popular governments, and their different understandings of the Constitution and Union were connected with their respective diagnoses and remedies to the problem of majority tyranny. One of Madison's principal aims going into the Constitutional Convention of 1787 was to remedy the "Vices of the Political System of the United States," and one of the chief vices was the danger that the majority would commit "unjust violations of the rights and interests of the minority, or of individuals."[29] In *Federalist* Nos. 10 and 51 Madison famously argued that the greater extent of territory and diversity of interests in the large republic, along with the separation of powers that the Constitution established, would make it more difficult for an unjust majority to acquire and hold power. "In the extended republic of the United States," Madison wrote in No. 51, "and among the great variety of interests, parties and sects which it embraces, a coalition of a majority of the whole society could seldom take place upon any other principles than those of justice and the general good."[30]

Calhoun also intended his own reinterpretation and reconstruction of the Constitution to remedy the danger of majority tyranny. In the *Exposition* Calhoun quoted the following passage from Madison's *Federalist* No. 51 (though attributing it to Hamilton): "It is of the greatest importance in a republic, not only to guard society against the oppression of its rulers but to guard one part of society against the injustice of the other part. Different interests necessarily exist in different classes of citizens. If a majority be united by a common interest, the rights of the minority will be insecure."[31] Calhoun immediately added that "the AMERICAN SYSTEM"—meaning the political coalition behind the protective tariff of 1828—was exactly the kind of majority faction warned against in *Federalist* No. 51. Calhoun obviously believed that he was, in a different time and context, addressing the same general problem that had preoccupied the author of *Federalist* No. 51, and also No. 10, though Calhoun did not specifically mention the latter.

That Madison's and Calhoun's remedies to the problem were radically different is clear from Madison's own response to the nullification doctrine. Madison's explanation of the Virginia Resolutions makes clear that his purpose was to use the states (in the plural) to build a national majority against oppressive federal measures, and thus to replace a bad national majority with a good one. Madison was equally committed to the principle of majority rule a decade earlier when drafting the Constitution and writing the *Federalist*. Because Madison presupposed that one way or another the majority would rule in a popular government, the challenge was to design ways to *slow down* the majority, preventing any national majority from forming too quickly so that, once formed, it would act deliberately rather than quickly and passionately. This is what Madison meant by a "coalition of a majority of the whole society" forming only around principles of "justice and the general good." A just and deliberate national majority ceases to be a majority *faction,* since factions were by definition unjust.

Calhoun, in contrast, did not believe that making the majority slow-moving and deliberate could remedy majority tyranny. On the contrary, a slow, deliberate, long-in-forming majority was precisely the greatest danger. "To form combinations in order to get the control of the government, in a country of such vast extent—and consisting of so many States, having so great a variety of interests, must necessarily be a slow process, and require much time, before they can be firmly united, and settle down into two organized and compact parties. But the motives to obtain this control are sufficiently powerful to overcome all these impediments."[32] Calhoun here argued, contrary to Madison, that extensive territory and great variety of interests would not permanently prevent the formation of oppressive national majorities but would only slow down the pace at which they will form.

The specific historical development that Calhoun thought rendered the Madisonian solution to majority faction obsolete was the emergence of national, patronage-based political parties. In the *Discourse* Calhoun prefaced his diagnosis of the problem by quoting Madison himself from *Federalist* No. 38 to the effect that there may be "errors . . . contained in the plan of the convention" that will not be discovered "until an actual trial will point them out." Calhoun then extended Madison's own point. One of the errors the framers failed to guard against was that "most corrupting, loathsome and dangerous disease, that can infect a popular government . . . known by the name of 'the Spoils.'" The "increased power and patronage of the federal government"—which for Calhoun was closely connected with the protective tariff and the revenues it generated—had the effect of rendering "the struggle between the two parties more and more intense. . . . To secure the desired object, the concentration of party action and the stringency of party discipline were deemed indispensable."[33] Disciplined national political parties organized for the purpose of exploiting the fiscal powers of government gradually reduce the initial political and economic diversity of a large republic, which Madison assumed, to two entrenched interests, a majority and a minority interest. Because these interests were regionally concentrated, the effect of party conflict was to turn one section of the country dangerously against another.

One of the key differences between Madison's and Calhoun's diagnoses is that Madison viewed the interests that generate faction (creditors, debtors, farmers, manufacturers, different opinions concerning religion, etc.) as already existing in society prior to any action of government. The use of government power may give one of these groups an unfair advantage over another, but Madison did not view government action as the principal cause of faction. For Calhoun, on the contrary, the fiscal action of government was itself the principal cause of factional divisions. In the *Disquisition on Government* he argued that "even if it were possible to find a community, where the people were all of the same pursuits . . . and in every respect, so situated, as to be without inequality of condition or diversity of interests," the "action of the government itself" along with its "honors and emoluments" would suffice to "divide even such a community into two great hostile parties." For as soon as government begins collecting tax revenues and spending them, society is transformed into two fundamental groups, taxpayers and tax recipients, with fundamentally different political interests.[34]

Calhoun argued that this unequal fiscal action of government would divide even the most homogeneous community into two hostile parties. But the more "various and diversified" are the interests in a community, the more "extensive and populous the country" and the "more diversified the conditions and pursuits of its population," the more pronounced will be the unequal effect of government action. For "nothing is more difficult than to equalize the action of the government, in reference to the various and diversified interests of the community"; at the same time it will be easier pervert the powers of government "to aggrandize and enrich one or more interests by oppressing and impoverishing the others."[35] Calhoun thus turned Madison's argument on its head. Because Madison thought that differences of interest arose independently of the action of government, he expected the diversity of interest and extensive territory to guard against majority tyranny by preventing any single interest from gaining exclusive control of government. Because Calhoun thought that the control of government was itself the key interest and the principal source of faction, diversity of interest and extensive territory only make the problem worse.

Calhoun did not and could not argue that the solution was to make the fiscal action of government exactly equal in its effects on all interests and sections, which would be both logically and politically impossible. Nor could he resort, as Madison did, to the distinction between majority factions and enlightened, deliberate, just majorities. Instead, the momentum of his argument in this section pushed inexorably toward a minority veto / consensus model of government, which he first articulated immediately following the diagnosis outlined above. Calhoun's solution was to give to each "interest or portion of the community, which may be unequally and injuriously affected by the action of the government . . . either a concurrent voice in making and executing the laws, or a veto on their execution."[36]

Thus, beginning with a diagnosis of majority tyranny that in its general outlines resembled Madison's, Calhoun proceeded via an analysis of faction rather different from Madison's to a proposed remedy radically different from Madison's. Calhoun himself believed that to insist upon a consensus rule—and, in the American context, upon each state's right to nullify federal law—was to rise above both minority rule and majority rule and achieve a truly just and perfect form of government. Madison himself regarded Calhoun's proposed remedy as a violation of the fundamental principle of republican government, a formula for minority rule or anarchy, or both.

Analysis of Madison's Criticisms of Nullification

James Madison made two different types of criticism of the doctrine of nullification. As the self-appointed guardian of the founders' legacy, Madison claimed that the "innovating constructions" of the Constitution upon which nullification rested radically diverged from the Constitution as understood by those who drafted and ratified it.[37] He also argued that nullification in practice meant a small minority imposing the law and its own version of the Constitution on the vast majority, thus violating the first principle of republican government.

On the first point Madison was certainly correct: Calhoun's doctrine of nullification, and his whole method of reading the Constitution, would indeed qualify as an "innovating construction." But one must also ask how much fidelity to the intentions of the framers actually mattered to a new generation, facing new problems and driven by new passions. Despite the verbal tributes they paid to their venerable ancestors, the answer is: probably not much. Calhoun, for instance, invoked the authority of Jefferson and Madison when it supported positions Calhoun had arrived at on his own, for his own reasons. But when the still-living Madison rejected Calhoun's use of his Virginia Resolutions, Calhoun shifted easily enough from veneration to measured criticism. Neither Madison nor Jefferson, nor for that matter any of those who framed the Constitution, could have foreseen the political, economic, and ideological developments to which Calhoun himself was responding. Individuals persuaded by Calhoun in 1832 that nullification was the solution to the country's problems would be unlikely to change their minds simply upon hearing that Madison had denounced nullification as a newfangled doctrine.

However, Madison's claim that nullification amounted in practice to the rule of the minority over the majority is a far more powerful argument that taps a deep emotional vein in a republic. Calhoun's own reformulation of the Union as a compact of fully sovereign states, each of them armed with the power to block any federal law or policy it opposed, raised this central question—is it consensus, or is it minority domination?—to a higher level. Following Calhoun's lead, the slave states increasingly insisted during the decades preceding the Civil War that they were entitled to have their way on every federal question, regardless of either majority rule or constitutional text. Madison's claim that Calhoun's supposed consensus was in fact a minority imposing its will on the majority helps explain why white citizens of northern states who cared little for the authority of "original intention," and even less for the rights of persons of African descent, were willing to fight to the death against what they called "the Slave Power."

Notes

1. For a comprehensive portrait of the elderly Madison's self-conscious role as guardian of the founders' legacy, see Drew McCoy, *The Last of the Fathers: James Madison and the Republican Legacy* (New York: Cambridge University Press, 1989).

2. Don E. Fehrenbacher, ed., *Abraham Lincoln: Speeches and Writings, 1832–1858* (New York: Library of America, 1989).

3. For a detailed portrait of the first generation of Americans born under independence (to which generation Calhoun belonged), see Joyce Appleby, *Inheriting the Revolution: The First Generation of Americans* (Cambridge, MA: Belknap, 2000).

4. On the nullification controversy itself, see William W. Freehling, *Prelude to Civil War: The Nullification Controversy in South Carolina, 1816–1836* (New York: Oxford University Press, 1965).

5. John C. Calhoun, *Rough Draft of What Is Called the South Carolina Exposition* (1828), in *Union and Liberty: The Political Philosophy of John C. Calhoun,* ed. Ross M. Lence (Indianapolis, IN: Liberty Fund, 1992).

6. *Federalist* No. 10, in *James Madison: Writings,* ed. Jack N. Rakove (New York: Library of America, 1999), 167 (hereafter cited as *Writings*).

7. James Madison, "Virginia Resolutions against the Alien and Sedition Acts," December 21, 1798, ibid., 589.

8. Calhoun, *Exposition,* 349.

9. Charles J. McDonald to Calhoun, May 30, 1831, in *The Papers of John C. Calhoun,* ed. Clyde N. Wilson (Columbia: University of South Carolina Press, 1959–2003), 11:396–97 (hereafter cited as *Calhoun Papers*).

10. Calhoun, *Exposition,* 349.

11. Madison to Joseph Cabell, September 18, 1828, *Writings,* 813–23.

12. Madison to Edward Everett, August 28, 1830, ibid., 848.

13. Ibid., 842–51. Emphasis in original.

14. Ibid., 844, 849.

15. Ibid., 845.

16. Ibid., 846–48.

17. Madison to Nicholas P. Trist, December 23, 1832, *Writings,* 861–63. It is possible that, in saying "until of late, there is not a State that would have abhorred such a doctrine more than South Carolina," Madison had in mind South Carolina's dependence on federal power to suppress slave uprisings, but the author has no direct evidence for this. James Monroe, in his retirement, did raise exactly this issue in his correspondence with Calhoun during the nullification crisis. See Monroe to Calhoun, August 4, 1828, in *Calhoun Papers,* 10:410.

18. Madison, *Report [of 1800] on the Alien and Sedition Acts, Writings,* 660–61.

19. See Adrienne Koch and Harry Ammon, "The Virginia and Kentucky Resolutions: An Episode in Jefferson's and Madison's Defense of Civil Liberties," *William and Mary Quarterly,* 3rd ser., 5, no. 1 (April 1948): 145–76. See also McCoy, *Last of the Fathers,* 145–46.

20. Madison to Nicholas P. Trist, May 1832, *Writings,* 860.

21. Madison to Nicholas P. Trist, December 23, 1832, *Writings,* 862. Madison was correct in claiming that Jefferson supported the right of Congress under the Articles of Confederation to coerce delinquent states. See Jefferson's "Answers and Observations for Demeunier's Article," in *Thomas Jefferson: Writings,* ed. Merrill D. Peterson (New York: Library of America, 1984), 579.

22. Madison to Edward Everett, August 28, 1830, *Writings,* 864, 849. Emphasis in original.

23. Madison to William Cabell Rives, March 12, 1833, *Writings,* 864.

24. Madison, "Advice to My Country," *Writings,* 866.

25. In 1837, during Senate debate over the proposed governmental purchase of Madison's notes on the Constitutional Convention, which Calhoun opposed, he remarked that in Madison's *Report of 1800* [Calhoun gave the year as 1799] Madison "had given his views . . . in the prime of his life and vigor of his manhood," implying that

his denunciation of nullification thirty years later was the result of failing mental powers. See *Calhoun Papers,* 13:447.

26. Calhoun, Speech on the Force Bill, February 15, 1833, *Calhoun Papers,* 12:75. Madison praised Rives's "very able and enlightening speech" in his debate with Calhoun over the meaning of the Virginia Resolutions. Madison to Rives, March 12, 1833, *Writings,* 863–64. It should also be pointed out that in 1798 the right to form an organized "out-of-doors" political opposition for the purpose of overturning a ruling group through an election was by no means universally accepted; Calhoun is incorrect to claim that in 1798 "no one denied" this right.

27. Calhoun, Discourse on the Constitution, in Lence, *Union and Liberty,* 109.

28. Calhoun, Speech on the Force Bill, February 15, 1833, *Calhoun Papers,* 12:71. In fact, a bisected triangle forms two new triangles, so Calhoun's metaphor here misses the mark. (He was correct about half a square.)

29. Madison, "Vices of the Political System of the United States" (1787), *Writings,* 77.

30. Madison, *Federalist* No. 51, *Writings,* 298.

31. Calhoun, *Exposition,* 338. The original passage, which Calhoun quoted accurately, may be found in *Writings,* 297.

32. Calhoun, *Discourse on the Constitution,* in Lence, *Union and Liberty,* 164.

33. Ibid., 244, 259.

34. Calhoun, *Disquisition on Government,* in Lence, *Union and Liberty,* 16–17.

35. Ibid., 15.

36. Ibid., 21.

37. Madison to Joseph Cabell, September 18, 1828, *Writings,* 819.

Selected Bibliography

Abraham, Henry J. *Justices, Presidents, and Senators: A History of the U.S. Supreme Court Appointments from Washington to Clinton.* Lanham, MD: Rowman and Littlefield, 1999.

Adair, Douglass. *Fame and the Founding Fathers: Essays by Douglass Adair.* Edited by Trevor Colbourn. New York: W. W. Norton, 1974.

Adams, Henry. *History of the United States of America during the Administrations of James Madison.* 1889–91. New York: Library of America, 1986.

Alley, Robert S. *James Madison on Religious Liberty.* Amherst, NY: Prometheus Books, 1985.

Amar, Akhil Reed. *America's Constitution: A Biography.* New York: Random House, 2005.

Appleby, Joyce. *Inheriting the Revolution: The First Generation of Americans.* Cambridge, MA: Belknap, 2000.

Baily, Thomas A. *Presidential Greatness: The Image and the Man from George Washington to the Present.* New York: Appleton-Century, 1969.

Bailyn, Bernard, ed. *The Debate on the Constitution: Federalist and Antifederalist Speeches, Articles, and Letters during the Struggle over Ratification.* 2 vols. New York: Library of America, 1993.

Ball, Terence, and J. G. A. Pocock, eds. *Conceptual Change and the Constitution.* Lawrence: University Press of Kansas, 1988.

Banning, Lance. "The Hamiltonian Madison: A Reconsideration." *Virginia Magazine of History and Biography* 92 (January 1984): 3–28.

———. *The Sacred Fire of Liberty: James Madison and the Founding of the Federal Republic.* Ithaca, NY: Cornell University Press, 1995.

Berkin, Carol. *A Brilliant Solution: Inventing the American Constitution.* New York: Harcourt, 2002.

Borneman, Walter R. *1812: The War That Forged a Nation.* New York: Harper Collins, 2004.

Brant, Irving. *The Fourth President: A Life of James Madison.* Indianapolis, IN: Bobbs-Merrill, 1970.

———. *James Madison: Father of the Constitution, 1787–1800.* Indianapolis, IN: Bobbs-Merrill, 1950.

———. "Madison: On the Separation of Church and State." *William and Mary Quarterly,* 3rd ser., 8 (January 1951): 3–24.

Brown, Roger H. *The Republic in Peril: 1812.* New York: Columbia University Press, 1964.

Cerami, Charles. *Young Patriots: The Remarkable Story of Two Men, Their Impossible Plan and the Revolution That Created the Constitution.* Naperville, IL: Sourcebooks, 2005.

DeGregorio, William A. *The Complete Book of U.S. Presidents: From George Washington to George W. Bush.* New York: Gramercy Books, 2001.

Donovan, Frank R. *Mr. Madison's Constitution: The Story behind the Constitutional Convention.* New York: Dodd, Mead, 1965.

Drakeman, Donald L. "Religion and the Republic: James Madison and the First Amendment." *Journal of Church and State* 25 (Autumn 1983): 427–45.

Draper, Theodore. "Hume and Madison: The Secrets of Federalist Paper No. 10." *Encounter* 58 (February 1982): 34–57.

Edling, Max M. *A Revolution in Favor of Government: Origins of the U.S. Constitution and the Making of the American State.* Oxford: Oxford University Press, 2003.

Elkins, Stanley, and Eric McKitrick. *The Age of Federalism.* New York: Oxford University Press, 1993.

Ellis, Joseph J. *Founding Brothers: The Revolutionary Generation.* New York: Alfred A. Knopf, 2001.

Epstein, David. *The Political Theory of the* Federalist. Chicago: University of Chicago Press, 1984.

Farrand, Max. *The Fathers of the Constitution: A Chronicle of the Establishment of the Union.* New Haven, CT: Yale University Press, 1921.

———. *The Records of the Federal Convention of 1787.* 4 vols. New Haven, CT: Yale University Press, 1937.

Ferling, John. *Adams vs. Jefferson: The Tumultuous Election of 1800.* New York: Oxford University Press, 1971.

Finkelman, Paul. "James Madison and the Bill of Rights: A Reluctant Paternity." In *The Supreme Court Review, 1990,* edited by Gerhard Casper, Dennis J. Hutchinson, and David Strauss, 301–47. Chicago: University of Chicago Press, 1991.

Fleet, Elizabeth, ed. "Madison's Detached Memoranda." *William and Mary Quarterly,* 3rd ser., 3 (October 1946): 534–68.

Forber, Duncan. *Hume's Philosophical Politics.* Cambridge: Cambridge University Press, 1975.

Freehling, William W. *Prelude to Civil War: The Nullification Controversy in South Carolina, 1816–1836.* New York: Oxford University Press, 1965.

Gibson, Alan. "Impartial Representation and the Extended Republic: Towards a Comprehensive and Balanced Interpretation of the Tenth *Federalist,*" *History of Political Thought* 12 (Summer 1991): 263–304.

———. *Interpreting the Founding: Guide to the Enduring Debates over the Origins and Foundations of the American Republic.* Lawrence: University Press of Kansas, 2006.

———. "Lance Banning's Interpretation of James Madison." *Political Science Reviewer* 32 (2003): 291–96.

———. "Veneration and Vigilance: James Madison and Public Opinion, 1785–1800." *Review of Politics* 67 (Winter 2005): 5–36.

Goldwin, Robert. *From Parchment to Power: How James Madison Used the Bill of Rights to Save the Constitution.* Washington, DC: AEI Press, 1997.

Gutzman, K. R. "The Virginia and Kentucky Resolutions Reconsidered: 'An Appeal to the Real Laws of Our Country.'" *Journal of Southern History* 66 (August 2000): 473–96.

Hamilton, Alexander, James Madison, and John Jay. *The Federalist Papers.* Edited by Clinton Rossiter. New York: New American Library, 1961.

Hendrickson, David C. *Peace Pact: The Lost World of the American Founding.* Lawrence: University Press of Kansas, 2003.

Hickey, Donald R. *The War of 1812.* Urbana: University of Illinois Press, 1989.

Hobson, Charles F. "The Negative on State Laws: James Madison, the Constitution, and the Crisis of Republican Government." *William and Mary Quarterly,* 3rd ser., 36 (April 1979): 214–35.

Hofstader, Richard. *The Idea of a Party System: The Rise of Legitimate Opposition in the United States, 1780–1840.* Berkeley: University of California Press, 1969.

Holmes, David L. *The Faiths of the Founding Fathers.* New York: Oxford University Press, 2006.

Holton, Woody. "'Divide et Impera': *Federalist* 10 in a Wider Sphere." *William and Mary Quarterly,* 3rd ser., 62 (April 2005): 175–212.

Horsman, Reginald. *The Causes of the War of 1812.* Philadelphia: University of Pennsylvania Press, 1962.

Howe, David Walker. "The Political Psychology of *The Federalist.*" *William and Mary Quarterly* 44 (June 1987): 485–509.

Hume, David. *Essays Moral, Political and Literary,* Rev. ed. Edited by Eugene F. Miller. Indianapolis, IN: Liberty Classics, 1987.

Hunt, Gaillard. "James Madison and Religious Liberty." *Annual Report of the American Historical Association* 1 (1901): 665–71.

Israel, Fred L., ed. *The State of the Union Messages of the U.S. Presidents, 1790–1966*. New York: Chelsea House, 1966.

Jennings, Paul. *A Colored Man's Reminiscences of James Madison*. Brooklyn, NY: G. C. Beadle, 1865.

Jillson, Calvin C. *Constitution Making: Conflict and Consensus in the Federal Convention of 1787*. New York: Agathon, 1988.

Jillson, Calvin C., and Cecil L. Eubanks. "The Political Structure of Constitution Making: The Federal Convention of 1787." *American Journal of Political Science* 28 (August 1984): 435–58.

Jones, Conover Hunt. *Dolley and the "Great Little Madison."* Washington, DC: American Institute of Architects Foundation, 1977.

Kaminski, John P. *James Madison: Champion of Liberty and Justice*. Madison, WI: Parallel, 2006.

Kelly, Brent P., and Arthur M. Schlesinger. *James Madison: Father of the Constitution*. Philadelphia: Chelsea House, 2001.

Kernell, Samuel. *James Madison: The Theory and Practice of Republican Government*. Stanford, CA: Stanford University Press, 2003.

Ketcham, Ralph. *Framed for Posterity: The Enduring Philosophy of the Constitution*. Lawrence: University Press of Kansas, 1993.

———. *James Madison: A Biography*. New York: Macmillan, 1971. Charlottesville: University Press of Virginia, 1990.

Koch, Adrienne. *Jefferson and Madison: The Great Collaboration*. New York: Alfred A. Knopf, 1950.

———. *Madison's "Advice to My Country."* Princeton, NJ: Princeton University Press, 1966.

Koch, Adrienne, and Harry Ammon, "The Virginia and Kentucky Resolutions: An Episode in Jefferson's and Madison's Defense of Civil Liberties," *William and Mary Quarterly*, 3rd ser., 5 (April 1948): 145–76.

Kramer, Larry. "Madison's Audience." *Harvard Law Review* 112 (January 1999): 611–79.

Kurland, Philip B., and Ralph Lerner. *The Founders' Constitution*. 5 vols. Chicago: University of Chicago Press, 1987.

Labunski, Richard. *James Madison and the Struggle for the Bill of Rights*. New York: Oxford University Press, 2006.

Langguth, A. J. *Union 1812: The Americans Who Fought the Second War of Independence*. New York: Simon and Schuster, 2006.

Lash, Kurt T. "James Madison's Celebrated Report of 1800: The Transformation of the Tenth Amendment." *George Washington Law Review* 74 (February 2006): 165–200.

Leibiger, Stuart. *Founding Friendship: George Washington, James Madison, and the Creation of the American Republic.* Charlottesville: University Press of Virginia, 1999.

Lee, Emery G., III. "Representation, Virtue, and Political Jealousy in the Brutus-Publius Dialogue." *Journal of Politics* 49 (November 1997): 1073–95.

Lence, Ross M., ed. *Union and Liberty: The Political Philosophy of John C. Calhoun.* Indianapolis, IN: Liberty Fund, 1992.

Levy, Leonard W. *The Establishment Clause: Religion and the First Amendment.* 2nd rev. ed. Chapel Hill: University of North Carolina Press, 1994.

Locke, John. *Two Treatises of Civil Government.* Rev. ed. Edited by Peter Laslett. New York: New American Library, 1960.

Loconte, Joseph. "Faith and the Founding: The Influence of Religion on the Politics of James Madison." *Journal of Church and State* 40 (Autumn 2003): 699–715.

Madison, James. *A Brief System of Logick.* The James Madison Papers. Library of Congress.

———. *James Madison: A Biography in His Own Words.* Edited by Merrill D. Peterson. New York: Newsweek, 1974.

———. *James Madison: Writings.* Ed. Jack N. Rakove. New York: Library of America, 1999.

———. *Notes of Debates in the Federal Convention of 1787 Reported by James Madison.* Edited by Adrienne Koch. New York: W. W. Norton, 1987.

———. *The Papers of James Madison.* Edited by William T. Hutchinson et al. 17 vols. Chicago: University of Chicago Press; Charlottesville: University Press of Virginia, 1962–91.

———. *The Writings of James Madison.* Edited by Gaillard Hunt. 9 vols. New York: G. P. Putnam's Sons, 1900–1910.

Malone, Dumas. *Jefferson the Virginian.* Boston: Little, Brown, 1948.

Martin, Robert W. T. *The Free and Open Press: The Founding of American Democratic Press Liberty, 1640–1800.* New York: New York University Press, 2001.

Mattern, David B., and Holly C. Shulman. *The Selected Letters of Dolley Payne Madison.* Charlottesville: University Press of Virginia, 2003.

Matthews, Richard K. *If Men Were Angels: James Madison and the Heartless Empire of Reason.* Lawrence: University Press of Kansas, 1995.

McCoy, Drew R. *The Last of the Fathers: James Madison and the Republican Legacy.* New York: Cambridge University Press, 1989.

McDonald, Forrest. *Alexander Hamilton: A Biography.* New York: W. W. Norton, 1979.

———. *Novus Ordo Seculorum: The Intellectual Origins of the Constitution*. Lawrence: University Press of Kansas, 1985.

Meyers, Marvin, ed. *The Mind of the Founder: Sources of the Political Thought of James Madison*. Indianapolis, IN: Bobbs-Merrill, 1973.

Meyerson, Michael I. *Liberty's Blueprint: How Madison and Hamilton Wrote the Federalist Papers, Defined the Constitution, and Made Democracy Safe for the World*. New York: Basic Books, 2008.

Miller, William Lee. *The Business of May Next: James Madison and the Founding*. Charlottesville: University Press of Virginia, 1992.

Mitchell, Barbara, and Alex Tavoularis. *Father of the Constitution: A Story about James Madison*. Minneapolis, MN: Carolrhoda Books, 1994.

Moore, John Allphin, Jr., and John E. Murphs, eds. *A Grand Experiment: The Constitution at 200: Essays from the Douglass Adair Symposia*. Wilmington, DE: Scholarly Resources, 1987.

Morgan, Edmund S. "Safety in Numbers: Madison, Hume and the Tenth *Federalist*." *Huntington Library Quarterly* 49 (Spring 1986): 95–112.

Morgan, Robert J. *James Madison on the Constitution and the Bill of Rights*. New York: Greenwood, 1988.

Morris, Richard, ed. *Alexander Hamilton and the Founding of the Nation*. New York: Dial, 1957.

Peterson, Merrill D., and Robert C. Vaughn, eds. *The Virginia Statute for Religious Freedom: Its Evolution and Consequences in American History*. New York: Cambridge University Press, 1988.

Pocock, J. G. A. *The Machiavellian Moment: Florentine Political Thought and the Atlantic Republican Tradition*. Princeton, NJ: Princeton University Press, 1975.

Rakove, Jack. "The Great Compromise: Ideas, Interests, and the Politics of Constitution Making." *William and Mary Quarterly* 44, 3rd ser., no. 3 (1987): 424–57.

———. *James Madison and the Creation of the American Republic*. 3rd ed. New York: Pearson Longman, 2007.

———. *Original Meanings: Politics and Ideas in the Making of the Constitution*. New York: Alfred A. Knopf, 1996.

Rehnquist, William. *Grand Inquests: The Historic Impeachments of Justice Samuel Chase and President Andrew Johnson*. New York: Morrow, 1992.

Reiss, David. "Jefferson and Madison as Icons in Judicial History: A Study of Religion Clause Jurisprudence." *Maryland Law Review* 61 (Winter 2002): 94–176.

Richardson, James D., ed. *Messages and Papers of the Presidents*. New York: Bureau of National Literature, 1908.

Rosen, Gary. *American Compact: James Madison and the Problem of Founding.* Lawrence: University Press of Kansas, 1999.

Rossiter, Clinton. *1787: The Grand Convention.* New York: W. W. Norton, 1966.

Rutland, Robert A. *James Madison: The Founding Father.* New York: Macmillan, 1987.

———. *The Presidency of James Madison.* Lawrence: University Press of Kansas, 1990.

———. "The Virginia Plan of 1787: James Madison's Outline of a Model Constitution." *This Constitution* 4 (Fall 1984): 23–30.

Sheehan, Colleen. "Madison v. Hamilton: The Battle over Republicanism and the Role of Public Opinion." *American Political Science Review* 98 (August 2004): 405–24.

Sheldon, Garrett Ward. *The Political Philosophy of James Madison.* Baltimore: Johns Hopkins University Press, 2001.

Simon, Sheila S. *Odd Couple of the Constitution: James Madison and Alexander Hamilton.* Baltimore, MD: Publish America, 2005.

Skowronek, Stephen. *The Politics Presidents Make: Leadership from John Adams to George Bush.* Cambridge, MA: Belknap, 1993.

Smith, James Morton. *Freedom's Fetters: The Alien and Sedition Laws and American Civil Liberties.* Ithaca, NY: Cornell University Press, 1956.

———. "The Sedition Law, Free Speech, and the American Political Process." *William and Mary Quarterly,* 3rd ser., 9 (October 1952): 497–511.

Smith, Stephen D. "Blooming Confusion: Madison's Mixed Legacy." *Indiana Law Review* 75 (Winter 2000): 61–75.

Spitzer, Robert. *The Presidential Veto: Touchstone of the American Presidency.* Albany: State University of New York Press, 1988.

Stagg, J. C. A. *Mr. Madison's War.* Princeton, NJ: Princeton University Press, 1983.

Staloff, Darren. *Hamilton, Adams, Jefferson: The Politics of Enlightenment and the American Founding.* New York: Hill and Wang, 2005.

Stathis, Stephen W. *Landmark Legislation, 1774–2002.* Washington, DC: CQ Press, 2003.

Stewart, John B. *The Moral and Political Philosophy of David Hume.* New York: Columbia University Press, 1963.

Tulis, Jeffrey K. *The Rhetorical Presidency.* Princeton, NJ: Princeton University Press, 1988.

Vile, John R. *The Constitutional Convention of 1787: A Comprehensive Encyclopedia of America's Founding.* 2 vols. Santa Barbara, CA: ABC-CLIO, 2005.

Vile, John R., David Hudson, and David Schultz, eds. *Encyclopedia of the First Amendment.* 2 vols. Washington, DC: CQ Press, 2008.

Waldman, Steven. *Founding Faith: Providence, Politics, and the Birth of Religious Freedom in America.* New York: Random House, 2008.

Weber, Paul. "James Madison and Religious Equality: The Perfect Separation." *Review of Politics* 44 (April 1982): 163–86.

Whitney, David C., and Robin Vaughn Whitney. *The American Presidents.* Pleasantville, NY: Reader's Digest Association, 2001.

Wilkie, Katharine E., and Elizabeth R. Moseley. *Father of the Constitution: James Madison.* New York: Messner, 1963.

Wills, Garry. *Explaining America: The Federalist.* Garden City, NY: Doubleday, 1981.

———. *James Madison.* New York: Times Books, 2002.

Witherspoon, John. *Lectures on Moral Philosophy.* In vol. 4, *The Works of the Rev. John Witherspoon.* Philadelphia: Woodward, 1802.

Wolfe, Christopher. "On Understanding the Constitutional Convention of 1787." *Journal of Politics* 39 (February 1977): 97–118.

Wood, Gordon S. *The Creation of the American Republic, 1776–1787.* Chapel Hill: University of North Carolina Press, 1969.

———. *Revolutionary Characters: What Made the Founders Different.* New York: Penguin, 2006.

Yoho, James. "Madison on the Beneficial Effects of Interest Groups: What Was Left Unsaid in *Federalist* 10," *Polity* 27, no. 4 (1995): 587–605.

Zuckert, Michael. "Federalism and the Founding: Toward a Reinterpretation of the Constitutional Convention." *Review of Politics* 48 (Spring 1968): 166–210.

———. "The Political Science of James Madison." In *History of American Political Thought,* edited by Bryan-Paul Frost and Jeffrey Skikkanga, 149–66. Lanham, MD: Lexington Books, 2003.

Contributors

Henry J. Abraham, James Hart Professor emeritus, University of Virginia

Steven P. Brown, associate professor of political science, Auburn University

Byron W. Daynes, William J. Clinton Distinguished Fellow, University of Arkansas Clinton School of Public Service, and professor of political science, Brigham Young University, with Mark Hopkins, Brigham Young University

Alan Gibson, associate professor of political science, California State University at Chico

Craig Grau, professor of political science, University of Minnesota, Duluth

Rodney A. Grunes, professor of political science, Centenary College

Gordon P. Henderson, associate professor of government and politics, Widener University

Samuel B. Hoff, George Washington Distinguished Professor of History and Political Science, Delaware State University

Stefano Luconi, professor of American history, Universities of Padova and Pisa, Italy

John Allphin Moore, Jr., professor emeritus of history, California State Polytechnic University, Pomona

David Nordquest, assistant professor of philosophy, Gannon University

James H. Read, professor of political science, College of St. Benedict and St. John's University

Mary Stockwell, associate professor of history, Lourdes College

John R. Vile, professor of political science and dean of the University Honors College, Middle Tennessee State University

Index

Abbott, Philip, 253
Act for Establishing Religious Freedom. *See* Virginia Act for Establishing Religious Freedom
Adair, Douglass: on fame and founders, 50–51; on influence of Hume, 214
Adams, Henry, 220
Adams, John, 261
Adams, John Quincy, 203, 263
Adams, Samuel, 176
"Address of the General Assembly to the People of the Commonwealth of Virginia" (Madison), 139, 141
"Address to the States" (Madison), 178
"Advice to My Country" (Madison), 53n4, 276
Agostini v. Felton, 126
Albany Plan of Union, 49
Alien and Sedition Acts, 97, 134, 271
Allegheny v. American Civil Liberties Union, 127
Amar, Akhil Reed, 65–66, 78
American Whig Society, 28
Ames, Fisher, 113, 187
Ammon, Harry, 134
Annapolis Convention, vii, 185, 251
annual messages, 253
Armstrong, John, 237, 241–42
Articles of Confederation, 43, 67, 157–58, 271

Bailey, Thomas, 258
Bailyn, Bernard, 78
balance of power, 218, 230
Banning, Lance, 15, 106, 108, 110
Baptists, 24–25, 112, 114
Barbary pirates, 251
Barber, James, 229–30, 245
Barber, Philip, 266
Barron v. Baltimore, 164
Bayard, James A., 197
Beard, Charles, 50, 75
Beasley, Frederick, 107
Beer, Samuel H., 211
Benson, Egbert, 195
Benton, Thomas Hart, 31
Berkin, Carol, 45
Bill for Establishing Religious Freedom in Virginia. *See* Virginia Act for Establishing Religious Freedom
Bill of Rights: adoption of, 162–64; advantages of, 91–92; father of, 52n3; Jefferson correspondence regarding, 95; and second convention, avoidance of, 111–12; state governments, attempt to limit, 113, 133, 164; wording of provisions in, 163
Black, Hugo, 122, 144–45
Bladensburg, battle of, 242
Bloom, Sol, 45
Blount, William, 196–98
Bonaparte, Napoleon, 238
Brackenridge, Hugh Henry, 203
Bradford, William, 3, 22, 24
Brant, Irving, 5, 38, 108, 110, 125
Brennan, William, 145–46
Briggs, C. N., 30
Brutus, 63–64, 168
Burgess, John, 51
Burr, Aaron, 188, 202–3

Calhoun, John C.: on Madison's ability to control cabinet, 252; on nullification, xiii–xiv, 270
Canada, 241
Cantwell v. Connecticut, 122
chaplaincies: congressional, 115, 118–19; military, 115, 119–20
Chapman, Reynolds, 14
"Charters" (Madison), 95–96
Chase, Samuel, 201–2, 262
Chicago Sun-Times survey, 230, 237
Chicago Tribune poll, 230
churches: Episcopal, 106; grants of public lands to, 116–17; incorporation of, 116–17; Protestant Episcopal Church of Alexandria, 114; tax exemptions for, 117–18. *See also* freedom of religion; separation of church and state
Church of the Holy Trinity v. United States, 127
City of Boerne v. Flores, 125
Clay, Henry, 258
Cliosophic Society, 28
Coke, Edward, 18n19
College of New Jersey. *See* Princeton
College of William and Mary, ix, 106
Commentaries on the Constitution of the United States (Story), 264
common law, 135–42
conscience, right to. *See* freedom of religion
Constitution (U.S.): amending process, 44; Article I, Section 8, 137, 187; Article I, Section 10, 76; Article II, Section 4, 196; Article III, Section 2, 136; Article VI, prohibition of religious tests, 110; Eleventh Amendment, 136; First Amendment, 113, 137–42; Fourteenth Amendment, 146; House of Representatives, direct election of, 77; necessary and proper clause, 187; preamble, 137; signatures on, 42; supremacy clause, 159
Constitutional Convention of 1787: extended republic, influence of Madison's view, 67–73; joint work of Madison and Hamilton, 181; universal negative, 71, 158
Continental Congresses, 251
Cooper v. Aaron, 168
Corwin, Edwin S., 159
Council of Revision, 42
"Court" and "Country" parties, 212
Creation of the American Republic (Wood), 80
C-Span poll, 230, 237
Cunningham, Noble, Jr., 31
Curtis, George Ticknor, 45
Cushing, William, 262
Cutter v. Wilkinson, 125

Dartmouth College v. Woodward, 265
Dearborn, Henry, 241
Declaration of Independence, 41
Deity, in government documents, 118
Democratic-Republican Party, 217, 243–44
Detached Memoranda (Madison), 115–20
Diamond, Martin, 67–68
Discourse on the Constitution (Calhoun), 277
Disquisition on Government (Calhoun), 279
Drakeman, Donald L., 115
Duane, James, 29
Duvall, Gabriel, 264–65

ecclesiastical monopolies, 116
election of 1800, 199
Elkins, Stanley, 211
Ellis, Joseph, 22–23, 40, 210
Embargo Act of 1807, 234, 252, 263
Episcopal Church, 106
Epstein, David, 213
Erikson, Erik, 245
Essay Concerning Human Understanding (Locke), 4
Eustis, William, 236
Eve, George, 112
Everett, Edward, 273
Everson v. Board of Education, 122
extended republic, 63–87

Faber, Charles F., 237
Faber, Richard B., 237
fame, 50–51
Farrand, Max, 39, 45
Faschingbauer, Thomas, 252
Federalist No. 10 (Madison): and extended republic, 63–87; and factions, 7, 17, 23, 91–93, 95, 212, 215–16; leaders, role of, 50, 99; and liberty, 90, 167; mutual influence of opinions and passions, 10–11; republican remedy, 271; work of political science, 51

Federalist No. 14 (Madison): nationhood, 93; wisdom and action, 95
Federalist Nos. 18–20 (Madison and Hamilton), 182–83
Federalist No. 37 (Madison): and blending institutional virtues, 15; and language, 8–9, 13; people's political wisdom, 95
Federalist No. 38 (Madison): on constitutional convention, 41; on discovery of errors, 279
Federalist No. 39 (Madison): Calhoun's critique, 277; republican fidelity, 15; U.S. partly "national" and partly "federal," 276
Federalist No. 40 (Madison): farmers as patriotic and respectable, 99
Federalist No. 42 (Madison): piracies on high seas, 140
Federalist No. 43 (Madison): association of states after ratification, 94
Federalist No. 44 (Madison): on necessary and proper clause, 187
Federalist No. 46 (Madison): citizens' attachments to their states, 94
Federalist No. 48 (Madison): on wariness of legislature, 98; on parchment barriers, 213
Federalist No. 49 (Madison): passions, role of, 11; veneration, role of, 49–50
Federalist No. 51 (Madison): auxiliary precautions, 213; breaking of factions, 212, 277–78; Calhoun's interpretation, 278; interests, 216; religions, multiplicity of, 111; separation of powers, 15–17
Federalist No. 52 (Madison): House representation and liberty, 96; religious oaths, prohibition on,110
Federalist No. 62 (Madison): blending forms of government, 14; wisdom of Senate, 15
Federalist No. 65 (Hamilton): on impeachable offenses, 194
Federalist No. 84 (Hamilton): on power over press, 140
Federalist Nos. 84 and 85 (Hamilton): Constitution as guarantor of rights; weakness of parchment barriers, 216
Federal Republican, 233
Few, Francis, 30
Finkelman, Paul, 111–12
Fleet, Elizabeth, 115–16
Forefathers' Day, 39
Fort Hill address (Calhoun), 272
Foster, Augustus J., 240
Founding Brothers (Ellis), 22
founding fathers, derivation of term, 39–40
France, relations with, 238
Franklin, Benjamin, 41–42, 46–48
freedom of religion: First Amendment, 113, 165–67; Madison's views on, 9, 24–26, 107–14, 114–15, 115–22, 242–43; mere toleration, inadequacy of, 107. *See also* churches; separation of church and state
Freneau, Philip, 28, 188

Gallatin, Albert: cabinet, service in, 235–36; on Madison, 30
Germany, 183
Gerry, Elbridge, 43, 46, 237
Giles, Branch, 199
Gitlow v. New York, 164
Goldwin, Robert, 162
grants of public lands to churches, 116–17
Great Britain, relations with, 239
Greek city-states, 183, 214

Habermas, Jürgen, 96
Hamilton, Alexander: Constitutional Convention, role at, 47; death in duel with Burr, 188; on fame, 50; impeachment, proposals for, 198–99; Madison, relationship with, 175–92; *Report on Manufactures*, 186–89; *Report on Public Credit*, 176–85; *Report on the Bank*, 186; Yorktown, battle of, 176. *See also specific numbers of the* Federalist; Hamilton, Alexander, relationship with Madison
Hamilton, Alexander, relationship with Madison: Annapolis Convention, joint work at, 180; Articles of Confederation, joint work on finances under, 177; bank, disagreement over, 186–87; at Constitutional Convention, 181; "discrimination," disagreement over, 185; early friendship, 175–76; *Federalist Papers*, joint work on, 182;

Hamilton, Alexander, relationship with Madison (*cont.*):
Report on Public Credit (Hamilton), Madison's response to, 176–85; rift, perspectives on, 185–86, 189–90; state debt, disagreement over, 185; tariff, disagreement over, 186–87; and taxation, 184; veterans, experiences with, 179. *See also* Hamilton, Alexander
Hamilton, Paul, 236
Harding, Warren G., 39
Harvey, John, 193–94
Henry, Patrick: as Antifederalist, 8; as opponent of Madison's election to House of Representatives, 112, 161; revenue proposals in Virginia, 180; support for religious assessments, 25, 108; and Virginia Declaration of Rights, 108
Hickey, Donald R., 239
Hobson, Charles, 71
Holmes, David L., 107
Holton, Woody, 78
Howe, Daniel Walker, 12
Hull, William, 241
Hume, David: *Essays,* 7; "Idea of a Perfect Commonwealth," 81n2, 214, 222n22, 222n25; influence on Madison, 209–19; on moderation, 215; "That Politics May Be Reduced to a Science," 215, 221n21
Hutcheson, Francis, 10

"Idea of a Perfect Commonwealth" (Hume), 81n2, 214, 222n22, 222n25
Ideological Origins of the American Revolution (Bailyn), 78
impeachment: of Blount, 196–99; in colonial period, 193–94; and Constitutional Convention, 194–95; of federal judges, 199–202; and Hamilton, 198–99; Madison on, 195–96, 203–4; mechanism, 193–208; origins of, 193–94; scope of, 195–96
inaugural messages, 253
incorporation of churches, 116–17
internal improvements, 257
interposition, 271

Jackson, Andrew, 244
Jackson, Robert, 167
Jay, John: and *Federalist Papers,* 182; on Supreme Court, 261
Jefferson, Thomas: Act for Establishing Religious Freedom, 110, 166; appointments to Supreme Court, 261; assessment of Madison, 5, 30; association with Madison, 30; and Bill of Rights, 91–92; and Blount impeachment, 198; books for Madison, 7; election of 1800, 199; and Madison-Hamilton relationship, 185–86, 188–89; and *National Gazette,* 188; Story, opposition to appointment of, 263; Virginia and Kentucky Resolutions, differences with Madison on, 275–76
Jenkins, David, 134
Jennings, Paul, 31
Jensen, Merrill, 45
judicial review: exercises prior to *Marbury v. Madison,* 160; and Madison, 159
Judiciary Act of 1801, 199, 201

Kauffmann, Bruce G., 38
Kent, James, 152n59, 264
Ketcham, Ralph, 26, 29, 30, 107–8, 112–13, 214, 235, 252
King, Rufus, 202
Koch, Adrienne, 3–5, 134
Kramer, Larry, 66, 73–75, 78

Labunski, Richard, 31, 112
Lansing, John, 43
Lash, Kurt, 134
Latrobe, Mary, 232
Lee, Arthur, 195
Lee, Henry (Light Horse Harry), 28, 40, 161
Lee v. Weisman, 123
Leland, John, 30, 112
"Letter to a Member of Congress; Respecting the Alien and Sedition Laws" (Tucker), 134
Levy, Leonard, 145
liberalism and the founders, 211–12
Lincoln, Abraham, 39–40, 49, 88, 269
Lincoln, Levi, 262
Lind, Michael, 40
Livermore, Samuel, 113

Livingston, Edward, 119, 128
Livingston, Henry, 265
Locke, John, 4–6, 90, 109
Loconte, Joseph, 106, 121
logic, natural and artificial, 6
Logick (Watt), 4
Logic or the Art of Thinking (Arnaud and Nicole), 4
Lonergan, Bernard, 5
Louisiana Purchase, 251
Lowell, John, 233
Lynch v. Donnelly, 127
Lyon, Bryce, 193

"Machiavellian Moment," 212
Macon's Bill Number 2, 234, 252
Madison, Dolley: inaugural balls, 232; as social facilitator, 245; and White House socials, 232
Madison, James (Jr.): "Address to the States," 178; "Advice to My Country," 53n4, 276; appeal to scholars, 51–52; approach to Congress, 252–57; Articles of Confederation, critique of, 67, 157–58; on authorship of Constitution, 41; biographical background, vii, 250–51; and Burr, 202–3; cabinet, 235–37, 252; "Charters," 95–96; and Committee of Safety (Orange County), 26; on common law, 135–42; at Constitutional Convention, 46; Continental Congress, 29; correspondence not saved, 22; Council of Revision, vii, 159; as cultural anthropologist, 89, 93–96; extended republic and ratification of constitution, 74–75, 77; as father of the Bill of Rights, 133; as father of the Constitution, 37–62, 81, 87n61; "Government of the United States," 96; on governments, British and American, 138–40; Governor's Council (Virginia), 26, 251; Hamilton, relationship with, 175–90; health and physical characteristics, viii, 22, 53n5, 231–32, 251; Henry, arguments with, 8; Hume and political parties, 209–26; identity crisis, 23–24; and Jefferson, 275–76; justice, concern for, 218; on libel, state power over, 141–42; liberty as major concern, 90; *Memorial and Remonstrance,* 25, 92, 95, 97, 98, 108–10; Montpelier, xiv, 23; and national bank, 186–87, 243, 257; *National Gazette* essays, 79; nationalism of, 26–27, 93–94; nullification, response to, 269–83; occupation, choice of, 27–28; original intent interpretations, 151n52; as party leader, xii–xiii; as philosophe, 252; and politics, 29–31, 89, 90–92, 96–98; popular government, views on, 88–102; press, relations with, 233–34; Princeton, studies at, 3–20; on religion and passions, 110, 213; religious faith of, 105–7; *Report on Restoring Public Credit,* 178; and Republican Party, creation of, 217; *Robert Smith's Address to the People of the United States,* 236; as scholarly philosopher, 23; secession, opposition to, 273–74; on separation of powers vs. nullification, 274; socials, 232; speeches, 233, 250–60; travels, 232–33; on universal negative, 71, 158; "Universal Peace," 97; vetoes, 256–58; "Vices of the Political System of the United States," 91–92, 100; 213; Virginia Act for Establishing Religious Freedom, 30, 166; Virginia Convention, work at, 25, 251; Virginia House of Delegates, work in, 251; Virginia Plan, authorship of, 158; Virginia ratifying convention (1788), 8, 31, 37, 80, 111, 146n1, 195; *See also* Bill of Rights; *Federalist;* freedom of religion; Hamilton, Alexander, relationship with Madison; impeachment; messages to Congress (Madison); nullification; *Report of 1800;* Supreme Court (U.S.)
Madison, James (Rev.), 23
Marbury v. Madison, 159–60, 168, 201
Marshall, John, 49, 139, 164, 201
Mason, George, vii, 43, 46, 107, 155n85, 194
McConnell, Michael, 125
McCoy, Drew, 30, 38
McCreary County v. American Civil Liberties Union, 124
McDonald, Forrest, 42
McKitrick, Eric, 211
Melville, Lord, 193

Memorial and Remonstrance against Religious Assessments (Madison): arguments in, 25, 92, 95, 97, 98, 108–10; assessment of, 108, 166; empiricism of, 9; Supreme Court, use by, 122
messages to Congress (Madison): evaluations of, 258; inaugural and annual messages, 253; proclamations, 254–55; special messages, 253–54; veto messages, 256–58
Meyers, Marvin, 38
Miller, David, 215
Monroe, James: correspondence with Madison, 12, 239; on invasion of Canada, 241; as opponent to Madison in election to House, 161, 183; as secretary of state, 30, 234–35; as secretary of war, 234; and southern Republicans, 234
Montesquieu, Baron de, 63–87, 214
Morgan, Robert, 134, 141–42
Morris, Gouverneur, 46–47, 50
Morrison, Jeffrey, 10
Muñoz, Vincent Philip, 107, 125
Murray-Blessing poll, 230

national bank, 186–87
National Gazette, 79, 95–96, 188, 213
Netherlands, United, 183
Neustadt, Richard, 245
New England, opposition to War of 1812, 234–35, 239
Newton, Isaac, 218
New York Daily Advertiser, 63
New York Evening Post, 233
New York Times Co. v. Sullivan, 142, 145–46
Nicholas, Robert C., 25
Non-Intercourse Act, 234, 252
nullification, 269–83

O'Connor, Sandra Day, 124–25
Orange County, Virginia, 25
Orfield, Lester, 44
Otis, Gray, 197

Peck, James Hawkins, 204
Pendleton, Edmund, 24–25, 27, 29, 200
Pfeffer, Leo, 117, 125–26
Pickering, John, 200–01
Pickering, Timothy, 47
Pierce, William, 29
Pilgrims, 39
Pinckney, Charles, 48, 251
Plumer, William, 199, 202–3
pocket veto, 257
Pocock, J. G. A., 212
presidency of James Madison: positive contributions, 242–44; roles, 130–42
Princeton, vii, ix, 3–20, 23, 106
proclamations, 114–15, 120–21, 254–58
Protestant Episcopal Church of Alexandria, 114

Rakove, Jack, 68–69, 74
Randolph, Edmund, 28, 43, 134
Randolph, John, 202, 236
Ranney, Austin, 211
Rehnquist, William, 38, 123
Reid, Thomas, 12
Reiss, David, 123
religion. *See* churches; freedom of religion; separation of church and state
religious proclamations by the government, 120–21
Report of 1800 (Madison): First Amendment bar to Sedition Act, 137–41; libel laws, 142–44, 167; nondelegated powers, exercise of, 135–37; nullification by single state, 275
Report on Manufactures (Hamilton), 186–89.
Report on Public Credit (Hamilton), 176–85
Report on Restoring Public Credit (Madison), 178
Report on the Bank (Hamilton), 186–87
republicanism and the founding generation, 211
Riccards, Michael, 252
Roberts, Owen, 122
Robertson, David Brian, 47–48
Robertson, Donald, 29, 196
Rodney, Caesar A., 236
Rosen, Gary, 22
Rosenberger v. University of Virginia, 124
Rossiter, Clinton, 45, 47
Rubenzer, Steven, 252

Rutland, Robert, 38, 235
Rutledge, Wiley, 122

Sacred Fire of Liberty (Banning), 15
Sanford, Edward, 164
Scalia, Antonin, 124–25
Schachner, Nathan, 39
Schlesinger, Arthur, Jr., 230
Schlesinger, Arthur, Sr., 230
Scott, Jack, 10
secession, 274–75
Second Continental Congress, 42
Second Treatise on Government (Locke), 6
Sedition Act. *See* Alien and Sedition Acts
separation of church and state: and vetoes, 114–15; wall of separation metaphor, 122–23, 167. *See also* churches; Deity, in government documents; freedom of religion
Sherman, Roger, 47–48
Sisson, Daniel, 211
Sitgreaves, Samuel, 197
Skowronek, Stephen, 252
Smith, Robert, 236–37, 241–42
Smith, Samuel Stanhope, 28
social contract, 109
Souter, David, 123–24
South Carolina Exposition (Calhoun), 270, 272
sovereignty, 44
Sparks, Jared, 38
special messages to Congress, 253–54
Stagg, J. C. A., 4, 237–38
Stanwood, Edward, 210
St. Clair, Arthur, 188
Stevens, John Paul, 125
Storing, Herbert, 163
Story, Joseph: appointment of, 263–64; Senate confirmation of, 204
Suarez, Ray, 38
Supreme Court (U.S.): *Detached Memoranda* and, 126–27; and First Amendment, 165–67; Madison's appointments to, 261–66; Madison's influence on, 121–27, 157–71; as mirror of Madison's views, 164–65; reliance on Madison, 122–26
Sutherland, George, 154n82
System of Moral Philosophy (Hutcheson), 10
tariffs: controversy over, 272–73; Tariff of 1789, 184, 186; Tariff of 1790, 186; Tariff of 1792, 188
tax exemptions for religious entities, 117–18
Taylor, Hannis, 48
Taylor, John (of Caroline), 25
Tazewell, Henry, 198–99
Thomas, Clarence, 124–25
Thompson, James, 3
toleration, 107
Treaty of Paris, 180
Trist, Nicholas, 160, 282n17
Tucker, George, 30, 134
Tulis, Jeffrey K., 233, 253
Turberville, G. L., 162

Umbreit, Kenneth B., 39
United States v. Eliza, 200
United States v. Hudson and Goodwin, 145
universal negative, 71, 158
"Universal Peace" (Madison), 97

Valley Forge Christian College v. Americans United for Separation of Church and State, 126
Van Orden v. Perry, 125
"Vices of the Political System of the United States" (Madison), 91–92, 100, 213, 277
Vidal v. Girard's Executors, 127
Virginia Act for Establishing Religious Freedom, 30, 110, 166
Virginia and Kentucky Resolutions, 97, 134, 143, 270–75
Virginia Constitutional Convention, 107–8
Virginia Convention of 1829, 12
Virginia Declaration of Rights, 25, 107
Voltaire, 106

Wallace, Caleb, 28
Wallace v. Jaffree, 123
wall of separation metaphor, 122–23, 167. *See also* churches; separation of church and state
Walsh, Robert, 128
Walzer, Michael, 90
Walz v. Tax Commission, 126
War Hawks, 239, 241

War of 1812: and civil liberties, 243; invasion of Canada, 241; Madison's actions leading to, 252; Madison's popularity after, 244; Proclamations of Prayer and Thanksgiving, 114–15, 256; public opinion during, 217, 231, 239; votes on, 240, 254
Warren, Charles, 45
Washington, George: Constitutional Convention, role at, 46; correspondence with Madison, 158, 161; as father of the nation, 40–41, 49; and Hamilton, 198; Madison's work with, 30
Watson v. Jones, 154n80
Watt, Isaac, 4, 6
Webster, Daniel, 39, 49, 258
Webster, Pelatiah, 48
Welliver, Judson, 39
White, Leonard D., 232
White House, burning of, 242
William and Mary. *See* College of William and Mary
Williams, Selma R., 39
Wills, Garry, 22, 128, 229, 240, 258
Wilson, James, 44–46, 48, 52, 69, 74, 78, 230
Winder, William H., 241
Witherspoon, John: courses at Princeton, 3–16; as role model, 29
Wolcott, Alexander, 262
Wolfe, Christopher, 66, 70
Wood, Gordon, 31, 80, 211
Woodbury, Levi, 266

Yazoo compromise, 202
Yoho, James, 31

Zelman v. Simmons-Harris, 126
Zuckert, Michael, 66, 71–73, 76